Communications in Computer and Information Science 1243

Commenced Publication in 2007
Founding and Former Series Editors:
Simone Diniz Junqueira Barbosa, Phoebe Chen, Alfredo Cuzzocrea,
Xiaoyong Du, Orhun Kara, Ting Liu, Krishna M. Sivalingam,
Dominik Ślęzak, Takashi Washio, Xiaokang Yang, and Junsong Yuan

More information about this series at http://www.springer.com/series/7899

Tarmo Robal · Hele-Mai Haav ·
Jaan Penjam · Raimundas Matulevičius (Eds.)

Databases and Information Systems

14th International Baltic Conference, DB&IS 2020
Tallinn, Estonia, June 16–19, 2020
Proceedings

 Springer

Editors
Tarmo Robal (ID)
Department of Computer Systems
Tallinn University of Technology
Tallinn, Estonia

Hele-Mai Haav (ID)
Department of Software Science
Tallinn University of Technology
Tallinn, Estonia

Jaan Penjam
Department of Software Science
Tallinn University of Technology
Tallinn, Estonia

Raimundas Matulevičius (ID)
Institute of Computer Science
University of Tartu
Tartu, Estonia

ISSN 1865-0929   ISSN 1865-0937   (electronic)
Communications in Computer and Information Science
ISBN 978-3-030-57671-4   ISBN 978-3-030-57672-1   (eBook)
https://doi.org/10.1007/978-3-030-57672-1

This Springer imprint is published by the registered company Springer Nature Switzerland AG
The registered company address is: Gewerbestrasse 11, 6330 Cham, Switzerland

Preface

This volume gathers the papers presented at the 14th International Baltic Conference on Databases and Information Systems (DB&IS 2020), held in Tallinn, Estonia, during June 16–19, 2020. The Baltic DB&IS 2020 conference continued the series of biennial conferences, which were previously held in Trakai (1994, 2018), Tallinn (1996, 2002, 2008, 2014), Riga (1998, 2004, 2010, 2016), and Vilnius (2000, 2006, 2012). The 14th Baltic DB&IS conference was organized by Tallinn University of Technology (TalTech) in cooperation with University of Tartu.

Unfortunately, due to the escalation of the COVID-19 pandemic and the antiCOVID-19 regulations in Europe and the rest of the world, the planned physical meeting in Tallinn and in Tartu (June 18, 2020) had to be re-formatted and the conference was held online as a virtual conference featuring live and semi-live presentations during the same period of time.

Since its inception in 1994, the Baltic DB&IS series of conferences have served as an international forum for researchers, practitioners, and PhD students to exchange research findings and ideas on crucial matters of engineering reliable, secure, and sustainable information systems with data and data analysis in the central role. The 14th edition of the Baltic DB&IS conference continued this tradition and featured original research and application papers on the theory, design, implementation, and security of today's information systems on a set of themes and issues, with an emphasis on artificial intelligence and knowledge engineering in the central role.

The Baltic DB&IS 2020 program included three invited keynote talks on trending topics actual to the conference series, given by Prof. Claudia Hauff (TU Delft, The Netherlands), Prof. Marite Kirikova (Riga Technical University, Latvia), and Dr. Jan Willemson (Cybernetica, Estonia), the latter two are also included in this volume. The call for papers for the 14th Baltic DB&IS welcomed original unpublished research and application experience papers on enterprise, web and information systems engineering, architectures, quality and security of information systems, spatial data science, artificial intelligence, and data and knowledge engineering in information systems. For Baltic DB&IS 2020, we received 52 submissions with authors coming from 16 countries. Each paper was reviewed (single-blind) by at least three members of the Program Committee. The International Program Committee consisted of 74 members from 26 countries. The reviewers were assigned based on placed bids and highlighted topics of interest after careful consideration of all potential conflicts. Papers were not assigned to Program Committee members originating from the same country or having known conflicting interests. After the review process, papers with consistent negative evaluations were rejected, whereas papers with mixed ratings (negative and positive) were additionally evaluated by program and general chairs prior to the meeting, where all the papers and final decisions regarding them were thoroughly discussed. The evaluation process resulted in the selection of 22 papers (acceptance rate of 42%), which were accepted for presentation at the conference and publication in these conference proceedings.

The original research results presented in this volume concern well-established fields such as information systems architectures and quality, machine learning and data science for artificial intelligence, data and knowledge representation and engineering, ontology modeling and semantic data, enterprise and information systems engineering, information retrieval, social web and web engineering, and security of data, information, and processes. The volume also includes two keynote talks.

Finally, we express our deep gratitude to the members of the Program Committee and the external reviewers for their time, comments, and constructive evaluations. We also sincerely thank the members of the International Steering Committee for their continued support of the conference. We would like to thank everyone from the Organizing Committee for their time and dedication in helping to make this conference a success. We also thank the organizers and mentors of the Doctoral Consortium, especially Dr. Riina Maigre and Prof. Eduard Petlenkov. We are also grateful to the authors and all the participants who truly made the conference a success, even within the short time frame we had to re-organize the conference due to the COVID-19 outbreak to face the new reality and hold a conference virtually from a safe distance. Stay safe!

July 2020

Tarmo Robal
Hele-Mai Haav
Jaan Penjam
Raimundas Matulevičius

Organization

General Chairs

Hele-Mai Haav   Tallinn University of Technology, Estonia
Jaan Penjam   Tallinn University of Technology, Estonia

Program Committee Chairs

Tarmo Robal   Tallinn University of Technology, Estonia
Raimundas Matulevičius   University of Tartu, Estonia

Steering Committee

Janis Bubenko
(Honorary Member)   Royal Institute of Technology and Stockholm University, Sweden
Arne Sølvberg
(Honorary Member)   Norwegian University of Science and Technology, Norway
Guntis Arnicāns   University of Latvia, Latvia
Juris Borzovs   University of Latvia, Latvia
Albertas Čaplinskas   Vilnius University, Lithuania
Jānis Grundspeņķis   Riga Technical University, Latvia
Hele-Mai Haav   Tallinn University of Technology, Estonia
Mārīte Kirikova   Riga Technical University, Latvia
Audronė Lupeikienė   Vilnius University, Lithuania
Raimundas Matulevičius   University of Tartu, Estonia
Tarmo Robal   Tallinn University of Technology, Estonia
Olegas Vasilecas   Vilnius Gediminas Technical University, Lithuania

Program Committee

Witold Abramowicz   Poznań University of Economics and Business, Poland
Rajendra Akerkar   Western Norway Research Institute, Norway
Alla Anohina-Naumeca   Riga Technical University, Latvia
Guntis Arnicans   University of Latvia, Latvia
Irina Astrova   Swedbank Eesti, Estonia
Marko Bajec   University of Ljubljana, Slovenia
Josef Basl   University of West Bohemia, Czech Republic
Janis Bicevskis   University of Latvia, Latvia
Mária Bieliková   Slovak University of Technology in Bratislava, Slovakia
Ilze Birzniece   Riga Technical University, Latvia
Juris Borzovs   University of Latvia, Latvia

Robert Buchmann	Babes-Bolyai University, Romania
Ahto Buldas	Tallinn University of Technology, Estonia
Albertas Caplinskas	Vilnius University, Lithuania
Tania Cerquitelli	Politecnico di Torino, Italy
Emma Chavez Mora	Universidad Catolica de la Santisima Concepcion, Chile
Guanliang Chen	Monash University, Australia
Christine Choppy	University of Paris, France
Gintautas Dzemyda	Vilnius University, Lithuania
Dale Dzemydiene	Vilnius University, Lithuania
Johann Eder	Universität Klagenfurt, Austria
Olga Fragou	Hellenic Open University, Greece
Flavius Frasincar	Erasmus University Rotterdam, The Netherlands
Wojciech Froelich	University of Silesia, Poland
Janis Grundspenkis	Riga Technical University, Latvia
Saulius Gudas	Vilnius University, Lithuania
Hyoil Han	Illinois State University, USA
Claudia Hauff	TU Delft, The Netherlands
Mirjana Ivanovic	University of Novi Sad, Serbia
Hannu Jaakkola	Tampere University, Finland
Dimitris Karagiannis	Universität Wien, Austria
Marite Kirikova	Riga Technical University, Latvia
Arne Koschel	Hannover University of Applied Sciences and Arts, Germany
Dalia Kriksciuniene	Vilnius University, Lithuania
Olga Kurasova	Vilnius University, Lithuania
Mart Laanpere	Tallinn University, Estonia
Dejan Lavbic	University of Ljubljana, Slovenia
Marion Lepmets	SoftComply, Germany/Estonia
Innar Liiv	Tallinn University of Technology, Estonia
Christoph Lofi	TU Delft, The Netherlands
Audrone Lupeikene	Vilnius University, Lithuania
Hui Ma	Victoria University of Wellington, New Zealand
Olaf Maennel	Tallinn University of Technology, Estonia
Riina Maigre	Tallinn University of Technology, Estonia
Saulius Maskeliunas	Vilnius University, Lithuania
Mihhail Matskin	Royal Institute of Technology, Sweden
Alexander Mädche	Karlsruhe Institute of Technology, Germany
Timo Mäkinen	Tampere University, Finland
Martin Necaský	Charles University, Czech Republic
Laila Niedrite	University of Latvia, Latvia
Christophoros Nikou	University of Ioannina, Greece
Jyrki Nummenmaa	Tampere University, Finland
Jens Myrup Pedersen	Aalborg University, Denmark
Eduard Petlenkov	Tallinn University of Technology, Estonia
Gunnar Piho	Tallinn University of Technology, Estonia

Jaroslav Pokorny	Charles University in Prague, Czech Republic
Achilleas Psyllidis	TU Delft, The Netherlands
Jolita Ralyte	University of Geneva, Switzerland
David Jose Ribeiro Lamas	Tallinn University, Estonia
José Raúl Romero	University of Cordoba, Spain
Gunter Saake	Otto von Guericke University of Magdeburg, Germany
Imen Ben Sassi	Tallinn University of Technology, Estonia
Janis Stirna	Stockholm University, Sweden
Jelena Zdravkovic	Stockholm University, Sweden
Jaak Tepandi	Tallinn University of Technology, Estonia
Helgi Thorbergsson	University of Iceland, Iceland
Ahto Truu	Guardtime, Estonia
Kadri Umbleja	Tallinn University of Technology, Estonia
Olegas Vasilecas	Vilnius Gediminas Technical University, Lithuania
Kristiina Vassiljeva	Tallinn University of Technology, Estonia
Damjan Vavpotic	University of Ljubljana, Slovenia
Tatjana Welzer	University of Maribor, Slovenia
Algimantas Venckauskas	Kaunas University of Technology, Lithuania
Markus Westner	OTH-Regensburg, Germany

Organizing Committee

Kristiina Kindel	Tallinn University of Technology, Estonia
Grete Lind	Tallinn University of Technology, Estonia
Madis Raaper	University of Tartu, Estonia
Uljana Reinsalu	Tallinn University of Technology, Estonia
Margarita Spitšakova	Tallinn University of Technology, Estonia

Additional Reviewers

Dominik Bork
Gabriel Campero Durand
Jasper Feine
Damjan Fujs
Minsung Hong
Kristiina Kindel
Julius Köpke
Grete Lind
Hoang Long Nguyen
Kęstutis Normantas

René Pihlak
Aurora Ramírez
Uljana Reinsalu
Ruben Salado-Cid
Titas Savickas
Eike Schallehn
Sven Scheu
Margarita Spichakova

Contents

Data and Knowledge Engineering

Enterprise and Information Systems Engineering

Security of Information Systems

Invited Talks

Continuous Requirements Engineering in the Context of Socio-cyber-Physical Systems

Marite Kirikova[✉] [ID]

Department of Artificial Intelligence and Systems Engineering,
Riga Technical University, Riga, Latvia
`marite.kirikova@rtu.lv`

Abstract. Continuously changing business situations and technologies have produced a need for continuous requirements engineering. The challenges in continuous requirements engineering for socio-cyber-physical systems stem from the differences in approaches to systems design and development that can be applied simultaneously at the same time and in the same context, on the one hand; and, on the other hand, from the frequent changes that can appear in objects and the interactions of all three types of systems involved: social, cyber and physical, that form the context of solutions to be developed. This paper addresses complexity, emergence, and fluent borders of systems – the challenges that may occur in continuous requirements engineering in the context of socio-cyber-physical systems. The FREEDOM framework is discussed as one of the tools that can help to meet these challenges.

Keywords: Continuous requirements engineering · Socio-cyber-physical systems · Systems engineering

1 Introduction

New technologies, related to Internet of Things (IoT), Industry 4.0, microservice architectures etc., have opened new opportunities and brought new challenges regarding the scope of elements to be considered in requirements engineering. While in the previous century we mainly were concerned with information systems development and enterprises as their context; nowadays the situation has changed twofold. First, systems that are smaller than enterprises have become so complex that they require their own information systems (e.g. cloud services, robotic systems), and, second, the enterprises have started to utilize technologies that go beyond traditional database management systems and software applications. Obviously, these new contexts of systems to be developed have more and different change generation objects than was the case in traditional enterprise systems. Therefore, in this paper we will ponder over the assumption that clear analytical distinction between social, cyber, and physical (abstract) types of systems is helpful in meeting the challenges of requirements engineering in socio-cyber-physical system contexts. One more issue that influences requirements engineering to a higher

© Springer Nature Switzerland AG 2020
T. Robal et al. (Eds.): DB&IS 2020, CCIS 1243, pp. 3–12, 2020.
https://doi.org/10.1007/978-3-030-57672-1_1

extent than previously – continuous changes inside and outside the stated borders of a system to be developed, will also be placed at the centre of the discussion.

The main purpose of this paper is to identify the main challenges in continuous requirements engineering in socio-cyber-physical system contexts and suggest some possible means of meeting these challenges.

Section 2 of the paper explores system types behind socio-cyber-physical systems and their potential to generate change, and identifies requirements engineering challenges related to these. In Sect. 3, the continuity in requirements engineering is addressed from two perspectives. In Sect. 4, the way in which one of the continuous engineering frameworks could be applied to meet the challenges of continuous requirements engineering is discussed in the context of socio-cyber-physical systems. Section 5 consists of brief conclusions.

2 Socio-cyber-Physical Systems

There are two popular system combinations often mentioned as contexts in information systems development, namely, socio technical systems [1], and, the new trend, cyber-physical systems [2, 3] (see Fig. 1).

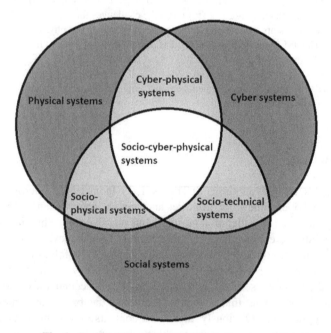

Fig. 1. Positioning socio-cyber-physical systems [4].

The schema in Fig. 1 shows that putting in focus socio-cyber-physical systems yields 3 two-system type combinations, namely, socio-technical systems (as a combination of social and cyber systems), cyber-physical systems and socio-physical systems. Socio-physical systems are not discussed so often in information technology and computer science literature, but the two other types of systems are popular subjects of research. In the 21st century it is rarely the case that a system is purely socio-physical, as the main objects of social systems (homo-sapiens) almost always use some computational resources.

Looking at it from a different point of view – the definitions of social, cyber, and physical systems – we will see that these definitions are not self-exclusive. For instance, the Merriam-Webster Dictionary [5] explains the *social system* as follows: "the patterned series of interrelationships existing between individuals, groups, and institutions and forming a coherent whole" and the social structure is defined as "the internal institutionalized relationships built up by persons living within a group (such as a family or community) especially with regard to the hierarchical organization of status and to the rules and principles regulating behaviour". Here we can take into account that persons are also physical objects, so the elements of a physical system are included in the social system. But when robots are "socializing" then the social system of artificial objects comprises the cyber component together with the physical one. Similarly, there is a close relationship between cyber systems and social systems, as a cyber system cannot initially originate without the involvement of persons – the main elements of social systems. According to [6] "a cyber-system is a system that makes use of a cyberspace" and "a cyberspace is a collection of interconnected computerized networks, including services, computer systems, embedded processors, and controllers, as well as information in storage or transit". Thus, it includes physical objects. The term "physical" is used to describe the things which affect our bodily senses, possess a continuing public character and, together, constitute the spatio-temporal system which we call 'the world' [7]. A physical system is regarded as a portion of the physical universe chosen for analysis [8]. The above-cited definitions show that when, conceptually, a socio-cyber-physical system is taken as a core system, the types of systems it is composed of can be viewed as abstractions. In this paper we will use these abstractions for deeper analysis of a core system. The assumption is that structured templates for modeling via these abstractions can help to continuously define requirements in socio-cyber-physical contexts.

The main challenges in considering socio-cyber-physical systems, as well as social, cyber, and physical systems are their complexity [9] and emergence (unpredicted changes in structure and behaviour) [10]. Distinguishing between the elements of each type of system separately gives us an opportunity to define interdependencies or relationships between these elements, inside and outside of each abstraction, more clearly [11, 12]. This, in turn, facilitates analysis of possible change propagation both inside the system and from the outside, if the environmental change generation source is identified and its relationships with the system known.

One more challenge in socio-cyber-physical systems is fluent borders between the systems [10]. We can illustrate this by mapping between the socio, cyber, and physical system types and one of the most popular enterprise architecture description languages: ArchiMate [13] (see Fig. 2).

Figure 2 illustrates that it is a problem to distinguish between three types of systems using the ArchiMate language. The way to partly solve this problem, by introducing the same scope of elements in all layers of the language, is suggested in [15]. Similar problems are encountered with other enterprise modeling methods which might be used

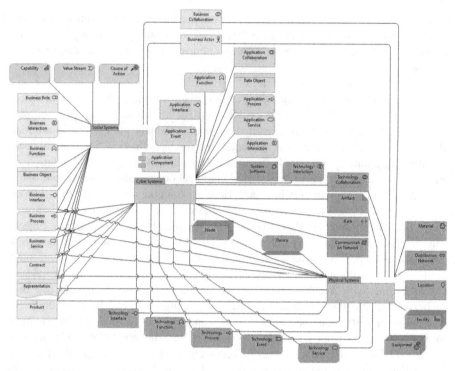

Fig. 2. Mapping between ArchiMate elements and abstract system types. Elements of Strategic, Business, Application, Technology, and Physical layers of ArchiMate language are considered. Archi tool is used for the representation [14].

for modeling of soicio-cyber physical contexts [16]. Therefore some adjustments in these methods would be needed in order to be able to distinguish clearly between different types of systems when addressing the elements of socio-cyber-physical systems.

3   Continuity in Requirements Engineering

Two perspectives of continuity of requirements engineering have been recognized [17]. The first perspective relates to continuous changes in the environment. The second perspective relates to requirements engineering activities in each phase of the system's development lifecycle.

In the context of socio-cyber-physical systems *the first perspective* refers to changes in any elements of abstract systems (social, cyber or physical ones) as well as to changes in the interrelations among the elements of these systems. To identify these changes in requirements engineering, appropriate modeling methods and tools for system representation are to be chosen: these allow the elements of the systems that can become the objects of changes (change generators) to be reflected. Enterprise architectures used as such tools of system representation are discussed in [15]. The use of 4EM approach based enterprise models [16] will be discussed in the next section of this paper. A novel approach about how to model interactions is suggested in [12].

Regarding *the second perspective* of continuity, there can be several projects running simultaneously in the context of socio-cyber-physical systems; and each of them may have a different project lifecycle; for instance, a plan-driven, rigidly phased, project can co-exist with several DevOps projects in one and the same context. Requirements engineering performed through iterative cycles of contemporary software development methods [18] is a special case of the second perspective. This case is most widely discussed in scientific literature and used in practice, however, as stated before, it is not the only alternative for systems development activity phases in the socio-cyber-physical systems context. Therefore, to handle several projects simultaneously, the engineering frameworks that can accommodate several lifecycle models are required.

The approaches and methods of continuous requirements engineering may handle either only one or both of the continuity perspectives. In most cases the approaches and methods are oriented to a particular application area (e.g. self-adaptive systems [19]) or specific requirements engineering aspects [20]. An application domain independent framework FREEDOM will be discussed in the next section as one of the alternatives for meeting challenges of socio-cyber-physical contexts.

4 Applying FREEDOM Framework

The continuous requirements engineering framework FREEDOM emerged as a result of the application of the viable systems model in requirements engineering [21, 22]. The FREEDOM framework consists of several functional units (see the top item in Fig. 3): Future representation, Reality representation, requirements Engineering, fulfillment Engineering, Design and implementation, and Operations, and Management. All these units are related by a number of links that correspond to monitoring, analysis, and analytics ("maa" in Fig. 3), feedback, and change request information. The framework is flexible with respect to the number of its units and the number of links between the units. The requirements engineering function represents requirements engineering activities as a whole; other functions include requirements engineering, fractally, on a smaller scale [23]. The framework has been validated against other continuous software and systems engineering approaches [24]. For analysis of applicability of the architecture of the framework three continuous requirements engineering methods were developed and applied [23].

In the context of socio-cyber-physical systems, the FREEDOM framework is applicable from both project life cycle and system changes perspectives. Regarding the project life cycle perspective, the FREEDOM framework can be flexibly adjusted to different life cycles, by explicitly addressing each of the functions defined in the framework, or merging several functions into one. The flexibility of the framework is illustrated in Fig. 3. Here the top level item would correspond to the plan driven approach, but the bottom line option corresponds to a small project with no distinction among project phases. Moreover, it is possible to have several different lifecycle projects integrated by a common requirements engineering function, if a framework is architected as a fractal system with several heterogeneous branches. This flexibility of the framework helps to reduce requirements engineering complexity of socio-cyber-physical systems by having an appropriate development approach for each specific situation that has common

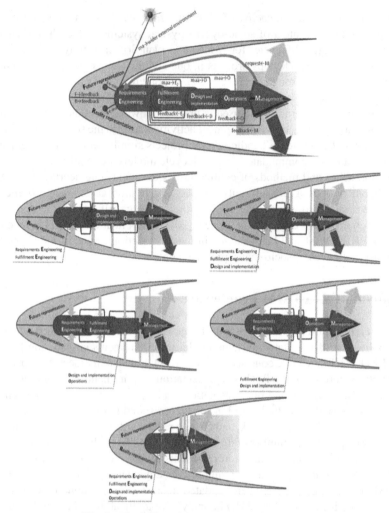

Fig. 3. Flexibility of the FREEDOM framework

means for being integrated in the overall requirements engineering process. It also helps to address the emergence challenge, as the framework is easily adjustable to new project situations by choosing the most appropriate combination of merged and independent functions.

From the system changes perspective, the framework can help to address all three challenges discussed in Sect. 2. The complexity is addressed by the architecture of the framework that has two (reality and future) representation functions. These functions basically involve development of models of systems; and do not restrict the scope of models to be used. For instance, if a 4EM approach [16] would be used for the representations, it could be extended by specific templates for socio-cyber-physical systems. The 4EM method works with six interrelated models (goals model, business processes model, concepts model, actors and resources model, business rules model, and information systems requirements and components model). In Fig. 4 an example of a template for one of the models (business rules model) of 4EM is illustrated. The pre-defined template can help to identify the scope of requirements where all three abstract systems (social, cyber, and physical) are taken into account. The depth of the template would depend on the level of abstraction at which the system is considered.

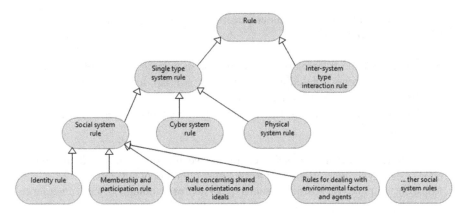

Fig. 4. Rule model template.

The template in Fig. 4 reflects the class hierarchy of rules. The subclasses of rules and subclasses of single type system rules would be common to all cases of socio-cyber-physical systems. However, lower levels of hierarchy can be designed for specific types of systems or can be populated by a theoretically complete number of lower level rule types. To obtain such models existing research in rule models can be examined and new research works performed. In Fig. 4, the bottom level of the rule class hierarchy is taken from [25], where the following key types of rule categories, specifying group conditions, structures, and processes have been identified: (1) identity rules, (2) membership and participation rules, (3) rules concerning shared value orientations and ideals, (4) rules concerning shared beliefs and models, (5) social relational and structural rules, (6) procedures and production rules, (7) rules for dealing with environmental factors and agents, (8) rules for changing core group bases, in particular the rule regime itself, (9) technology and resource rules, and (10) time and place rules. While in [25] all ten categories of rules are regarded as social system rules, we can see that some of these categories (e.g. the ninth category) would belong to inter-system type interaction rules. This shows that the analytical distinction between rule types suggested in this paper is not a common way of system rule representation in current research. However, we can assume that the proposed typology could help to handle the complexity of the systems by ensuring relatively equal treatment of all three types of systems at a chosen level of abstraction. The templates, if populated, would produce an opportunity to predict what new system combinations can emerge. And they obviously help to handle the challenge of fluent borders of system types, by enforcing system element consideration in respect of all three base abstract systems and their interactions.

5 Conclusions

The paper addresses three challenges of continuous requirements engineering in the context of socio-cyber-physical systems: complexity, emergence, and fluent borders among the abstract types of systems.

The paper, with the help of the FREEDOM framework, illustrates the way in which these challenges might be met by the following means:

1. The use of flexible requirements engineering frameworks which can produce the following opportunities:

   a. Using the same framework for all projects in a given context of socio-cyber-physical systems (including projects that overlap in their execution time) – addresses complexity and emergence
   b. Integrating all projects in one common requirements engineering function – addresses complexity.

2. At an abstract level, distinguishing clearly between system types, and considering inter-system type interactions – addresses fluent borders of systems.
3. Applying templates for abstract system types – addresses complexity and emergence.

In this paper we did not discuss the differences regarding the model templates of different systems of one type. For instance, there are specific rules for chemical systems, biological systems, mechanical systems, their components and combinations. Probably it is possible to derive requirements engineering patterns for different types of systems of one abstract type and then apply them according to the substances that are to be modeled in the socio-cyber-physical system context under consideration.

Another issue not discussed in this paper is the differences regarding the scope of requirements. The requirements can be defined for software systems only, or for software and hardware; also they may concern physical objects or even social norms. Each of these situations would require different distributions between abstract templates and constraints in the requirements engineering process.

The preliminary results presented in this paper are derived from the previous research and related works in (1) continuous requirements engineering and (2) modeling of social, cyber, and physical systems. It was shown that the models currently available in the body of scientific knowledge about a domain cannot be directly incorporated in the frame of continuous requirements engineering and the proposed template. Therefore further research is necessary to see whether methods can be established for transferring existing models into templates that are useful for continuous requirements engineering, or whether new modeling approaches will be established that consider socio-cyber-physical systems from perspectives of abstraction and granularity that are not yet common.

References

1. Baxter, G., Sommerville, I.: Socio-technical systems: from design methods to systems engineering. Interact. Comput. **23**(1), 4–17 (2011). https://doi.org/10.1016/j.intcom.2010.07.003

2. Yang, L., Cormican, K., Yu, M.: Ontology-based systems engineering: a state-of-the-art review. Comput. Ind. **111**, 148–171 (2019). https://doi.org/10.1016/j.compind.2019.05.003
3. Allgöwer, F.: Position paper on the challenges posed by modern applications to cyber-physical systems theory. Nonlinear Anal. Hybrid Syst. **34**, 147–165 (2019). https://doi.org/10.1016/j.nahs.2019.05.007
4. Berovskis R.: Designing a communication device in the soci-cyber-physical context. Ph.D.thesis, RTU, Riga (2019). In Latvian
5. Merriam-webster Dictionary. https://www.merriam-webster.com/dictionary/social%20system. Accessed 3 June 2020
6. Refsdal, A., Solhaug, B., Stølen, K.: Cyber-systems. In: Cyber-Risk Management. Springer-Briefs in Computer Science, pp. 25–27 (2015). https://doi.org/10.1007/978-3-319-23570-7_3
7. Whiteman, M.: Philosophy of Space and Time And the Inner Constitution of Nature (2014). https://doi.org/10.4324/9781315830117
8. Your Dictionary. https://www.yourdictionary.com/physical-system. Accessed 3 June 2020
9. Mittal, S., Tolk, A.: The complexity in application of modeling and simulation for cyber physical systems engineering (2019). https://doi.org/10.1002/9781119552482
10. Report on the AMADEOS workshop on emergence in cyber-physical systems-of-systems. https://publik.tuwien.ac.at/files/PubDat_249527.pdf
11. Vissers, C.A., Ferreira Pires, L.: Architectural design: conception and specification of interactive systems, Springer, Cham (2016). https://doi.org/10.1007/978-3-319-43298-4
12. Saurin, T.A., Patriarca, R.: A taxonomy of interactions in socio-technical systems: a functional perspective. Appl. Ergon. **82**, 102980 (2020). https://doi.org/10.1016/j.apergo.2019.102980
13. ArchiMate enterprise architecture modeling language. https://www.opengroup.org/archimate-forum/archimate-overview
14. Archi tool. https://www.archimatetool.com/
15. Kirikova, M.: Challenges in enterprise and information systems modeling in the contexts of socio cyber physical systems. In: Pergl, R., Babkin, E., Lock, R., Malyzhenkov, P., Merunka, V. (eds.) EOMAS 2019. LNBIP, vol. 366, pp. 60–69. Springer, Cham (2019). https://doi.org/10.1007/978-3-030-35646-0_5
16. Sandkuhl, K., Stirna, J., Persson, A., Wißotzki, M.: Enterprise modeling. tackling business challenges with the 4EM method (2014). https://doi.org/10.1007/978-3-662-43725-4
17. Pohl, K.: Requirements Engineering, Springer, London (2010). https://doi.org/10.1007/978-1-84996-405-0
18. Rodriguez, P., et al.: Continuous deployment of software intensive products and services: a systematic mapping study. J. Syst. Softw. **123**, 263–291 (2017). https://doi.org/10.1016/j.jss.2015.12.015
19. Qureshi, N.A., Perini, A., Ernst, N.A., Mylopoulos, J.: Towards a continuous requirements engineering framework for self-adaptive systems. In: Proceedings of the 1st International Workshop on Requirements@Run.Time, IEEE, pp. 9–16 (2010). https://doi.org/10.1109/reruntime.2010.5628552
20. Fitzgerald, B., Stol, K.J.: Continuous software engineering: a roadmap and agenda. J. Syst. Softw. **123**, 176–189 (2017). https://doi.org/10.1016/j.jss.2015.06.063
21. Kirikova, M.: Continuous requirements engineering in FREEDOM framework: a position paper. In: Joint Proceedings of REFSQ-2016 Workshops, Doctoral Symposium, Research Method Track, and Poster Track co-located with the 22nd International Conference on Requirements Engineering: Foundation for Software Quality (REFSQ 2016), March 14–17, 2016, Gothenburg, Sweden, vol. 1564. CEUR-WS.org (2016). http://ceur-ws.org/Vol-1564/paper10.pdf
22. Beer, S.: Diagnosing The System for Organisations, Wiley, Hoboken (1985)

23. Kirikova, M.: Continuous requirements engineering. In: Proceedings of the 18th International Conference on Computer Systems and Technologies – CompSysTech 2017, Ruse, Bulgaria — June 23–24 2017, pp. 1–10. ACM Press (2017). https://doi.org/10.1145/3134302.3134304
24. Kirikova, M.: Towards framing the continuous information systems engineering. In: Joint Proceedings of the BIR 2016 Workshops and Doctoral Consortium co-located with 15th International Conference on Perspectives in Business Informatics Research (BIR 2016), Managed Complexity, vol. 1684. CEUR-WS.org (2016). http://ceur-ws.org/Vol-1684/paper18.pdf
25. Burns, T.: Machado des Johansson, N.: Social rule system theory: universal interaction grammars (2014)

Developing Requirements for the New Encryption Mechanisms in the Estonian eID Infrastructure

Mart Oruaas[1] and Jan Willemson[1,2(✉)]

[1] Cybernetica AS, Mäealuse 2/1, 12618 Tallinn, Estonia
{mart.oruaas,jan.willemson}@cyber.ee
[2] STACC, Narva mnt 20, 51009 Tartu, Estonia

Abstract. After the Estonian ID-card crisis in 2017, it became apparent that the document encryption-decryption functionality built on top of the ID-card infrastructure requires major rethinking. This paper describes the starting points of this process and reviews some of the requirements that have been identified in the first phase. We study the main usage scenarios and process flows, and discuss the need to distinguish transport encryption from storage encryption.

Keywords: Electronic identity · Document encryption · Requirements engineering

1 Introduction

Digital communication has become an integral part of our everyday life. However, as such communication is mostly happening over open Internet, extra measures need to be taken if the messages require security in some sense.

In this paper, we will be concentrating on one aspect of security, namely confidentiality. Confidentiality protection is built into many communication protocols, and is typically achieved via encryption. Encryption, however, does not solve the message protection problem cleanly, but rather reduces it to key management. The latter, in turn, is not necessarily an easy task to solve.

One option for key distribution is to use cryptographic chip cards. In Estonia, for example, a specific instance of such a card (called ID-card) is even made mandatory since 2002, so virtually all the Estonian residents have one.

Even though message encryption was originally not a planned usage scenario of the ID-cards, it was added later. The current paper deals with some of the issues that the present solution (code-named CDOC) has, and discusses requirements for the next-generation message encryption framework (code-named CDOC2.0).

© Springer Nature Switzerland AG 2020
T. Robal et al. (Eds.): DB&IS 2020, CCIS 1243, pp. 13–20, 2020.
https://doi.org/10.1007/978-3-030-57672-1_2

2   Background

In Estonia, there are currently three main electronic identity solutions.

- **ID-card**, first launched in 2002, was historically the first one and is the only compulsory form of identification in Estonia. It features a smart card chip capable of asymmetric cryptographic operations, and it comes with pre-generated and certified public-private key pairs. There is also digi-ID card that is digitally equivalent to ID-card, but can not be used for physical identification. For the sake of this paper we will use the name ID-card for both of them.
- **Mobile-ID**, first launched in 2007, relies on the mobile phone SIM card as the key storage and cryptographic coprocessor.
- **Smart-ID**, first launched in 2016, is a software-only solution making use of a specific cryptographic scheme [5] where the signature key is split between the mobile device and server.

As of May 2020, there were about 1.35 million active ID-cards, more than 230,000 mobile-ID users and more than 500,000 Smart-ID users[1].

All of the three solutions listed above provide two basic functionalities, *authentication* and *digital signature*. From the cryptographic point of view, both of them actually rely on digital signature primitive, but since their legal context is different, authentication and digital signing make use of different key pairs.

Originally, ID-cards and mobile-ID SIM cards used 1024-bit RSA, but around 2010 it became clear that advances in computing power would make it too weak at some point in foreseeable future [2], so it was gradually phased out in favour of RSA2048 on ID-cards and elliptic curve P256 on mobile-ID. After the ID-card crisis in 2017, ID-cards started to make use of the elliptic curve P384. Smart-ID originally used 4-kilobit multi-prime RSA, which is today replaced by 6-kilobit keys.

Besides digital signatures, there is another major application of public key cryptography, namely public key encryption. Since more and more Estonian citizens had access to strong cryptographic tokens in the form of ID-cards, the idea of providing encryption functionality emerged naturally. Along with the general growth of digital data exchange, also the need for private communication increased, so there was also demand for such a service.

Thus, in 2005, encryption-decryption functionality was added to the base software package of the Estonian ID-card [8]. Originally, the package featured a standalone application *DigiDoc Krüpto*, but today this functionality is integrated into the main DigiDoc4 Client (see Fig. 1).

In order to send an encrypted file, recipient's authentication public key certificate is required. This is fetched from the LDAP server of Estonia's main Certification Authority by supplying the recipient's (public) Personal Identity Code. In fact, supporting the encryption service is the only reason why all the public key certificates are available in a public LDAP server in the first place [7].

---

[1] https://www.id.ee/?lang=en. Accessed 7 May 2020.

Fig. 1. DigiDoc4 Client with decryption functionality (Image source: https://www.id.ee/)

Out of the three eID solutions available in Estonia, only the ID-card can be used for decryption, and there is a good technical reason for that. Namely, ID-card is the only form of eID directly connected to the user's computer via a wired card reader.[2] Mobile-ID and Smart-ID requests are, on the other hand, server-mediated. This is OK for signature-based applications (including authentication), but transferring decrypted material (essentially symmetric transport keys) via a server would break message confidentiality.

Estonian eID ecosystem has had a number of challenges throughout the years [7], but by far the most severe of them was the ROCA vulnerability found by a group of Czech researchers in 2017 [6]. It turned out that prime number generation algorithm used to create the RSA public moduli was using a very small seed space, hence it became feasible to factor the moduli by full inspection of that space. The lab experiments conducted by the Czech researchers were also independently verified in Estonia on a real ID-card belonging to Margus Arm, the leader of Estonian eID project[3].

As an aftermath of the ROCA case, several analyses were conducted [1,4]. One of the conclusions drawn in these analyses was that out of the three main application scenarios of the ID-card – authentications, signing and encryption – it was encryption that was hit the hardest. Indeed, authentication is a short-

---

[2] As of 2019, also ID-cards with NFC interface started to roll out, but the support for NFC operations is still very limited.

[3] https://epl.delfi.ee/eesti/id-kaart-murti-lahti-ria-toestas-et-kara-id-kaardi-turvanor kuse-parast-polnud-asjata?id=81807683. Accessed 11 May 2020.

lived protocol anyway, and once the affected keys are revoked, breaking them becomes useless. Digital signatures, on the other hand, are protected by time-stamps. Thus, even if factoring some RSA modulus becomes possible in the future, we can still reasonably argue that at the time of signing such an attack was infeasible.

However, encryption is a scenario requiring long-term secrecy. In the most common use case, a document is encrypted using the recipient's public key, the cryptogram is saved into a special .cdoc container file and sent as an email attachment. The problem is that, from the end user perspective, it is very hard to control the actual chain of intermediate servers that the email together with its attachments travels through. Every one of them is in principle capable of retaining a copy of the .cdoc file until the time when breaking the underlying cryptography becomes feasible.

3   Setting Requirements for the New Encryption Solution(s)

After the ROCA crisis, it became clear that, in order to prevent similar problems in future, better-designed document encryption features were needed for the Estonian eID ecosystem. Of course, the design phase needs to be preceded by an analysis phase. The respective project was initiated by the Estonian Information System Authority, seeking questions to the following broad questions.

- What are the common usage scenarios where CDOC infrastructure is used, and what are the corresponding user requirements?
- What are the core shortcomings of the present CDOC infrastructure, and how should a new system be built to avoid them?

The authors of the current paper were involved in this analysis project, and this paper presents a high-level summary of the final report of the project.

3.1   Usage Scenarios

In order to map the main usage scenarios of document/data encryption in Estonian public and private sectors, a series of interviews were conducted with eight large organisations, presumably having the need for secure communication. The organisations included law enforcement agencies, state defence structures, health information management, certification authority and one of the main banks active in Estonia.

As a result, we identified the following scenarios.

- Inter-organisational communication requiring an extra layer of confidentiality
  - System administrators transferring passwords
  - Handling sensitive incidents
- Intra-organisational confidential communication
  - Law enforcement data exchange

- Restricted access data exchange
- Time-critical information required by courts and criminal investigations
- Contracts, official data queries
- Confidential communication between the citizens and organisations
  - Some *ad hoc* health data transfer
  - Whistle blowing (from citizen to law enforcement)
  - Contracts, official data queries
  - Fines (from law enforcement to citizens)
  - Getting excerpts from bank statements
- Confidential document exchange between citizens
- Confidential document exchange with foreign partners

The last scenario was not directly in scope of the study, but potential interest was expressed by several interviewees. E.g., after establishment of the eIDAS framework in the European Union, it is a natural question to ask whether it could also be extended to confidential data exchange, much like a similar question arose in Estonia after the introduction of ID-card.

4   Transport Cryptography *vs* storage cryptography

One of the problems identified during the analysis was that the same `.cdoc` files were used both for transport and long-term storage of confidential documents. Such usage brings along several issues.

1. Relying on the implicit heuristic assumption that CDOC is secure (without actually specifying the security definition), users kept the `.cdoc` files in their mailboxes, on unencrypted hard drives, removable media, etc. After the underlying cryptography turned out to be weak, it was very hard to control all the copies of the `.cdoc` files.
2. ID-card was efficiently used as the private decryption key management token. However, the ID-card does not (and should not) provide any key back-up mechanism, so when it becomes dysfunctional (e.g. due to physical ageing, being lost, etc.), all the `.cdoc` containers are left un-decryptable.

To address these issues, it is necessary to make a more clear distinction between transport and storage encryption. The first item above translates to the requirement that transport encryption should provide *forward-secrecy* [3], i.e. that compromise of the long-lived keys should not cause breaching the secrecy of all the exchanged messages. There are a few ways how this property can be achieved, but the most popular approach in practice is using ephemeral (i.e. short lived, temporary) encryption keys. For example, in the latest TLS version 1.3, only key agreement protocols resulting in ephemeral transport keys are allowed[4].

On the other hand, if a confidential document sent via the CDOC infrastructure needs to be accessed for a longer period of time, ephemeral encryption keys are not a good solution. Another aspect of information access arises from

---

[4] https://tools.ietf.org/html/rfc8446. Accessed 14 May 2020.

a number of organisational scenarios listed in Sect. 3.1. Currently, documents can only be encrypted for decryption with ID-cards of physical persons. However, in many occasions, the intended recipient is not a person, but rather an organisation or a specific role within the organisation.

This aspect can be observed also in the long-term storage scenario. There are documents with legally required confidentiality periods lasting for decades. The person who once will possibly be filling the role that needs access to the document is perhaps not even born yet at the time the document gets stored.

Thus, the new CDOC2.0 infrastructure needs to make a clear distinction between the transport and storage encryption. The component where this distinction manifests itself most clearly is the key management. Ephemeral keys will be generated and maintained just for one session or for a short period of time, and after expiry they should be deleted. If a document needs longer-term access, it needs to be re-encrypted with a different key that is managed according to the needs and regulations of the specific organisation.

This re-encryption step is something that probably requires a paradigm shift from the users who are currently used to saving `.cdoc` files on their hard-drives, or just leaving them in mailboxes. In order to break this habit, CDOC2.0 should change the process flow in a way that such insecure behaviour would become impossible, or at least quite inconvenient.

5   Main Classes of Process Flow

In fact, CDOC2.0 would anyway need to support several process for transport encryption, as the requirements of different usage scenarios differ. We have identified the following main types of process flows.

- **Ad hoc data exchange with low confidentiality requirements** where data exchange is not agreed upon beforehand, the data itself is not very sensitive and it may expire quite fast (e.g. situational updates).
- **Synchronous data exchange** where both of the communicating parties can be expected to be online at the same time.
- **Information exchange within an organisation**, where we can typically also assume some perimeter protection measures.
- **Highly confidential data exchange between different organisations**, where the communication occurs over open Internet, but on the other hand, the sender and recipient may be motivated to use methods that require extra efforts (say, specific ephemeral key generation and distribution).
- **Confidential data exchange between citizen and an organisation**, e.g. a bank or a law enforcement agency.

On one hand, the requirements of different scenarios are different, but on the other hand, so do the motivation and technical capabilities of the communicating parties. Thus, future DigiDoc client will need to provide a list of encryption options, and the sender will need to choose between them based on the concrete scenario.

Also, the long-term storage processes can be divided into two large categories depending on the needs and capabilities of the recipients.

- **Personal data access**, where just one person needs the decryption capability which is the case with personal data or the data for a one-man-organisation.
- **Role-based data access**, which is the case for larger organisations where different physical persons may be fulfilling a certain role at different points of time.

The needs of the first category can be satisfied with a number of readily-available solutions like encrypting the hard-drive of the user's main computer and backing up the key in one's physical safe deposit box.

For the second scenario, however, extra development is necessary. Large organisations already have existing document management systems (DMS), possibly also integrated with email exchange functionality. Assuming that CDOC2.0 containers are still mostly transferred via email, the following additional activities need to be enabled for a typical DMS.

1. The DMS must be capable of decrypting the CDOC2.0 container from the transport encryption scheme.
2. The person fulfilling the respective role must have access to the encryption functionality using an in-house long-term secure storage solution.
3. Later, a (possibly different) person fulfilling the role must have access to the in-house solution's decryption functionality.

There are a number of ways the encryption-decryption key management can be implemented in a company. There can be employee badges in the form of cryptographic chip cards, or there can be a dedicated in-house key distribution server. The specific implementation depends on the needs and capabilities of the organisation.

One interesting aspect to note is that the CDOC2.0 container format can be the same for both transport and storage process flows, but it is the key management process that makes all the difference.

6   Conclusions

Being initiated about 20 years ago, Estonian eID infrastructure has matured. It is used every day to provide authentication and signature functionality for public and private e-services.

However, there is also a third kind of cryptographic e-service required by the end users, namely document encryption. For the last 15 years it has been technically implemented as an add-on to authentication, but this has caused several problems (with the ROCA case of 2017 being the best known one).

The root of these problems lies within different requirements that authentication and encryption keys have. Authentication keys can be instantly revoked and hence potential vulnerabilities due to, say, key compromise are easy to limit.

Decryption functionality, on the other hand, has to be maintained over a long period of time (years, perhaps even decades), and thus it is impossible to mitigate key compromises by just revoking them.

This means that encryption-decryption key management has to be designed much more thoroughly, and this is a process that the Estonian Information System Authority has initiated in 2019. The current paper summarised the main findings of the first, analysis and requirement gathering phase. The next steps will include design, development and deployment. All of these remain the subject of further work, parts of which have already started by the time of this writing (May 2020).

Acknowledgements. We are grateful to the Estonian Information System Authority for their initiative on the CDOC2.0 process. This paper has been supported by the Estonian Personal Research Grant number 920 and European Regional Development Fund through the grant number EU48684.

References

1. Ansper, A., Buldas, A., Willemson, J.: Cryptographic algorithms lifecycle report, Cybernetica research report A-101-9 (2018). https://www.ria.ee/sites/default/files/content-editors/publikatsioonid/cryptographic-algorithms-lifecycle-report-2017.pdf. Accessed 11 May 2020
2. Babbage, S., et al.: ECRYPT II Yearly Report on Algorithms and Keysizes (2009–2010) (2010). https://www.ecrypt.eu.org/ecrypt2/documents/D.SPA.13.pdf. Accessed 11 May 2020
3. Boyd, C., Mathuria, A., Stebila, D.: Protocols for Authentication and Key Establishment. Information Security and Cryptography, 2nd edn. Springer, Heidelberg (2020). https://doi.org/10.1007/978-3-662-58146-9
4. Buldas, A., et al.: ID-kaardi kaasuse õppetunnid (2018). (in Estonian) https://www.ria.ee/sites/default/files/content-editors/EID/id-kaardi_oppetunnid.pdf. Accessed 11 May 2020
5. Buldas, A., Kalu, A., Laud, P., Oruaas, M.: Server-supported RSA signatures for mobile devices. In: Foley, S.N., Gollmann, D., Snekkenes, E. (eds.) ESORICS 2017. LNCS, vol. 10492, pp. 315–333. Springer, Cham (2017). https://doi.org/10.1007/978-3-319-66402-6_19
6. Nemec, M., Sýs, M., Svenda, P., Klinec, D., Matyas, V.: The return of coppersmith's attack: practical factorization of widely used RSA moduli. In: Thuraisingham, B.M., Evans, D., Malkin, T., Xu, D. (eds.) Proceedings of the 2017 ACM SIGSAC Conference on Computer and Communications Security, CCS 2017, Dallas, TX, USA, 30 October–03 November 2017, pp. 1631–1648. ACM (2017). https://doi.org/10.1145/3133956.3133969
7. Paršovs, A.: Estonian Electronic Identity Card and its Security Challenges. Ph.D. thesis draft (2020)
8. Sinivee, V., Uukkivi, K.: Encrypted DigiDoc Format Specification (2012). https://www.id.ee/public/SK-CDOC-1.0-20120625_EN.pdf

Architectures and Quality
of Information Systems

Change Discovery in Heterogeneous Data Sources of a Data Warehouse

Darja Solodovnikova$^{(\boxtimes)}$ ⬥ and Laila Niedrite ⬥

Faculty of Computing, University of Latvia, Riga 1050, Latvia
{darja.solodovnikova,laila.niedrite}@lu.lv

Abstract. Data warehouses have been used to analyze data stored in relational databases for several decades. However, over time, data that are employed in the decision-making process have become so enormous and heterogeneous that traditional data warehousing solutions have become unusable. Therefore, new big data technologies have emerged to deal with large volumes of data. The problem of structural evolution of integrated heterogeneous data sources has become extremely topical due to dynamic and diverse nature of big data. In this paper, we propose an approach to change discovery in data sources of a data warehouse utilized to analyze big data. Our solution incorporates an architecture that allows to perform OLAP operations and other kinds of analysis on integrated big data and is able to detect changes in schemata and other characteristics of structured, semi-structured and unstructured data sources. We discuss the algorithm for change discovery and metadata necessary for its operation.

Keywords: Data warehouse · Evolution · Metadata · Big data

1 Introduction

In recent years, the concept of big data has attracted increasing attention and interest from researchers and companies around the world. The demand to analyze big data is increasing and one of the analysis options is to use data warehousing and OLAP methods. Due to dynamic and heterogeneous nature of big data new challenges have appeared related to schema evolution of big data sources of a data warehouse. The evolution problem arises when the structure of data evolves or new data items are added to data records. Besides, to handle changes in user requirements, a great developer effort must be devoted to adapt the existing data structures and metadata. Existing solutions of evolution problems developed for relational data bases are not applicable directly to semi-structured or unstructured data sources that are generated at the higher rate.

Several recent review papers [1–3] outline research directions and challenges that must be solved with the emergence of big data sources. The authors in [1] mention dynamic design challenges for big data applications, which include data expansion that occurs when data becomes more detailed. A review paper [2]

© Springer Nature Switzerland AG 2020
T. Robal et al. (Eds.): DB&IS 2020, CCIS 1243, pp. 23–37, 2020.
https://doi.org/10.1007/978-3-030-57672-1_3

indicates research directions in the field of data warehousing and OLAP. Among others, the authors mention the problem of designing OLAP cubes according to user requirements. Another recent vision paper [3] discusses the variety of big data stored in the multi-model polystore architectures and suggests that efficient management of schema evolution and propagation of schema changes to affected parts of the system is a complex task and one of the topical issues.

In this paper, we present our solution that addresses the current problem of evolution of heterogeneous data sources and user requirements of a data warehouse. Our approach employs a data warehouse architecture that on one hand provides various methods for data analysis and on the other hand is capable of detecting and propagating evolution.

The rest of the paper is organized as follows. In Sect. 2 the recent studies related to the topic are discussed. In Sect. 3 we outline the proposed data warehouse architecture. Section 4 is devoted to the description of the metadata employed in the architecture to handle evolution. We briefly overview the supported atomic changes in the structure and other characteristics of data sets utilized in the architecture in Sect. 5. The main contribution of this paper is presented in Sect. 6, where the algorithm for change discovery is presented. Section 7 is dedicated to the description of the case study system. Finally, we conclude with directions for future work in Sect. 8.

2   Related Work

Several recent studies have been devoted to solving various evolution problems in the big data context. In the paper [4], we summarized the research made in the field of big data architectures and analyzed available approaches with the purpose to identify the most appropriate solution for the evolution problem. The most relevant studies are also discussed in this section.

A solution to handling data source evolution in the integration field was presented in the paper [5]. The authors propose the big data integration ontology for the definition of integrated schema, source schemata, their versions and local-as-view mappings between them. When a change at a data source occurs, the ontology is supplemented with a new release that reflects the change. Our approach differs in that the proposed architecture is OLAP-oriented and is capable of handling not only changes in data sources, but also requirements.

Another study that considers evolution is presented in the paper [6]. The author proposes a data warehouse solution for big data analysis that is implemented using MapReduce paradigm. The system supports two kinds of changes: slowly changing dimensions are managed with methods proposed in [7] and fact table changes are handled by schema versions in metadata. Unlike our proposal, the system does not process changes in big data sources that may significantly influence analysis process and results.

An architecture that exploits big data technologies for large-scale OLAP analytics is presented in the paper [8]. The architecture supports source data evolution by means of maintaining a schema registry and enforcing the schema to remain the same or compatible with the desired structure.

In the paper [9] we analyzed studies dedicated to metadata employed to describe heterogeneous data sources of data lakes and we concluded that none of the examined metadata models reflect evolution. For our solution, we adapted the metadata model proposed in [10] to describe data sources of a data lake. The authors distinguish three types of metadata: structure metadata that describe schemata of data sources, metadata properties and semantic metadata that contain annotations of source elements. In our approach, we extended the model presented in [10] with metadata necessary for evolution support.

3   Data Warehouse Architecture

In this section, a data warehouse architecture that we propose to perform big data analysis using different methods and facilitate evolution treatment is presented. The detailed description of the architecture is given in the paper [11]. The architecture components and their interaction are demonstrated in Fig. 1.

The main component of the architecture is a data processing pipeline (*Data Highway*). The idea and the concept of the data highway was first presented in [7]. Our proposed architecture implies that data from data sources are first extracted and loaded into the 1st raw source data level of the highway in their original format. Other levels of the highway are obtained from data sets at other data highway levels by ETL (Extract, Transform, Load) processes by means of performing transformation, aggregation and integrating related data items. The number and contents of the levels of the data highway depend on the requirements of the individual system. The final level of the highway is a data warehouse which stores structured aggregated data. If data volume does not allow to meet the desirable query performance, a set of precomputed OLAP cubes may be generated by the cube engine component of the architecture.

The unique feature of the architecture is the adaptation component that is aimed at handling changes in data sources or other levels of the data highway. The main idea of the adaptation component is to automatically detect changes in data sources or analyze changes introduced manually by means of a metadata management tool and generate several potential change propagation scenarios for each change. Then a developer can choose appropriate scenarios that are to be implemented or define preferences regarding change propagation scenarios that should be chosen automatically in case of streaming data sources.

To support the operation of the main components of the architecture and to allow to handle evolution, the metastore consisting of six types of interconnected metadata is included in the architecture. Schematic metadata describe schemata of data sets stored at different levels of the highway. Mapping metadata define the logic of ETL processes. Information about changes in data sources and data highway levels is accumulated in the evolution metadata. Cube metadata describe schemata of precomputed cubes. Potential change metadata accumulate proposed changes in the data warehouse schema. Finally, adaptation rules store additional information provided by the developer required for some change propagation and preferences of the developer regarding change propagation scenarios.

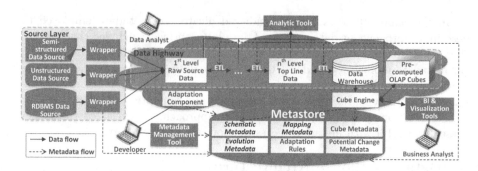

Fig. 1. Data warehouse architecture

4 Metadata

To describe schemata of data sources and data highway levels necessary for the analysis along with changes in structure and other properties of involved data sets we developed the metadata shown in Fig. 2.

The table *DataSet* is used to represent a collection of *DataItems* that are individual pieces of data. A data set may be obtained from a *DataSource* or it may be a part of a *DataHighwayLevel*. Data sets may have multiple instances that share the same data structure, for example, files of the same type. Data sets are characterized by format types grouped into parent types in the table *Types*. Each data item is associated with an item type determined by the format type of its data set. We distinguish three parent types of data sets:

- The parent type *Structured Data Set* represents a relational database table where data items correspond to table columns.
- The parent type *Semi-structured Data Set* reflects files where data items are organized into a schema that is not predefined. This type consists of such format types as XML, JSON, CSV, RDF, etc. The type of a data item incorporated into such data set indicates the position of it in the schema. For example, XML documents are composed of *Elements* and their *Attributes*, JSON documents may contain *Objects* and *Arrays*.
- The parent type *Unstructured Data Set* includes data that do not have any acknowledged schema. This type incorporates such format types as text, images, other multimedia content, etc. Usually, an unstructured data set is represented by a single data item. However, pieces of supplementary information like keywords or tags may be available. They are represented as additional data items associated with the corresponding data set in the metadata.

In addition to data set formats, we describe data sets by the velocity type that defines the rate of information retrieval from the data set, being batch, near real-time, real-time and stream. If a data set is a part of a data warehouse, a *Role* in the multidimensional model is assigned to such data set (dimension or fact) and corresponding data items (attribute or measure).

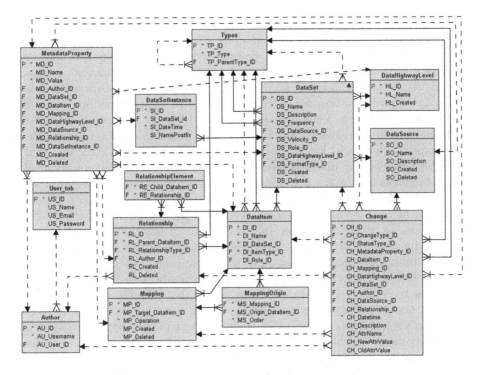

Fig. 2. Metadata for evolution support

There usually exist relationships between data items in the same data set or across integrated data sets. For example, elements in XML files are composed of other sub-elements and attributes, objects in JSON files may contain other objects as property values, foreign keys relate columns of relational tables. The same information may be reflected in different data sets in the related data items. To represent such relationships in the metadata, we introduced the tables *Relationship* and *RelationshipElement* that connect child and parent data items and assign the corresponding relationship type, for instance, composition, foreign key or equality. Certain relationships may be obtained in a machine-processible form automatically, but others may be only entered manually. For the latter case, we associate a relationship with the Author who created relationship metadata.

Since data sets are either extracted from data sources or obtained from other levels, the information about provenance of data sets within the data highway must be maintained to make it possible to follow their lineage. For this purpose, mappings were introduced in the metadata. A record in the table *Mapping* defines a transformation saved in the column *Operation* by which a target data item is derived from origin data items associated via the table *MappingOrigin*.

Up to this point, we discussed mainly the schematic metadata of data sets employed in the architecture whereas other characteristics of data should also be collected. To this end, we included the table *MetadataProperty*. Any Name:Value pair relevant to schema elements present in the model can be added to the metadata. Considering that various elements may possess different properties, such approach allows for some flexibility. Examples of metadata properties include physical file name, size, character set, check constraints for data sets; type, length, precision, scale, nullable for data items; mechanism used to retrieve data from a data source (for instance, API request), etc. Although many properties of schema elements may be identified automatically by ETL procedures, there still might be certain characteristics that have to be added manually, for instance, by semantic annotation. Furthermore, some new properties of data sets that might be valuable may be discovered during data analysis. Such conversational metadata properties are associated with the *Author* who recorded the property.

The main feature of the proposed architecture is evolution support. Therefore, we identified a set of atomic changes that are discussed in more detail in the next section. In order to maintain information about any changes in data sets discovered automatically or introduced manually, the metadata model incorporates the table *Change*. Every record of this table is associated with a schema element affected by the change. For each change, we store the date and time when the change took place, *Type* of the change, *Status* that determines whether that change is new, already propagated in the system or being currently processed. For changes that involve modification of an attribute or property value, we also store the name of the changed attribute (*AttrName*), and both the value before and after the change (*OldAttrValue* and *NewAttrValue*). If the change was produced manually, we associate it with the corresponding *Author*.

5   Atomic Changes

In this section, we will overview atomic changes supported in the proposed solution. The changes are classified according to the part of the metadata they affect. Most of the changes may be identified automatically by the change discovery algorithm described in the next section. Manually created changes are processed by the metadata management tool. For changes that can only be implemented manually, we present metadata tables that are referenced by the record in the table *Change*, the key columns of the table *Change* with their values and additional metadata that must be recorded in Table 1. The detailed discussion of all atomic changes is available in the paper [9]. The following automatically discoverable changes are supported in the proposed approach:

- *Schematic changes*: addition of a data source, deletion of a data source, addition of a data highway level, deletion of a data highway level, addition of a data set, deletion of a data set, change of data set format, addition of a data item, change of a data item type, deletion of a data item from a data set, addition of a relationship, deletion of a relationship, modification of a relationship, deletion of a mapping;
- *Changes in metadata properties*: addition of a metadata property, deletion of a metadata property, update of an attribute value.

Table 1. Manual atomic changes

Change	Referenced table	Key column values	Additional information
Renamed data set	*DataSet*	Type: Attribute value update AttrName: Name	The columns *OldAttrValue* and *NewAttrValue* of the table *Change* are filled with the previous and updated name of the data set
Renamed data item	*DataItem*	Type: Attribute value update AttrName: Name	The columns *OldAttrValue* and *NewAttrValue* of the table *Change* are filled with the previous and updated name of the data item
Addition of a new mapping	*Mapping*	Type: Addition	A new record in the table *Mapping* that references target and origin data items and defines the way the target data item is obtained in the column *Operation* is added

6   Algorithm for Change Discovery

In this section, the algorithm for schema change discovery in the metadata is described. The algorithm is implemented as a part of the adaptation component of the data warehouse evolution architecture. It is triggered automatically when any new data are loaded from data sources into the data highway by wrappers or during ETL processes. The high-level pseudocode of the algorithm is presented as follows:

Input: TM - temporary metadata describing current schemata and
   properties of all data sets. SM - metadata at the metastore.
foreach *schema element E in TM or SM* **do** E.processed ← false;
while *exists DataSource S where S.processed = false* **do**
ProcessDataSourceChanges(S);
while *exists DHighwayLevel L where L.processed = false* **do**
ProcessDataHighwayLevelChanges(L);
while *exists Mapping M where M.processed = false* **do**
ProcessMappingChanges(M);
while *exists Relationship R where R.processed = false* **do**
ProcessRelationshipChanges(R);

Initially, the change detection algorithm gathers schema metadata and properties of existing data sources and data highway levels in temporary metadata (*TM*). The model of the temporary metadata is identical to the one presented in Sect. 4 except for the table *Change*. For metadata collection, special procedures are used depending on the format of data sets. The algorithm then processes each data source and each data highway level separately, then processes mappings between data items and finally relationships. Treatment of changes in mappings and relationships can be done only after processing of all data sources and data highway levels so that all data items required for the mapping or relationship are already available in the schema metadata.

The procedure *ProcessDataHighwayLevelChanges* is identical to the procedure *ProcessDataSourceChanges*. The difference is that the former handles changes in data highway levels instead of data sources. Therefore, only the source change detection procedure is explained in the following section.

6.1   Detection of Data Source Changes

The following pseudocode demonstrates the procedure *ProcessDataSource Changes*:

> **Procedure** *ProcessDataSourceChanges(S: data source, TM, SM)*
> > **if** *S is present in TM and S is not present in SM* **then**
> > > Copy metadata describing the data source S from TM to SM;
> > > Create a change with the type *Addition of a data source*;
> > > S.processed ← true;
> >
> > **else if** *S is present in SM and S is not present in TM* **then**
> > > Create a change with the type *Deletion of a data source*;
> > > S.processed ← true;
> >
> > **else**
> > > **foreach** *data set DS belonging to S from TM or SM* **do**
> > > ProcessDataSetChanges(DS) ;
> > > ProcessChangesInMetadataProperties(S);
> > > S.processed ← true;
> > **end**
> **end**

This procedure discovers new data sources and unavailable data sources as well as detects changes in data sets of data sources. The input of the procedure is the metadata describing a schema and properties of a data source that are present in the schema metadata (SM) at the metastore or temporary schema metadata (TM). The input metadata also include properties and data sets of a data source. To discover changes in a data source, the procedure distinguishes 3 cases.

The metadata describing the data source are present in TM and not present in SM. This means that the data source is newly added to the system. In this case, metadata about the new data source and all its properties are created in SM at the metastore by copying it from TM. For each data set included in the new data source, the corresponding schematic metadata and metadata properties must be added too. The change with the Type: Addition is inserted in the table *Change* and associated with the new data source record in the table *DataSource*.

The metadata describing the data source are present in SM and not present in TM. This means that the data source is no longer available. In this case, the data source is marked as deleted in the table *DataSource*. The change with the Type: Deletion is inserted in the table *Change* and associated with the corresponding data source record in the table *DataSource*.

The metadata describing the data source are present both in *TM* and *SM*. This means that the data source is not new and is still available, so any changes in its data sets and properties have to be discovered. So to do that, at first metadata about all data sets of the data source are selected from *SM* or *TM* and each data set is treated with the procedure *ProcessDataSetChanges*. After that, the procedure *ProcessChangesInMetadataProperties* is executed for all properties of the data source.

6.2   Detection of Changes in Metadata Properties

The following pseudocode demonstrates the procedure *ProcessChangesInMetadataProperties*:

Procedure *ProcessChangesInMetadataProperties(E: schema element, TM, SM)*

> **foreach** *property P of E from TM or SM* **do**
>> **if** *P is present in TM and P is not present in SM* **then**
>>> | Create a change with the type *Addition of a property*;
>> **else if** *P is present in SM and P is not present in TM* **then**
>>> **if** *P.Author is null* **then**
>>>> | Create a change with the type *Deletion of a property*;
>>> **else if** *P is present in SM and P is present in TM and P.value in SM* $\neq$ *P.value in TM* **then**
>>>> | Create a change with the type *Update of an attribute value*;
>>> **end**
>> **end**
> **end**

end

The procedure is capable of detecting new properties, no longer available properties and changes in automatically discoverable property values. The input of the procedure is the metadata describing properties of any schema element that are present in *SM* or *TM*. The operation of the procedure is similar to the previously described procedure for detection of data source changes with some specifics. The procedure categorizes each of the properties into three cases based on the availability of metadata in *SM* and *TM*.

If the property metadata are available only in *TM* and not in *SM*, a new record with property information is created in the table *MetadataProperty* and the change with the Type: Addition is inserted in the table *Change* and associated with the corresponding record in the table *MetadataProperty*.

If the property metadata are available only in *SM* and not in *TM*, this means that the property is either not valid any more or is not discoverable automatically. So the procedure checks whether the property was previously entered in the metastore manually and has a reference to the corresponding record in the table *Author*. If that is the case, the property may only be deleted manually. Otherwise, the property is marked as deleted in the table *MetadataProperty* and the change with the Type: Deletion is inserted in the table *Change* and associated with the corresponding record in the table *MetadataProperty*.

If the property metadata are available both in *TM* and *SM*, this means that the property is still valid and is discoverable automatically and its value is compared in *SM* and *TM*. If the values differ, the property value is updated in the table *MetadataProperty*. The change is created with the Type: Attribute value update in the table *Change*. The property values before and after the update are recorded in the attributes *OldAttrValue* and *NewAttrValue*. The change record is associated with the corresponding record in the table *MetadataProperty*.

6.3   Detection of Changes in Data Sets

The procedure *ProcessDataSetChanges* implements discovery of three atomic changes: new data set, no longer available data set and change in data set format. The pseudocode of the procedure is not included since it resembles the pseudocode of the procedure *ProcessDataSourceChanges*. It also runs a procedure for detection of changes in data items included in the data set. The procedure *ProcessDataSetChanges* is also executed for the detection of changes in data sets belonging to data highway levels. As an input, the procedure receives metadata describing a data set that were obtained either from *SM* or *TM*. These metadata also contain properties of a data set and its data items. Just as other change detection procedures, the procedure for change detection in data sets analyzes the origin of metadata about the data set and distinguishes three cases.

If the data set metadata are present only in *TM*, they are copied into *SM* and the change with the Type: Addition is inserted in the table *Change* and associated with the corresponding record in the table *DataSet*.

If the data set metadata are present only in *SM*, the change with the Type: Deletion is inserted in the table *Change* and associated with the corresponding record in the table *DataSet* that in turn is marked as deleted.

If the metadata are present both in *TM* and *SM*, first it must be verified whether the format of the data set is the same in both metadata. If the format differs, such change must be recorded as two changes: deletion and addition of a data set. After that, new relationships with the type *Equality* between the equivalent data items of the removed data set and the new data set must be added to *SM*. If the format of the data set is the same in *TM* and *SM*, these metadata have to be compared to discover changes in data items as described in Sect. 6.4. Finally, changes in properties of the data set are analyzed by the procedure *ProcessChangesInMetadataProperties*.

6.4   Detection of Changes in Data Items

The procedure *ProcessDataItemChanges* is used to identify such changes in data items as addition of a new data item, deletion of a data item and change of a data type of a data item. The pseudocode of the procedure is not included since it resembles the pseudocode of the procedure for detection of data source changes. The input to the procedure *ProcessDataItemChanges* is the metadata describing a data item obtained either from *TM* or *SM*. Here again the procedure identifies three cases according to the existence of the metadata in *SM* or *TM*.

The first case when the metadata describing the processed data item are available only in *TM* is processed as an addition of a new data item to the existing data set. The procedure inserts a new record with information about the data item in the table *DataItem* and associates it with the corresponding data set. Then a new record is inserted in the table *Change* with the Type: Addition and associated with the previously created record in the table *DataItem*.

When the metadata are present only in *SM*, the deletion of a data item from a data set has to be registered. In this case, the procedure creates a record in the table *Change* with the Type: Deletion and associates it with the corresponding record in the table *DataItem* that in turn is marked as deleted.

Finally, if the data item is present both in *SM* and *TM*, the procedure compares the data type of the data item in both metadata. Such comparison also considers length, scale, precision and nullable properties. If any of these properties differs, the change is processed as an update of the attribute value. The data type is reflected as a pre-defined property in the metadata, so its value is updated according to the new data type. Then, a new record in the table *Change* is created with the Type: Attribute value update, the columns *OldAttrValue* and *NewAttrValue* are filled with the previous and updated type of the data item. The change record is associated with the property record in the table *MetadataProperty*. Lastly, the procedure *ProcessChangesInMetadataProperties* is executed for other properties of the data item.

6.5   Detection of Changes in Mappings

The following pseudocode demonstrates the procedure *ProcessMappingChanges*:

```
Procedure ProcessMappingChanges(M: mapping, SM)
    foreach data item I used in M from SM do
        if I.deleted = true then
            Create a change with the type Deletion of a mapping;
        ProcessChangesInMetadataProperties(I);
    end
end
```

The objective of this procedure is to automatically identify mappings that are no longer valid because of the absence of the data items used in them. The input to the procedure is the mapping metadata obtained from *SM*. First, the procedure selects all data items used to calculate the mapping target data item via the table *MappingOrigin*. Then it is verified whether any of these data items are marked as deleted by the previous steps of the algorithm. If at least one such data item is identified, the mapping is marked as deleted and the change with the Type: Deletion is inserted in the table *Change* and associated with the corresponding record in the table *Mapping*. If none of the data items necessary for the mapping was deleted, the mapping is still usable in ETL processes and does not have to be changed. In this case, the procedure *ProcessChangesInMetadataProperties* is executed on properties of the processed mapping.

6.6   Detection of Changes in Relationships

Due to space limitations the pseudocode of the procedure *ProcessRelationship-Changes* is not included. This procedure analyzes relationships between data items that are obtained either from *TM* or *SM* and detects new relationships, relationships that are no longer present in data or modified relationships as well as discovers changes in relationship properties. As an input, the procedure receives relationship information from *SM* or *TM*. Th processing of this information begins with distinction of three cases based on the availability of metadata.

If the information about the relationship is present only in *TM*, the procedure copies this information into the tables *Relationship* and *RelationshipElement* in *SM*, creates the change with the Type: Addition in the table *Change* and associates it with the new relationship metadata.

The second case is when information about the relationship is present only in *SM* and the procedure has to identify whether the relationship is still valid or it was deleted. Three situations are analyzed:

1. The relationship is with the type *Equality* and it was created between two data items by the change discovery algorithm when the format of a certain data set was modified. In this situation, the procedure verifies if any of the related data items are still available and not deleted. If that is the case, the relationship is considered to be still valid. Otherwise, the relationship is considered obsolete and the deletion of a relationship has to be registered. To implement this change, a record with the Type: Deletion is created in the table *Change* and associated with the relationship record in the table *Relationship* that in turn is marked as deleted.
2. The relationship was created manually and is associated with a certain user via the table *Author*. In this case, the procedure has to verify that all data items involved in the relationship are still present in *SM* and were not deleted. If that is the case, the relationship is no longer valid and the deletion of a relationship has to be registered according to the operations described in the previous situation.
3. If the relationship was not added to the metastore manually or created by the change discovery algorithm, the procedure just records the deletion of a relationship according to the above mentioned process.

Finally, if the information about the relationship is available in both *TM* and *SM*, it has to be checked that data items involved in the relationship and relationship type have not changed. If modification of the relationship is detected, it must be recorded as two changes: deletion and addition of a relationship according to the operations discussed in the previous cases. If the relationship has not changed, the procedure continues with the discovery of changes in properties of the relationship.

7   Case Study

As a proof of concept, we applied the architecture and change discovery approach to the case study data warehouse. The example model and metadata fragments of this system are available in [9]. The data warehouse integrates data about research papers published by the faculty of the University of Latvia. The system gets data from four data sources of various formats. One of these sources is the university management system LUIS implemented in Oracle database. We extract data about the academic staff and students as well as publications entered by LUIS users from this source. Other three data sources are external systems that offer API for data retrieval in XML format. We extract bibliographical data, authors, affiliations, and publication citation metrics from SCOPUS and Web of Science data sources as well as from the library data management system if publications are not indexed by SCOPUS or Web of Science.

We implemented the case study data warehouse according to the proposed architecture. Three levels of the data highway were created to transform and integrate publication data. First, data from the sources are ingested and loaded into the 1st raw data level. We use Scoop to extract data from the relational database LUIS into Hive tables. Semi-structured data from other sources in XML format are first pulled from the API and saved in Linux file system as multiple files and then data are transferred into HDFS using a script with HDFS commands. Then XML data are transformed into the structured Hive tables at the 2nd level of the data highway. Finally, at the 3rd level all data are integrated and loaded into the data warehouse implemented in Hive.

We gathered the metadata about data sources and data highway levels of the case study system into the metastore implemented in Oracle database according to the model presented in Sect. 4. Since we have a full access to LUIS data source, we embedded a procedure directly into LUIS that collects the necessary metadata. To process data extracted from external sources in XML format, we created a procedure that analyses the structure of XML documents and other properties and generates the necessary metadata in the metastore. We developed a prototype of the metadata management tool that currently displays the metadata gathered in the metastore, allows a developer to track all changes discovered in data automatically and add information about changes manually.

During the operation of the publication data warehouse, several changes in data sources and data highway levels were detected by the change discovery algorithm and introduced manually via the metadata management tool. Several examples of these changes are following.

A new XML element *citeScoreYearInfoList* was added to the data set *Scopus_metrics* obtained from SCOPUS. It was composed of several subelements that were also absent in the previously gathered data sets. The algorithm detected that change automatically and processed it as an addition of a data item.

An XML element IPP was removed from the same data set *Scopus_metrics*. This change was also detected automatically and processed as a deletion of a data item from a data set. Since this change invalidated the data loading process, the algorithm also discovered mappings affected by the removal of the data item and implemented the change Deletion of a mapping for each of them.

In line with new requirements, the system was supplemented by a new data source *DSpace* that contained text files and metadata associated with them as tags. This change was implemented by the metadata management tool since the data source along with all necessary metadata were added manually.

8   Conclusions

In this paper, we presented a data warehouse solution for big data applications. Not only our proposed solution allows to perform various kinds of analysis on big data, but also the unique feature of it is support for change discovery in data sources and user requirements. We described the main components of the system architecture, metadata necessary for its operation and supported changes in the structure of data caused by evolution of data sources or user requirements. The main contribution of this paper is the algorithm for automatic detection of most of the changes. We also outlined our experience with application of our approach in the case study system.

The directions for future work include full implementation of the adaptation component of the data warehouse architecture where we will develop algorithms for automatic and semi-automatic change treatment.

Acknowledgments. This work has been supported by the European Regional Development Fund (ERDF) project No. 1.1.1.2./VIAA/1/16/057.

References

1. Kaisler, S., Armour, F., Espinosa, J.A., Money, W.: Big data: issues and challenges moving forward. In: 46th International Conference on System Sciences, pp. 995–1004 (2013)
2. Cuzzocrea, A., Bellatreche, L., Song, I.: Data warehousing and OLAP over big data: current challenges and future research directions. In: 16th International Workshop on Data Warehousing and OLAP, pp. 67–70 (2013)
3. Holubová, I., Klettke, M., Störl, U.: Evolution management of multi-model data. In: Gadepally, V., et al. (eds.) DMAH/Poly -2019. LNCS, vol. 11721, pp. 139–153. Springer, Cham (2019). https://doi.org/10.1007/978-3-030-33752-0_10
4. Solodovnikova, D., Niedrite, L.: Handling evolution in big data architectures. Balt. J. Mod. Comput. **8**(1), 21–47 (2020)
5. Nadal, S., Romero, O., Abelló, A., Vassiliadis, P., Vansummeren, S.: An integration-oriented ontology to govern evolution in big data ecosystems. In: Workshops of the EDBT/ICDT 2017 Joint Conference (2017)
6. Chen, S.: Cheetah: a high performance, custom data warehouse on top of MapReduce. VLDB Endow. **3**(2), 1459–1468 (2010)
7. Kimball, R., Ross, M.: The Data Warehouse Toolkit: The Definitive Guide to Dimensional Modeling, 3rd edn. Wiley, Indiana (2013)
8. Sumbaly, R., Kreps, J., Shah, S.: The "big data" ecosystem at LinkedIn. In: ACM SIGMOD International Conference on Management of Data, pp. 1125–1134 (2013)

9. Solodovnikova, D., Niedrite, L., Niedritis, A.: On metadata support for integrating evolving heterogeneous data sources. In: Welzer, T., et al. (eds.) ADBIS 2019. CCIS, vol. 1064, pp. 378–390. Springer, Cham (2019). https://doi.org/10.1007/978-3-030-30278-8_38

10. Quix, C., Hai, R., Vatov, I.: Metadata extraction and management in data lakes with GEMMS. Complex Syst. Inform. Model. Q. **9**, 67–83 (2016)

11. Solodovnikova, D., Niedrite, L.: Towards a data warehouse architecture for managing big data evolution. In: Proceedings of the 7th International Conference on Data Science, Technology and Applications (DATA 2018), Porto, Portugal, pp. 63–70 (2018)

Floor Selection Proposal for Automated Travel with Smart Elevator

Uljana Reinsalu$^{(\boxtimes)}$, Tarmo Robal , and Mairo Leier

Tallinn University of Technology, 12618 Tallinn, Estonia
{uljana.reinsalu,tarmo.robal,mairo.leier}@taltech.ee

Abstract. Elevators have been used for centuries to convey material and people, with a history going back to 19th century. Modern elevators as we use them today became widely used some 150 years ago, and regardless of many improvements and technological advancements, the general concept has remained the same. The typical elevator still needs traveller's input to take the passenger from one floor to another. In this paper we explore the possibility to predict elevator passenger destination floor. For this task we use passenger profiles established through deep learning, and elaborate on the passenger's trip history to predict the floor the passenger desires to travel. The study is based on a smart elevator system set up in a typical office building. The aim is to provide personalised elevator service in the context of a smart elevator.

Keywords: Smart elevator · Prediction · Personalization

1 Introduction

The history of modern elevators goes back to 19th century, although mechanisms for vertical transportation have existed even for a longer term. Elevators are used to meet the vertical transportation needs of people (and goods) in buildings. Since the advancement in engineering has enabled to establish ever higher buildings, elevators have become an important mean of vertical transportation, allowing people to move from one floor to another quickly and without any extra physical effort. In modern buildings today – either commercial, or residential – elevators are a necessity many people rely on, especially in mid- and high-rise buildings, as climbing several floors is tiring, and in some cases even impossible, e.g., elderly people and people with disabilities.

Most of today's elevators are operated manually from inside the elevator car by its passengers by selecting the desired destination floor from the switch panel. This is a simple, yet really efficient approach, and provides a lot of liberty to the passengers. Yet, once a destination is set, it cannot be cancelled. The main problem of conventional elevators is that the passenger destination floor is unknown until the passenger has boarded the elevator car. This issue has been addressed by some more advanced elevator systems, which allow to pre-register

© Springer Nature Switzerland AG 2020
T. Robal et al. (Eds.): DB&IS 2020, CCIS 1243, pp. 38–51, 2020.
https://doi.org/10.1007/978-3-030-57672-1_4

destination floor together with an elevator call [20], providing also a way to group and schedule the passengers moving to the same floor.

With the advancement of technology and overall computerization, Cyber Physical Systems (CPS) [25] and Cyber Physical Social Systems (CPSS) [7,9,43], emphasizing the crucial role of humans in highly computerized systems, have gained an importance in our lives. This is in turn complemented with an explosive growth of Artificial Intelligence (AI) technologies [32] such as facial image recognition [30,34,36,41] and human speech recognition [2,19,22,31]. A smart elevator is a CPSS advantaging of data mining, AI, and machine learning to deliver personalized travel experience to its passengers.

Although, a lot of works can be found on CPSS, smart elevators as CPSS have received little attention. Most of the research around elevators falls into the scope of reducing waiting time and energy consumption [3,4,8,13,14,39], the latter being an emerging focus since the need to reduce our carbon footprint. Optimal parking in group elevator control was explored in [5], whereas the use of floor sensors and RFID for elevator scheduling in [24], and the use of mobile phones to improve flow of people in [38]. Optimization of elevator evacuation in smart high-rise buildings in [27]. Thorough overview of elevator control systems is provided in [13]. Intelligent elevator systems have been addressed in [17], and passenger behavioral patterns while using elevators in [26].

The majority of the prior research work on elevator scheduling systems has explored possibilities of using genetic algorithms [21] and networks [10], artificial neural networks [42], and DNA computing methods [40], or exploiting the context of elevator usage [17,18,37]. In these works the passengers are mostly addressed as anonymous units having any prior knowledge about them in the system. In our work, on the contrary, we will be addressing elevator passengers about whom the elevator system has some prior knowledge stored and available for future decisions. Thus, with our smart elevator system we are aiming on a personalized travel experience for an elevator passenger, which distinguishes our work from prior research.

Providing personalized services has been a research ground for many studies. Mostly, these approaches facilitate from systems of information retrieval (IR), extraction of user context, modelling and establishing user profiles [11,16], re-ranking items and providing recommendations [1,6,15,29,33,35], e.g. personalized news recommendations or Web personalization, delivering significant improvement to services provided. In this article, we take this approach towards CPSS, in particular to a smart elevator system.

In this paper our main focus is on elevator passengers for whom a user profile has been established (discussed in Sect. 3.3) in the system, and some travel history is available. For passengers who remain unidentified by the system, the travel with the smart elevator remains conventional, and the smart elevator floor prediction system does not provide any prediction nor floor pre-selection for the passenger. The utmost aim is to provide a personalized service for smart elevator passengers.

The objectives of the research described in this paper are to investigate elevator passengers' travel behaviour and establish a baseline for floor prediction. To accomplish this, data about travels with an elevator is collected to a special log together with actual travel information. We also explore whether traveller behaviour data can be used to extract some travel patterns and apply these to improve destination floor predictions. These objectives take us to the following research questions to be studied:

RQ1: *How likely are elevator travellers willing to take the elevator to travel just one floor?* We hypothesize that the majority of people prefer to take stairs to transit one floor, as it is not a big effort and usually the elevator waiting time exceeds this effort time.

RQ2: *To what extent does the most frequently travelled floor describes elevator passenger behaviour and travel needs?* To answer this question we look at passengers' travels and compare those to the baseline prediction based on the most probable floor within passenger travel history.

RQ3: *How dependent are elevator passengers' travel needs on their daily activities in a typical office building, and can this be used to improve floor prediction for a profiled passenger?* To answer this question, we explore passengers daily travel patterns and include them to floor prediction. We hypothesize that including these daily travel patterns will improve prediction accuracy for profiled elevator passengers in a typical office building.

The results of our studies indicate that potential travel distance, as well as frequently travelled floors and the travel time are important attributes of smart elevator passenger profile, and serve as a valuable input for our future studies.

The rest of the paper is organized as follows. In Sect. 2 we discuss related works in the domain of elevators, Sect. 3.2 is dedicated to a discussion on smart elevator system, while in Sect. 4 we address personalized elevator travel. Finally, in Sect. 5 we draw conclusions and discuss ideas for future work.

2   Related Works

The research on elevators has mainly focused on dispatch problems and alleviating the waiting time problem. Bharti et al. [4] established a cognitive model for dispatch systems like smart elevators to reduce wait time and predict a necessity of an elevator on a particular floor, using machine learning. Their solution could be applied to other dispatch systems like bus and train to maximize the utilization of provided services. In their system travellers were identified using ID card's location, and persons were registered within the system with their regular destination floor. These two pieces of data were used to minimize elevator waiting time by making an automatic call to elevator based upon prediction of user's arrival into elevator area. Fujimura et al. [14] on the other hand explored a similar problem of reducing passenger waiting time in the context of multi-car elevators in single shaft for high-rise buildings. Their control algorithm allocated requests to elevator cars by using a local search method to reduce the waste time during which cars cannot transport passengers. The algorithm was evaluated by simulation and showed improved performance compared to earlier algorithms used for multi-car elevators. Luo and colleagues [12] described elevator traffic flow as a time series set, and predicted the latter using the least squares support vector machines, providing promising results and good performance.

Cameras and deep learning were used by Chou et al. [8] not only to minimize the average waiting time for passengers but also decrease energy consumption by re-scheduling elevator movements. In this research cameras were placed in front of elevators and Region Based Convolutional Neural Network (R-CNN) was used to detect the number of passengers queuing for an elevator, and dispatch elevators according to the detected demand such that the elevator with the smallest energy consumption was serving the waiting passengers.

Ge and colleagues [17] took the concept of a smart elevator even further by turning a conventional elevator system into a IoT based elevator system, and proposed Intellevator - an intelligent elevator system able to proactively provide passengers assistive information (e.g., real-time waiting time) based on real-time context sensing and awareness. Passengers perceived Intellevator as useful. In parallel, another smart elevator system was proposed by Ge and colleagues [18] – a pre-call enabled elevator system in smart building called the PrecaElevator, where elevator could be pre-called within office room using a special user interface, reducing significantly passenger waiting times on a conventional office elevator. While Ge and colleagues relied on IoT, Strang and Bauer [37] applied context-awareness to elevator system by exploiting available contextual knowledge (e.g., weather vs lunch-time, upcoming events in the building, etc), and made it available for control systems for elevator scheduling. Their work indicated that including the context can improve system performance.

While in [18] passengers could pre-call elevator from their office, Turunen et al. [38] explored a novel concept of using mobile interaction with elevators. They allowed passengers to indicate in advance where they are going through a special smartphone app, whereas the application handled the corresponding elevator calls on behalf of them. The app also allowed to define default departure and destination floors. The important finding of this study is that mobile apps can be used to place elevator calls in advance, and it can shorten the perceived waiting time and expedite the movement of passengers in buildings.

Human behavioural patterns in elevator usage were investigated by Liang et al. [26]. Based on real-world traces collected from 12 elevators in an 18-story office building, they argue that understanding human behavioral patterns is an important step towards better elevator usage efficiency, and behavioral patterns affect the service the most in high-rise buildings with several elevators, as in low-rise buildings the elevators can reach all floors quickly and the effect of service time therefore is rather small.

Compared to this earlier work, our work focuses on delivering the profiled passenger to a floor that suites her travelling needs the most, without any effort required from the passenger, i.e., no need to use the switch panel in the elevator car to dial the destination floor. To the best of our knowledge, personalization has not yet been applied in the context of smart elevator travels in such a way.

3 Smart Elevator System

3.1 Elevator System Background

The elevator system we use as a basis for the smart elevator is a conventional simple elevator system with a single car running in its allocated elevator shaft in a typical 8-floor office building. The building resides at university campus and hosts offices for university staff, labs, computer classes, and start-up companies. The entrance floor of the building is Floor 1, whereas Floor 0 allows access to secured parking area. Floors 1–7 are used for offices, Floors 1, 3, 4, 5, and 6 have also labs and computer classes, and Floors 2 and 7 are occupied by companies. Thereby, besides employees who have offices in the building, the regular visitors of this building are students. The travel needs of university academic staff and students are affected by the time and location of classes taking place.

Let us now turn to the elevator system. An *elevator call* (a trip) is a ride between two floors, where at least one passenger is present in the elevator car. The elevator call is defined by its departure and destination floor, and the number of passengers on the call. Herein, we do not consider empty calls – trips without passengers – of interest. An *elevator event* is defined as any action a passenger takes with an elevator, and events are logged. In the context of the smart elevator voice commands and floor predictions are additional events captured.

In our elevator model the building is defined to consist of F floors such that $F = \{f_0, f_1, ..., f_7\}$, there is a single elevator car E running Up or $Down$ in its own shaft. Floor calls C are initiated by passengers P pressing either the Up or $Down$ button indicating their desired travel direction. These buttons are located outside the elevator car on each floor. The elevator car makes a stop on the floor for which a call on its travel direction exists, or a travel destination has been selected by a passenger from the switch panel inside the car. If the destination floor chosen by passenger is not on the car's travel direction, the elevator continues to serve calls on its travel direction before serving calls on the opposite direction.

3.2 Smart Elevator System Architecture

The smart elevator system is based on the existing conventional elevator built by KONE Corporation – a global leader in the elevator and escalator industry. Our building has two independent KONE elevators, each running in its own shaft. For the smart elevator, we use only one of these elevators. In addition to the existing elevator system, the following devices were installed in the elevator car to add the main features of Smart elevator (Fig. 1):

– A RGB camera from Basler with Ethernet communication, 4MP resolution and global shutter. The camera is installed in the corner of the elevator facing the doors, and is able to capture video stream up to 15 fps covering the area of elevator entrance and most of the cabin. The images captured by the camera are used as an input for face detection algorithm to detect human faces.

The latter is based on HOG feature extractor [23] with linear classifier. Extracted face descriptions are then compared to existing face profiles using Radius Neighbour Classifier [28] to detect and distinguish different passengers.

– Four Intel Real Sense depth cameras with dual infrared light sensors located over the elevator ceiling cover. These are used to detect passenger movement and locations within the elevator car, including exiting the elevator car.
– Microphone and speaker (Sennheiser SP20) which allow the passengers to control the elevator through voice commands using either Estonian or English as the command language. Presently, the passengers can request the elevator to take them to a specific floor (e.g., by giving the command *Go to the first floor!*), to a floor of an employee by stating employee name, and in addition ask about weather forecast and current date and time.

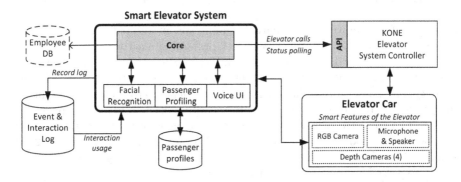

Fig. 1. The Smart elevator system architecture.

To comply with privacy and security requirements, passengers of the smart elevator are informed about the existence of these devices in accordance with the law using notices near elevator entrance. To preserve passengers privacy the captured biometric data is only stored as encoded feature vectors, and used on an anonymous basis by machine learning algorithm.

The orchestration of different smart elevator components and subsystems is the responsibility of the *Core* (Fig. 1), written in Python. In particular, the *Core* takes care of interacting with the KONE API (the elevator API) with the aim of making elevator calls and polling its status. The *Core* is also responsible for logging elevator event data, associating passenger identificators received through facial recognition, tracking passengers' entry and exit floors, predicting destination floors for passengers for automatic floor pre-selection and call, and lastly moving the elevator near floors with high volume of entry traffic while its idle.

The Smart elevator databases store the following data: passenger profiles, facial fingerprints, audio queries performed as voice commands to the elevator, passenger travel history together with departure and destination floor, elevator event log containing all elevator travels. All interactions and events with the Smart elevator are logged with timestamps added by the database management system (DBMS). We have used the PostgreSQL DBMS ver.11.4 for data storing.

Regardless of the installed smart elevator features, the passengers of this elevator are still able to manually operate it using the switch panel in the elevator car and select their desired destination floor. As our aim in this paper is the automatic passenger destination floor selection, we will limit our discussion on the system here.

3.3   Passenger Profiles

Once a passenger enters the smart elevator, the system captures a video stream with the in-car RGB camera, and facial recognition is carried out to detect whether a passenger has already been profiled, or a new profile should be created. This identification is based on facial fingerprints stored as 128-member vectors. The database of passenger profiles is created based upon arrival of new passengers from scratch. If no match is found for an entered passenger, a new passenger profile is created. No passenger profile is linked to an actual person with name and other data making her identifiable. With this approach, the smart elevator system operates around passengers, who's identity remains anonymous.

In general passenger profile consist of profile identificator, which distinguishes the passenger from others, and facial fingerprints, used to identify a passenger whenever she uses the elevator. These profiles are generated automatically. During the test period of three months from November 2019 to February 2020, around 450 profiles were established. In addition, the passenger profile is connected to passenger interactions history. In our research we use the travel history to forecast passenger travel floor and make a personalized floor pre-selection for a profiled passenger.

Each of the profiles is related to a passenger interaction log, where an entry is made every time a passenger is successfully identified with facial recognition. This log links together profiled passengers with elevator interactions, and forms the basis for providing personalization and smart features for profiled passengers. Presently, personalized floor pre-selection on elevator entry is provided for known (profiled) passengers, based on the most frequently travelled floor from a departure floor. Yet, this approach is not sufficient, and has provoked us to find ways to improve it through user profiling, as discussed in Sect. 4.

4   Towards Personalized Elevator Travel

In this section we address the personalized travel experience for profiled passengers. For passengers that remain unidentified by the system, the travel with the smart elevator remains conventional – they call the elevator, enter the elevator car, and select the desired destination floor from the switch panel within the car. In addition, all passengers can use voice commands to set the destination floor.

Vision of Personalized Travel: For profiled passengers we have envisioned that commuting between two floors should be possible without a need to press any buttons inside the car. Once a profiled passenger enters the elevator and is identified, the system is able to predict the floor the passenger wants to reach, pre-selects the floor for the passenger and initiates travel – all this without any need from a passenger to press buttons or interact in any other way with the elevator within the car.

In the present set-up, the simplest solution has been taken and the smart elevator system predicts the most visited destination floor for a departure floor. For this, the smart elevator system pulls the passenger's travel history from the repository. The floor to which the passenger has travelled from the departure floor the most, is deemed to be the most probable destination floor. The precondition for this is that the floor has to have been visited by a passenger from the departure floor as a destination at least 10 times, in all other cases the departure-destination floor pair is not considered for the prediction. Thus, the smart elevator floor prediction system looks at floor pairs FP such that $FP = f_n \times D$, where $f_n \in F$ and $D \subset F$ such that $f_n \notin D$, and f_n is the departure floor and D is a set of destination floors.

The feedback we got during the initial smart elevator test period indicated that the initial approach taken for floor predictions is not perceived useful, and in some cases even considered annoying. Thereby, we are now looking for ways to improve the system, including passenger context, travel behaviour patterns, also by time, and any other additional information to be included in anonymous passenger profiles to deliver better desired destination predictions and quality of personalized elevator service.

Herein, we focus on these anonymous passenger profiles for which we construct daily travel patterns. We then investigate, whether including these daily travel needs improves the present simple approach of destination floor prediction, and to what extent. For the latter, we first answer ***RQ1*** to investigate the travel distances and likelihood of making short one-floor transits in Sect. 4.1. We then proceed to set the baseline for ***RQ2*** and look at the extent the most travelled floor describes passenger behaviour (Sect. 4.2), followed by the study where we include time patterns (***RQ3***) in Sect. 4.3.

4.1   RQ1: Likelihood of Short-Distance Transit

The first question to consider is the likelihood that elevator passengers transit only one floor. In particular, how likely an elevator is used just to travel one floor up or down. The motivation is to identify whether this aspect of travel behaviour could be used for floor prediction. If the hypothesis that passengers tend to prefer stairs to elevator to transit one floor holds true, this can be used as a valuable input for the decision process and should be included in passenger profiles. This would help, for example in the case an equal or almost equal choice between two floors exists, to decide over whether the long or short distance transit should be preferred for the floor prediction.

To answer RQ1, we take a look on all the trips made with our smart elevator. Presently, our database holds data about 36,526 such trips collected over a time period of three months. These trips are the transits in between two floors without any intermediate stops. We do not consider 'ferry' trips – trips without any passengers – of value here.

In parallel, we also look at transits of profiled passengers – these however may contain several trips. The typical scenario for the latter case is that there are more than one passenger in the elevator car with different destination floors, or the elevator makes an intermediate stop to serve additional calls on its way. We look at passenger transits as these describe the real needs of elevator passengers for travel within a particular building. The passenger transits are formed based on the identified elevator passengers according to their profiles.

Figure 2 describes the results of this study. In case of individual trips, which also include intermediate stops, we see that in 16% of cases the elevator car moves only one floor up or down, while the majority of trips are either 3 or 4 floors distance. However, when considering the actual passenger travel needs, we see that only a small amount of travels (6%) are between two floors on top of each other, and the majority of travels are derived by the need to transit between several floors. Thereby, we conclude that this information should be included in passenger profiles to personalize the floor prediction decision for a particular passenger.

These findings also confirm our hypothesis on passengers' travel behaviour. Evidently, taking stairs to transit one floor up or down suits for most of the visitors of the building. It is highly likely that this is due to the fact that taking a floor by stairs is generally faster than waiting for the elevator to take the same trip. The waiting time problem has been a source for many research works [4,8,14].

We acknowledge that these findings apply to the particular building – the building where our smart elevator is located, and are also somewhat dependant on the floor context. Even though for another building these statistics might be different, for our smart elevator system, these results provide a valuable input for the floor prediction, and confirm the necessity to include this data into passenger profiles for personalizing elevator travel.

4.2   RQ2: Frequent Destination Floor as Prediction Basis

The second question we consider is to what extent does the most frequently travelled floor describes passengers' behaviour and travel needs. In an 8-floor building, the probability to travel from one floor to any other floor is theoretically $p = 1/(8-1) = 14.3\%$. Obviously, this is purely theoretical and does not count the context of the floor, and the passenger's travel habits and needs.

We now proceed to investigate whether using the most travelled floor from the passengers profile is more accurate than assuming that the passenger takes one of the floors randomly. For this we investigated the interaction logs for profiled passengers. After data cleaning we ended up with only 497 trips for which the

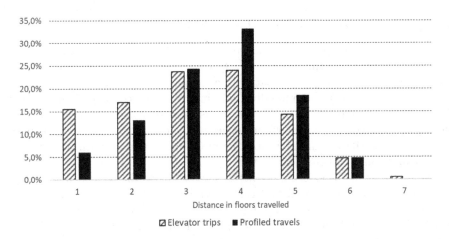

Fig. 2. Elevator car travel distances for trips, and passenger travel needs by distance.

prediction data was correctly available, due to the malfunction of the KONE API. Unfortunately, KONE API is beyond our authorized capabilities.

Table 1 describes the results of the study. Here the profiled trip is defined as a travel of a profiled passenger between two floors (even if the elevator car had intermediate stops) for which the smart elevator system proposed a predicted destination floor. As observed, there is a great variability of 30% in prediction accuracy over different profiles – apparently some profiled passengers have more fixed travel behaviour than others. Evidently, the approach of using the most frequently travelled floor for prediction is more accurate than just randomly picking a floor to predict. Interestingly, the approach has better accuracy for downwards travel (to entrance floor) than for travels going upwards. Further analysis on a larger data set over a longer period could bring insights into this aspect. All in all, most frequently travelled floor cannot singly meet the need to reliably predict destination floor for a known passenger, and thus additional measures are needed.

Table 1. Using frequently travelled floor for floor prediction for known passengers.

Characteristic	Value
# trips with predictions	497
# profiles covered	91
# profiles total	453
Average prediction accuracy for passenger profiles	$65.7 \pm 30.2\%$
Average prediction accuracy over profiled trips	64.5%
Average prediction accuracy over profiled trips (downwards travel)	73.1%
Average prediction accuracy over profiled trips (upwards travel)	59.6%

4.3   RQ3: The Value of Daily Travel Needs

Next, we investigate passengers' travel needs and their dependency on daily activities expressed by time of day in a typical office building. We aim to show that the inclusion of daily travel patterns, e.g, going for a lunch in the canteen on the first floor, or outside the building, will improve the accuracy of the present floor prediction approach. As a baseline we use already collected prediction data on real elevator travels for known passengers. We define four separate time periods throughout the working day, starting of 6 a.m. (Table 2), with period start time inclusive and end time exclusive.

We now look at the existing predictions according to the context and defined period of day (Table 2 col.3), and run a simulation where the floor prediction is made based on the passenger's travel history for that particular time context (col.4). Table 2 outlines the findings. As indicated, there is no particular improvement for predictions made for morning arrivals – passengers arrive and depart to upper floors, however a small improvement of ca 6% can be observed for predictions in the Midday and Leaving context. Interestingly, an improvement of 25% is found for 'Night-owls', calling for further investigation. In summary, including the daily moving patterns of known users into floor prediction has the potential to improve the prediction accuracy and provide a better personalization. Thereby, we conclude that this information must be included for floor prediction and passenger profiles extended to indicate daily travel needs by time.

Table 2. Using frequently travelled floor for floor prediction for known passengers.

Period of day (24 h)	Context	Prediction accuracy [%]	Periodic prediction accuracy [%]	Improvement [%]
06–11	Arrival	70.2	70.8	0.8
11–15	Midday/Lunch	66.5	70.4	5.8
15–19	Leave	65.8	69.8	6.2
19–06	'Night-owls'	43.9	54.9	25.8
	Overall	64.5	68.6	6.1

5   Conclusions

In this paper we have explored the possibility to provide personalized travel experience for profiled passengers of a smart elevator – a cyber physical social system. Namely, of our interest was how and with what information to complement existing passenger profiles so that the present destination floor prediction, based simply on the most frequently visited floor, could be significantly improved.

For this we investigated passengers' travel needs and behaviour within a 8-story office building where the smart elevator system was set up based on a conventional KONE elevator. Our studies indicated that passengers are likely to take stairs instead of travelling a distance of one floor by elevator, possibly as this saves time. This can be used as a valuable aspect for floor prediction decision. We also explored the extent the most frequently travelled floors describe passengers travel needs, and even though this gives suggestions for predictions, it is not merely enough, and additional information must be included in passenger profiles for better destination floor prediction accuracy. Such information could be the time context of daily activities. We do have to keep in mind that our options are limited to anonymous passenger profiles. As our study showed, including time context can provide a small lift for the accuracy. We will continue working on the prediction accuracy for improved personalized travel experience with the smart elevator. The smart elevator approach described in this article could also be applicable for other types of buildings with regular visitors or permanent inhabitants, e.g., apartment buildings, hotels, and hospitals.

For the future we continue collecting interaction data from the smart elevator, and experiment with various approaches to improve destination floor prediction. For example, we would like to have the elevator ask the passenger, if she wants to travel to the predicted floor, or wants to point another destination floor. Also, of interest is to study how the schedule of classes affects passengers' travel needs in the building. And lastly, what of personal information would passengers be willing to provide to get personalized elevator service even further.

References

1. Adomavicius, G., Tuzhilin, A.: Toward the next generation of recommender systems: a survey of the state-of-the-art and possible extensions. IEEE Trans. Knowl. Data Eng. **17**(6), 734–749 (2005)
2. Allen, J.: Speech Recognition and Synthesis, pp. 1664–1667. Wiley, Chichester (2003). GBR
3. Bamunuarachchi, D.T., Ranasinghe, D.N.: Elevator group optimization in a smart building. In: 2015 IEEE 10th International Conference on Industrial and Information Systems (ICIIS), pp. 71–76, December 2015
4. Bharti, H., Saxena, R.K., Sukhija, S., Yadav, V.: Cognitive model for smarter dispatch system/elevator. In: 2017 IEEE International Conference on Cloud Computing in Emerging Markets (CCEM), pp. 21–28, November 2017
5. Brand, M., Nikovski, D.: Optimal parking in group elevator control. In: IEEE International Conference on Robotics and Automation, Proceedings. ICRA 2004, vol. 1, pp. 1002–1008, April 2004
6. Brocken, E., et al.: Bing-CF-IDF+: a semantics-driven news recommender system. In: Giorgini, P., Weber, B. (eds.) CAiSE 2019. LNCS, vol. 11483, pp. 32–47. Springer, Cham (2019). https://doi.org/10.1007/978-3-030-21290-2_3
7. Cassandras, C.G.: Smart cities as cyber-physical social systems. Engineering **2**(2), 156–158 (2016)
8. Chou, S., Budhi, D.A., Dewabharata, A., Zulvia, F.E.: Improving elevator dynamic control policies based on energy and demand visibility. In: 2018 3rd International Conference on Intelligent Green Building and Smart Grid (IGBSG), pp. 1–4 (2018)
9. Dressler, F.: Cyber physical social systems: towards deeply integrated hybridized systems. In: 2018 International Conference on Computing, Networking and Communications (ICNC), pp. 420–424, March 2018

10. Eguchi, T., Hirasawa, K., Hu, J., Markon, S.: Elevator group supervisory control systems using genetic network programming. In: Proceedings of the 2004 Congress on Evolutionary Computation (IEEE Cat. No. 04TH8753), vol. 2, pp. 1661–1667, June 2004

11. Eirinaki, M., Vazirgiannis, M.: Web mining for web personalization. ACM Trans. Internet Technol. **3**(1), 1–27 (2003)

12. Luo, F., Xu, Y.-G., Cao, J.-Z.: Elevator traffic flow prediction with least squares support vector machines. In: 2005 International Conference on Machine Learning and Cybernetics, vol. 7, pp. 4266–4270, August 2005

13. Fernandez, J.R., Cortes, P.: A survey of elevator group control systems for vertical transportation: a look at recent literature. IEEE Control Syst. Mag. **35**(4), 38–55 (2015)

14. Fujimura, T., Ueno, S., Tsuji, H., Miwa, H.: Control algorithm for multi-car elevators with high transportation flexibility. In: 2013 IEEE 2nd Global Conference on Consumer Electronics (GCCE), pp. 544–545, October 2013

15. Gauch, S., Chaffee, J., Pretschner, A.: Ontology-based personalized search and browsing. Web Intell. Agent Syst. **1**(3–4), 219–234 (2003)

16. Gaudioso, E., Boticario, J.G.: User modeling on adaptive web-based learning communities. In: Palade, V., Howlett, R.J., Jain, L. (eds.) KES 2003. LNCS (LNAI), vol. 2774, pp. 260–266. Springer, Heidelberg (2003). https://doi.org/10.1007/978-3-540-45226-3_36

17. Ge, H., Hamada, T., Sumitomo, T., Koshizuka, N.: Intellevator: a context-aware elevator system for assisting passengers. In: 2018 IEEE 16th International Conference on Embedded and Ubiquitous Computing (EUC), pp. 81–88, October 2018

18. Ge, H., Hamada, T., Sumitomo, T., Koshizuka, N.: PrecaElevator: towards zero-waiting time on calling elevator by utilizing context aware platform in smart building. In: 2018 IEEE 7th Global Conference on Consumer Electronics (GCCE), pp. 566–570, October 2018

19. Goetsu, S., Sakai, T.: Voice input interface failures and frustration: developer and user perspectives. In: The Adjunct Publication of the 32nd Annual ACM Symposium on User Interface Software and Technology, UIST 2019, pp. 24–26. Association for Computing Machinery, New York (2019)

20. Hikita, S., Iwata, M., Abe, S.: Elevator group control with destination call entry and adaptive control. IEEJ Trans. Electron. Inf. Syst. **124**(7), 1471–1477 (2004). https://doi.org/10.1541/ieejeiss.124.1471

21. Kim, J.-H., Moon, B.-R.: Adaptive elevator group control with cameras. IEEE Trans. Industr. Electron. **48**(2), 377–382 (2001)

22. Ketkar, S.S., Mukherjee, M.: Speech recognition system. In: Proceedings of the Intl Conference & Workshop on Emerging Trends in Technology, ICWET 2011, pp. 1234–1237. Association for Computing Machinery, New York (2011)

23. King, D.E.: Dlib-ml: a machine learning toolkit. J. Mach. Learn. Res. **10**, 1755–1758 (2009)

24. Kwon, O., Lee, E., Bahn, H.: Sensor-aware elevator scheduling for smart building environments. Build. Environ. **72**, 332–342 (2014)

25. Lee, E.A., Seshia, S.A.: Introduction to Embedded Systems: A Cyber-Physical Systems Approach, 2nd edn. The MIT Press, Cambridge (2016)

26. Liang, C.J.M., Tang, J., Zhang, L., Zhao, F., Munir, S., Stankovic, J.A.: On human behavioral patterns in elevator usages. In: Proceedings of the 5th ACM Workshop on Embedded Systems for Energy-Efficient Buildings, BuildSys 2013, pp. 1–2. Association for Computing Machinery, New York (2013)

27. Ding, N., Chen, T., Luh, P.B., Zhang, H.: Optimization of elevator evacuation considering potential over-crowding. In: Proceeding of the 11th World Congress on Intelligent Control and Automation, pp. 2664–2668, June 2014
28. Pedregosa, F., et al.: Scikit-learn: machine learning in python. J. Mach. Learn. Res. **12**, 2825–2830 (2011)
29. Robal, T., Kalja, A.: Conceptual web users actions prediction for ontology-based browsing recommendations. In: Papadopoulos, G., Wojtkowski, W., Wojtkowski, G., Wrycza, S., Zupancic, J. (eds.) Information Systems Development: Towards a Service Provision Society, pp. 121–129. Springer, Boston (2010). https://doi.org/10.1007/b137171_13
30. Robal, T., Zhao, Y., Lofi, C., Hauff, C.: Webcam-based attention tracking in online learning: A feasibility study. In: 23rd International Conference on Intelligent User Interfaces, IUI 2018, pp. 189–197. ACM, New York (2018)
31. Ross, S., Brownholtz, E., Armes, R.: Voice user interface principles for a conversational agent. In: Proceedings of the 9th International Conference on Intelligent User Interfaces, IUI 2004, pp. 364–365. Association for Computing Machinery, New York (2004). https://doi.org/10.1145/964442.964536
32. Russell, S., Norvig, P.: Artificial Intelligence: A Modern Approach, 3rd edn. Prentice Hall Press, Upper Saddle River (2009)
33. Sieg, A., Mobasher, B., Burke, R.D.: Learning ontology-based user profiles: a semantic approach to personalized web search. IEEE Intell. Inf. Bull. **8**(1), 7–18 (2007)
34. Silva, E.M., Boaventura, M., Boaventura, I.A.G., Contreras, R.C.: Face recognition using local mapped pattern and genetic algorithms. In: Proceedings of the International Conference on Pattern Recognition and Artificial Intelligence, PRAI 2018, pp. 11–17. Association for Computing Machinery, New York (2018)
35. Speretta, M., Gauch, S.: Personalized search based on user search histories. In: 2005 IEEE/WIC/ACM International Conference on Web Intelligence (WI 2005), pp. 622–628. IEEE Computer Society (2005)
36. Stark, L.: Facial recognition is the plutonium of AI. XRDS **25**(3), 50–55 (2019)
37. Strang, T., Bauer, C.: Context-aware elevator scheduling. In: 21st International Conference on Advanced Information Networking and Applications Workshops (AINAW 2007), vol. 2, pp. 276–281, May 2007
38. Turunen, M., et al.: Mobile interaction with elevators: improving people flow in complex buildings. In: Proceedings of International Conference on Making Sense of Converging Media, AcademicMindTrek 2013, pp. 43–50. ACM, New York (2013)
39. Wang, F., Tang, J., Zong, Q.: Energy-consumption-related robust optimization scheduling strategy for elevator group control system. In: 2011 IEEE 5th Intl Conference on Cybernetics and Intelligent Systems (CIS), pp. 30–35, September 2011
40. Zhao, H.-C., Liu, X.-Y.: An improved DNA computing method for elevator scheduling problem. In: Zu, Q., Hu, B., Elçi, A. (eds.) ICPCA/SWS 2012. LNCS, vol. 7719, pp. 869–875. Springer, Heidelberg (2013). https://doi.org/10.1007/978-3-642-37015-1_76
41. Zhao, W., Chellappa, R., Phillips, P.J., Rosenfeld, A.: Face recognition: a literature survey. ACM Comput. Surv. **35**(4), 399–458 (2003)
42. Zhu, D., Jiang, L., Zhou, Y., Shan, G., He, K.: Modern elevator group supervisory control systems and neural networks technique. In: 1997 IEEE International Conference on Intelligent Processing Systems (Cat. No. 97TH8335), vol. 1, pp. 528–532, October 1997
43. Zhuge, H.: Cyber-physical society-the science and engineering for future society. Fut. Gener. Comput. Syst. **32**, 180–186 (2014)

Artificial Intelligence in Information Systems

Application Development for Hand Gestures Recognition with Using a Depth Camera

Dina Satybaldina[1,2(✉)] ⓘ, Gulziya Kalymova[2] ⓘ, and Natalya Glazyrina[2] ⓘ

[1] National Research Nuclear University "MEPhI", 31 Kashirskoe Road, 115409 Moscow,
Russian Federation
[2] L.N. Gumilyov Eurasian National University, 11 Pushkin Street, 010008 Nur-Sultan,
Kazakhstan
satybaldina_dzh@enu.kz

Abstract. The aim of the work is to develop an application for hand gestures identification based on a convolutional neural network using the TensorFlow & Keras deep learning frameworks. The gesture recognition system consists of a gesture presentation, a gesture capture device (sensor), the preprocessing and image segmentation algorithms, the features extraction algorithm, and gestures classification. As a sensor, Intel® Real Sense™ depth camera D435 with USB 3.0 support for connecting to a computer was used. For video processing and extraction both RGB images and depth information from the input data, functions from the Intel Real Sense library are applied. For pre-processing and image segmentation algorithms computer vision methods from the OpenCV library are implemented. The subsystem for the features extracting and gestures classification is based on the modified VGG-16, with weights previously trained on the ImageNet database. Performance of the gesture recognition system is evaluated using a custom dataset. Experimental results show that the proposed model, trained on a database of 2000 images, provides high recognition accuracy (99.4%).

Keywords: Gesture recognition · Deep Learning · Machine learning · Convolutional neural network

1 Introduction

Creation and implementation of efficient and accurate hand gesture recognition systems are aided to development of the human computer interaction (HCI) technologies [1]. The term, Hand Gesture Recognition is collectively referred as the process of tracking human gestures and conversion their representation to semantically meaningful commands for devices control [2]. Tracking technologies for this tasks use the contact based and vision based devices. Restrained by the dependence on experienced users the contact based devices (for example, accelerometers, multi-touch screen) do not provide much acceptability [3].

The most common approach to vision-based gesture recognition is to extract low-level features from hand RGB images, and then employ statistical classifiers to classify

© Springer Nature Switzerland AG 2020
T. Robal et al. (Eds.): DB&IS 2020, CCIS 1243, pp. 55–67, 2020.
https://doi.org/10.1007/978-3-030-57672-1_5

gestures according to the features [2–5]. Also some additional techniques are applied (e.g. cybergloves and magnetic trackers [6], a colored glove [7]). RGB-D sensors (such as Microsoft Kinect and CSEM Swissranger) can greatly reduce various restrictions on experimental conditions as they obtain both RGB images and depth information an actual time altogether.

In this work we use Intel RealSense D435, a stereoscopic depth camera, which enables a whole new generation of intelligent vision-based systems for more application as robotics or augmented and virtual reality. Because of the great succeed Deep Learning (DL) in computer vision [8], a pre-trained deep convolutional neural network is applied for features extraction and gesture classifying. RealSense libraries from Intel, OpenCV and open-source DL frameworks Keras and TensorFlow are used for software implementation of the gesture recognition system on Python. To determine the performance of our approach we collected a database of 1,000 images, which consists of 40 different types for 5 gestures, which were presented to the sensor by 5 people, and tested the recognition system on this database.

The rest of this paper is structured as follows. Section 2 describes some related work proposed so far in the gesture recognition area. The details of the proposed method are described in Sect. 3. In Sect. 4, we briefly introduce our newly collected database and show the experimental results. Conclusion and future research are presented in Sect. 5.

2   Related Work

A gesture can be defined as a physical movement of the hands, arms, face and body that expresses an emotion, intention or command [9]. A set of gestures and their meanings form the gestures vocabulary. Hand gestures can be to divide into two types: static and dynamic gestures [4]. In static gestures the hand position does not change during the gesture demonstration. Static gestures mainly rely on the shape and flexure fingers angles. In second case the hand position changes continuously and dynamic gestures rely on the hand trajectories and orientations, in addition to the shape and fingers angles [10].

Most of the hand gesture recognition systems are comprised of three fundamental phases: hand detection and the segmentation of the corresponding image regions, tracking (for dynamic gestures) and recognition [3]. Hand gestures detection is a difficult task due to objective and subjective differences associated with a large number of degrees of freedom of the hand and fingers bones, the differences in articulation, a relatively small area of he hands, and a different skin color. In addition, reliable algorithms for segmentation and detection of the hands and fingers positions should have invariance with respect to the size, speed and orientation of the gesture, the scene brightness, the background heterogeneity and other parameters.

Pisharady et al. [4] reviewed RGB cameras as well as the new generation RGB-D cameras used for hand detection and segmentation. They provided a comprehensive analysis of integration of sensors into gesture recognition systems and their impact on the system performance. It was shown that the RGB-D sensors enable extraction of invariant features in spite of complex backgrounds and variations in scale, lighting, and view-points.

Depth sensors due to their versatility, accuracy and compactness such sensors and depth-sensing technology provided a significant boost for medicine [11], robotics [12], education [13] and Apple Face ID realization [14].

Intel Inc. also created its own RealSense deep vision technology and developed (in collaboration with Microsoft) the tool for 3D face recognition, which provides access to Windows10 devices [15]. RealSense technology supported by an open source multi-platform software development kit (SDK) [16].

The second generation RealSense cameras were introduced in January 2018 and its use stereo vision to calculate depth [17]. Despite the fact that Intel RealSense D400 series devices appeared on the market only in recent years, they began to be used in many areas, for example, in security systems [18], robotics [12], medicine [19], and agriculture [20]. At the same time, there are few works that report on the depth camera using for recognizing hand gestures that can be integrated into effective HCI systems.

A comparison of the extraction features of hand gesture and posture recognition algorithms using depth cameras, including one paper with the using on RealSense SR300 sensor are provided in Table 1 [21–25]. As can be seen from Table 1, the used methods for features extraction and gestures classification provides high recognition accuracy of both static and dynamic gestures. It should be noted that in the majority of paper, the effectiveness of recognition systems is obtained for the small gestures sets. It limits their mass application. This is confirmed by the fact that there are many open source developments for face, mouth and eye recognition (OpenCV), but there reliable hand detectors absence. Therefore, the problem of improving the static and dynamic posture recognition on a photo image or in a video stream remains relevant.

3 Proposed Method

3.1 General Framework of the Hand Static Gesture Recognition System

In the work we propose a recognizing static hand gestures system based on the digital processing of the color and depth images from a video stream in real time and extracting classification features from them inside a convolutional neural network. The structure of the proposed system is shown in Fig. 1, and operation principle of the each stage is described in detail in the following subsections.

3.2 Capture Images with Hand Gestures

The purpose of the gesture capture sensor is to digitize the gesture. The input sensor is a RGB-D camera (Intel® RealSense ™ D435) that gives us an RGB image as well as depths for each point [17].

RealSense D435 is a compact (99 mm × 25 mm × 25 mm; weight 72 g) peripheral RGB-D device supporting USB 3.1 standard and a range of up to 10 m. The camera consists of Vision Processor D4, Depth Module and RGB camera. The characteristics of an active stereo depth deep resolution and RGB resolution are up to 1280 × 720 and 1920 × 1080, respectively.

Table 1. Comparison of gesture recognition methods based on the depth cameras using.

Works	Static (S) or Dynamic (D) gesture	Sensor	Features	Classification method	Number of classes	Accuracy
[21]	D	CSEM Swissranger SR-2	Motion primitives	Probabilistic edit distance classifier	4	92.9
[22]	S	ToF and RGB camera	Haarlets	Nearest Neighbor	6	99.54
[23]	S	Kinect	Hand/finger shape	Template matching using FEMD (finger earth mover's distance)	10	93.9
[24]	D	Kinect	Extended-Motion-History-Image	Maximum correlation coeffcient	8	Not reported
[25]	S	Kinect	Depth pixel values	Randomized classification forests and voting	24	84.3
[26]	S	RealSense SR300	Depth and colour pixel values	Generalized Hough transform and double channel Convolution Neural Network	24	99.4

A pair of identical cameras referred as imagers (left and right) and an infrared (IR) projector are used to stereo vision realization and calculate depth (see Fig. 2) [17]. The infrared projector projects non-visible static IR pattern to improve depth accuracy in scenes with low texture. The left and right imagers capture the scene and sends imager data to the depth imaging (vision) processor, which calculates depth values for each pixel in the image by correlating points on the left image to the right image and via shift between a point on the Left image and the Right image. The depth pixel values are processed to generate a depth frame. Subsequent depth frames create a depth video stream.

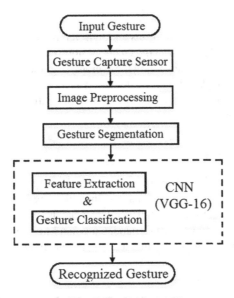

Fig. 1. Block diagram of proposed static hand gesture recognition system

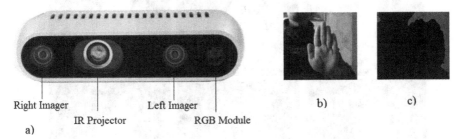

Fig. 2. RealSense D435 (a) and output data from the sensor: RGB- (b) and Depth-Image (c)

Open library RealSense SDK 2.0 has standard functions for camera initialization, parameters setting, functions and methods for reading frames from the video stream, calculating the distance from the hand to the depth camera, RGB images and depth maps saving methods [16]. It is possible to modify the algorithms available in the source code of the RealSence SDK 2.0. The methods and functions from RealSence SDK 2.0 were used to implement gestures image. Some additional functions for gesture capture were coded by the authors.

3.3 Image Preprocessing

Performing various operations in the subsequent steps of the gesture recognition system, such as segmentation and feature extraction, is much easier for pre-processed images. At this stage, usually the interferences and external noise are reduced by applying the operations of averaging and histograms leveling, color normalization is also carried out in accordance with the lighting conditions and light temperature [22].

In this paper, a bilateral filter from the OpenCV library is used to remove noise in the frame. Additional method for determining the average brightness of pixels in an image is applied. We implemented a function for calculating average brightness using non-linear conversion from RGB color model to the HSV (Hue, Saturation, Value), where Value is the brightness parameter [27].

3.4 Segmentation Methods

Segmentation is an extraction of an interest object (hand) from the background and determining its location in the scene. At this step, the following operations are performed: searching for a Region of Interest (ROI) to detect hands, removing the background, converting the color image to grayscale frame, Gaussian filtering for cleaning of noised grayscale images, contouring the segmented object and final binary thresholding to isolate the hand (see Fig. 3).

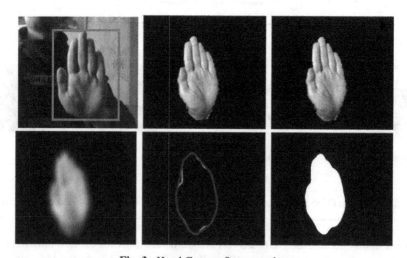

Fig. 3. Hand Gesture Segmentation

To implement these operations, we used both methods from the OpenCV library and own code development.

3.5 Basic Architecture VGG-16 and Transfer Training

A classification or recognition mechanism is a computational algorithm that takes an object representation and correlates (classifies) it as an instance of some known class type.

In proposed method for hand static gestures recognition we have used Deep Convolutional Neural Network (DCNN) with VGG-16 model pre- trained on big image dataset.

The VGG network architecture was developed by K. Simonyan and A. Zisserman [28]. Designing architecture with small convolution filters with 3×3 size shows a significant improvement on the neural networks can be achieved by pushing the depth to 16–19 weight layers. The 5 convolutional blocks are followed by 5 max-pooling layers, and three fully-connected layers. The final 1000-way layer is a soft-max layer that outputs class probabilities. Basic architecture VGG-16 is shown in Fig. 4a. VGG-16 was trained and tested on ImageNet database to classify the 1.3 million images to the 1000 classes with accuracy of 92.7% [8].

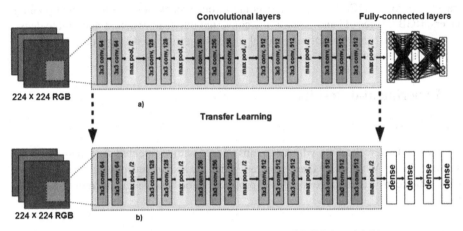

Fig. 4. VGG16 architecture (a) and proposed DCNN model (b)

DCNN with fixed weights of the convolutional layers, obtained by training on large-scale sets of natural images (ImageNet) shows the high accuracy of classifying images from other subject areas. Such approach on based on VGG-16 and concept of a transfer learning and fine-tuning was used for classification of malware samples represented as byte plot grayscale images [29].

Transfer learning consists in transferring the parameters of the neural network trained with one dataset and task to another problem with a different dataset images and task [30]. When the target dataset is significant smaller than the base dataset, transfer learning can be a powerful tool to enable training a large target network without overfitting.

Fine-tuning is associated with the need to change and retrain fully connected layers in the classifier. The basic architecture of VGG-16 contains 1000 output neurons in the last layer according to the number of the objects classes. In a new classification task (for example, in the gesture recognition problem), the number of classes may differ from that in the original data set. In this case, the last layer in the VGG-16 architecture must be removed, and a new classifier with the required number of output neurons must be added. It is also necessary to replace the previous fully connected layers, since their output vectors do not correspond to the new classification layer.

For static hand gesture recognition system we use the modified VGG-16 architecture, in which fully connected layers with a large number of neurons are replaced by 4 dense layers with fewer neurons (see Fig. 4 b). The dropout layer has 5 output channels for 5 gestures from the training and test sets.

The new layers weights are initialized with random values, after which the learning process on the training data set begins. We use an end-to-end approach proving surprisingly powerful. With minimum training data from humans the neuron's weights were corrected and recognition system learns to identify hand gestures.

The input data to VGG-16 model is an RGB image with the fixed size of 224 × 224. Therefore, at the segmentation stage, processed frames with a segmented gesture saved in a different color resolution RGB model are converted to 224 × 224 format and transferred to the DCNN input. After going through stack of convolution and pooling layers, RGB images of hand gestures are converted into features maps and sent to dense layers. In the last step, the softmax model is used to gesture predict and output the result as a confusion matrix.

4   Experimental Results

4.1   Datasets

We prepared a new database which contains images with segmented static hand gestures shown in Fig. 5. We selected these gestures, which are also included in alternative dataset [31], which can be used to cross-validate proposed static hand gesture recognition system model.

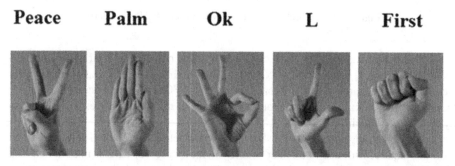

Fig. 5. Dataset samples

Depth camera Intel RealSense D435 placed over a table, the subjects sat close to it, and moved their right hand over the sensor at a distance between 10 and 75 cm in front of it (see Fig. 6). The gestures were performed by 10 different subjects (5 women and 5 men).

Our dataset has a total of 2,000 pictures, including 1,000 RGB images and 1,000 depth maps, collected under different backgrounds in a few rooms with illumination changes. In order to increase the diversity of the database, we also tried image augmentation by using of flips, skews, rotations and etc. The static hand gestures database was used only for the training of the modified VGG-16. At the validation/testing stage RGB and depth images from RealSense D435 used directly to predict gesture.

Fig. 6. Samples human hand gesture tracking from RealSense D435 sensor

DCNN training is the fine-tuned process based on the pre- trained models VGG-16 on ImageNet. At the start, the learning rate is 0.01 and decreases by 10 times every 2000 iterations. Weight decay is set to 0.0004. At most 10,000 iterations were needed for the fine-tuning on training set. The experiments were done on Intel(R) Core(TM) i3-8100 CPU, NVIDIA GeForce GTX 1050 Ti, 16 GB RAM desktop. After performing transfer learning with a fine tuned last activation layer we were able to achieve an average accuracy of 95.5% on the 5 class subset of the static hand gesture.

4.2 Performance Metrics

The confusion matrix (CM) has been used for obtaining quantitative results. The precision, recall, and F-Score measures are used as metrics for evaluation.

CM of size $n \times n$ associated with a classifier shows the predicted and actual classification, where n is the number of different classes [32]. Table 2 shows a confusion matrix for $n = 2$, whose entries have the following meanings:

- a is the number of correct negative predictions;
- b is the number of incorrect positive predictions;
- c is the number of incorrect negative predictions;
- d is the number of correct positive predictions.

We use an alternative construction of CM: each column represents the percentage of hand gestures that belongs to each class, and along the first diagonal are the correct classifications, whereas all the other entries show misclassifications [31].

From CM matrix two measurements can be directly observed, the precision and the recall, which can be expressed as follows:

$$Precision = \frac{d}{d+b}, \tag{1}$$

$$Recall = 100 \times \frac{d}{d+c}. \tag{2}$$

Recall demonstrates the ability of the algorithm to detect a given class in general, and precision demonstrates the ability to distinguish this class from other classes. F-Score is a harmonic mean of the precision and recall:

$$F - Score = 2 \times \frac{Precision \times Recall}{Precision + Recall} \tag{3}$$

The F-Score reaches its maximum with precision and recall equal to unity, and is close to zero if one of the arguments is close to zero.

Table 2. Confusion matrix for two-class classification problem

	Predicted negative	Predicted positive
Actual negative	a	b
Actual positive	c	d

4.3 Results and Discussion

Table 3 presents the CM obtained by using the proposed static hand gesture recognition system on test stage. As it can be seen, for all the gestures the precision, elements of the main diagonal, are over 97% and just a small percentage of samples are detected as belonging to other gestures, but an amount less than 0.2%. This indicates that our algorithm is quite accurate in two measurements, precision and recall. The exception is recognition of palm, where the classification error is greater than 2.5%. This can be explained by a certain similarity between this gesture and the gesture of Peace. The average accuracy of gesture recognition (according to the first diagonal of the CM) reaches 99.4%.

Table 3. Confusion matrix for the proposed static hand gesture recognition system

Gesture	Predicted Gesture				
	First	L	Ok	Palm	Peace
First	99.899	0.0039	0.0502	0.039	0.0829
L	0	99.9989	0.0005	0	0.0006
Ok	0.0001	0.0074	99.9924	0	0.0001
Palm	0.0578	0.0319	0.0559	97.6184	2.236
Peace	0.0007	0.0815	0.0689	0.2034	99.6455

The proposed hand gesture recognition system has been compared with the one proposed in [31]. The near-infrared images of the same gestures acquired by a Leap Motion sensor. Along with the CM values, the F-Score measure is also used to compare the results of both solutions. This measure is present in Table 4.

Table 4. F-Score results for the proposed system and for system from [31]

	Hand Gesture Recognition System	
Gesture	Proposed	[31]
First	1	0.99
L	1	0.99
Ok	1	0.99
Palm	0.99	1
Peace	1	0.99

As it can be seen in Table 4, proposed system is the one that achieves comparable results. The recognition system proposed in [31] use RGB sensor and a global image descriptor, called Depth Spatiograms of Quantized Patterns (DSQP), without any hand segmentation stage. And image descriptors reduced from DSQP are analyzed by a set of Support Vectors Machines to gesture classification. This comparison also allows us to notice that a depth maps and convolution neural networks allow achieving same high performance.

5   Conclusion

We proposed static hand gesture recognition system that utilizes both RGB and depth information from Intel® Real Sense™ depth camera D435. We utilized depth sensor's unique property to segment hand poses and perform background denoising on images with gesture. Features extraction and gesture classification was performed on the deep convolution neural networks (DCNN) with VGG network architecture, pre- trained on the ImageNet database. Our training database was collected manually using both RGB and depth images from depth sensor. This database consists of 2,000 samples performed by 5 women and 5 men.

Modified VGG-16 model delivered the high accuracy on training set of images from. Obtained recognition scores on the test stage prove the efficiency of the presented recognition framework, and claim a higher prominence of the depth camera D435 for future HMI applications.

However, the static hand gestures recognition is insufficient for effective HCI systems. Therefore, future research is related to the method development for recognizing dynamic hand gestures and the expansion of the database and object classes.

Acknowledgements. This work has been supported by the Ministry of Digital Development, Innovations and Aerospace Industry of the Kazakhstan Republic under project № AP06850817.

References

1. Jaimes, A., Sebe, N.: Multimodal human–computer interaction: a survey. Comput. Vis. Image Underst. **108**, 116–134 (2007)
2. Bhame, V., Sreemathy, R., Dhumal, H.: Vision based hand gesture recognition using eccentric approach for human computer interaction In: Proceedings of 2014 International Conference on Advances in Computing, Communications and Informatics (ICACCI), pp. 949–953. IEEE (2014)
3. Rautaray, S.S., Agrawal, A.: Vision based hand gesture recognition for human computer interaction: a survey. Artif. Intell. Rev. **43**(1), 1–54 (2015)
4. Pisharady, P.K., Saerbeck, M.: Recent methods and databases in vision-based hand gesture recognition: a review. Comput. Vis. Image Underst. **141**, 152–165 (2015)
5. Chakraborty, B.K., Sarma, D., Bhuyan, M.K., MacDorman, K.F.: Review of constraints on vision-based gesture recognition for human–computer interaction. IET Comput. Vision **12**(1), 3–15 (2017)
6. Kevin, N.Y.Y., Ranganath, S., Ghosh, D.: Trajectory modeling in gesture recognition using CyberGloves and magnetic trackers. In: Proceedings of IEEE Region 10 Conference TENCON, pp. 571–574 (2004)
7. Zhao, H.-C., Liu, Xi-Yu.: An improved DNA computing method for elevator scheduling problem. In: Zu, Q., Hu, B., Elçi, A. (eds.) ICPCA/SWS 2012. LNCS, vol. 7719, pp. 869–875. Springer, Heidelberg (2013). https://doi.org/10.1007/978-3-642-37015-1_76
8. Sree, S.R., Vyshnavi, S.B., Jayapandian, N.: Real-world application of machine learning and deep learning. In: 2019 International Conference on Smart Systems and Inventive Technology (ICSSIT), pp. 1069–1073. IEEE (2019)
9. Mitra, S., Acharya, T.: Gesture recognition: a survey. IEEE Trans. Syst. Man Cybern. Part C (Appl. Rev.) **37**(3), 311–324 (2007)
10. Kendon, A.: Current issues in the study of gesture. In: The Biological Foundation of Gestures: Motor and Semiotic Aspects, pp. 23–47. Psychology Press (1986)
11. Chiu, C.Y., Thelwell, M., Senior, T., Choppin, S., Hart, J., Wheat, J.: Comparison of depth cameras for 3D reconstruction in medicine. J. Eng. Med. **233**(9), 938–947 (2019)
12. Fang, Q., Kyrarini, M., Ristic-Durrant, D., Gräser, A.: RGB-D camera based 3D human mouth detection and tracking towards robotic feeding assistance. In: Proceedings of the 11th Pervasive Technologies Related to Assistive Environments Conference, pp. 391–396 (2018)
13. Satybaldina, D.Zh., Kalymova, K.A.: Development a gesture-based application using Microsoft Kinect sensor. In: 21th International Conference Proceedings on Digital signal processing, DSPA 2019, Moscow, Russia, pp. 525–529 (2019). (in Russian)
14. Zhang, S.: High-speed 3D shape measurement with structured light methods: a review. Opt. Lasers Eng. **106**, 119–131 (2018)
15. Keselman, L., Woodfill, J.I., Grunnet-Jepsen, A., Bhowmik, A.: Intel R RealSense TM stereoscopic depth cameras. In: Proceedings of the IEEE Conference on Computer Vision and Pattern Recognition Workshops, pp. 1–10 (2017)
16. Intel® RealSense™ SDK 2.0. https://www.intelrealsense.com/developers/. Accessed 24 Jan 2020
17. Intel RealSense D400 Series Product Family. Datasheet. 2019 Intel Corporation. Document Number: 337029-007. https://www.intel.com. Accessed 24 Jan 2020

18. Bock, R.D.: Low-cost 3D security camera. In: Autonomous Systems: Sensors, Vehicles, Security, and the Internet of Everything. International Society for Optics and Photonics, vol. 10643, pp. 106430E (2018)
19. Aoki, H., Suzuki, A., Shiga, T.: Study on non-contact heart beat measurement method by using depth sensor. In: Lhotska, L., Sukupova, L., Lacković, I., Ibbott, Geoffrey S. (eds.) World Congress on Medical Physics and Biomedical Engineering 2018. IP, vol. 68/1, pp. 341–345. Springer, Singapore (2019). https://doi.org/10.1007/978-981-10-9035-6_62
20. Syed, T.N., et al.: Seedling-lump integrated non-destructive monitoring for automatic transplanting with Intel RealSense depth camera. Artif. Intell. Agricult. **3**, 18–32 (2019)
21. Holte, M.B., Moeslund, T.B., Fihl, P.: Fusion of range and intensity information for view invariant gesture recognition. In: 2008 IEEE Computer Society Conference on Computer Vision and Pattern Recognition Workshops, pp. 1–7. IEEE (2008)
22. Van den Bergh M., et al.: Real-time 3D hand gesture interaction with a robot for understanding directions from humans. In: 2011 Ro-Man, pp. 357–362. IEEE (2011)
23. Ren, Z., Yuan, J., Zhang, Z.: Robust hand gesture recognition based on finger-earth mover's distance with a commodity depth camera. In: Proceedings of the 19th ACM International Conference on Multimedia, pp. 1093–1096 (2011)
24. Wu, D., Zhu, F., Shao, L.: One shot learning gesture recognition from RGBD images. In: 2012 IEEE Computer Society Conference on Computer Vision and Pattern Recognition Workshops, pp. 7–12. IEEE (2012)
25. Keskin, C., Kirac, F., Kara, Y., Akarun, L.: Randomized decision forests for static and dynamic hand shape classification. In: 2012 IEEE Computer Society Conference on Computer Vision and Pattern Recognition Workshops, pp. 31–36. IEEE (2012)
26. Liao, B., Li, J., Ju, Z., Ouyang, G.: Hand gesture recognition with generalized hough transform and DC-CNN using RealSense. In: 2018 Eighth International Conference on Information Science and Technology (ICIST), pp. 84–90. IEEE (2018)
27. Chernov, V., Alander, J., Bochko, V.: Integer-based accurate conversion between RGB and HSV color spaces. Comput. Electr. Eng. **46**, 328–337 (2015)
28. Simonyan, K., Zisserman. A.: Very deep convolutional networks for large-scale image recognition. arXiv preprint arXiv: 1409. 1556. (2014)
29. Rezende, E., Ruppert, G., Carvalho, T., Theophilo, A., Ramos, F., Geus, Pd: Malicious software classification using VGG16 deep neural network's bottleneck features. In: Latifi, S. (ed.) Information Technology - New Generations. AISC, vol. 738, pp. 51–59. Springer, Cham (2018). https://doi.org/10.1007/978-3-319-77028-4_9
30. Liu, Z., et al.: Improved kiwifruit detection using pre-trained VGG16 with RGB and NIR information fusion. IEEE Access, pp. 2327–2336 (2019)
31. Mantecón, T., del-Blanco, Carlos R., Jaureguizar, F., García, N.: Hand gesture recognition using infrared imagery provided by leap motion controller. In: Blanc-Talon, J., Distante, C., Philips, W., Popescu, D., Scheunders, P. (eds.) ACIVS 2016. LNCS, vol. 10016, pp. 47–57. Springer, Cham (2016). https://doi.org/10.1007/978-3-319-48680-2_5
32. Visa, S., Ramsay, B., Ralescu, A.L., Van Der Knaap, E.: Confusion matrix-based feature selection. MAICS **710**, 120–127 (2011)

Features and Methods for Automatic Posting Account Classification

Zigmunds Beļskis[1], Marita Zirne[1], and Mārcis Pinnis[1,2(✉)]

[1] Tilde, Vienibas Gatve 75A, Riga 1004, Latvia
{zigmunds1belskis,marita.zirne,marcis.pinnis}@tilde.lv
[2] University of Latvia, Raina blvd 19-125, Riga 1586, Latvia

Abstract. Manual processes in accounting can introduce errors that affect business decisions. Automation (or at least partial automation of accounting processes) can help to minimise human errors. In this paper, we investigate methods for the automation of one of the processes involved in invoice posting – the assignment of account codes to posting entries – using various classification methods. We show that machine learning-based methods can reach a precision of up to 93% for debit account code classification and even up to 98% for credit account code classification.

Keywords: Accounting · Machine learning · Classification

1 Introduction

Machine learning and artificial intelligence technologies develop opportunities for humans to create a methodology for automation of processes where human mistakes are common. The use of machine learning and artificial intelligence technologies in the accounting field has had a history of more than 30 years [1]. According to a study by the International Association of Chartered Certified Accountants, many accounting processes will be automated in the future, which will allow accountants to focus more on high-value tasks rather than on routine accounting activities [7].

The work of accountants is highly dynamic because the accounting procedures of a company are affected by a series of factors that are in a continuous flow and interacting with each other: accounting and tax legislation, professional standards, good practices, sector specificities, business volumes, types of transactions and their complexity, the internal culture of companies, and the experience and knowledge of accountants.

Accounting process automation helps accountants processing large-scale uniform transactions effectively and accurately over a short period and minimise the risk of material errors. For a company, automation helps to increase efficiency by reducing costs or using accountants' services for higher-value jobs, such as performance analysis and forecasting, or improving business processes.

© Springer Nature Switzerland AG 2020
T. Robal et al. (Eds.): DB&IS 2020, CCIS 1243, pp. 68–81, 2020.
https://doi.org/10.1007/978-3-030-57672-1_6

Unfortunately, the possibility of process automation can be limited by the fact that not all accounting processes are subject to objective and unambiguous criteria. For example, determining the recoverable value of assets is a very subjective process. It is further complicated by the fact that the calculation requires the use of data that is not entered into the accounting system and which, as time passes, changes.

In practice, the most demanding time for accountants is the processing, posting, and control of initial information. These time-consuming manual tasks can introduce errors. For example, errors, which are related to incorrect postings, appear in the processing of both supplier and customer invoices. The causes of errors may vary depending on the situation. For instance, when an accountant enters a new invoice for an existing customer or supplier, he/she uses a copy from the previous invoice of the same partner that may have had the nature of another transaction. Thereby the accountant can end up using different accounts that are not up to date for the new invoice. Another common mistake is, for example, when an accountant copies an invoice from another partner by mistake, and the posting is performed for the incorrect partner. Such and similar errors when posting transactions lead to incorrect financial reports, which require a lot of time to be corrected, as the causes of errors may be the most varied.

Invoice posting process automation can help reduce human errors by either providing automatic suggestions or by at least performing automatic validation of the different human accountant actions and indicating of possible mismatches with and deviations from the standard and intended practices. Therefore, to help reduce human error, in the scope of this paper, we investigate methods for the automation of one of the processes involved in invoice posting – the assignment of account codes to accounting entries – using various classification methods.

The paper is further structured as follows: Sect. 2 discusses related work on account code classification, Sect. 3 describes the data used in our experiments, Sect. 4 describes the rule-based and machine learning methods that we used for account code classification, Sect. 5 discusses features that were used to train machine learning models, Sect. 6 documents the results of our experiments, Sect. 7 provides a brief discussion on data quality, and the paper is concluded in Sect. 8.

2   Related Work

Automatic or semi-automatic account classification for invoices has received considerable attention in related work. Bengtsson and Jansson (2015) [2] analysed two classification methods (support vector machines and feed-forward neural networks) for the classification of financial transactions using historical data. The authors concluded that machine learning methods are not able to surpass a simple method that looks at the previous invoice from the same supplier to the same buyer. Mateush et al. (2018) [10] used a hybrid classification method with three types of rules (userindependent, user-defined, and manually labelled transaction rules) to create a multi-class classifier for classification of money transfers and credit card transactions. The authors relied on the following features: party, transaction amount, country, bank, comment text, transaction type codes and card payment types. They used a data set from 50 thousand customers and showed that the XGBoost [12] classifier can reach higher recall levels compared to a rule-based method while maintaining comparable precision levels. Bergdorf (2018) [3] investigated the generation of rules for automatic account code classification. The authors compared two rule generation methods, the Fuzzy Unordered Rule Induction Algorithm (FURIA) and MODLEM [17], with other machine-learning methods (i.e., random forest and support vector machine classifiers) and two simple classifiers that perform classification based on the last or the most frequently used account codes for each supplier. The authors achieved the best results using the random forest classifier, however, the quality difference was not significant compared to the rule generation methods. Smith (2018) [16] describes methods for the automation of the various accounting processes, including the problem of automatic account code classification. The author suggests using Naive Bayes or random forest classifiers for account code classification. However, the author has not investigated a representative set of machine learning methods.

Unlike Bengtsson and Jansson (2015) [2], Mateush (2018) [10] and Bergdorf (2018) [3], we attempt to create account code classification models that can be applied for multiple companies simultaneously with the goals to analyse whether the models can also support new companies (either on the buyer or the supplier side). Although Bergdorf (2018) [3] acknowledges the existence of double-entry bookkeeping systems, they analyse only single-entry bookkeeping systems. We present work for a double-entry bookkeeping system that has two classification targets – a debit account and a credit account.

3   Data for Automatic Posting Account Classification

3.1   Overall Description of Data

For our experiments, we use a data set that consists of 2,054,280 real posting entries from 1,194,266 supplier invoices from a total of 958 different companies. The entries feature a total of 27,653 suppliers. The supplier invoices span over a 10-year time-frame from 2010 to 2020. Every supplier invoice consists of up to 94 posting entries with an average of 2 posting entries per document. The supplier invoices are from a double-entry bookkeeping system, which means that the data has two multi-class classification targets:

- Debit account (279 unique values)
- Credit account (186 unique values)

The debit/credit classifiers that are used in the accounting software, from which the data set was acquired, are based on Latvia's (now deprecated) Law On the Unified Book-Keeping Chart of Accounts of Companies, enterprises, and Organisations [11]. Nowadays accounts can contain sub-accounts, however, each company can freely devise their own sets of sub-accounts. Assignment of sub-accounts often depends on external knowledge, which is not stored in the accounting software's database (e.g., information about projects to which certain invoices belong). As it is not feasible to predict sub-accounts in the absence of information that would allow predicting sub-accounts, we trimmed each account such that only the main account (up to four digits) would remain. After trimming, the data set contained up to seven (with an average of 1.6) unique debit accounts for each supplier and up to five (with an average of 1.1) unique credit accounts.

Each posting entry in the data set consisted of 11 items: 1) the year of the financial document, 2) the registration number of the company, 3) the companies statistical classification of economic activities in the European Community (i.e., NACE code), 4) the registration number of the supplier, 5) the supplier's NACE code, 6) the reverse value-added tax (VAT) indicator, 7) the payable amount, 8) a number indicating the proportion of the payable amount from the total amount of the financial document 9) the currency of the document, 10) the debit account, and 11) the credit account.

3.2 Training/Evaluation Data Sub-sets

For machine learning experiments, we randomised the data set and split it into two parts such that:

- 1,954,280 posting entries (95.13% of all data) were used to train classification models;
- 100,000 posting entries (4.87% of all data) were used to evaluate the quality of the trained models.

4540 (or 4.54%) posting entries of the evaluation set feature suppliers that are not present in the training data. It is also expected that new companies will want to use the automatic account code classification method. This means that the classification models will have to be able to classify posting entries featuring unknown parties. To enable the possibility for machine learning models to learn classifying posting entries that feature unknown parties, we created also two training data sets with synthesized data. The three data sets used for training were as follows:

- Original training data (set 1; 1,954,280 posting entries)
- Supplemented training data (set 2; 7,217,120 entries), which consist of:
  - set 1;
  - set 1 with masked company registration numbers;
  - set 1 with masked supplier registration numbers;
  - set 1 with masked supplier registration numbers and masked company registration numbers;
- Supplemented training data (set 3; 9,771,400 entries), which consist of:
  - set 1;
  - set 1 with masked company registration numbers;
  - set 1 with masked company NACE codes;
  - set 1 with masked supplier registration numbers;
  - set 1 with masked supplier NACE codes.

4 Methods

To train multi-class classification models for automatic account code classification, we compared several machine-learning-based methods (both rule-based and statistical). We selected most of the classification methods such that we could validate findings found in related work. For some of the classification methods, which are typically binary classification methods, one versus all classification models were trained. Further, we describe the configurations used for training the different classification models.

4.1 ZeroR

The simplest classification method used was the ZeroR classifier, which always returns the most frequent class that is found in the training data set. In our training data set those are:

- 5721 for debit account code classification (found in 48.45% of posting entries)
- 5310 for credit account code classification (found in 82.96% of posting entries)

This method shows the lower-bound (or baseline) performance that must be reached by any useful classification method.

4.2 OneR

Considering that the average occurrence of account codes per each supplier is relatively small (1.1 for credit accounts and 1.6 for debit accounts), it is obvious that a method that outputs the majority account for each supplier seperately would be a stronger baseline and also show whether application of machine learning for this task even makes sense. To simulate this approach, we used the OneR classifier. The OneR classifier performs grouped ZeroR predictions for each separate feature and uses the one best-performing feature effectively building a one-level decision tree. Despite our expectation, the best feature for the OneR classifier was the relative sum instead of the supplier registration number. However, to show that relying just on supplier registration numbers does not allow achieving high classification precision, we masked the relative sum and re-calculated OneR results, which now used the supplier registration number as the one best-performing feature. The results are as follows:

- OneR results with relative sum hidden (supplier registration number used):
  - 55.42% for debit account code
  - 86.87% for credit account code
- OneR results using all features (relative sum used):
  - 59.05% for debit account code
  - 88.09% for credit account code

This shows that simple rule-based methods achieve a maximum precision of 59.05% for debit account classification, and machine learning-based methods (as we will see further) will improve beyond these results.

4.3 Averaged Perceptron

Next, we used an averaged perceptron (AP) classifier [4], which allows training multi-class classifiers using large feature sets. For instance, the feature set used in our experiments consists of 143,580 different features. The averaged perceptron is a simple feed-forward neural network that does not contain any hidden layers and accepts only categorical (0- or 1-valued) features. This means that to support numeric features, all numeric values are treated as separate features. For our experiments, we used the averaged perceptron implementation by Pinnis (2018) [14], however, we extended it to support features listed in Sect. 5. All models were trained for 10 epochs.

4.4 Feed-Forward Neural Network

Next, we used a feed-forward neural network (FFNN) (or multi-layer perceptron) classifier. We limited our experiments to one hidden layer that uses the rectified linear unit activation function and consists of 50 neurons. All layers are fully connected. To train the FFNN models, we used the scikit-learn [13] implementation. The parameters were optimised using the Adam [8] optimisation algorithm. The models were trained until convergence or up to 200 epochs for the training data set 1 and 10 epochs for the training data set 2 and training data set 3. Similarly to the averaged perceptron classifier, all features were treated as categorical.

4.5 Decision Tree

Next, we used a decision tree classifier. For our experiments, we used the custom *TreeLearner* algorithm from the machine learning toolkit Orange3 [5] to train the decision tree models. All decision trees feature a minimum of two instances in leaves, have an unlimited depth, and used a stopping criterion of 98% for majority classes in nodes.

4.6 Linear Support Vector Machine

Next, we used a linear support vector machine (LSVM) classifier. For our experiments, we used the Fan et al. (2008) [6] implementation from the scikit-learn [13] Python library. All categorical features were transformed into boolean features using scikit-learn's [13] *OneHotEncoder*. All parameters were set to their default values.

4.7 Bernoulli Naïve Bayes Classifier

Finally, we used the Bernoulli Naïve Bayes classifier by Manning et al. (2008) [9] from the scikit-learn [13] Python library. Similarly to the averaged perceptron classifier, all features were treated as categorical. Features were transformed into categorical features using scikit-learn's [13] *OneHotEncoder* and binarization was disabled. All other parameters were set to their default values.

5   Feature Engineering

We created categorical and numerical features for the various machine learning methods by using the nine data fields from the posting entry data set (except the two target values - debit/credit account codes). For the methods that did not support numerical features, numerical values were treated as categorical features. As the numerical feature for the document sum can become very sparse when transformed into numerous categorical features, we introduced also three rounded features for the document sum (rounded to ones, rounded to tens, and rounded to hundreds).

In our experiments, we used two sets of features: 1) set 1 where we used the eight features except the document sum and the relative amount (see Table 1), and 2) set 2 (see Table 2) where we used also the document sum, the three additional rounded features for the methods that did not use numerical features, and the relative amount.

Table 1. Feature set 1, (C - categorical features, N - numerical features, $\#$ - distinct feature count for categorical features, AP - averaged perceptron, $FFNN$ - feed-forward neural network, DT - decision tree, $LSVM$ - linear support vector machine, BNB - Bernoulli Naive Bayes)

Feature\method	$\#$	AP	FFNN	DT	LSVM	BNB
Company registration number	958	C	C	C	C	C
Company NACE code	235	C	C	C	C	C
Supplier registration number	27266	C	C	C	C	C
Supplier NACE code	521	C	C	C	C	C
Year	9	C	C	N	N	C
Reverse VAT	2	C	C	C	C	C
Currency	22	C	C	C	C	C

6   Results

The results of our experiments for debit account code classification are given in Table 3. It is evident that the best overall results were achieved using the decision tree and feed-forward neural network classifiers. The results also show that the various classifiers achieve the best results when using the first training data set (without synthetic data) and the second feature set (with numerical value features). However, the evaluation data features mostly known (i.e., present in the training data) companies and suppliers. This means that these results do not show how the various classifiers will perform when encountering new (or unknown) companies or suppliers. Therefore, we masked all buyers and all suppliers in the evaluation set and ran all classifiers. The results (see Table 4) show

Table 2. Feature set 2, (C - categorical features, N - numerical features, N/A - not used features, $\#$ - distinct feature count for categorical features, AP - averaged perceptron, $FFNN$ - feed-forward neural network, DT - decision tree, $LSVM$ - linear support vector machine, BNB - Bernoulli Naive Bayes)

Feature\method	#	AP	FFNN	DT	LSVM	BNB
Company registration number	958	C	C	C	C	C
Company NACE code	235	C	C	C	C	C
Supplier registration number	27266	C	C	C	C	C
Supplier NACE code	521	C	C	C	C	C
Year	9	C	C	N	N	C
Relative amount	764	C	C	N	N	C
Reverse VAT	2	C	C	C	C	C
Currency	22	C	C	C	C	C
Document sum	187628	C	C	N	N	C
Document sum rounded to ones	20459	C	C	N/A	N/A	C
Document sum rounded to tens	6279	C	C	N/A	N/A	C
Document sum rounded to hundreds	1775	C	C	N/A	N/A	C

Table 3. Evaluation results (precision scores) of the debit account code classification experiments

Method	Training data			
	Set 1		Set 2	Set 3
	Features			
	Set 1	Set 2		
ZeroR	49%	49%	49%	49%
OneR	59%	59%	59%	59%
Averaged perceptron	63%	91%	90%	90%
Decision tree	27%	92%	**93%**	**93%**
Feed-forward neural network	64%	**93%**	92%	92%
Linear support vector machine	63%	63%	61%	61%
Bernoulli Naïve Bayes	53%	79%	75%	76%

that both training data sets that featured synthetic data allowed training models that handle posting entries from unknown companies and suppliers better.

The results for credit account code classification are given in Table 5. Since the lower-bound (or baseline) classification precision was significantly higher than for the debit account code classification, the overall results for all classification methods are considerably higher with the averaged perceptron, decision tree, and feed-forward neural network classifiers all reaching 98% precision.

Table 4. Evaluation results (precision scores) of the debit account code classification experiments with masked suppliers and buyers

Method	Masked buyer				Masked supplier			
	Training Data				Training Data			
	Set 1		Set 2	Set 3	Set 1		Set 2	Set 3
	Features				Features			
	Set 1	Set 2			Set 1	Set 2		
ZeroR	49%	49%	49%	49%	49%	49%	49%	49%
OneR	59%	59%	59%	59%	59%	59%	59%	59%
Averaged perceptron	56%	79%	87%	87%	57%	83%	87%	87%
Feed-forward neural network	53%	76%	89%	89%	53%	76%	89%	89%
Linear support vector machine	56%	54%	59%	59%	54%	56%	57%	52%
Bernoulli Naïve Bayes	50%	75%	75%	76%	48%	75%	76%	76%

Table 5. Evaluation results (precision scores) of the credit account code classification experiments

Method	Training data			
	Set 1		Set 2	Set 3
	Features			
	Set 1	Set 2		
ZeroR	83%	83%	83%	83%
OneR	88%	88%	88%	88%
Averaged perceptron	97%	**98%**	**98%**	**98%**
Decision tree	74%	**98%**	**98%**	**98%**
Feed-forward neural network	**98%**	**98%**	**98%**	**98%**
Linear support vector machine	97%	97%	97%	97%
Bernoulli Naïve Bayes classifier	95%	95%	95%	95%

Next, we analysed how the frequency of companies and suppliers in the training data affects the classification precision. For this analysis, we grouped each company and each supplier by counting its posting entries in the training data, taking the base 10 logarithm of the count, and rounding the final number down. Using this method, we grouped all companies into six groups and all suppliers into five groups. Then, we calculated the debit account code classification precision using the evaluation data for each frequency group. The results for companies (see Fig. 1) show that the precision for companies with higher numbers of posting entries is in general higher (even up to 99%). At the same time, the precision for companies that are rare in training data is still above 70%. The results for suppliers (see Fig. 2) exhibit a similar tendency. However, the results for the most frequent suppliers are lower. This is because the training data features entries for unknown suppliers (i.e., the supplier registration number is equal to *"NONE"*, and *"NONE"* is frequent in the training data). When excluding these unknown suppliers, the precision for the most frequent suppliers increases to 90.2% and 91.5% for the averaged perceptron and feed-forward neural network classifiers respectively.

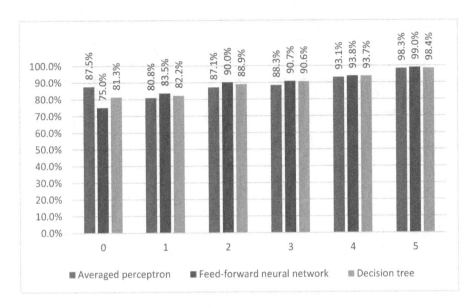

Fig. 1. Debit account code classification precision based on company log frequency in the training data set

Finally, we performed also an ablation study to identify whether all features that we devised for the debit and credit account code classification tasks are complementary to improving the overall classification precision. The results of the ablation study for the averaged perceptron classifier are given in Table 6. It is evident that most of the features except two rounded document sum features are needed for the debit account code classification. Credit account code classification can be improved (both quality-wise and speed-wise) by not using all three rounded document sum features. The study also revealed that the most important features for account code classification are the relative sum, the registration number of the supplier, and the registration number of the company.

Further, we analysed the feature set using the ReliefF feature selection algorithm [15]. The results (see Table 6) show that the feature rankings are similar to the findings of the ablation study.

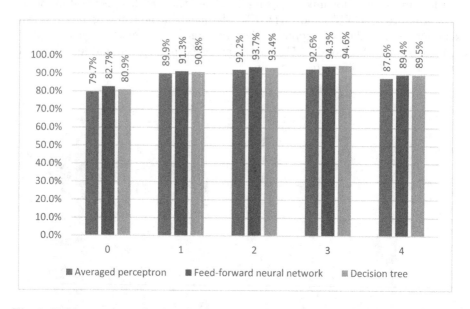

Fig. 2. Debit account code classification precision based on supplier log frequency in the training data set

Table 6. Ablation study for the averaged perceptron classifier. F - ReliefF feature ranking value

Skipped feature	Debit			Credit		
	Precision	Diff.	F	Precision	Diff.	F
None	90.84	0.00	-	98.09	0.00	-
Relative sum	79.42	−11.42	0.67	97.60	−0.50	0.34
Supplier registration number	87.47	−3.37	0.59	97.36	−0.74	0.68
Company registration number	87.90	−2.94	0.55	96.64	−1.46	0.81
Reverse VAT	89.98	−0.86	0.10	96.73	−1.36	0.28
Document sum	90.24	−0.60	0.18	98.05	−0.04	0.10
Supplier NACE code	90.59	−0.25	0.59	98.04	−0.05	0.65
Year	90.73	−0.11	0.05	98.07	−0.02	0.11
Currency	90.74	−0.09	0.00	98.07	−0.02	0.00
Company NACE code	90.74	−0.09	0.47	98.08	−0.01	0.78
Document sum rounded to 100	90.00	−0.07	0.04	98.10	0.00	−0.03
Document sum rounded to 10	90.84	0.00	−0.01	98.09	0.00	−0.09
Document sum rounded to 1	90.92	0.08	0.02	98.12	0.02	−0.11

7   Discussion

When analysing evaluation results, we noticed that the evaluation data contain contradictory entries that were identical when comparing feature values, but had different classification targets. There were 2091 (or 2.1%) conflicting debit account classification entries and 1729 (or 1.7%) conflicting credit account classification entries in the evaluation data. This does not necessarily mean that the data is wrong. Since we do not have access to all information that is available in the financial documents and since all information that could explain why certain account codes are assigned to posting entries is not stored in the accounting system (i.e., accountants often assign account codes to posting entries based on external knowledge), the data may contain a certain percentage of contradictory entries. However, this also means that it is not possible to reach 100% classification precision neither for debit account code classification nor credit account code classification using the available data and feature sets. Nevertheless, the classification methods still allowed achieving high results (93% for debit account code classification and 98% for credit account code classification). The results for credit account code classification are even very close to the theoretic maximum (of ~99%).

8   Conclusion

In the paper, we described our experiments on debit and credit account code classification using six different methods (rule-based and machine-learning-based methods). Our experiments on an ~2 million posting entry data set showed that the best results for debit account code classification (a precision of 93%) were achieved by decision tree and feed-forward neural network classifiers. Results for credit account code classification showed that the best results (a precision of 98%) were achieved using the same methods as for the debit account code classification as well as by the averaged perceptron classifier.

We also showed that supplementing original training data with synthetic training data where companies and suppliers are masked allows training models that are better suited for classification of posting entries for new companies and new suppliers.

The ablation study for the features used in the averaged perceptron classifier showed that most features (apart from the generated features) that were available for the posting entries were useful for classification.

The automation of posting of supplier invoices makes the posting process more fluid and understandable and increases confidence in the correctness of the process. We believe that using the automated posting functionality will allow shortening the time spent on invoice processing and have a positive impact on the accounting cycle as a whole because it will reduce the number of errors in financial statements and tax reports that would otherwise require additional time for corrections.

In the future, we plan to expand the feature set to incorporate also textual information that may be available (although not always) for posting entries, as well as other information from the financial documents.

Acknowledgements. The research has been supported by the ICT Competence Centre (www.itkc.lv) within the project "2.6. Research of artificial intelligence methods and creation of complex systems for automation of company accounting processes and decision modeling" of EU Structural funds, ID n° 1.2.1.1/18/A/003.

References

1. Baldwin, A.A., Brown, C.E., Trinkle, B.S.: Opportunities for artificial intelligence development in the accounting domain: the case for auditing. Intell. Syst. Account. Finan. Manage. **14**(3), 77–86 (2006). https://doi.org/10.1002/isaf.277. http://doi.wiley.com/10.1002/isaf.277
2. Bengtsson, H., Jansson, J.: Using classification algorithms for smart suggestions in accounting systems. Master's thesis, Department of Computer Science & Engineering, Chalmers University of Technology (2015)
3. Bergdorf, J.: Machine learning and rule induction in invoice processing: Comparing machine learning methods in their ability to assign account codes in the bookkeeping process (2018)
4. Collins, M.: Discriminative training methods for hidden Markov models: theory and experiments with perceptron algorithms. In: Proceedings of the ACL-02 Conference on Empirical Methods in Natural Language Processing, vol. 10, pp. 1–8. Association for Computational Linguistics (2002)
5. Demšar, J., et al.: Orange: data mining toolbox in python. J. Mach. Learn. Res. **14**, 2349–2353 (2013). http://jmlr.org/papers/v14/demsar13a.html
6. Fan, R.E., Chang, K.W., Hsieh, C.J., Wang, X.R., Lin, C.J.: Liblinear: a library for large linear classification. J. Mach. Learn. Res. **9**(Aug), 1871–1874 (2008)
7. Chua, F. (2013 ACCA): Digital Darwinism: thriving in the face of technology change Acknowledgements (2013). https://www.accaglobal.com/content/dam/acca/global/PDF-technical/futures/pol-afa-tt2.pdf
8. Kingma, D.P., Ba, J.: Adam: a method for stochastic optimization (2014). arXiv preprint arXiv:1412.6980
9. Manning, C.D., Raghavan, P., Schütze, H.: Introduction to Information Retrieval. Cambridge University Press, Cambridge (2008)
10. Mateush, A., Sharma, R., Dumas, M., Plotnikova, V., Slobozhan, I., Übi, J.: Building payment classification models from rules and crowdsourced labels: a case study. In: Matulevičius, R., Dijkman, R. (eds.) CAiSE 2018. LNBIP, vol. 316, pp. 85–97. Springer, Cham (2018). https://doi.org/10.1007/978-3-319-92898-2_7
11. Ministry of Finance of the Republic of Latvia: Par "uzņēmumu, uzņēmējsabiedrbu un organizāciju vienoto grāmatvedbas kontu plānu" (May 1993). https://likumi.lv/doc.php?id=232076
12. Nielsen, D.: Tree boosting with xgboost. NTNU Norwegian University of Science and Technology (2016)
13. Pedregosa, F., et al.: Scikit-learn: machine learning in Python. J. Mach. Learn. Res. **12**, 2825–2830 (2011)

14. Pinnis, M.: Latvian tweet corpus and investigation of sentiment analysis for Latvian. In: Human Language Technologies - The Baltic Perspective - Proceedings of the Seventh International Conference Baltic HLT 2018, pp. 112–119. IOS Press, Tartu, Estonia (2018). https://doi.org/10.3233/978-1-61499-912-6-112
15. Robnik-Šikonja, M., Kononenko, I.: An adaptation of relief for attribute estimation in regression. In: Proceedings of the Fourteenth International Conference on Machine Learning, ICML'97, vol. 5, pp. 296–304 (1997)
16. Smith, L.: User considerations when applying machine learning technology to accounting tasks. Ph.D. thesis. Stellenbosch University, Stellenbosch (2018)
17. Stefanowski, J.: The rough set based rule induction technique for classification problems. In: Proceedings of 6th European Conference on Intelligent Techniques and Soft Computing EUFIT, vol. 98 (1998)

Mobile Phone Usage Data
for Credit Scoring

Henri Ots[1(✉)], Innar Liiv[1], and Diana Tur[2]

[1] Tallinn University of Technolgoy, Akadeemia tee 15a, 12618 Tallinn, Estonia
`henriots@online.ee, innar.liiv@taltech.ee`
[2] Warsaw School of Economics, aleja Niepodległości 162, 02-554 Warszawa, Poland
`tur.diana@gmail.com`

Abstract. The aim of this study is to demostrate that mobile phone usage data can be used to make predictions and find the best classification method for credit scoring even if the dataset is small (2,503 customers). We use different classification algorithms to split customers into paying and non-paying ones using mobile data, and then compare the predicted results with actual results. There are several related works publicly accessible in which mobile data has been used for credit scoring, but they are all based on a large dataset. Small companies are unable to use datasets as large as those used by these related papers, therefore these studies are of little use for them. In this paper we try to argue that there is value in mobile phone usage data for credit scoring even if the dataset is small. We found that with a dataset that consists of mobile data based only on 2,503 customers, we can predict credit risk. The best classification method gave us the result 0.62 AUC (area under the curve).

Keywords: Supervised learning · Mobile phone usage data · Credit risk

1 Introduction

Credit scoring helps in increasing the speed and consistency of the loan application processes and allows lending firms to automate their lending processes [26]. In this case, credit scoring significantly reduces human involvement in credit evaluation and lessens the cost of delivering credit [34]. Moreover, by using credit scores, financial institutions are able to quantify risks associated with granting credit to a particular applicant in a shorter period of time. According to Leonard [19], a study done by a Canadian bank found that the time it took to process a consumer loan application was shortened from nine days to three after credit scoring was used. As such, the optimisation of the loan processing time means that time saved on processing could be utilised to address more complex aspects in the firm. Banaslak and Kiely [4] concluded that with the help of credit scores, financial institutions are able to make faster, better and higher quality decisions.

© Springer Nature Switzerland AG 2020
T. Robal et al. (Eds.): DB&IS 2020, CCIS 1243, pp. 82–95, 2020.
https://doi.org/10.1007/978-3-030-57672-1_7

There are more than 2 billion people in world who do not have a bank account [17]. This makes it difficult to perform a credit evaluation exercise for these individuals. With the rise of big data and especially new kinds of novel data sources, various data alternatives can be used to explain the financial inclusion of these unbanked individuals. For instance, mobile usage data is a novel data source that can be employed successfully. Mobile phone usage data can been considered as good alternative data for credit scoring.

To what extent can one tell your personality by simply looking at how you use your mobile phone? The use of standard carrier logs to determine the personality of a mobile phone user is a hot topic, which has generated tremendous interest. The number of mobile phone users has reached 6 billion worldwide and [18] service providers are allowing increasing access to phone logs to researchers and [10] commercial partners [12]. If predicted accurately, mobile phone datasets could provide a valuable and cost-effective method of surveying personalities. For example, marketers and phone manufacturing companies might seek to access dispositional information about their customers so as to design customised offers and promotions [23]. The human-computer interface field uses personality. Thus, it benefits from the appraisal of user dispositions using automatically collected data. Lastly, the ability to extract personality and other psychosocial variables from a large population might lead to unparalleled discoveries in the field of social sciences [2].

The use of mobile phones to predict people's personalities is a result of advancement in data collection, machine learning and computational social science which has made it possible to infer various psychological states and traits based on how people use their cell phones daily. For example, some studies have shown that people's personality can be predicted based on the pattern of how they use social media such as Facebook or Twitter [3,8,31]. Other researchers have used information about people's usage of various mobile applications such as YouTube, Internet Calendar, games and so on to make conclusions about their mood and personality traits [7,11,25,30,33]. While these approaches are remarkable, they require access to a wide-ranging information about a person's entire social network. These limitations greatly weaken the use of such classification methods for large-scale investigations [22].

The main contribution of this paper is to demonstrate that mobile phone usage data, instead of classical loan application data collection and other semi-manual processes, can be successfully used to predict credit risk even if the dataset is small (2,503 customers). Such contribution is novel and necessary for academic discussions as well as practical applications in relevant industries. From practical engineering point of view, the final selection of important features (Table 2) can be considered an equally strong contribution besides the main results.

The general outline of the paper is as follows: first, related work in this area is introduced (Sect. 2), secondly, experimental set-up is explained regarding data, measures, and experiment design (Sect. 3), followed by experimental results (Sect. 4) and conclusions (Sect. 5).

2   Related Work

Credit scoring can be best explained as the use of statistical models in the transformation of relevant data into numerical measures, which inform organisations assessing the credit trustworthiness of clients. Essentially, credit scoring is simply an industrialisation or proxy of trust; a logical and further development of the subjective credit ratings first provided by 19th century credit bureaus [1].

Numerous literature review focus on the development, application and evaluation of predictive models used in the credit sector [9]. These models determine the creditworthiness of an applicant based on a set of descriptive variables. Corporate risk models use data from a statement on financial position, financial ratios or macro-economic pointers, while retail risk models use data captured in the application form such as the customer's transaction history [32]. The difference between variables used in corporate and retail models indicates that more challenges arise in consumer than corporate credit scoring. This paper focuses on the retail business.

There are several indications about the use of mobile phone usage data in credit scoring corporate world. However, only very few relevant papers [6,20,24, 27–29] are open to wider research community.

Björkegren and Grissen [6] use behavioural signatures in mobile phone data to predict default with an accuracy almost similar to that of credit scoring methods that use financial history. The approach was validated using call records matched to loan results for a sample of borrowers in a Caribbean country. Applicants in the highest quartile of risk according to the authors' measure were six times more likely to default in payment than those in the lowest quartile. They used two different algorithms, Random Forest and Logistic regression. The result obtained with the Random Forest algorithm was 0.710 AUC (area under the curve) and with Logistic regression 0.760 AUC. The dataset included information on 7,068 customers from a South-American country [6]. Jose San Pedro et al. developed MobiScore [27], a methodology used to build a model of the user's financial risk using data collected from mobile usage. MobiScore [27] was using data on 60,000 real people obtained from telecommunication companies and financial service providers in a Latin American country. They used gradient boosting, support vector machine and linear regression models to solve the problem. AUC results with different combinations were between 64.1 and 72.5 [27]. Speakman et al. demonstrated [29] how to use boosted decision trees to create a credit score for underbanked populations, enabling them to access a credit facility that was previously denied due to the unavailability of financial data. Their research result was a 55% reduction in default rates while simultaneously offering credit opportunities to a million customers that were given a 0 credit limit in the bank's original model. The dataset contained 295,926 labelled examples with over 30 categorical and real-valued features. AUC results with the boosted decision trees algorithm were 0.764 and with logistic regression 0.74 [29].

3   Experimental Set-Up

3.1   Data

The dataset comprises of information on 2,503 customers who have obtained a consumer loan, and allows one to understand their previous payment behaviour. Any means of identification have been entirely removed from the data and consequently anything personal has been remove. Information was initially obtained with the consent of the customers. The mobile phone usage dataset was collected from an anonymous European consumer lending company whose customers used their mobile application to submit digital loan applications and gave explicit data permissions to the app.

Using their payment behaviour we are able to separate the trustworthy customers from the untrustworthy ones. The target varibale is calculated from previous payment behavior data originating from the payment monitoring information system, which identifies untrustworthy customers as those, who have got a 90-day delay in payment of their instalments. Additionally, the dataset will include about 1,516 trustworthy customers without debts that exceed the 90-day limit. Conclusively, this will result in the percentages of the trustworthy and untrustworthy customers being 60.57 % and 39.43 %, respectively.

Android phone users can be requested to yield the following data about their device (see Table 1). For this research we did not use phone numbers, calendar body texts or text messages (SMS).

From among all the varying parameters, 22 variables were selected to be used in the experiments necessary for the research (the variables are shown in Table 2). The variables were chosen by using manual review and statistical analysis of dependencies. We chose variables that were less dependent on each other. Using these variables, one of them is a categorical variable while others are numerical. In some experiments we discretized some numerical variables into bins so that their data type changed to categorical.

3.2   Measures

Harris [14] notes that in the process of developing and reporting the credit scoring models it is pragmatic to differentiate between the training and the reporting phase. This is due to the need of the person to provide clarity on the type of the metric that was initially applied in the selection of model parameters. When denoting the metric adopted, it would be sensible to use the term evaluation metric in the training process. On the other hand, to report the model performance during the performance phase, the term performance metric will be adopted [14].

In this analysis, both the performance metric and the primary model evaluation metric are represented by the region under the ROC (Receiver Operating Characteristic) curve called AUC. The ROC curve, often adopted by the AUC, illustrates a two-component aspect of differential performance where the sensitivity (1) (i.e. the relative amount of the actual positives which is forecasted as positive) and the specificity (2) (i.e. the proportion of actual negatives that

Table 1. Raw data from Android phones.

Data group	Data description
Device	Device ID
Device	OS (operating system) version
Device	SDK (software development kit) version
Device	Release version
Device	Device
Device	Model
Device	Product
Device	Brand
Device	Display
Device	Hardware
Device	Manufacturer
Device	Serial
Device	User
Device	Host
Network	Network ID
Network	Carrier
Network	Operator
Network	Subscriber
Calendar	Calendar ID
Calendar	Title
Calendar	Date
Calendar	Body
Call info	Caller ID
Call info	Receiver (contact/unknown)
Call info	Type (incoming/outgoing/missed/unanswered)
Call info	Number
Call info	Date
Call info	Duration
Contact info	Contact ID
Contact info	Contact number
Installed apps	App ID
Installed apps	Package name
Installed apps	Label
Installed apps	Version name
Installed apps	Version code
Installed apps	Install date
SMS info	SMS ID
SMS info	Type (incoming/outgoing)
SMS info	Conversation
SMS info	Number
SMS info	Message lenght
SMS info	SMS date
SMS info	SMS ID
Images	Image ID
Images	Image date
Images	Image location
Data storage	Data storage ID
Data storage	Path
Data storage	Last modifed

Table 2. Variables for experiments.

Data group	Calculated data points	Data type
Call info	Average number of calls per month	Numerical
Call info	Average number of incoming calls per month	Numerical
Call info	Average number of outgoing calls per month	Numerical
Call info	Average number of missed calls per month	Numerical
Call info	Average number of unanswered calls per month	Numerical
Call info	Average call duration	Numerical
Call info	Average outgoing call duration	Numerical
Call info	Average incoming call duration	Numerical
Call info	Maximum outgoing call duration	Numerical
Call info	Maximum incoming call duration	Numerical
Images	Average number of images per month	Numerical
Images	Average number of images made in distinct places per month	Numerical
SMS info	Average number of SMSs per month	Numerical
SMS info	Average number of incoming SMSs per month	Numerical
SMS info	Average number of incoming SMSs per month from contacts	Numerical
SMS info	Average number of incoming SMSs per month	Numerical from an unknown number
SMS info	Average number of outgoing SMSs per month	Numerical
SMS info	Average number of outgoing SMSs per month from a contact	Numerical
SMS info	Average number of outgoing SMSs per month	Numerical from an unknown number
SMS info	Average number of SMS conversations per month	Numerical
Contacts	Number of contacts	Numerical
Device	SDK version	Categorical

are forecasted as being negative) are plotted on the Y and X axis, respectively. Normally, the AUC figure is demonstrated as in (3) the figure below where S1 illustrates the total sum of the customer's creditworthiness rank. In this, a score of 100% shows that the person classifying can impeccably differentiate between the classes, and a score of fifty percentage shows a classifier possessing a minor quality of differentiation [15].

$$Sensitivity = \frac{true\,positive}{true\,positive + false\,negative} \tag{1}$$

$$Specificity = \frac{true\,negative}{true\,positive + true\,negative} \tag{2}$$

$$AUC = \frac{(S1 - sensitivity) + [(sensitivity + 1) + 0.5]}{sensitivity + specificity} \tag{3}$$

$$Test\,accuracy = \frac{true\,positive}{true\,positive + false\,positive} + \frac{true\,negative}{false\,negative + true\,negative} \tag{4}$$

Different metrics can also be applied and used to produce the working of the categories used herein. For instance, to check for the correctness (4) it can also be taken to be the measure of how correct those applying for credit on a held back data test are classified. Several performances are often applied when reporting the performance of the classifier developed in this analysis. For instance, the test accuracy below has also been reported to be a measure of how precise the applicants of credit is. Subsequently, the slanted datasets are familiar, similar to what is happening with actual world credit, which scores the datasets making it irrelevant [15].

3.3   Experiment Design

We carried out three experiments with five different classification methods and considered AUC to be the performance parameter. As the author's previous experiences have illustrated, there are no specific rules for working with alternative data. Accordingly, we carried out three experiments based on different pre-processing techniques.

In the first experiment we included all the calculated variables. The SDK variable, which is categorical, needs to be encoded. The SDK data has to be converted into numbers to make them comparable. The SDK version comprises six different values (19, 20, 21, 22, 23, 24, 25), for which we generated dummy variables. The values of these parameters are either 1 or 0. As a result, there can be no missing information in the dataset. The second step in the data pre-processing is to scale all variables to make them comparable with each other.

In the second experiment we used the same pre-processing techniques as in the first experiment, but we added backward elimination. The principle of Occam's razor states that the [16] model needs to be as simple as possible until it achieves an acceptable level of performance on training data. This will help to avoid over-fitting the model. With backward elimination we can throw out variables with p-value (probability value) >0.05 and the highest p value. After that we can calculate a new combination of p values and continue the same process until we have a set of variables, all with p lower than 0.05.

In the third experiment we used the same pre-processing method as before but modified the variables. We used the optimal binning technique to group the variables. Optimal binning is a method of pre-processing categorical predictors where we set values for variables by grouping them into optimal bins. Its purpose is to reduce the impact of statistical noise [21].

In order to choose the classifier methods for the experimental part we used three parameters:

- How have they functioned in previous credit scoring research?
- How have they functioned in previous credit scoring research using mobile data?
- How have they functioned in the author's practical work in credit scoring models?

According to these three parameters we chose for our experiments the following methods: logistic regression, decision tree, random forest, SVM and neural networks.

When organising benchmarks in pattern recognition, there is often the problem of determining the size of the test set that would give statistically significant results. The commonly adopted ratio is 8:2 according to the Pareto principle.

According to research by Isabelle Guyon and the formula she found we can determine the example test size. The fraction of patterns reserved for the validation set should be inversely proportional to the square root of the number of free adjustable parameters. The ratio of the validation set (v) to the training set (t) is v/t, and the scales are ln(N/h-max), where N is the number of families of recognizers, and h-max is the largest complexity of those families. Each family of recognizers is characterised by its complexity, which may or may not be related to the VC-dimension (Vapnik–Chervonenkis dimension), the description length, the number of adjustable parameters, or other measures of complexity [13]. According to a small sample size of customers we chose three different test size examples for this research. The test sizes we chose were 10%, 25% and 40%.

Testing any combination of variables first results in all variables. We then chose only the variables with $p < 0.05$ and finally binned the variables with $p < 0.05$. The intervals of the variables can be determined in a variety of ways. For example, by using prior knowledge on the data. The boundaries of the intervals are usually defined beforehand.

3.4 Experiments

The experiments described in this chapter were done using the Python programming language and the Spyder environment. We also used numpy, matplotlib, panda and scikit-learn Python libraries for statistical analyses.

Tables 3, 4 and 5 show a representation of the performance of classification methods using mobile data. The results in Table 3 show the classifiers' performances with all variables. The results in Table 4 show the classifiers' performance with only the variables whose p value is lower than 0.05. Table 5 shows binned variables whose p value is lower than 0.05. The tables suggest the models created for the prediction of creditworthiness as illustrated by AUC on the suppressed datasets. To determine the importance of the variation in performance between the models we can take AUC as the main parameter to see which model had the best performance. Tables 3, 4 and 5 can also be compared for training accuracy, test accuracy and training time(s). The training time is measured using a MacBook Air (1.6GHz Dual-Core Intel Core i5, RAM 8GB RAM).

The target variable chosen was 0 for a performing customer and 1 for a non-performing customer. A non-performing customer in this research is set as one who is 90 or more days overdue in paying their debt. According to Barisitz, [5] the rule of being 90 days overdue is most common in the European country from which the data for this research were collected.

Table 3. Showing comparative classifier performances with all variables.

Classifier	Test size	Training accuracy	Test accuracy	AUC	Training time (s)
Logistic regression	Test size = 0.10	0.62	0.62	0.51	0.005
Logistic regression	Test size = 0.25	0.61	0.62	0.55	0.005
Logistic regression	Test size = 0.40	0.63	0.61	0.56	0.001
Decision tree	Test size = 0.10	1.00	0.57	0.54	0.093
Decision tree	Test size = 0.25	1.00	0.56	0.54	0.074
Decision tree	Test size = 0.40	1.00	0.56	0.54	0.052
Random forest	Test size = 0.10	0.98	0.63	0.62	0.103
Random forest	Test size = 0.25	0.98	0.60	0.52	0.076
Random forest	Test size = 0.40	0.98	0.61	0.58	0.059
SVM	Test size = 0.10	0.61	0.65	0.56	3.330
SVM	Test size = 0.25	0.60	0.59	0.56	2.150
SVM	Test size = 0.40	0.60	0.59	0.57	1.220
Neural networks	Test size = 0.10	0.69	0.60	0.59	100.630
Neural networks	Test size = 0.25	0.67	0.59	0.57	69.790
Neural networks	Test size = 0.40	0.69	0.61	0.55	51.710

4 Experimental Results

The empirical results consist of the performance estimates of five classifiers with three different combinations. The tables on the previous page report the AUCs of all five classifiers with all three experiment combinations.

Random forest provides the best average AUC level across experiments with different test sizes. Random forest also ranks the best AUC at 0.62 with all variables and a test size of 10. The second-best method was neural networks with the highest AUC and all variables using 10 for the test size.

According to the author's previous know-how as regards choosing a test size for a small dataset of 2,503 customers, we were able to take the most stable

Table 4. Showing comparative classifier performances with variables were p-value is lower than 0.05.

Classifier	Test size	Training accuracy	Test accuracy	AUC	Training time (s)
Logistic regression	Test size = 0.10	0.68	0.62	0.54	0.004
Logistic regression	Test size = 0.25	0.76	0.56	0.53	0.003
Logistic regression	Test size = 0.40	0.77	0.55	0.50	0.003
Decision tree	Test size = 0.10	1.00	0.56	0.53	0.032
Decision tree	Test size = 0.25	1.00	0.55	0.53	0.029
Decision tree	Test size = 0.40	1.00	0.58	0.55	0.023
Random forest	Test size = 0.10	0.98	0.66	0.56	0.064
Random forest	Test size = 0.25	0.98	0.62	0.59	0.056
Random forest	Test size = 0.40	0.98	0.60	0.58	0.045
SVM	Test size = 0.10	0.60	0.65	0.53	1.305
SVM	Test size = 0.25	0.60	0.59	0.56	1.094
SVM	Test size = 0.40	0.60	0.59	0.57	0.678
Neural networks	Test size = 0.10	0.64	0.61	0.57	84.360
Neural networks	Test size = 0.25	0.63	0.60	0.55	89.720
Neural networks	Test size = 0.40	0.65	0.60	0.58	62.620

Table 5. Showing comparative classifier performances with variables are binned and p-value is lower than 0.05.

Classifier	Test size	Training accuracy	Test accuracy	AUC	Training time (s)
Logistic regression	Test size = 0.10	0.68	0.62	0.54	0.004
Logistic regression	Test size = 0.25	0.76	0.56	0.53	0.003
Logistic regression	Test size = 0.40	0.77	0.55	0.50	0.003
Decision tree	Test size = 0.10	0.74	0.59	0.53	0.060
Decision tree	Test size = 0.25	0.76	0.56	0.53	0.003
Decision tree	Test size = 0.40	0.78	0.55	0.50	0.003
Random forest	Test size = 0.10	0.73	0.58	0.54	0.220
Random forest	Test size = 0.25	0.75	0.53	0.52	0.022
Random forest	Test size = 0.40	0.76	0.54	0.50	0.021
SVM	Test size = 0.10	0.60	0.65	0.49	0.007
SVM	Test size = 0.25	0.59	0.59	0.48	0.238
SVM	Test size = 0.40	0.60	0.59	0.48	0.168
Neural networks	Test size = 0.10	0.61	0.63	0.51	84.400
Neural networks	Test size = 0.25	0.61	0.62	0.54	63.330
Neural networks	Test size = 0.40	0.62	0.58	0.45	53.820

results at a 40 test size. With the test size being 40, we gained the best result from the first experiment with the random forest algorithm AUC = 0.58, and the same result from the neural networks algorithm in the second experiment with only the variables where p < 0.05.

The weakest result overall was obtained from the SVM algorithm, which yielded very poor results in the second and third experiment, where AUC was below 0.50. The decision tree algorithm shows the most stable results across experiments and test sizes, having AUC between 0.50 and 0.55.

Table 6. Comparing related works.

Work	Test set size	Method	AUC
Behavior Revealed in Mobile Phone Usage Predicts Loan Repayment", authors: Björkegren and Grissen, 2017	7,068	Random Forest	0.710
Behavior Revealed in Mobile Phone Usage Predicts Loan Repayment", authors: Björkegren and Grissen, 2017	7,068	Logistic regression	0.760
Mobile phone-based Credit Scoring", authors: Skyler Speakman, Eric Mibuari, Isaac Markus, Felix Kwizera, 2017	60,000	Linear regression	0.725
MobiScore: Towards Universal Credit Scoring from Mobile Phone Data", authors: Jose San Pedro, Davide Proserpio and Nuria Oliver, 2015	295,926	Boosted decision trees algorithm	0.740
MobiScore: Towards Universal Credit Scoring from Mobile Phone Data", authors: Jose San Pedro, Davide Proserpio and Nuria Oliver, 2015	295,926	Logistic regression	0.760
Current research	2,503	Logistic regression	0.540
Current research	2,503	Decision tree	0.550
Current research	2,503	Random forest	0.620
Current research	2,503	SVM	0.570
Current research	2,503	Neural networks	0.590

Comparing the results with related works in Table 6, it is apparent that in this research, the AUC results are lower than in others. There is high correlation between the test size and AUC, and seeing how our sample size is only 2,503 customers compared to 7,068, 60,000 and 295,926 we can consider our results to be good.

This study has two important theoretical contributions. First, based on the use of mobile data for credit scoring research, we can see that all the tested methods with all variables yielded a better result than in a random study.

Secondly, we empirically demonstrate that the best method for credit scoring based on mobile data is the random forests classification method with AUC 0.62.

Our research on mobile data scoring will make it possible for other organizations in the financial sector to use mobile data for their credit scoring. While prior three researches on this subject showed that mobile data is only useful with big datasets, we maintain that it can yield positive results even with a small dataset. Thus, this knowledge can now be used in small or medium-sized companies as well.

5 Conclusions

For the past three decades, financial risk forecasting has been one of the main areas of growth in statistics and probability modelling. People often think of the term 'financial risk' in relation with portfolio management when it comes to pricing of options among other financial instruments. The main challenge for consumer loan firms over the past years has been reaching the huge sector of unbanked customers. There are more than 2 billion people in world who do not have a bank account [17] and the number of mobile phone users has reached 6 billion worldwide [18]. Few conceptual works have been posited with a research subject that brings together credit scoring and mobile data.

This paper is based on a synthesis of earlier academic research with new experiments and argues that mobile phone usage data can give positive results for credit scoring even with a small dataset. Our findings also reveal that the best model in terms of mobile data usage for credit scoring is the decision tree method.

If finance companies want to have more accurate data on those customers who are more likely to pay back their loans, they need to find alternative data sources such as mobile phone data. This will a give huge advantage to finance companies in third world countries where most people do not have any bank history – the only data they have is their mobile phone data.

We hope this study opens up further discussion and advances theory to generate a more accurate understanding of how we can use mobile data to make predictions and added value. This paper could spark discussion not only for financial sector companies but also in the field of insurance or fraud prevention, where mobile data can help make predictions.

There are many ways in which future studies could elaborate on this subject. One way is to look at algorithms in more depth and try to come up with more accurate models. Making predictions on mobile data can be used in other sectors as well, not only in finance. It is very probable that if we can predict customers' payment behaviour based on mobile data, we could also predict their insurance or fraud risk. There are multiple research possibilities in the field of alternative data sources such as mobile data that could add value for businesses. In the modern world we have many technical solutions at our disposal that create and gather data every day.

References

1. Anderson, R.: The Credit Scoring Toolkit: Theory and Practice for Retail Credit Risk Management and Decision Automation. Oxford University Press, New YorK (2007)
2. Arteaga, S.M., Kudeki, M., Woodworth, A.: Combating obesity trends in teenagers through persuasive mobile technology. ACM SIGACCESS Accessibility Comput. **94**, 17–25 (2009)
3. Back, M.D., Stopfer, J.M., Vazire, S., Gaddis, S., Schmukle, S.C., Egloff, B., Gosling, S.D.: Facebook profiles reflect actual personality, not self-idealization. Psychol. Sci. **21**(3), 372–374 (2010)
4. Banasiak, M.J., Kiely, G.: Predictive collection score technology. Bus. Credit **102**(2), 18–34 (2000)
5. Barisitz, S., et al.: Nonperforming loans in cesee-what do they comprise. Focus Eur. Econ. Integr. Q **4**, 46–68 (2011)
6. Björkegren, D., Grissen, D.: The development of credit scoring quality measures for consumer credit applications. In: Netmob (2013)
7. Chittaranjan, G., Blom, J., Gatica-Perez, D.: Mining large-scale smartphone data for personality studies. Pers. Ubiquit. Comput. **17**(3), 433–450 (2013)
8. Counts, S., Stecher, K.: Self-presentation of personality during online profile creation. In: Third International AAAI Conference on Weblogs and Social Media (2009)
9. Crook, J.N., Edelman, D.B., Thomas, L.C.: Recent developments in consumer credit risk assessment. Eur. J. Oper. Res. **183**(3), 1447–1465 (2007)
10. De Montjoye, Y.A., Hidalgo, C.A., Verleysen, M., Blondel, V.D.: Unique in the crowd: the privacy bounds of human mobility. Sci. Rep. **3**, 1376 (2013)
11. Do, T.M.T., Gatica-Perez, D.: By their apps you shall understand them: mining large-scale patterns of mobile phone usage. In: Proceedings of the 9th International Conference on Mobile and Ubiquitous Multimedia, pp. 1–10 (2010)
12. Goldman, D.: Your phone company is selling your personal data. CNN Money **1** (2011)
13. Guyon, I.: A scaling law for the validation-set training-set size ratio. AT&T Bell Laboratories, vol. 1, p. 11 (1997)
14. Harris, T.: Quantitative credit risk assessment using support vector machines: broad versus narrow default definitions. Expert Syst. Appl. **40**(11), 4404–4413 (2013)
15. Harris, T.: Credit scoring using the clustered support vector machine. Expert Syst. Appl. **42**(2), 741–750 (2015)
16. Blumer, A., Ehrenfeucht, A., Haussler, D., Warmuth, M.K.: Occam's razor. Inf. Process. Lett. **24**, 377–380 (1987)
17. Hodgson, C.: The world's 2 billion unbanked, in 6 charts, Business Insider UK (2017). www.businessinsider.com/the-worlds-unbanked-population-in-6-charts-2017-8
18. Lance, W.: 2011 ends with almost 6 billion mobile phone subscriptions, CNET News (2012). www.cnet.com/news/2011-ends-with-almost-6-billion-mobile-phone-subscriptions/
19. Leonard, K.J.: The development of credit scoring quality measures for consumer credit applications. Int. J. Qual. Reliab. Manage. **12**, 79 (1995)
20. Ma, L., Zhao, X., Zhou, Z., Liu, Y.: A new aspect on p2p online lending default prediction using meta-level phone usage data in China. Decis. Support Syst. **111**, 60–71 (2018)

21. Mironchyk, P., Tchistiakov, V.: Monotone optimal binning algorithm for credit risk modeling. Technical report, Utrecht: Working Paper (2017)
22. de Montjoye, Y.-A., Quoidbach, J., Robic, F., Pentland, A.S.: Predicting personality using novel mobile phone-based metrics. In: Greenberg, A.M., Kennedy, W.G., Bos, N.D. (eds.) SBP 2013. LNCS, vol. 7812, pp. 48–55. Springer, Heidelberg (2013). https://doi.org/10.1007/978-3-642-37210-0_6
23. de Oliveira, R., Karatzoglou, A., Concejero Cerezo, P., Armenta Lopez de Vicuña, A., Oliver, N.: Towards a psychographic user model from mobile phone usage. In: CHI 2011 Extended Abstracts on Human Factors in Computing Systems, pp. 2191–2196 (2011)
24. Óskarsdóttir, M., Bravo, C., Sarraute, C., Vanthienen, J., Baesens, B.: The value of big data for credit scoring: enhancing financial inclusion using mobile phone data and social network analytics. Appl. Soft Comput. **74**, 26–39 (2019)
25. Pianesi, F., Mana, N., Cappelletti, A., Lepri, B., Zancanaro, M.: Multimodal recognition of personality traits in social interactions. In: Proceedings of the 10th International Conference on Multimodal Interfaces, pp. 53–60 (2008)
26. Rimmer, J.: Contemporary changes in credit scoring. Credit Control **26**(4), 56–60 (2005)
27. Pedro, J.S., Proserpio, D., Oliver, N.: MobiScore: towards universal credit scoring from mobile phone data. In: Ricci, F., Bontcheva, K., Conlan, O., Lawless, S. (eds.) UMAP 2015. LNCS, vol. 9146, pp. 195–207. Springer, Cham (2015). https://doi.org/10.1007/978-3-319-20267-9_16
28. Shema, A.: Effective credit scoring using limited mobile phone data. In: Proceedings of the Tenth International Conference on Information and Communication Technologies and Development, pp. 1–11 (2019)
29. Speakman, S., Mibuari, E., Markus, I., Kwizera, F.: Mobile phone-based credit scoring. NetMob Book of Abstracts (2017)
30. Staiano, J., Lepri, B., Aharony, N., Pianesi, F., Sebe, N., Pentland, A.: Friends don't lie: inferring personality traits from social network structure. In: Proceedings of the 2012 ACM Conference on Ubiquitous Computing, pp. 321–330 (2012)
31. Stecher, K.B., Counts, S.: Spontaneous inference of personality traits and effects on memory for online profiles. In: International AAAI Conference on Weblogs and Social Media (ICWSM) (2008)
32. Thomas, L.C.: A survey of credit and behavioural scoring: forecasting financial risk of lending to consumers. Int. J. Forecast. **16**(2), 149–172 (2000)
33. Verkasalo, H., López-Nicolás, C., Molina-Castillo, F.J., Bouwman, H.: Analysis of users and non-users of smartphone applications. Telematics Inform. **27**(3), 242–255 (2010)
34. Wendel, C., Harvey, M.: Credit scoring: best practices and approaches. Commercial Lending Rev. **18**, 4 (2003)

Review of Non-English Corpora Annotated for Emotion Classification in Text

Viktorija Leonova[✉]

University of Latvia, Riga, Latvia
vk15061@lu.lv

Abstract. In this paper we try to systematize the information about the available corpora for emotion classification in text for languages other than English with the goal to find what approaches could be used for low-resource languages with close to no existing works in the field. We analyze the corresponding volume, emotion classification schema, language of each corresponding corpus and methods employed for data preparation and annotation automation. We've systematized twenty-four papers representing the corpora and found that corpora were mostly for the most spoken world languages: Hindi, Chinese, Turkish, Arabic, Japanese etc. A typical corpus contained several thousand of manually-annotated entries, collected from a social network, annotated by three annotators each and was processed by a few machine learning methods, such as linear SVM and Naïve Bayes and (more recent ones) a couple of neural networks methods, such as CNN.

Keywords: Review · Emotion classification · Emotion annotation · Machine learning · Text corpus

1 Introduction

In recent times we have witnessed the advent of modern technologies: dramatically increasing storage and processing capacities, high-resolution equipment generating massive amounts of data, such as imaging technologies used in medicine, sequencers used in biology and so forth. Similarly, the forthcoming of Web 2.0 gave rise to the generation of an unprecedented amount of text. Such volumes presented a problem, as those could not be possibly processed by humans. Thus, as machine learning techniques have come into play, they were immediately employed for text analysis. And of all machine learning methods, neural networks are currently looking especially fitting the task. However, there is one peculiarity to machine learning methods that hampers their advance: unfortunately, they require relatively big training data corpus in order to produce a viable model. Creation of such corpora is an arduous task, especially if it should be done from scratch.

Above, we have mentioned the analysis of text, however, the text can be analyzed for a dozen of different purposes. For example, it can be semantic annotation, named entity recognition, sentiment analysis and so forth. And while some of those are relatively well-studied, other are still underrepresented, despite the keen interest towards them. With

© Springer Nature Switzerland AG 2020
T. Robal et al. (Eds.): DB&IS 2020, CCIS 1243, pp. 96–108, 2020.
https://doi.org/10.1007/978-3-030-57672-1_8

recent development of all kinds of chat bots, virtual assistants and similar intelligent agents, the analysis of emotions in text has seen ever-increasing interest, both because the feedback from customers and users can prove valuable and because people prefer dealing with agents that express emotions. Although, while there is a considerable number of works involving sentiment analysis, there are much less works on emotion analysis. And logically, the corpora annotated for emotion classification, are very rare, both because the emotion analysis in text is underdeveloped and because creating such corpus requires considerable amount of resources from a researcher. We would like to note that there are considerably more works on emotion recognition in speech, even in relatively low-resource languages such as Russian (an example is provided in [1]).

The situation is even worse when we look at the languages other than English, which has several emotion-annotated corpora available [2]. From the point of view of emotion analysis, virtually all languages are either low-resource or extremely low-resource. In this paper, we are gathering and analyzing the available corpora in non-English languages as a part of preparation for engaging in emotion recognition project in Latvian and Russian, to investigate the approaches taken, tools and models and methods used by researchers for low-resource languages belonging to different language groups before taking up a toilsome task of building such corpus and to provide the possibility to any other who would be willing to involve into a similar task to consult this paper for references and compare the employed approaches.

2 Related Works and Background

2.1 Modelling Emotions

In order to classify emotions in text, one must find the way to represent the emotions in a psychologically justified way. However, there is no emotion representation concepts univocally agreed by specialists, and there coexist several different models. One of the most popular between those is Ekman's six basic emotions: happiness, anger, sadness, fear, disgust and surprise [3], which addresses emotions as a discrete set, and the variations of this model. These variants sometimes include neutral value denoting the absence of any pronounced emotions added to the list and Plutchik's wheel of emotions that views emotions as four [4] pairs of opposing emotions: happiness–sadness, anger–fear, trust–disgust, anticipation–surprise.

However, occasionally, a more unorthodox approach is adopted: for example, unique model used in compiling YACIS dataset consisting of ten discrete emotions, more fitting for Japanese language, as claimed by authors [5]. Another example includes Yahoo's 8 emotions model [6] intended for Chinese readers' emotion classification and employed for creation of Ren-CECps1.0 dataset [7]. Yet another model, discriminating between five discrete emotions was used by authors without a reference to any particular author [8]. Section 3.2 reviews the discrete emotion models and relations between those in detail.

Completely different approach is employed by PAD emotional state model [9], which represents emotions as continuous values on axes of valence, arousal and dominance, where valence marks how pleasant an emotion may be, arousal denotes the intensity of emotion and dominance represents the level of control and dominance.

2.2 Information Collection

As the machine learning has gained popularity among researchers, the need for datasets that could be used for training models, is naturally growing. People are actively looking for such datasets and as a result, the articles like "20 Best German Language Datasets for Machine Learning" [26] are plentiful. However, there are specifics that make those unusable in the case examined in this paper. First, as we have mentioned above, the works that focus on emotion detection in text are low-numbered per se, and the majority of this few are in English. Second, naturally, belonging to a language-detecting domain, emotion detection datasets tend to be organized by language. To the best of our knowledge, there are currently no available reviews that would try to systematize non-English corpora for emotion classification task from text. There is also no straightforward way to exclude results for English, as most authors either reference works done for English texts or compare results for their language of choice and for English, or both.

So, in order to find the relevant works for this research, we have incorporated the following strategy: we would look for works dedicated to emotion-annotated corpora/datasets, including language names into search terms. After finding relevant works, we would examine their related works section in order to find other possible candidates for including into the list. As to the set of languages we used in our search, we have looked for twenty most spoken languages as well as European national languages. Besides, we have perused the general search results without including any specific language, to make sure we haven't overlooked any major works. The results are summarized in the next section.

3 Corpora

3.1 Datasets Size and Source

Not surprisingly, the corpora we have discovered, are mostly representing the most-spoken languages of the world: Chinese, Arabic, Hindi etc. Many authors have referred to the scarceness of resources in those languages and the absence of emotion-annotated corpora as a motivation for creating the corpus. Thus, they had to work from scratch and manually annotate the training set to be able to train their model. As a result, the sizes of these manually annotated datasets are limited by the availability of human resources. For example, Gohil et al. [10] mentions that the dataset was annotated by three annotators, while Lapitan et al. [11] and Araque et al. [12] employed crowdsourcing approach: the former used CrowdFlower platform for annotation, while the latter has collected the data from the portal that already had emotions annotated by the visitors. Yet another approach is to use machine learning methods to annotate the dataset, one of the most impressive examples of which can be seen in [5] with 5-billion word corpus.

As to the source of emotion-charged utterances, it is no surprise that most of the authors have turned to social media that have expanded immensely during the last decade. Twitter and Facebook are the most popular choices (see [33] and [28], respectively, for example), while various blog platforms are also a valid option (and example can be seen in [16]). A few works turn to completely different domain, namely, literature, and analyze fairy tales, probably, because being intended for children, they provide richer emotional content, like [24]. Some works use texts, written specifically for the purpose of model training, such as [32]. Figure 1 illustrates the distribution of different data sources.

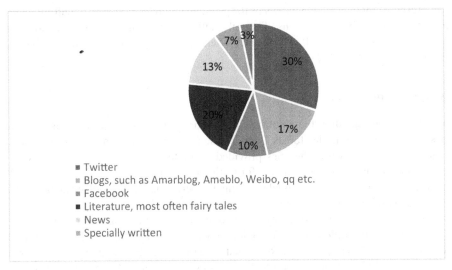

Fig. 1. The relative ratio of different data sources

3.2 Emotions Classification Models

For classification of emotions, Ekman's 6 emotions (anger, disgust, fear, happiness, sadness, surprise) model was the most popular, being used in about half of works. However, a number of variations to this model was introduced by several authors:

- Disgust was removed from the list, so the final variant included only anger, fear, happiness, sadness and surprise [12, 27];
- Neutral emotion was added [24, 25];
- Fondness was added [16];
- Embarrasment and pride for achievement were additionally selected from Ekman's extended set of emotions [38].

Plutchik's 8-emotions model (happiness, sadness, anger, fear, trust, disgust, anticipation and surprise) was employed in two works: [10] and [11]. It can be considered an extension of Ekman's model with anticipation and trust added. Several other authors used their own sets: Kumar et al. [8] used "popular emotion categories", namely anger, happiness, suspense, sad, and neutral. Minato et al. [30] used the following "basic emotions": happiness, hate, love, sorrow, anxiety, surprise, anger, and respect[1]. Ptaszynski et al. used "a classification of emotions that reflects the Japanese culture": happiness, anger,

---

[1] The authors cite Tanaka et al. 2004 (in Japanese) [13] as a source for their schema.

sorrow (sadness, gloom), fear, shame (shyness), fondness, dislike, excitement, relief, and surprise. Boynukalin et al. [23] used happiness, sadness, fear and anger for classification.

We can see that virtually all authors used one or the other discrete set of emotions, mostly revolving around Ekman's model, with happiness, sadness, and anger appearing in all presented models, which allows us to speculate that independently of culture these three are the most basic emotions. The only authors who don't use discrete emotion models is Cakmak et al. [23], who used PAD emotional state model in addition to the variation of Ekman's.

3.3   Information Summary

The information regarding the emotion classification model, size and language of the dataset is summarized in the Tables 1 and 2. The difference between the corpora listed in those table is that while the ones provided in Table 1 are built by the authors for the purposes of making those available for further research, the sources listed in Table 2 were created in order to train a model or testing the performance of a tool, even though at least in one case, the authors have declared an intention to share it (however, we weren't able to locate it) [24]. Those possibly can be obtained by contacting the authors.

Table 1 uses the following abbreviations for machine learning and statistical data processing methods: Hereinafter: LR – Logistic Regression, RF – Random Forests, CNN – Convolutional Neural Networks, LSTMN – Long Short-Term Memory networks, DT – Decision Tree, (M/C) NB – (Multinomial/Complement) Naïve Bayes, ME – Maximum Entropy, AA - annotations agreement, NP – Naïve Possibilistic.

Table 1. Emotion models used in corpora.

Dataset	Language	Emotion model	Corpus size	Font size and style
BHAAV	Hindi	Authors' own 5-emotion model	20 304 sent.	linear SVM LR, RF, CNN Bi-LSTM
Minato's dialog corpus	Japanese	Non-standard 8-emotion model	1 200 sent.	NB, DT, NP, ME
YACIS	Japanese	Nakamura 10-emotion model [14]	5 billion words	CAO [41], ML-Ask [42]
Danielewicz-Betz twitter corpus	Japanese	Ekman + pride and embarrassment	813 English, 5335 Japanese tweets	–

(*continued*)

Table 1. (*continued*)

Dataset	Language	Emotion model	Corpus size	Font size and style
SemEval-2018 Task 1 [36]	Arabic, Spanish, English	Ekman, VAD model	10 983 Arabic, 7 094 Spanish tweets	SVM/SVR, LSTM, Bi-LSTM, CNN LR, RF
ACTSEA [17]	Tamil, Sinhala	Ekman	1 800 Tamil, 1 200 Sinhala	AA
Ren-CECps1.0	Chinese	Yahoo's 8-emotion model	12 742 sent.	AA
Yao's microblog corpus	Chinese	Ekman + fondness	45 431 sent.	AA
Lee's code-switching corpus [29]	Chinese, English	Turner 5 motion model [15] (Ekman – disgust)	4 195 posts	ME classifiers
IAEC [28]	Arabic	Ekman	1 365 Fb posts	J48, ZeroR, NB, MNB, SMO
TREMO [32]	Turkish	Ekman	27 350 entries	CNB, RF, DT C4.5 and SVM
TURTED [33]	Turkish	Ekman	205 278 tweets	ANN, CNN, LSTM, SVM, NB, RF, DT, kNN
UIT-VSMEC [20]	Vietnamese	Ekman	6 927 sent.	RF, SVM, CNN and LSTM
Vietnamese dialog act [21]	Vietnamese	Ekman	23 803 words	AA
Das' Bengali blog corpus	Bengali	Ekman	12 149 sentences	CRF, SVM
EMOTERA [11]	Filipino, English	Plutchik	647 Filipino, 499 English tweets	AA

3.4 Description of Corpora

Tables 1 and 2 concisely systematize the most important technical characteristics of the corpora. The most corpora are in the most spoken world languages, and, mostly, the more popular the language, the more corpora are available. Figure 2 gives the overview of the number of datasets for each language, included in this review.

Here we provide a more detailed description of each dataset.

Table 2. Emotion models used in corpora of unknown availability.

Dataset	Language	Emotion model	Corpus size	ML methods
Jain's blog corpus [18]	Punjabi	Ekman	Not indicated	ME, SVM
Wang's multi-source dataset [40]	Chinese	Ekman	1 135 news, 1223 tales, 100 blog posts	ME, SVM
Rahman's social media dataset [19]	Bangla	Ekman	6 314 Fb comments	NB, kNN, DT, kMC and RBF SVM
Araque's news dataset [12]	Italian, English	Ekman – disgust	53 226 English documents, 12 437 Italian	LR, DT, RF, MLP
Gohil's tweet dataset	Gujarati, Hindi, English	Plutchik	1822 Gujarati tweets, 5833 Hindi, 5000 English	Supervised Learning, LR, MNB, SVC
Burget's newspaper headlines [25]	Czech	Ekman + neutral	Approx. 1000 headlines	LR, kNN, DT, Bayes Net, LRA, various SVM
Scorzewski's book dialog corpus [37]	Polish	Plutchik	598 entries	Various LSTM con-figurations
Cakmak's fairy tales [24]	Turkish	Ekman + neutral, PAD model	83 120 sentences	AA
Boynukalin's translated ISEAR and Turkish fairy tales [23]	Turkish	happiness, sadness, fear and anger	4 265 entries, 25 tales	CNB, NB, and SVM
Martinazzo's short text dataset [38]	Portuguese	Ekman	1002 short texts	Singular Value De-composition
Harikrishna's stories dataset [35]	Hindi	Happiness, sadness, anger and neutral	780 sentences	NB, kNN and SVM

BHAAV [8]. A corpus in Hindi language, consisting of approximately twenty thousand sentences from 230 short stories, covering different genres, such as Patriotic or Mystery. Those sentences were annotated manually, by at least three annotators each. Authors also provide the result of application of different leaning methods, namely SVM with a linear kernel, Logistic Regression, Random Forests, shallow Convolutional Neural Network with a single input channel, and Bidirectional Long Short-Term Memory networks, to this dataset.

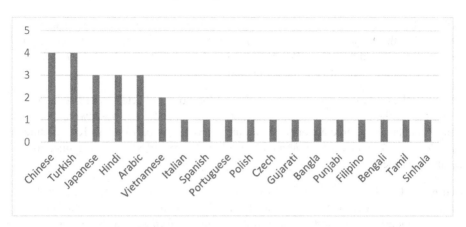

Fig. 2. Number of datasets by language.

Minato's dialog corpus [30]. A Japanese corpus of 1200 manually entered bilingual (Japanese and English) sentences from [31], automatically tagged for emotion words and idioms, as well as for emotion modifiers (plus, minus, neutral and negative), and statistical analysis was performed on the dataset.

YACIS [5]. A five-billion-word corpus consisting of blog posts, automatically acquired from Ameblo blog platform with the help of web crawler and automatically annotated with ML-Ask, a keyword-based system for affect annotation in Japanese, detecting emotive expressions and annotating those with high precision, but with low recall.

Danielewicz-Betz Twitter Corpus [39]. A Japanese and English corpora of tweets, collected from TREC'2011 dataset (for the reason of supposed lesser degradation in comparison with recent ones) and manually annotated by three annotators.

ACTSEA [15]. A Tamil and Sinhala corpus, obtained by collecting emotional tweets from year 2018, selected by the keywords for main emotions. It was annotated manually as classified correctly, misclassified, objective and not applicable. The final version contains 1962 tweets annotated for emotion and classified or misclassified.

Ren-CECps1.0 [7]. A large-scale Chinese corpus, sourced from sina, sciencenet blog, baidu, qzone, qq, and other blog platforms and consisting of 1487 posts and 35096 sentences. The corpus is manually annotated for emotions at document, paragraph and sentence levels. Annotations agreement analysis is provided.

Yao's Microblog Corpus [16]. A Chinese corpus, consisting of 14000 micro-blogs (45431 sentences) sourced from sina blog platform annotated for primary (all) and secondary (some) emotions. The corpus was used as the standard resource in the NLP&CC2013 Chinese micro-blog emotion analysis evaluation.

Lee's Code-Switching Corpus [29]. A Chinese-English code-switching corpus, consisting of 4195 posts from Weibo blog platform, manually annotated with the help of annotation tool. Multiple Classifier System, consisting of Maximum Entropy classifiers for Chinese and English texts separately and together was tried on this corpus.

ArSEL [27]. An Arabic corpus, consisting of 32196 lemmas sourced from ArSenL and annotated with authors-developed version of DepecheMood expanded with the help of English WordNet (dubbed EmoWordNet) and evaluated using SemEval 2007 Affective Task dataset translated into Arabic using Google Translate.

IAEC [28]. An Arabic corpus, consisting of 1365 posts collected from Facebook by searching for the posts declaring the relevant emotional state. The posts were independently annotated by three annotators with the pairwise comparison. WEKA classifiers J48, ZeroR, Naïve Bayes, Multinomial Naïve Bayes Text and SMO were applied to the resulting dataset.

SemEval-2018 Task 1 [36]. A English, Arabic and Spanish dataset, consisting of Twitter posts, randomly selected by querying the relevant language keywords and annotated for four emotions with the help of crowdsourcing platform Figure Eight (previously CrowdFlower). As the name suggests, was used as a dataset for SemEval 2018.

TREMO [32]. A Turkish dataset created by asking 5000 volunteers to write their memories and life experiences for each of six Ekman's emotions. 27350 entries were collected from 4709 participants then validated manually by annotation of each entry for emotions by three different annotators. The dataset was automatically annotated by Complement Naïve Bayes, Random Forest, Decision Tree C4.5 and SVM, and the results are provided.

TURTED [33]. A Turkish dataset obtained by collecting posts from Twitter using Tweepy application for five days in 2019 right after the local government election. It was automatically annotated using TEL, a Turkish lexicon-based annotation tool. ANN, CNN, and LSTM were applied, and the results were compared to SVM, Naïve Bayes, Random Forest, Decision Tree and k-Nearest Neighbor. The performance was validated by applying the same methods to human-annotated TREMO.

UIT-VSMEC [20]. A Vietnamese corpus sourced from Facebook with the help of Facebook API. The obtained 6927 entries were annotated by three annotators each with the help of specially developed annotation guideline. Random Forest, SVM, CNN and LSTM are used on this corpus for classification with results provided.

Vietnamese Dialog Act Corpus [22]. A Vietnamese corpus, consisting of 28 transcripts of Vietnamese conversations obtained by an automatic speech recognition in IARPA Babel program and manually annotated for emotions within functional segments by two annotators.

Das's Blog Corpus [18]. A Bengali corpus, consisting of 12 149 sentences acquired from Amarblog blog platform manually annotated with the help of illustrated samples from annotated sentences in a way of instruction. Conditional Random Field and SVM methods were applied to the small subsets and the result were described.

EMOTERA [11]. A Filipino and English corpus sourced from Twitter for the three days in 2012 and consisting of 647 Filipino and 499 English tweets with the help of crowdsourcing assisted by CrowdFlower platform with at least three annotators each. Hashtag Emotions Lexicon was tried for classification.

Jain's Blog Corpus [19]. A Punjabi corpus, sourced from Punjabi Tribute Online, Parchanve Wordpress and Daily Punjab Times, was annotated for emotions and a hybrid approach, combining SVM and Maximum Entropy classifiers was used for the dataset.

Wang's multi-source Dataset [40]. A Chinese corpus, obtained by collection of news and blog posts and manually annotating those by two annotators each, translation of already annotated Alm's Dataset and separating anger and disgust emotions. SVM and Maximum Entropy approaches were tested on the dataset.

Rahman's Social Media Dataset [20]. A Bangla dataset, consisting of 6314 Facebook comments from three different groups, manually annotated for emotions. Naïve Bayes, k-Nearest Neighbors, Decision Tree, k-Means Clustering and SVM with a Non-Linear RBF-Kernel were applied to the dataset for emotion classification with results described.

Araque's Bilingual Dataset [12]. A bilingual, Italian and English, dataset obtained from corriere.it and rappler.com, respectively. The annotations are provided by the article readers with the help of built-in emotional reaction functionality. This dataset was used for creating DepecheMood++ – an expanded version of English-only DepecheMood [34].

Gohil's Tweet Dataset [10]. A Gujarati, Hindi and English dataset, collected from twitter using Twitter search API for the India's general election 2019 and consisting of 1557 (Gujarati), 1822 (Hindi) and 5000 (English) tweets. The tweets were manually annotated by three annotators. Supervised Learning, LR, Multinomial Naive Bayes and Linear SVC approaches were used for classification with the results provided.

Burget's Czech Newspaper Headlines [25]. A Czech dataset, consisting of approximately 1000 randomly chosen news headlines, manually annotated for emotions by eight annotators each. Logistic Regression, k-Nearest Neighbors, Decision Tree, Bayes Net, Linear Regression Analysis and SVM with different kernels were tested on the dataset.

Scorzewski's Book Dialog Corpus [37]. A Polish dataset, consisting of 598 utterances, sourced from dialogs, selected from Kubis' corpus and manually annotated by at least four annotators. Different configurations of neural networks were tried for emotion classification with results reported.

Cakmak's Fairy Tale Corpus [24]. A Turkish corpus incorporating 83120 sentences from 31 fairy tales, manually annotated by 31 annotators. For automated classification, word roots were extracted with Zemberek library and the Turkish lexicon was created by translating 171 words from EMO20Q into Turkish, adding 26 synonyms and surveying approximately 40 people for appraising the words on the list. Correlation between emotions calculated by word roots and between one of the whole sentences was studied.

Boynukalin's Translated ISEAR Dataset and Turkish Fairy Tale Dataset [23]. A Turkish dataset created by paraphrasing of ISEAR texts by 33 people (4265 items) and collecting 25 fairy tales. The collection was then manually annotated for emotions on sentence and paragraph level by three annotators and the agreement analysis was performed. Complement Naïve Bayes, Naïve Bayes and SVM were tried for classification.

Martinazzo Short Text Dataset [38]. A Brazilian Portuguese dataset obtained by collecting 1002 news articles from www.globo.com and manually annotated by three annotators each. Algorithm based on Latent Semantic Analysis was tried for the emotion classification.

Harikrishna's Story Corpus [35]. A Hindi dataset consisting of 730 sentences collected from short stories. Naïve Bayes, k-nearest neighbor and (SVM) approaches were tested.

4   Conclusions and Future Work

In this paper, we have provided an overview of available non-English emotion-annotated corpora. The languages represented in the list were mostly the languages with high number of speakers, such as Chinese or Filipino. With virtually no exceptions all have adopted discrete emotion models, the most popular among them being Ekman's. The advent of social media can be seen from the preferred sources of the corpora: in most cases the data was taken from Twitter or Facebook independently of the language or a blog platform preferred by the native speakers of the language. Due to the need of manual annotation, with a few exceptions, the corpus size revolved around a few thousand entries. The greater part of the authors tried one or the other machine learning or deep learning algorithm, the most popular choices being SVM and Naïve Bayes with ANN and CNN gaining popularity in more recent works. SVM typically outperformed other machine learning methods while Neural Networks outperformed ML. In works where the number of annotators was specified, the most popular number was three, to exclude the draw situation while allowing for difference in opinions.

We expect that in the future this work can be used by us and other researchers as a reference for state-of-the art datasets in low-resource languages and approaches the authors have taken to overcome this difficulty.

Acknowledgements. The research has been supported by the European Regional Development Fund within the joint project of SIA TILDE and University of Latvia "Multilingual Artificial Intelligence Based Human Computer Interaction" No.1.1.1.1/18/A/148.

References

1. Lyakso, E., Frolova, O., Dmitrieva, E., Grigorev, A., Kaya, H., Salah, A.A., Karpov, A.: EmoChildRu: emotional child Russian speech corpus. In: Ronzhin, A., Potapova, R., Fakotakis, N. (eds.) SPECOM 2015. LNCS (LNAI), vol. 9319, pp. 144–152. Springer, Cham (2015). https://doi.org/10.1007/978-3-319-23132-7_18
2. Bostan, L.A.M., Klinger, R.: An analysis of annotated corpora for emotion classification in text. In: Proceedings of the 27th International Conference on Computational Linguistics, pp. 2104–2119 (2018)
3. Ekman, P.: An argument for basic emotions. Cogn. Emot. **6**(3–4), 169–200 (1992)

4. Plutchik, R.: A general psychoevolutionary theory of emotion. In: Plutchik, R., Kellerman, H. (eds.) Emotion: Theory, research and experience, Theories of emotion, vol. 1, pp. 3–33. Academic Press, New York (1980)

5. Ptaszynski, M., Dybala, P., Rzepka, R., Araki, K., Momouchi, Y.: YACIS: a five-billion-word corpus of Japanese blogs fully annotated with syntactic and affective information. In: AISB/IACAP World Congress 2012: Linguistic and Cognitive Approaches to Dialogue Agents, Part of Alan Turing Year 2012, pp. 40–49 (2012)

6. Lin, K.H.Y., Yang, C., Chen, H.H.: What emotions do news articles trigger in their readers? In: Proceedings of the 30th Annual International ACM SIGIR Conference, pp. 733–734 (2007)

7. Quan, C., Ren, F.: A blog emotion corpus for emotional expression analysis in Chinese. Comput. Speech Lang. **24**(4), 726–749 (2010)

8. Kumar, Y., Mahata, D., Aggarwal, S., Chugh, A., Maheshwari, R., Shah, R.R.: BHAAV-A Text Corpus for Emotion Analysis from Hindi Stories (2019). arXiv preprint arXiv:1910. 04073

9. Mehrabian, A.: Basic Dimensions for A General Psychological Theory, pp. 39–53 (1980)

10. Gohil, L., Patel, D.: Int. J. Innovative Technol. Exploring Eng. (IJITEE) **9**(1) (2019). ISSN: 2278-3075

11. Lapitan, F.R., Batista-Navarro, R.T., Albacea, E.: Crowdsourcing-based annotation of emotions in Filipino and English tweets. In: Proceedings of the 6th Workshop on South and Southeast Asian Natural Language Processing (WSSANLP2016), pp. 74–82 (2016)

12. Araque, O., Gatti, L., Staiano, J., Guerini, M.: Depechemood ++: a bilingual emotion lexicon built through simple yet powerful techniques. IEEE Trans. Affect. Comput. (2019)

13. Tanaka, Y., Takamura, H., Okumura, M.: Research concerning facemarks in text based communication. In: Proceedings of the 10th Annual Natural Language Processing Conference (2004). (in Japanese)

14. Nakamura, A.: Kanjo hyogen jiten [Dictionary of Emotive Expressions]. Tokyodo Publishing, Tokyo (1993). (in Japanese)

15. Turner, J.H.: On the Origins of Human Emotions: A Sociological Inquiry into the Evolution of Human Affect. Stanford University Press, CA (2000)

16. Yao, Y., Wang, S., Xu, R., et al.: The construction of an emotion annotated corpus on microblog text. J. Chin. Inf. Process. **28**(5), 83–91 (2014). (in Chinese)

17. Jenarthanan, R., Senarath, Y., Thayasivam, U.: ACTSEA: annotated corpus for Tamil & Sinhala emotion analysis. In: 2019 Moratuwa Engineering Research Conference (MERCon), Moratuwa, Sri Lanka, pp. 49–53 (2019)

18. Das, D., Bandyopadhyay, S.: Labeling emotion in Bengali blog corpus – a fine grained tagging at sentence level. In: Proceedings of the 8th Workshop on Asian Language Resources (ALR8), COLING-2010, pp. 47–55 (2010)

19. Jain, U., Sandu, A.: Emotion detection from Punjabi text using hybrid support vector machine and maximum entropy algorithm. Int. J. Adv. Res. Comput. Commun. Eng. **4**(11), 5 (2015)

20. Rahman, M., Seddiqui, M.: Comparison of Classical Machine Learning Approaches on Bangla Textual Emotion Analysis, 18 July 2019. arXiv preprint arXiv:1907.07826

21. Ho, V.A., Nguyen, D.H., Nguyen, D.H., Pham, L.T., Nguyen, D.V., Van Nguyen, K., Nguyen, N.L.: Emotion Recognition for Vietnamese Social Media Text (2019). arXiv preprint arXiv: 1911.09339

22. Ngo, T.L., Linh, P.K., Takeda, H.: A Vietnamese dialog act corpus based on ISO 24617-2 standard. In: Proceedings of the Eleventh International Conference on Language Resources and Evaluation (LREC 2018) (2018)

23. Boynukalin, Z.: Emotion analysis of Turkish texts by using machine learning methods. Master thesis, Middle East Technical University (2012)

24. Cakmak, O., Kazemzadeh, A., Can, D., Yildirim, S., Narayanan, S.: Root-word analysis of Turkish emotional language. In: Corpora for Research on Emotion Sentiment & Social Signals (2012)
25. Burget, R., Karasek, J., Smekal, Z.: Recognition of emotions in Czech newspaper headlines. Radioengineering **20**(1), 39–47 (2011)
26. Nguen, A.: 20 Best German Language Datasets for Machine Learning. https://lionbridge.ai/datasets/20-best-german-language-datasets-for-machine-learning/ (2019). Accessed 18 Jan 2020
27. Badaro, G., Jundi, H., Hajj, H., El-Hajj, W., Habash, N.: ArSEL: a large scale arabic sentiment and emotion lexicon. In: Proceedings of the 3rd Workshop on Open-Source Arabic Corpora and Processing Tools (2018)
28. Al-Mahdawi, A., Teahan, W.J.: Automatic emotion recognition in English and Arabic text. Dissertation, Bangor University (2019)
29. Lee, S.Y.M., Wang, Z.: Emotion in code-switching texts: corpus construction and analysis. ACL-IJCNLP **2015**, 91 (2015)
30. Minato, J., Bracewell, B., Ren, F., Kuroiwa, S.: Japanese emotion corpus analysis and its use for automatic emotion word identification. Eng. Lett. **16**(1) (2008)
31. Hiejima, I.: Japanese-English Emotion Dictionary. Tokyodo Shuppan, Tokyo (1995)
32. Tocoglu, M.A., Alpkocak, A.: TREMO: a dataset for emotion analysis in Turkish. J. Inf. Sci. **44**(6), 848–860 (2018)
33. Tocoglu, M.A., Ozturkmenoglu, O., Alpkocak, A.A.: Emotion analysis from Turkish tweets using deep neural networks. IEEE Access **7**, 183061–183069 (2019)
34. Staiano, J., Marco, G.: Depechemood: a Lexicon for emotion analysis from crowd-annotated news. In: Proceedings of the 52nd Annual Meeting of the Association for Computational Linguistics (ACL), pp. 427–433 (2014)
35. Harikrishna, D., Rao, K.S.: Emotion-specific features for classifying emotions in story text. In: 2016 Twenty Second National Conference on Communication (NCC), pp. 1–4 (2016)
36. Mohammad, S., Bravo-Marquez, F., Salameh, M., Kiritchenko, S.: Semeval-2018 task 1: affect in tweets. In: Proceedings of the 12th International Workshop on Semantic Evaluation, pp. 1–17 (2018)
37. Skórzewski, P.: Using book dialogs to extract emotions from texts in Polish. In: Vetulani, Z., Paroubek, P. (eds.) Proceedings of the 9th Language and Technology Conference, pp. 252–257 (2019)
38. Martinazzo, B., Dosciatti, M.M., Paraiso, E.C.: Identifying emotions in short texts for Brazilian Portuguese. In: IV International Workshop on Web and Text Intelligence (WTI 2012), p. 16 (2011)
39. Danielewicz-Betz, A., Kaneda, H., Mozgovoy, M., Purgina, M.: Creating English and Japanese twitter corpora for emotion analysis. People **1634**, 5869 (2015)
40. Wang, Z.: Segment-based fine-grained emotion detection for Chinese text. In: Proceedings of The Third CIPS-SIGHAN Joint Conference on Chinese Language Processing, pp. 52–60 (2014)
41. Ptaszynski, M., Maciejewski, J., Dybala, P., Rzepka, R., Araki, K.: CAO: fully automatic emoticon analysis system. In: Proceedings of the 24th AAAI Conference on Artificial Intelligence (AAAI-10), pp. 1026–1032 (2010)
42. Ptaszynski, M., Dybala, P., Rzepka, R., Araki, K.: Affecting corpora: experiments with automatic affect annotation system - a case study of the 2channel forum. In: Proceedings of the Conference of the Pacific Association for Computational Linguistics (PACLING-09), pp. 223–228 (2009)

Simultaneous Road Edge and Road Surface Markings Detection Using Convolutional Neural Networks

René Pihlak$^{(\boxtimes)}$ and Andri Riid

Tallinn University of Technology, Ehitajate tee 5, 19086 Tallinn, Estonia
{rene.pihlak,andri.riid}@taltech.ee

Abstract. Accurate road surface markings and road edges detection is a crucial task for operating self-driving cars and for advanced driver assistance systems deployment (e.g. lane detection) in general. This research proposes an original neural network based method that combines structural components of autoencoders, residual neural networks and densely connected neural networks. The resulting neural network is able to concurrently detect and segment accurate road edges and road surface markings from RGB images of road surfaces.

Keywords: Road surface markings · Road edge · Neural networks · Segmentation · Machine learning · Autoencoder

1 Introduction

Road surface markings (RSMs) and road edges (REs) are among the most important elements for guiding autonomous vehicles (AVs). High-Definition maps with accurate RSM information are very useful for many applications such as navigation, prediction of upcoming road situations and road maintenance [23]. RSM and RE detection is also vital in the context of pavement distress detection to ensure that RSMs are not confused with pavement defects and to eliminate the areas where the cracks, potholes and other defects cannot possibly be found [17].

The detection of stationary objects of interest related to roadways is usually addressed by using video streams or still images acquired by digital cameras mounted on a vehicle. For example, Reach-U Ltd.—Estonian company specializing in geographic information systems, location based solutions and cartography—has developed a fast-speed mobile mapping system employing six high-resolution cameras for recording images of roads. The resulting orthoframes assembled from recorded panoramic images are available to Estonian Road

This study was partially supported by the Archimedes Foundation and Reach-U Ltd. in the scope of the smart specialization research and development project #LEP19022: "Applied research for creating a cost-effective interchangeable 3D spatial data infrastructure with survey-grade accuracy".

T. Robal et al. (Eds.): DB&IS 2020, CCIS 1243, pp. 109–121, 2020.
https://doi.org/10.1007/978-3-030-57672-1_9

Administration via a web application called EyeVi [16] and are used as the source data in present study.

RSM extraction methods are often based on intensity thresholds that are subject to data quality, including lighting, shadows and RSM wear. RE detection is generally considered even more difficult than lane mark detection due to lack of clear boundary between road and RE because of variations in road and roadside materials and colors [9]. Due to recent advances in deep learning, semantic segmentation of RSMs and REs is increasingly implemented within the deep learning framework [21].

The present study combines both RSM and RE detection by a hierarchical convolutional neural network to enhance the method's predictive ability. On narrow rural roads without RSMs, RE detection alone can provide sufficient information for navigation but REs might escape the field of view of cameras on wider highways and REs cannot provide sufficient information for lane selection. Simultaneous detection of REs and RSMs can also improve the accuracy of these tasks, e.g. RSMs suggested by the network outside the road can be eliminated either implicitly within the network or explicitly during the post-processing.

2   Related Work

In recent years, several studies have tackled tasks of RSM and RE detection for a variety of reasons. For example, [3,19] employ RSMs for car localization, [1] applies RSMs to detect REs, [2,4,6,26] classify RSMs whereas [7,9,12,20,21,27] focus on pixel level segmentation to detect the exact shapes and locations of RSMs.

These works have used different input data. For example, [12,22,24] use 3D data collected by LiDAR, [15,25] use 3D spacial data generated from images captured by stereo camera, [11] uses radar for detecting metal guardrails and [9,21,26] use 2D still images captured by a camera. Radars have an advantage over cameras as they can be deployed regardless of lighting conditions. However, metal guardrails are rarely found on smaller rural roads. LiDARs can also operate under unfavorable lighting conditions that can cause over- or under-lit road surface, however, high quality LiDARs are expensive. Both 2D cameras and 3D (stereo) cameras are adversely affected by shadows, over- and under-lit road surface and while 3D cameras can provide additional information, this information requires more processing power. Consequently, 2D cameras are still the most suitable equipment for capturing data for RSMs and RE detection provided that the detection method is "smart" enough to cope with even the most adverse lighting condition such as hard shadows, over- and under-lit surface of the road, etc. Thus the RSM and RE detection methods must address these issues.

Possible RSMs and RE detection methods and techniques include, for example, filtering [10] and (NN) based detection [26]. While filtering was the method of choice in older research, the NN based methods have started to dominate recent research. Even though the NN based methods have gained popularity, the way NNs are implemented for RSM and RE detection has evolved significantly over the years. Earlier approaches used classifier networks. The segmentation of images was achieved by applying a sliding window classifier over the whole input image. To improve quality of the predictions, fully convolutional (AEs) that can produce a segmented output image directly, have replaced the sliding window method. However, since the 'encoding' part of the AE is subject to data loss, the AEs have been phased out by residual networks (e.g., [5,8]) with direct forward connections between layers of *encoder* and *decoder* for higher quality image segmentation.

3 Methodology

3.1 Neural Network Design

The proposed architecture consists of three connected neural networks of identical structure (Fig. 1) that combines the architectures of symmetrical AE (with dimension reducing *encoder* and expanding *decoder*), (ResNet) [5] and DenseNet [8] having shortcut connections between *encoder* and *decoder* layers by feature map concatenation.

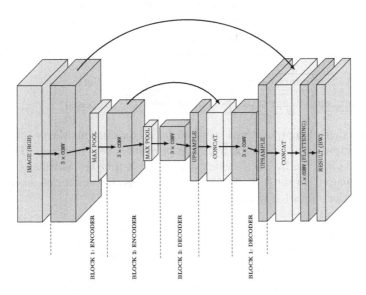

Fig. 1. Illustration of sub-neural network design using 2 blocks with 3 convolutional filters

This NN can be further divided into sub-blocks (hereafter *blocks*) that all have a similar structure. In essence, a block consists of a set of convolutional layers followed by a size transformation layer (either `max pooling` for *encoder* or `upsampling` for *decoder*). As the NN is symmetric, *encoder* and *decoder* have equal number of blocks. Thus a NN with "two blocks" would be a NN that has two encoding and two decoding blocks. Each of these blocks has an equal number of convolutional layers with 3×3 kernel. After each decoding block, there is a concatenation layer in order to fuse the upsampled feature map with the corresponding convolutional layer's feature map from the *encoder* part of the network.

The overall design of the sub-NN is as follows:

1. Input layer (RGB image)
2. $n\times$ encoding block
3. $n\times$ decoding block + concatenation layer
4. flattening convolutional layer
5. Output layer (gray scale image).

All the convolutional layers (except the last one) use LeakyReLU ($\alpha = 0.1$) as activation function. It is observed that a large gradient flowing through a more common ReLU neuron can cause the weights to update in such a way that the neuron will never activate on any datapoint again. Once a ReLU ends up in this state, it is unlikely to recover. LeakyReLU returns a small value when its input is less than zero and gives it a chance to recover [13]. The convolutional layers' padding is 'same', i.e., the height and width of input and output feature maps are the same for each convolutional layer within a block.

The U-Net architecture proposed in [18] utilizes a similar idea, however, the order of layers is different in the *decoder* part of their NN:

- $\boxed{\text{upsample}} \rightarrow \boxed{\text{concatenate}} \rightarrow \boxed{\text{convolution}}$ (U-Net)
- $\boxed{\text{convolution}} \rightarrow \boxed{\text{upsample}} \rightarrow \boxed{\text{concatenate}}$ (Proposed)

The number of computations required by a convolutional layer increases as the size of inputs (feature maps from the previous layer) increases. The size of layer's inputs is given by Eq. 1, where *width* and *height* are width and height of the feature map from the previous layer and *depth* is the number of convolutional filters in the previous (convolutional) layer.

$$V = width \times height \times depth \tag{1}$$

Because U-Net performs upsampling and concatenation before convolutional layer, the input size (hence the required computational power) is more than four times bigger (Eq. 2) than with the proposed NN. Upsampling with kernel size (2×2) doubles both height and width and concatenation further increases depth by adding $depth_{enc}$ layers from an encoder block to the feature map.

$$\begin{aligned} V_{\text{UNet}} &= width_{\text{UNet}} \times height_{\text{UNet}} \times depth_{\text{UNet}} \\ &= (2 \times width) \times (2 \times height) \times (depth + depth_{enc}) \end{aligned} \tag{2}$$

Since RSMs and REs have different characteristics, these two tasks are performed using two different NNs. Both NNs have a RGB input of size ($224 \times 224 \times 13$) and a single (224×13) output, i.e., a gray scale mask (Fig. 1). One pixel corresponds roughly to 3.37 mm, thus the width and height of the input segment are about 75.42 cm.

The resulting outputs from RE and RSMs detection are concatenated with the original input image and fed to a third NN (REFNET) to refine the final results (Fig. 2). Hence, the final structure of the whole NN combines three NNs: two parallel NNs (RENN and RSMNN) and a REFNET. REFNET has the same general design as the RENN and RSMNN but the number of blocks and number of convolutional filters per block differ (Table 1). It must be noted that adding REFNET incurs relatively small overhead because it has considerably smaller number of trainable parameters compered to RENN and RSMNN even though REFNET has higher block count. Table 1 describes the chosen architecture that had the best performance.

Table 1. Neural network parameters

Value	RENN	RSMNN	REFNET
Trainable parameters	148489	208201	66058
Block count	3	4	5
Conv layers per block	6	2	2
Number of filters	(8,16,32)	(8,16,32,64)	(8,8,16,16,32)

Both RENN and RSMNN are pre-trained for 20 epochs. Several combinations of blocks and layers were tested and best performing RENN and RSMNN were chosen. Next, all three NNs – RENN, RSMNN and REFNET – are trained for additional 60 epochs. The NNs were trained using Adadelta optimizer with initial learning rate of 1.0 and binary crossentropy as loss function. Automatic learning rate reduction was applied if validation loss did not improve in 15 epochs. Each reduction halved the current learning rate.

3.2   Evaluation Methodology

There are several metrics for evaluating segmentation quality. The most common of those is accuracy (Eq. 3) that calculates the percent of pixels in the image that are classified correctly

$$A_{cc} = \frac{TP + TN}{TP + FP + TN + FN}, \tag{3}$$

where TP = True Positives (pixels correctly predicted to belong to the given class), TN = True Negatives (pixels correctly predicted not to belong to the given class), FP = False Positives (pixels falsely predicted to belong to the given class), and FN = False Negatives (pixels falsely predicted not to belong to the given class). In cases where there is a class imbalance in the evaluation data,

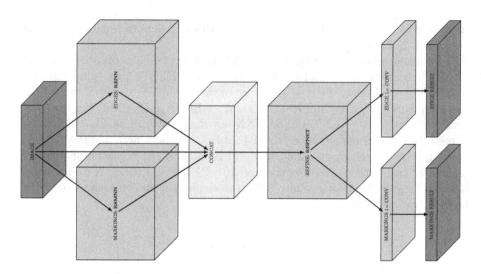

Fig. 2. Overall structure of the final neural network

e.g. TN ≫ TP, FP, FN (which is often the case in practice), accuracy is biased toward an overoptimistic estimate.

For class-imbalanced problems, precision (Eq. 4) and recall (Eq. 5) (showing how many of predicted positives were actually true positives and how many of true positives were predicted as positives, respectively)

$$P_r = \frac{TP}{TP + FP}, \tag{4}$$

$$R_c = \frac{TP}{TP + FN}, \tag{5}$$

or balanced accuracy that is an average of recall (also known a sensitivity or True Positive Rate) and specificity (also known as True Negative Rate) (Eq. 6)

$$Acc_{bal} = \frac{TPR + TNR}{2} = \left(\frac{TP}{TP + FN} + \frac{TN}{TN + FP} \right) \div 2, \tag{6}$$

give a better estimate

In addition, Jaccard similarity coefficient or Intersection over Union (IoU) (Eq. 7) can be used

$$IoU = \frac{|X \bigcap Y|}{|X \bigcup Y|} = \frac{TP}{TP + FP + FN}. \tag{7}$$

IoU is the area of overlap between the predicted segmentation (X) and the ground truth (Y) divided by the area of union between the predicted segmentation and the ground truth.

For binary or multi-class segmentation problems, the mean IoU is calculated by taking the IoU of each class and averaging them.

$$mIoU = n^{-1} \sum_{i=1}^{n} IoU_i \tag{8}$$

The same applies for the other metrics (Eq. 6, Eq. 4, Eq. 5).

4 Experimental Results

4.1 Setup of the Experiments

The proposed methods are evaluated on a dataset that contains a collection of 314 orthoframe images of Estonian roads that each have a size of 4096 × 4096 pixels.

The images in the dataset are manually annotated to generate ground truth masks for both RSMs and RE. The annotation is performed by using Computer Vision Annotation Tool (CVAT) (Fig. 3). These vector graphics annotations are then converted into image masks with separate masks for RSM and RE.

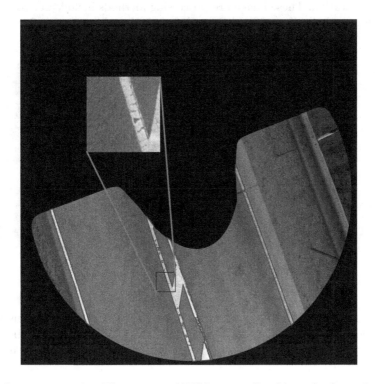

Fig. 3. Image annotation. The annotated RSMs are outlined by red color and the area outside the road masked out by the annotation mask is painted green for illustration. (Color figure online)

As a preliminary step before training and testing the proposed NN, automatic image pre-processing (i.e. white balancing) is applied to each individual input image by using gray world assumption with saturation threshold of (0.95). The goal of image pre-processing is to mitigate color variance (e.g. due to color difference of sun light).

Next, 249 of 314 pre-processed images are used to build the training/validation dataset of image segments. This training/validation dataset contains 36497 image segments and each segment has a size of 224 × 224 pixels (Fig. 3). It must be noted that not all segments of a pre-processed image are included in the training/validation dataset. Since large part of the 4096 × 4096 pixel image is masked out (depicted by black color in Fig. 3), only segments with 20% or more non-masked pixels are considered. These segments are then divided into two groups: 1) those that include annotations and 2) those that do not include annotations. A segment is considered to be annotated if and only if at least 5% of its pixels contain annotations. In order to prevent significant class imbalance in training data, the two groups (i.e., segments with and without annotations) have to be of equal size. The segments in the two groups do not overlap.

Built-in image pre-processing methods of TensorFlow/Keras library are randomly applied on each 224 × 224 × 3 segment before training in order to perform data augmentation. These image pre-processing methods include horizontal flip, vertical flip, width shift (±5%), height shift (±5%) and rotation (<90°).

Input:

Output:

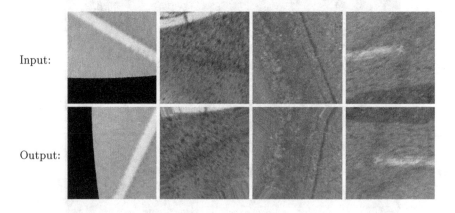

Fig. 4. Augmentation of input data

Rotation and/or shifting without zooming in can lead to situations where part of the modified segment does not include the pixels from the original segment. Therefore, these pre-processing methods are performed using 'nearest' fill method (Fig. 4).

4.2 Image Post-processing and Testing Results

Testing is performed on 65 images which were not included in training or validation data sets. The images are turned into $224 \times 224 \times 3$ RGB image segments similarly to the process described in Sect. 4.1. The main difference is that after pre-processing (i.e., white balance), the testable segments are generated from all segments that are not 100% black. These testable segments are then passed to the NNs and resulting output of the NNs is re-combined such that input segments that were 100% black are also fully black in the combined 4096×4096 output image. This process is repeated on each test image three times. Each time a different amount of padding is used. These three outputs are cropped to original size and averaged to assure that final generated masks/images are smooth.

Before the final evaluation, the re-combined outputs undergo image post-processing. First, thresholding using Otsu's method [14] is applied on both RE and RSM images to produce binary images (Fig. 5). Next, holes are filled in the RE image. Then RE contours are detected and small objects are filtered out based on their area. Next, the refined RE image is used as a mask to rule out false positive RSMs. Finally, RSM contours are detected and small objects are filtered out based on the object's area (Fig. 6)

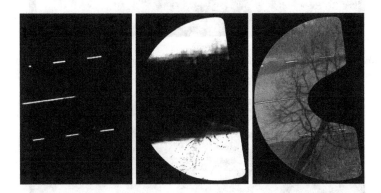

Fig. 5. Road surface markings and road edges masks before applying Otsu's method (left and middle, respectively) and the combined result after post-processing (right).

The number of pixels, classified as true positives (TP), true negatives (TN), false positives (FP) and false negatives (FN) are determined over all test images (Table 2). Based on the resulting figures, recall (R_c), precision (P_r), balanced accuracy (ACC_{bal}) and IoU are calculated and given in Table 3. The figures in Table 3 imply that RE detection has somewhat better quality than RSMs detection. This is, however, deceptive, because of the smaller overall size of RSMs (TP + FN in Table 2), minor detection imperfections result in a greater degradation of performance indices.

In contrast to performance measures over all test images in Table 3, Table 4 provides performance analysis on orthoframe basis. First, performance measures were calculated for each image separately. Next, statistical measures such as average, minimum, maximum value and standard deviation (σ) were calculated. These additional characteristics show that RE detection accuracy is in fact less consistent and more sensitive to hard shadows in particular as Fig. 7 demonstrates. Standard deviation (σ) for RSM detection is lower in all categories compared to RE detection.

Fig. 6. Near-perfect detection of road surface markings (outlined by blue color) and road edges (pale red). (Color figure online)

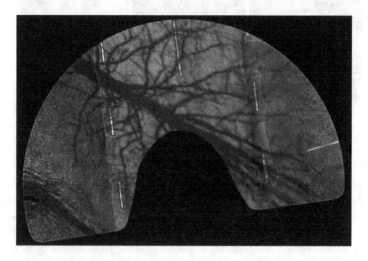

Fig. 7. Detection of road surface markings (outlined by blue color) and road edges (pale red) in presence of hard shadows. (Color figure online)

Table 2. Pixel classification after post-processing

Type	TP	TN	FP	FN
Edges	159647475	915666344	8170998	7034223
Markings	7501060	1081635670	581563	800747

Table 3. Detection performance indices after post-processing

Type	R_c	P_r	Acc_{bal}	IoU
Edges	0.96	0.95	0.97	0.88
Markings	0.90	0.93	0.95	0.84

Table 4. Detailed measures of per image results

Value	Edges				Markings			
	R_c	P_r	TNR	Acc_{bal}	R_c	P_r	TNR	Acc_{bal}
Avg	0.92	0.95	0.99	0.96	0.90	0.93	1.00	0.95
σ	0.18	0.08	0.02	0.09	0.06	0.06	0.00	0.03
Min	0.13	0.42	0.88	0.57	0.64	0.71	1.00	0.82
Max	1.00	0.99	1.00	1.00	0.98	1.00	1.00	0.99

This was expected because RE detection is considered to be harder problem to solve. The detection of RENN did not improve when NN size (block and/or convolutional layer count) were increased. However, adding contextual information (RSMNN) increased the proposed method's predictive ability for both RE and RSM detection when the outputs of RENN and RSMNN were combined in REFNET.

5   Conclusion

In this study, we proposed a convolutional neural network-powered method for concurrent road edge (RE) and road surface markings (RSMs) detection from orthoframes even under severely adverse conditions such as bad lighting conditions (shadows, over-lit road surface, etc) and RSM wear. The measures of IoU (88% and 84%, respectively) indicate that the network performs well in most conditions, however, hard shadows, cast either by trees or buildings alongside the road, present a problem, particularly for RE detection.

In future works, we intend to research how to improve the predictive ability of the method by using increased contextual awareness either by incorporating data about the neighboring image segments or by using the whole orthoframe image as input.

References

1. Álvarez, J.M., López, A.M., Gevers, T., Lumbreras, F.: Combining priors, appearance, and context for road detection. IEEE Trans. Intell. Transp. Syst. **15**(3), 1168–1178 (2014). https://doi.org/10.1109/TITS.2013.2295427
2. De Paula, M.B., Jung, C.R.: Automatic detection and classification of road lane markings using onboard vehicular cameras. IEEE Trans. Intell. Transp. Syst. **16**(6), 3160–3169 (2015). https://doi.org/10.1109/TITS.2015.2438714
3. Deng, L., Yang, M., Hu, B., Li, T., Li, H., Wang, C.: Semantic segmentation-based lane-level localization using around view monitoring system. IEEE Sens. J. **19**(21), 10077–10086 (2019). https://doi.org/10.1109/JSEN.2019.2929135
4. Gupta, A., Choudhary, A.: A framework for camera-based real-time lane and road surface marking detection and recognition. IEEE Trans. Intell. Veh. **3**(4), 476–485 (2018). https://doi.org/10.1109/tiv.2018.2873902
5. He, K., Zhang, X., Ren, S., Sun, J.: Deep residual learning for image recognition. In: 2016 IEEE Conference on Computer Vision and Pattern Recognition (CVPR), pp. 770–778 (2015)
6. Hoang, T.M., Nam, S.H., Park, K.R.: Enhanced detection and recognition of road markings based on adaptive region of interest and deep learning. IEEE Access **7**, 109817–109832 (2019). https://doi.org/10.1109/access.2019.2933598
7. Hu, J., Yang, M., Xu, H., He, Y., Wang, C.: Mapping and localization using semantic road marking with centimeter-level accuracy in indoor parking lots. In: 2019 IEEE Intelligent Transportation Systems Conference, ITSC 2019, pp. 4068–4073. Institute of Electrical and Electronics Engineers Inc. (October 2019). https://doi.org/10.1109/ITSC.2019.8917529
8. Huang, G., Liu, Z., Weinberger, K.Q.: Densely connected convolutional networks. In: 2017 IEEE Conference on Computer Vision and Pattern Recognition (CVPR), pp. 2261–2269 (2016)
9. Jiang, W., Wu, Y., Guan, L., Zhao, J.: DFNet: semantic segmentation on panoramic images with dynamic loss weights and residual fusion block. In: Proceedings - IEEE International Conference on Robotics and Automation, vol. 2019, pp. 5887–5892. Institute of Electrical and Electronics Engineers Inc. (May 2019). https://doi.org/10.1109/ICRA.2019.8794476
10. Kim, Z.W.: Robust lane detection and tracking in challenging scenarios (2008). https://doi.org/10.1109/TITS.2007.908582
11. Lin, J., Chien, S., Chen, Y., Chen, C.C., Sherony, R.: 24 GHz and 77 GHz radar characteristics of metal guardrail for the development of metal guardrail surrogate for road departure mitigation system testing. In: 2019 IEEE Intelligent Transportation Systems Conference, ITSC 2019, pp. 3340–3346. Institute of Electrical and Electronics Engineers Inc. (October 2019). https://doi.org/10.1109/ITSC.2019.8916960
12. Ma, L., Li, Y., Li, J., Zhong, Z., Chapman, M.A.: Generation of horizontally curved driving lines in HD maps using mobile laser scanning point clouds. IEEE J. Sel. Top. Appl. Earth Obs. Remote Sens. **12**(5), 1572–1586 (2019). https://doi.org/10.1109/JSTARS.2019.2904514
13. Maas, A.L., Hannun, A.Y., Ng, A.Y.: Rectifier nonlinearities improve neural network acoustic models. In: ICML Workshop on Deep Learning for Audio, Speech and Language Processing (2013)
14. Otsu, N.: A threshold selection method from gray-level histograms. IEEE Trans. Syst. Man Cybern. **9**(1), 62–66 (1979). https://doi.org/10.1109/TSMC.1979.4310076

15. Ozgunalp, U., Fan, R., Ai, X., Dahnoun, N.: Multiple lane detection algorithm based on novel dense vanishing point estimation. IEEE Trans. Intell. Transp. Syst. **18**(3), 621–632 (2017). https://doi.org/10.1109/TITS.2016.2586187

16. Reach-U Ltd.: Eyevi – mobile mapping based visual intelligence. https://www.reach-u.com/eyevi.html. Accessed 12 Feb 2020

17. Riid, A., Lõuk, R., Pihlak, R., Tepljakov, A., Vassiljeva, K.: Pavement distress detection with deep learning using the orthoframes acquired by a mobile mapping system. Appl. Sci. **9**(22), 4829 (2019)

18. Ronneberger, O., Fischer, P., Brox, T.: U-Net: convolutional networks for biomedical image segmentation. ArXiv (May 2015)

19. Rose, C., Britt, J., Allen, J., Bevly, D.: An integrated vehicle navigation system utilizing lane-detection and lateral position estimation systems in difficult environments for GPS. IEEE Trans. Intell. Transp. Syst. **15**(6), 2615–2629 (2014). https://doi.org/10.1109/TITS.2014.2321108

20. Suleymanov, T., Kunze, L., Newman, P.: Online inference and detection of curbs in partially occluded scenes with sparse LIDAR. In: 2019 IEEE Intelligent Transportation Systems Conference, ITSC 2019, pp. 2693–2700. Institute of Electrical and Electronics Engineers Inc. (October 2019). https://doi.org/10.1109/ITSC.2019.8917086

21. Tran, L.A., Le, M.H.: robust U-Net-based road lane markings detection for autonomous driving. In: Proceedings of 2019 International Conference on System Science and Engineering, ICSSE 2019, pp. 62–66. Institute of Electrical and Electronics Engineers Inc. (July 2019). https://doi.org/10.1109/ICSSE.2019.8823532

22. Uzer, F., Benmokhtar, R., Moujtahid, S., Perrotton, X.: Dempster shafer grid-based hybrid fusion of virtual lanes for autonomous driving. In: 2019 IEEE/RSJ International Conference on Intelligent Robots and Systems (IROS), pp. 3760–3765. IEEE (November 2019). https://doi.org/10.1109/IROS40897.2019.8967610, https://ieeexplore.ieee.org/document/8967610/

23. Wen, C., Sun, X., Li, J., Wang, C., Guo, Y., Habib, A.: A deep learning framework for road marking extraction, classification and completion from mobile laser scanning point clouds. ISPRS J. Photogramm. Remote Sens. **147**, 178–192 (2019). https://doi.org/10.1016/j.isprsjprs.2018.10.007

24. Yu, Y., Li, J., Guan, H., Jia, F., Wang, C.: Learning hierarchical features for automated extraction of road markings from 3-D mobile LiDAR point clouds. IEEE J. Sel. Top. Appl. Earth Obs. Remote Sens. **8**(2), 709–726 (2015). https://doi.org/10.1109/JSTARS.2014.2347276

25. Yuan, C., Chen, H., Liu, J., Zhu, D., Xu, Y.: Robust lane detection for complicated road environment based on normal map. IEEE Access **6**, 49679–49689 (2018). https://doi.org/10.1109/ACCESS.2018.2868976

26. Zhang, F., Wu, X., Gu, C.: Detection of road surface identifiers based on deep learning. In: 2019 International Conference on Artificial Intelligence and Advanced Manufacturing (AIAM), pp. 66–70. Institute of Electrical and Electronics Engineers (IEEE) (January 2020). https://doi.org/10.1109/aiam48774.2019.00020

27. Zhang, W., Mi, Z., Zheng, Y., Gao, Q., Li, W.: Road marking segmentation based on siamese attention module and maximum stable external region. IEEE Access **7**, 143710–143720 (2019). https://doi.org/10.1109/ACCESS.2019.2944993

Specialized Image Descriptors
for Signboard Photographs Classification

Aleksei Samarin[1,3] (ID), Valentin Malykh[2], and Sergey Muravyov[4(✉)] (ID)

[1] Saint-Petersburg State University, Saint-Petersburg, Russia
[2] Kazan Federal University, Kazan, Russia
[3] VK Research, Saint-Petersburg, Russia
[4] ITMO University, Saint-Petersburg, Russia
mursmail@gmail.com

Abstract. We propose several types of advertising sign photo descriptors that are useful for images classification. We also collected a dataset of commercial building facade photographs grouped by a type of provided services in order to perform comparison between different classification methods. Finally we performed comparison between methods based on the proposed descriptor usage and combined advertising sign classifier and obtained better performance using our system.

Keywords: Image descriptor · Image classification · Signboard dataset · Combined classifier · Optical character recognition

1 Introduction

Currently, a number of computer vision problems related to the field of applied marketing are urgent [10]. Among all problems, one can distinguish the problem of recognizing the type of the services provided from a photograph of an advertising poster [6]. That problem arises when analyzing a business segment using images of the studied area. It also should be noted the presence of circumstances that significantly complicate this issue. For example, advertising plates often contain non-standard fonts and are also painted in a wide range of colors and contain various elements of the underlay. It is also impossible not to note the fact of the influence of external shooting conditions on the resulting images, which also affects the complexity of the problem. It is noteworthy that we can classify a photograph of a building facade by the type of provided service basing on several aspects presented in the image. Firstly, we can be guided by the text presented at the signboard. In addition to the textual component, we can be guided by the visual design of the advertising signboard. Finally we can pay attention to the environment presented on the image and the visual component of the whole picture. In order to simultaneously cover all aspects of the image that are significant

S. Muravyov—The work of Sergey Muravyov was financially supported by the Government of the Russian Federation (Grant 08-08).

T. Robal et al. (Eds.): DB&IS 2020, CCIS 1243, pp. 122–129, 2020.
https://doi.org/10.1007/978-3-030-57672-1_10

for classification, it is possible to use a combined classifier [6]. Despite the fact that at the present time many methods have proven their effectiveness in solving problems of classifying general images [2,3,8], it should be noted that pictures in the datasets for classifying heterogeneous images [1,4] are very different from photographs of facades of buildings with advertising posters. Such visual features of posters as the lack of convex elements and a similar rectangular shape greatly complicate the classification of posters using classic image classification methods [6]. It also should be noted a weak visual difference between groups of advertising posters belonging to different types of business. In addition to the visual component, it is possible to use text information located on the poster using text recognition engines [7,9,11]. However signboards text recognition is often hampered by factors such as variable angles, fonts, styles of signage and lighting (Fig. 1). Since text-based classification also does not provide appropriate classification quality, there is a need to assess the presence of additional context on the facade of the building and its visual characteristics. Thus, the idea of constructing a combined classifier for classifying photographs of facades of commercial buildings with advertising signboards [6]. Unfortunately even model described in [6] does not demonstrate very high efficiency in a difficult context of the problem.

In order to achieve better performance in classifying advertising signboards photographs by the type of provided services, we propose a special type of image descriptors which we use as a part of a combined scheme, proposed in [6]. Our method demonstrates better efficiency than models that use only visual information or only recognized text during photo processing and also better than combined methods that uses visual features and explicit text information retrieval [6].

2   Problem Statement

In this article we present a study of the use of special types of descriptors as a part of a combined classifier scheme for advertising signboard photographs classifying by the type of provided services. The problem can be formulated as follows.

An input image containing a commercial building facade with a signboard Q should be assigned to one of the classes $C = C_i$, where $i \in [0, N]$.

We also use the following restrictions. Input images are captured in various conditions by different cameras with various intrinsic parameters, hence: a) may contain such visual defects as sun glare, noise, including those that greatly impede optical text recognition and visual features of input image; b) angle, framing, lighting and colour balance are unknown and can vary significantly from snapshot to snapshot; c) position of a signboard in frame can also vary greatly.

a)   b)   c)   d)

Fig. 1. Considered dataset illustration: a) photograph of a hotel; b) photograph of a store facade; c) image of a restaurant signboard; d) photograph of a signboard that does not belong to categories listed above.)

3 Proposed Method

We use similar combined classifier scheme, as described in [6]. The proposed architecture contains several modules: a visual features extraction module, text detection one, and the special image descriptor module (Fig. 2). It is remarkable that the proposed modular architecture does not require any special preprocessing stage since we use fairly stable and noise resistant approaches for significant information retrieval and we also make a decision based on an analysis of a wide range of features. We use CNN-based module for visual features extraction, since CNN-based image features extractors are effective in solving problems of general images classifying [2,3,8]. Unfortunately general images classifiers that are based only on CNN extracted features demonstrate poor results in advertising posters photographs classification [6]. In order to increase the performance of our classifier we introduce another special image descriptor that is obtained from original photo regions that contains text. Then we add some postprocessing to prepare general visual features and our special descriptor for concatenation. Then we project the result of the concatenation onto a space of dimension 4 (according to the number of classes). After that we apply SoftMax function to the obtained vector and interpret result values as the probabilities of target classes.

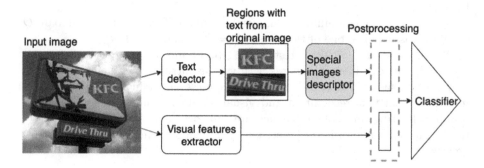

Fig. 2. General architectural diagram of the proposed combined classifier.

3.1   CNN-Based Feature Extractors

According to [6], we use MobileNet [2] for a whole image features extraction. Thus our visual features extractor is a sequence of convolutional, fully connected layers and residual connections [5]. We use that descriptor to retrieve significant information from background.

We also use CNN-based EAST [11] architecture for text detection on an input image. Advantages of using this method are its speed and resistance to an angle varying.

3.2   Special Image Descriptors

We present special types of descriptors for images containing textual information. The procedure for calculating proposed descriptors is parallelized naturally and does not require significant computing resources.

Our descriptors are based on the idea of obtaining the maximal information from the mutual arrangement of regions with the maximum brightness variation. We also intend to retrieve information from different locations simultaneously. Guided by the above considerations we construct image descriptors as traces of a certain number of agents moving from given initial positions on the image according to predefined strategies. We propose two strategies types that performed better on our datasets.

Image descriptor type A implies the special strategy for agent movement. At each step agent select movement type according to the following rule:

$$m^v_{i+1} = \arg\max_{m \in M_p}(|R^i_1 - R^i_2| + c_p * \mathbb{1}_{\{p\}}(m)),$$

$$(R^i_1, R^i_2) = \begin{cases} (R^i_{up}, R^i_{down}), & if \ |R^i_{up} - R^i_{down}| > |R^i_{left} - R^i_{right}| \\ (R^i_{left}, R^i_{right}), & otherwise, \end{cases}$$

$$R^i_{up} = I[x_i - s/2 : x_i + s/2; y_i - s : y_i],$$

$$R^i_{down} = I[x_i - s/2 : x_i + s/2; y_i : y_i + s],$$

$$R^i_{left} = I[x_i - s : x_i; y_i - s/2 : y_i + s/2],$$

$$R^i_{right} = I[x_i : x_i + s; y_i - s/2 : y_i + s/2],$$

where m^v_i stands for a movement direction, i stands for a step number, I denotes an input image, and (x, y) denotes position of a pixel on the input image, p stands for priority movement direction, M_p is a subset of $\{up, down, left, right\}$ that denotes allowed movements according to priority direction p, c_p denotes bonus for movement along the priority direction and s stands for a step size in pixels.

The trace of each agent with predefined movement direction can be formalized as follows:

$$T^p(x_0, y_0) = (m_1(x_0, y_0), ..., m_N(x_0, y_0)),$$

where $T^p(x_0, y_0)$ - trace of an agent with priority movement direction p and initial position (x_0, y_0), $m_i(x_0, y_0)$ stands for chosen agents movement at step i with predefined initial position and priority direction and N denotes the length of each trajectory (if an edge of the image achieved before making N steps then trace is padded with a special value). Thus trajectories of that descriptor type tends to be placed along contours of an input image (Fig. 3).

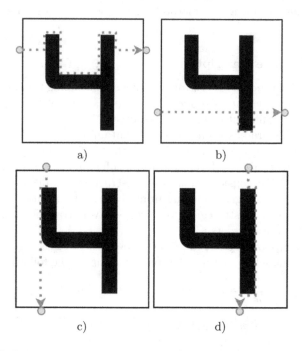

a)   b)

c)   d)

Fig. 3. Type A descriptors trace illustration: a,b) horizontal oriented trajectories; c,d) vertical oriented trajectories

All of trajectories are grouped by priority directions and initial positions:

$$T^{up} = (T^{up}(x_0, H), ..., T^{up}(x_A, H)),$$
$$T^{down} = (T^{down}(x_0, 0), ..., T^{down}(x_A, 0)),$$
$$T^{left} = (T^{left}(W, y_0), ..., T^{left}(W, y_B)),$$
$$T^{right} = (T^{right}(0, y_0), ..., T^{right}(0, y_B)),$$

where A and B stands for horizontal-oriented and vertical-oriented agents number, W denotes an input image width and H denotes image height. Finally we merge groups of trajectories for each direction into the complete image descriptor that can be described as follows:

$$T = (T^{up}, T^{down}, T^{left}, T^{right}).$$

From the above description, it is easy to construct a procedure that calculates the proposed descriptor for the number of steps that linearly depend on the number of pixels of an input image. It should also be noted that the algorithm for calculating our descriptor is parallelized with a small effort.

Image descriptor type B differs from type A only with movement direction rule:

$$m_{i+1}^v = \arg\max_{m \in M_p}(|R_1^i - R_2^i| + \alpha * c_p * \mathbb{1}_{\{p\}}(m)),$$

where equals 1 if movement direction was changed at least once and 0 otherwise. That modification allows agent to avoid priority direction influence if significant element was found during agents movement (Fig. 4).

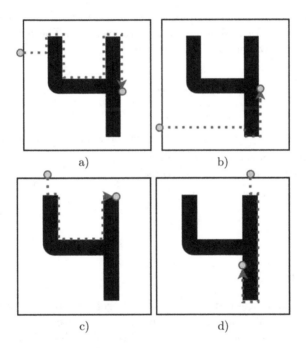

a)   b)

c)   d)

Fig. 4. Type B descriptors trace illustration: a,b) horizontal oriented trajectories; c,d) vertical oriented trajectories

4 Experiments

4.1 Datasets

We investigated performance of the proposed model and its variations using two datasets. The first dataset was presented in [6]. It contains snapshots from

Google Street View application captured mostly in U.S. The dataset contains only 357 images roughly split into the classes.

The second one is Signboard Classification Dataset (SCD). It was collected by ourselves from publicly available sources, namely from Flickr. This dataset contains photos from different authors who made their work available for research purposes. The number of images in the dataset is 1000. The class distribution is uniform in this dataset. We release the collected dataset and make it publicly available[1].

All of the images from datasets were obtained under different capture conditions and camera positions and grouped into 4 classes according to the type of services provided (hotels, shops, restaurants, and "other").

4.2   Performance Comparison

We used F_1 as a quality metric in all experiments. For multi-class classification estimation F_1 scores for individual classes are averaged. The results of comparative performance investigation are given in Table 1.

Table 1. Performance investigation results.

Model	Dataset	
	Malykh and Samarin, 2019 [6]	SCD
Malykh and Samarin, 2019 [6]	0.24	0.47
ours with descriptor type A	**0.38**	0.59
ours with descriptor type B	0.35	**0.63**

5   Conclusion

We propose special image descriptors that are useful for to classification images containing text. We also present a new open SCD dataset for advertising signboard classification by the type of provided services. The effectiveness of proposed descriptors usage is demonstrated on several datasets. It should be noted that performance of methods that use our descriptors significantly overcomes combined classifier baseline. Our solution demonstrated new state of the art result (0.38 in averaged F_1 score against 0.24 of previous best model over our dataset and 0.63 in averaged F_1 score against 0.47 over dataset from the original paper). According to obtained results, the further research could be focused on the study of new descriptors building new descriptors in order to better performance achievement.

---

[1] https://github.com/madrugado/signboard-classification-dataset.

References

1. Deng, J., Dong, W., Socher, R., Li, L., Li, K., Fei-Fei, L.: Imagenet: a large-scale hierarchical image database. In: 2009 IEEE Conference on Computer Vision and Pattern Recognition, pp. 248–255 (June 2009). https://doi.org/10.1109/CVPR. 2009.5206848

2. Howard, A.G., et al.: MobileNets: efficient convolutional neural networks for mobile vision applications (April 2017)

3. He, K., Zhang, X., Ren, S., Sun, J.: Deep residual learning for image recognition. In: 2016 IEEE Conference on Computer Vision and Pattern Recognition (CVPR), pp. 770–778 (June 2016). https://doi.org/10.1109/CVPR.2016.90

4. Lin, T.-Y., et al.: Microsoft COCO: common objects in context. In: Fleet, D., Pajdla, T., Schiele, B., Tuytelaars, T. (eds.) ECCV 2014. LNCS, vol. 8693, pp. 740–755. Springer, Cham (2014). https://doi.org/10.1007/978-3-319-10602-1_48

5. Liu, T., Fang, S., Zhao, Y., Wang, P., Zhang, J.: Implementation of training convolutional neural networks. CoRR abs/1506.01195 arxiv:1506.01195 (2015)

6. Malykh, V., Samarin, A.: Combined advertising sign classifier. In: van der Aalst, W.M.P., et al. (eds.) AIST 2019. LNCS, vol. 11832, pp. 179–185. Springer, Cham (2019). https://doi.org/10.1007/978-3-030-37334-4_16

7. Smith, R.: An overview of the tesseract OCR engine. In: Ninth International Conference on Document Analysis and Recognition (ICDAR 2007), vol. 2, pp. 629–633 (September 2007). https://doi.org/10.1109/ICDAR.2007.4376991

8. Szegedy, C., et al.: Going deeper with convolutions. In: 2015 IEEE Conference on Computer Vision and Pattern Recognition (CVPR), pp. 1–9 (June 2015). https:// doi.org/10.1109/CVPR.2015.7298594

9. Tian, Z., Huang, W., He, T., He, P., Qiao, Y.: Detecting text in natural image with connectionist text proposal network. In: Leibe, B., Matas, J., Sebe, N., Welling, M. (eds.) ECCV 2016. LNCS, vol. 9912, pp. 56–72. Springer, Cham (2016). https:// doi.org/10.1007/978-3-319-46484-8_4

10. Zhou, J., McGuinness, K., O'Connor, N.E.: A text recognition and retrieval system for e-business image management. In: Schoeffmann, K., et al. (eds.) MMM 2018. LNCS, vol. 10705, pp. 23–35. Springer, Cham (2018). https://doi.org/10.1007/978-3-319-73600-6_3

11. Zhou, X., et al.: East: an efficient and accurate scene text detector. In: 2017 IEEE Conference on Computer Vision and Pattern Recognition (CVPR), pp. 2642–2651 (July 2017). https://doi.org/10.1109/CVPR.2017.283

Text Extraction from Scrolling News Tickers

Ingus Janis Pretkalnins[1(✉)], Arturs Sprogis[1], and Guntis Barzdins[2]

[1] Institute of Mathematics and Computer Science, University of Latvia,
Raina blvd. 29, Riga 1459, Latvia
{ingus.pretkalnins,arturs.sprogis}@lumii.lv
[2] LETA, Marijas 2, Riga 1050, Latvia
guntis.barzdins@leta.lv

Abstract. While a lot of work exists on text or keyword extraction from videos, not a lot can be found on the exact problem of extracting continuous text from scrolling tickers. In this work a novel Tesseract OCR based pipeline is proposed for location and continuous text extraction from scrolling tickers in videos. The solution worked faster than real time, and achieved a character accuracy of 97.3% on 45 min of manually transcribed 360p videos of popular Latvian news shows.

Keywords: Tesseract OCR · OCR · Video text extraction · Text localization · Ticker text

1 Introduction

A ticker is a display of text commonly found at the lower third of the screen in news networks (examples in Fig. 3), which can contain weather reports, stock quotes, news headlines or other short pieces of text. Traditionally most tickers display text moving from right to left (opposite in right-to-left writing systems).

While work capable of reading static tickers exists [1,2,4], and even work capable of extracting keywords from scrolling tickers exists [4], at the time of writing, a ready-made solution for the problem of extracting the entire continuous text from a scrolling ticker was not found. This paper describes a solution to this problem built in collaboration with the largest Latvian news agency LETA, where the pipeline will be tested in production. A pipeline is proposed for finding the ticker text on screen, preprocessing images of the ticker text for better recognition by the Tesseract OCR engine [15], and combining the OCR readings into a continuous piece of text.

Attention was mostly paid to Latvian news shows, however with minor modifications the pipeline would likely work for any language written horizontally for which Tesseract OCR has been trained.

T. Robal et al. (Eds.): DB&IS 2020, CCIS 1243, pp. 130–143, 2020.
https://doi.org/10.1007/978-3-030-57672-1_11

2   Related Work

Work has been done in the area of static news video text extraction [1, 2, 4]. And work has even been done capable of keyword extraction from scrolling tickers [4]. However, there doesn't seem to be any work on extraction of the full continuous text from a scrolling ticker, which is the problem the pipeline described in this paper attempts to solve.

Most solutions to image or text extraction problems can be divided into five sub-steps: detection, localization, tracking, preprocessing, and recognition (OCR reading) [7]. So the pipeline described in this paper was designed similarly. Except for that the pipeline assumes the input video contains a ticker, which doesn't change its position throughout the video. So it is only concerned with the steps localization, preprocessing and recognition. In addition to that, due to the full text of a scrolling ticker never being completely visible on screen at any point in time, extra steps are taken after recognition, to construct a single continuous piece of text from OCR readings of multiple ticker images.

Although a lot of research is available on localizing text in videos [10], to locate the scrolling ticker text in a video, a novel simple method is proposed, which is designed specifically for scrolling ticker text localization, which uses an idea from [9].

Also the work proposes a method for constructing a single continuous piece of text from Tesseract OCR readings for individual ticker text images, which the authors believe to be novel.

3   Methodology

In this section each of the steps of the pipeline are described in detail. An overview of all the steps is shown in Fig. 1.

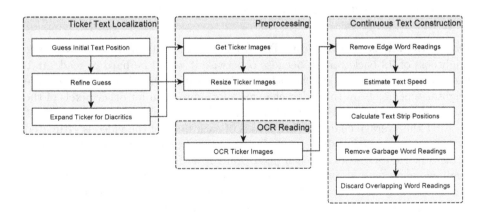

Fig. 1. Pipeline with arrows showing how information flows between steps.

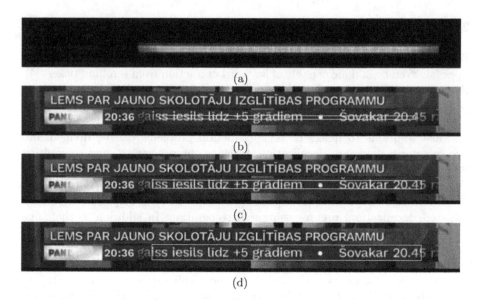

Fig. 2. Visualization of steps of ticker text localization for a section of the video containing a ticker. (a) Heat map of average change in brightness. (b) Initial window calculated in section "Guess Initial Text Position". (c) Window after line-by-line expansion in section "Refine Guess". (d) Window after expanding 1/3 to include possible diacritics and descenders in section "Expand Window for Diacritics".

3.1   Ticker Text Localization

In the ticker text localization steps the window where ticker text appears is found. It is assumed that there is exactly one ticker in the video, which doesn't change its position, and is visible throughout most of the video. An example of the intermediate results of the localization steps are shown in Fig. 2.

Guess Initial Text Position. The brightness of text differs a lot from the brightness of its background, because otherwise it would be hard to read. And, because the text printed on the ticker is constantly moving left, on average the brightness of pixels on the ticker changes a lot more than for other pixels of the video. This assumption is used in the ticker text location steps.

First the average change in brightness of each pixel of the video is estimated by reading a couple hundred pairs of consecutive frames from the video, calculating how the brightness of each pixel changes within each pair of frames, and then averaging over all pairs. Then, to get an initial guess for where ticker text can appear, the detector finds the smallest window containing all pixels whose average change in brightness passes a dynamic threshold Th_1 calculated as:

$$Th_1 = 0.9 \cdot MaxChange \tag{1}$$

where *MaxChange* is the maximum average change in brightness for a pixel in the sample.

This gives a window where ticker text frequently passes through and is usually smaller and contained within the actual window where ticker text appears.

Refine Guess. The initial guess is then expanded one line at a time, if the average change in brightness of a line directly adjacent to the window pass a threshold $Th_2 = 0.5 \cdot Th_1$.

The idea for line-wise expansion of the window is borrowed from [9] section IV.D.1.

A lower threshold $Th_3 = 0.15 \cdot Th_1$ is used for expansion upward, to include ascenders (e.g. letters h, k, A, l) which are usually much rarer than text between the baseline and mean line of the font (height spanned by x, e, c, o, a, etc.).

After this, the window height roughly corresponds to the region and height of a capital letter. This height value is later used when resizing ticker images in preprocessing.

Expand Window for Diacritics. The window is then expanded 1/3 vertically to each side to include possible diacritics (e.g. Ņ, Š, ļ) and descenders (e.g. g, y, j, p).

3.2 Preprocessing

Preprocessing is known to improve Tesseract OCR's output compared to just giving it raw images [6]. So first the pipeline crops the images to only the ticker text window calculated in the previous section. Then the images are resized so the font has a capital letter height of about 32 pixels.

Get Ticker Images. Images of the ticker are taken every 12 frames, which usually produces a lot of overlap in the text between consecutive images taken. This makes continuous text construction easier later on. The ticker images are then cropped to the ticker text window.

Resize Ticker Images. Tesseract OCR 4.0's LSTM line recognizer engine works best when the capital letter size is about 30–50 pixels in height [11, 16]. The ticker images are resized so the font is about 32 pixels in height. The interpolation method used when resizing is cubic interpolation.

3.3 OCR Reading

The OCR engine that was used for text recognition was the Tesseract OCR engine 4.0 with LSTM [15], because at the time of writing it was one of the most popular open source OCR engines, and shows comparable results to proprietary solutions [14].

The preprocessed ticker images from the previous section are run through Tesseract to get positions, text and confidence values of words for each ticker image. (From this point on the word "word" will be used to refer to a single word on a scrolling ticker as a human would interpret it, and the information that Tesseract OCR returns from reading a word from a ticker image will be referred to as a "word reading".)

The confidence values are later used for removing word readings that are the result of non-text symbols (Examples shown in Fig. 3) incorrectly interpreted by Tesseract as text. This is done in section "Remove Garbage Word Readings".

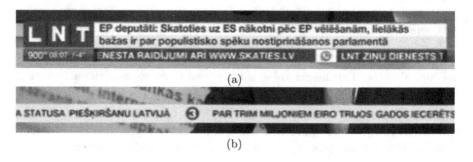

(a)

(b)

Fig. 3. Examples of scrolling tickers containing non-text symbols. (a) Ticker containing the icon of the social media platform *WhatsApp*. (b) Ticker containing the *TV3* logo.

3.4   Continuous Text Construction

After each ticker image has been read by Tesseract OCR, the resulting word readings are combined into one continuous piece of text. This process is divided into five parts:

- Remove word readings that might be clipping with the edges of the ticker text window. (section "Remove Edge Word Readings")
- Estimate leftward speed of text. (section "Estimate Text Speed")
- Use speed estimate to calculate the approximate position of each word reading on text strip, if the ticker is imagined to have an actual long strip of text scrolling through it. (section "Calculate Text Strip Positions")
- Remove word readings that come from non-text symbols being falsely interpreted as text by the Tesseract OCR engine. (section "Remove Garbage Word Readings")
- Pick words so that their calculated text strip positions don't overlap. (section "Discard Overlapping Word Readings")

Remove Edge Word Readings. When a word isn't fully visible in the ticker text window (either because it hasn't yet fully scrolled in, or has started to scroll out (e.g. the word "DIENESTA" on left side of ticker in Fig. 3a)), Tesseract will only read the part that it sees. These "partial" word readings can interfere with later steps in text construction, so any word readings that start or end within a word height of the left or right edge of the ticker text window, are discarded.

Estimate Text Speed. The text in the ticker moves leftward at constant speed. Tesseract OCR can return approximate positions of words in whole pixels. So if Tesseract reads the same text for a word at about the same position in consecutive ticker images, a rough estimate for the speed of the text can be calculated, by dividing the difference in position by the difference in frames.

Averaging these estimates for a couple hundred word readings gives a good approximation of the speed.

Calculate Text Strip Positions. Every word is read multiple times by the Tesseract OCR engine. To later understand which word readings correspond to the same word, it is imagined that a continuous text strip is actually scrolling through the ticker. Estimates for word reading positions on the text strip are then calculated. This is done by simply adding, how much we expect the text strip to have moved, to the position of the word reading reported by Tesseract. The speed approximation from section "Estimate Text Speed" is used as the speed of the text strip.

Even if the speed approximation is off by a bit, since a word only appears on screen for no more than a couple hundred frames, the difference in calculated text strip positions for the same word should be small compared to the word's size. Yet the difference in calculated text strip positions for different words should be similar to the difference between them on the actual text strip, at least for words close on the actual text strip. Which is mostly good enough for the methods used in later text construction steps.

Remove Garbage Word Readings. Occasionally symbols, that are not text, appear on the ticker. (Examples shown in Fig. 3).

In these situations Tesseract OCR may attempt to read them and usually return word readings whose text consists of random punctuation, or sometimes numbers or letters. These word readings make the result text worse if left in.

In order to lessen this problem, a method was worked out to remove word readings that are likely to be the result of Tesseract trying to read something that's not text.

Tesseract OCR supports returning confidence values. From the confidence values one can calculate the average character confidence:

$$charconf = \sqrt[len]{conf} \tag{2}$$

Where *len* is the length of the word reading in characters and *conf* is the Tesseract confidence value. The average character confidence of word readings that are the result of reading non-text symbols tends to be lower than the average for readings of legitimate text. However occasionally Tesseract returns high confidence values for individual non-text readings by chance.

To counteract this, the word readings corresponding to the same word/non-text symbol are clustered based on their left and right edge positions on the long text and character length. Two word readings are put in the same cluster, if their edge positions differ by less than the text height and their character length is equal. Then if the average character confidence of the cluster is less than 0.85, the cluster is discarded, otherwise the word reading with the highest Tesseract confidence value in the cluster is left in the text and the others are discarded.

Discard Overlapping Word Readings. Occasionally, because of small spaces between words, Tesseract OCR can misread two words as one (e.g. PAR TRIM → PARTRIM), or two letters can be interpreted as one or vice versa (e.g. LI ↔ U). This can create situations where, even after the clustering from last step, there are still word readings that overlap, and it is not clear which word reading to leave in the text and which to discard.

The method proposed for solving this problem, is to go through all the clustered words left to right based on their left edge. If the new clustered word doesn't overlap with the previous one, just add it. If it does, then pick the one that comes from the biggest cluster by count, and throw the other one out.

After the process has been finished simply concatenate the clustered words through spaces to get the final continuous text.

3.5 Limitations

The ticker text localization steps only work properly when exactly one ticker is present in the video, and is visible throughout most of the video. The OCR reading step also assumes the ticker is visible throughout the video. If the ticker is not present that can lead to garbage text insertions. It is also assumed the ticker has a solid or, at least, only partially translucent background.

It might also be possible that the ticker localization steps might fail, if a pixel from the background video is included in the initial text position guess. For instance, this might happen if the text is very spare, or it's contrast to the background is small, and the video contains moving high contrast footage (e.g. a panning checked tile pattern).

The pipeline only works for horizontally written scripts, with well defined word boundaries and spaces seperating them, for which Tesseract OCR has been trained.

The pipeline doesn't work in situations where the speed of scrolling of the scrolling ticker changes with time. Using it in such cases can lead to word deletion or duplication in the result text.

4   Dataset and Evaluation

4.1   Dataset

Ground truth data was gathered by manually transcribing scrolling ticker contents from 45 min of video. Data was gathered from popular Latvian news shows, more specifically *LNT Ziņas* (4 min), *LNT 900″* (16 min), *TV3 Ziņas* (10 min) and *Panorāma* (15 min).

All videos had a vertical resolution of 360 pixels, and horizontal resolutions varying from 450 to 640 pixels. The frame-rates of the videos were between 24 and 30 fps. Most videos were downloaded from *YouTube*. Each video contained exactly one scrolling ticker, which persisted throughout most of the video, and in total 6 different styles of scrolling tickers could be seen in the dataset. The ticker capital letter heights varied from 8 pixels to 14 pixels. The average font capital letter height for the videos was about 10.9 pixels. In total the data contained 24367 characters and 3089 words.

4.2   Evaluation

The main metric used for evaluation was character accuracy, which is used for OCR evaluation [3,13]. Character accuracy (*CAcc*) is an edit distance related metric calculated by the formula:

$$CAcc = 1 - \frac{EditDist}{N} \tag{3}$$

where N is the number of characters in the ground truth text, and *EditDist* is the Levenshtein edit distance [8], which calculates the minimum number of character edits (insertions, substitutions, deletions) to match the output of the pipeline to the ground truth. While calculating edit distance upper and lower case letters were considered different, and white spaces and punctuation were considered characters.

For analysis of results, the numbers of necessary insertions, substitutions and deletions are also displayed in experiment tables.

5   Experiments

The pipeline was hand tuned to good settings. Experiments were done to show that the pipeline works worse if a single parameter is changed, or a part of the system is disabled. All possible configurations weren't tested because that would take an enormous amount of computational resources.

5.1   Frame Step Experiment

An experiment was done to see how the results of the pipeline changed depending on how often ticker images are taken from the source video in section "Get Ticker Images". Results are shown in Table 1.

The number of substitutions somewhat decreases with the decrease in frame step likely because it reduces the chance that by accident the word reading with the highest Tesseract confidence will be an incorrectly read word.

The results don't improve much beyond decreasing the step to one image every 12 frames, so that was the default value chosen for the pipeline.

Table 1. Results of the pipeline depending on the step in frame number for taking a ticker image in section "Get Ticker Images".

Frame step	Character accuracy	Insertions	Substitutions	Deletions
6	97.6%	109	179	**287**
8	**97.7%**	106	**160**	288
12	97.4%	122	173	336
16	97.5%	**100**	167	341
24	97.1%	108	208	391
36	96.5%	108	186	562

5.2   Font Resizing Experiments

New Font Height Experiment. An experiment was done to see how the results of the pipeline changed depending on the capital letter height the ticker images were resized to have in section "Resize Ticker Images". Results are shown in Table 2 and Fig. 4.

The results are quite noisy. From Fig. 4 it looks like resizing the images to have a capital letter height between 30 and 50 pixels on average improves the character accuracy by about 0.3% (approximately 97.6%) compared to not resizing at all (approximately 97.3%).

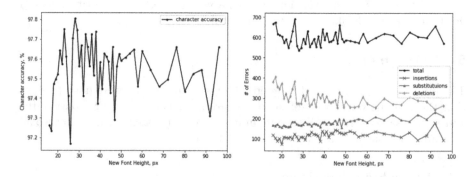

Fig. 4. Left - graph showing how character accuracy changes depending on capital letter height of text after resizing. Right - number of errors depending capital letter height of text after resizing.

Table 2. Results of the pipeline depending on capital letter height after resizing ticker images in section "Resize Ticker Images".

New height	Character accuracy	Insertions	Substitutions	Deletions
No Resizing	97.3%	78	148	440
16	97.3%	119	167	381
17	97.2%	104	165	405
18	97.5%	88	172	356
19	97.5%	102	161	347
20	97.5%	73	156	375
21	97.6%	109	167	298
22	97.6%	107	162	322
23	97.8%	105	158	285
24	97.6%	110	162	310
25	97.4%	100	185	346
26	97.2%	123	184	383
27	97.7%	111	174	274
28	97.8%	93	168	274
29	97.7%	109	167	273
30	97.6%	108	171	315
31	97.7%	96	183	289
32	97.4%	122	173	336
33	97.7%	118	174	262
34	97.7%	134	165	271
35	97.6%	123	176	295
36	97.7%	121	175	258
37	97.5%	116	168	321
38	97.7%	90	160	301
39	97.4%	140	182	318
40	97.6%	121	185	283
41	97.4%	137	175	310
42	97.6%	110	183	285
43	97.6%	128	174	280
44	97.6%	126	177	285
45	97.4%	143	192	292
46	97.7%	142	173	255
47	97.3%	132	200	328
48	97.6%	128	157	309
49	97.6%	125	197	257
50	97.6%	128	176	283
52	97.6%	138	188	257
54	97.6%	131	191	256
56	97.6%	111	200	262
58	97.5%	119	193	307
60	97.6%	119	182	274
64	97.5%	137	208	253
68	97.5%	126	193	300
72	97.5%	119	220	271
76	97.7%	108	193	269
80	97.4%	132	186	307
84	97.5%	95	220	288
88	97.5%	117	196	285
92	97.3%	178	232	245
96	97.7%	95	211	264

From Fig. 4 it looks like there is a small increase in character substitution errors with larger font sizes, which was also observed in [11]. For smaller font sizes word deletions seem to tend to go up. This might be because of words getting small Tesseract confidence values, and getting removed as garbage.

The experiment results are too noisy to tell which height brings the best results, so the value chosen for the capital letter height after resizing is 32 pixels, which seemed to give the good results in [11].

Interpolation Method Experiment. An experiment was done to see how the results of the pipeline changed depending on the interpolation method used for resizing the ticker images in section "Resize Ticker Images". Methods compared were—nearest neighbour, linear and cubic interpolation. Results are shown in Table 3.

Table 3. Results of the pipeline depending on the interpolation method used for ticker image resizing, when resizing to a capital letter height of 32 pixels, in section "Resize Ticker Images".

Method	Character accuracy	Insertions	Substitutions	Deletions
Nearest neighbour	97.3%	**114**	206	341
Linear	97.3%	127	179	355
Cubic	**97.4%**	122	**173**	**336**

There wasn't a large difference in character accuracy between interpolation methods. It was decided to stick with cubic interpolation as is proposed in [5].

5.3 Garbage Word Reading Removal Experiment

An experiment was done to see how the results of the pipeline changed depending on the average character confidence cutoffs for removing a word reading cluster in section "Remove Garbage Word Readings". Results are shown in Table 4.

Allowing word readings with lower average character confidence increases the amount of character insertions. Mostly because Tesseract OCR's attempts to read non-text symbols are not discarded. The amount of substitutions also increases, because, for low quality videos, Tesseract sometimes struggles to read long words correctly, instead splitting them into shorter incorrect word readings. They are then sometimes chosen over the correct readings in step "Discard overlapping word readings", which chooses based on cluster size. The spaces between these shorter readings are then sometimes interpreted as substitution errors.

However the amount of deletions of legitimate word readings decreases.

Requiring higher average character confidence leads to less insertions and substitutions, but increases the amount of deletions of legitimate text.

The cutoff that lead to the best character accuracy was 0.85.

Table 4. Results of the pipeline depending on the average character confidence cutoff for discarding a word reading cluster in section "Remove Garbage Word Readings".

Min confidence	Character accuracy	Insertions	Substitutions	Deletions
No garbage removal	93.3%	1131	339	**160**
0.7	96.8%	348	209	225
0.75	97.2%	259	199	236
0.8	**97.4%**	176	192	271
0.85	**97.4%**	122	173	336
0.9	96.9%	88	165	513
0.95	93.1%	**45**	**120**	1528

5.4   Overlapping Word Reading Choice Experiment

An experiment was done to see how the results of the pipeline changed depending on the method of choosing between word readings when they significantly overlap in section "Discard Overlapping Word Readings". The methods compared were:

– Choosing the one with highest average character confidence.
– Choosing the one with largest Tesseract confidence value.
– Choosing the one that comes from the largest cluster.
– Picking at random, as a baseline.

Results are shown in Table 5.

Table 5. Results of the pipeline depending on method for choosing between overlapping word readings in section "Discard Overlapping Word Readings".

Method	Character accuracy	Insertions	Substitutions	Deletions
Character confidence	93.8%	132	210	1173
Confidence	93.7%	124	239	1161
Merges	**97.4%**	**122**	**173**	**336**
Random	93.7%	149	228	1164

The only method that gave better results than random, was choosing the word reading that came from the largest cluster by word reading count. All other methods caused much more character deletions, but for different reasons:

– When using average character confidence, if two words are accidentally interpreted by Tesseract as correspond to one (e.g. PAR TRIM → PARTRIM), and if the first word (PAR in example) on average gets a lower average character confidence than the second one (TRIM), then the combined word reading

(PARTRIM) will have a higher average character confidence than word readings of the first word (PAR), because the second word (TRIM) raises the average character confidence. So, since the algorithm moves left to right, the combined word reading (PARTRIM) will be prioritized over the word readings of the first word (PAR). And after that, because of higher average character confidence, word readings of the second word (TRIM) will be prioritized over the combined word reading (PARTRIM). Overall this results in the deletion of the first word (PAR) from the result text.

- When using Tesseract confidence, problems arise when Tesseract accidentally reads only part of a word(e.g. Lielbritānija $\rightarrow$ nija). Shorter word readings tend to have a higher word confidence value than long word readings, So these shorter partial readings are prioritized over the longer correct word readings, which leads to character deletions.
- When picking at random, similarly as with average character confidence, a lot of word deletions happen because of two words getting read as one, and causing word deletions from the result text.

6   Conclusion and Future Work

The pipeline achieved 97.3% character accuracy on the dataset. The solution worked faster than real time on a regular computer, processing the 45 min of video in about 13 min on an Intel Pentium Gold G5400 CPU.

About a sixth of the errors were character insertions, mostly because of non-text symbols being read as text and not being removed in the garbage removal step. About a third of the errors were character substitutions, which mostly happened because Tesseract confuses one character for another because of low resolution and video compression. About half of the errors were character deletions. About half of the deletions happened because the word readings had small Tesseract confidence values so got removed as garbage.

There was a problem for videos from the channels *LNT 900″* and *LNT Ziņas* where occasionally the video froze and then skipped a couple tens of frames, this usually caused word deletions or some word duplication in the results text, because words were interpreted as having multiple positions on the text strip. Tickers of *LNT* also occasionally featured text, with inverted colors for background and text color, intermittently with regular text. Tesseract sometimes handled this incorrectly.

Other than that, less aggressive compression and a bigger font height in the original video seemed to lead to a better character accuracy.

The error rate could likely be halved if logos and other non-text symbols could be detected and removed perfectly, or if the garbage word removal method could perfectly tell which words are legitimate. So this is definitely a side where future work could focus on. Most character substitution errors are quite easy to resolve for a human reading the pipeline's output. So adding a dictionary check or contextual information analysis might reduce the error rate by about a third, which future work could also focus on.

Other useful functionality to add might be automatic detection of appearance or disappearance of tickers, or the ability to handle multiple tickers.

The code of the pipeline is available in a public Github repository [12].

Acknowledgements. The authors would like to thank the reviewers for their thought provoking comments.

The research was supported by ERDF project 1.1.1.1/18/A/045 at IMCS, University of Latvia.

References

1. Asif, M.D.A., et al.: A novel hybrid method for text detection and extraction from news videos. Middle-East J. Sci. Res. **19**(5), 716–722 (2014)
2. Bhowmick, S., Banerjee, P.: Bangla text recognition from video sequence: a new focus. arXiv preprint arXiv:1401.1190 (2014)
3. Carrasco, R.C.: An open-source OCR evaluation tool. In: Proceedings of the First International Conference on Digital Access to Textual Cultural Heritage, DATeCH 2014, pp. 179–184. Association for Computing Machinery, Madrid (2014). ISBN: 9781450325882. https://doi.org/10.1145/2595188.2595221
4. Ghosh, H., et al.: Multimodal indexing of multilingual news video. Int. J. Digit. Multimedia Broadcast. **2010**, 19 (2010)
5. How to Use Image Preprocessing to Improve the Accuracy of Tesseract. https://www.freecodecamp.org/news/getting-started-with-tesseract-part-ii-f7f9a 0899b3f/. Accessed 02 Mar 2020
6. Improving the Quality of the Output. https://tesseract-ocr.github.io/tessdoc/ ImproveQuality#Borders. Accessed 02 Mar 2020
7. Jung, K., Kim, K.I., Jain, A.K.: Text information extraction in images and video: a survey. Pattern Recogn. **37**(5), 977–997 (2004)
8. Levenshtein, V.I.: Binary codes capable of correcting deletions, insertions, and reversals. Sov. Phys. Dokl. **10**(8), 707–710 (1966)
9. Lienhart, R., Wernicke, A.: Localizing and segmenting text in images and videos. IEEE Trans. Circuits Syst. Video Technol. **12**(4), 256–268 (2002)
10. Lu, T., et al.: Video Text Detection. Springer, Heidelberg (2014). https://doi.org/ 10.1007/978-1-4471-6515-6
11. Optimal Image Resolution (DPI/PPI) for Tesseract 4.0.0 and eng.traineddata? https://groups.google.com/forum/#!msg/tesseract-ocr/Wdh_JJwnw94/ 24JHDYQbBQAJ. Accessed 02 Mar 2020
12. Pipeline Code Repository. https://github.com/IMCS-DL4media/DL4media_ ticker_extractor. Accessed 02 Mar 2020
13. Rice, S.V., Jenkins, F.R., Nartker, T.A.: The fourth annual test of OCR accuracy. Technical report 95 (1995)
14. Tafti, A.P., Baghaie, A., Assefi, M., Arabnia, H.R., Yu, Z., Peissig, P.: OCR as a service: an experimental evaluation of google docs OCR, Tesseract, ABBYY finereader, and transym. In: Bebis, G., et al. (eds.) ISVC 2016. LNCS, vol. 10072, pp. 735–746. Springer, Cham (2016). https://doi.org/10.1007/978-3-319-50835-1_66
15. Tesseract Documentation. https://tesseract-ocr.github.io/tessdoc/4.0-with-LSTM. Accessed 02 Mar 2020
16. Tesseract FAQ: Is there a minimum/maximum text size? https://tesseract-ocr. github.io/tessdoc/FAQ-Old#is-there-a-minimum-text-size-it-wont-read-screen-text. Accessed 02 Mar 2020

Using Machine Learning for Automated Assessment of Misclassification of Goods for Fraud Detection

Margarita Spichakova$^{(\boxtimes)}$ and Hele-Mai Haav

Department of Software Science, Tallinn University of Technology,
Akadeemia tee 15a, 12618 Tallinn, Estonia
margarita.spitsakova@taltech.ee,
helemai@cs.ioc.ee

Abstract. The paper is devoted to providing automated solutions to an actual problem of misclassification of goods in cross-border trade. In this paper, we introduce a hybrid approach to Harmonized System (HS) code assessment that combines the knowledge derived from textual descriptions of products, assigned to them HS codes and taxonomy of HS codes nomenclature. We use machine learning for providing HS code's predictions and recommendations on the basis of a model learned from the textual descriptions of the products. In order to perform an assessment of misclassification of goods we present a novel combined similarity measure based on cosine similarity of texts and semantic similarity of HS codes based on HS code taxonomy (ontology). The method is evaluated on the real open source data set of Bill of Lading Summary 2017 [1] using Gensim Python library [4].

Keywords: Machine learning · Doc2Vec · Harmonized system taxonomy · Cosine similarity of text · Semantic similarity

1 Introduction

In order to make the calculation and collection of the customs duties and import taxes, correct and speed up the customs clearance process the World Customs Organization (WCO) created the Harmonized Commodity Description and Coding System already in 1988 [18]. It is a system for identifying commodities in trade based on a six digits code. The HS is used by 179 countries covering about 98% of world trade for the assessment of customs duties and the collection of statistical data [5]. The HS nomenclature classifies products into 21 sections, 96 chapters, headings and subheadings giving possibility totally to classify about 8547 items [10].

For example, the correct HS code for the product described as "laptop computer" is 847130. In the HS code nomenclature it has the explanation as follows: "Portable automatic data processing machines, weighing not more than 10 kg, consisting of at least a central processing unit, a keyboard and a display" [7].

© Springer Nature Switzerland AG 2020
T. Robal et al. (Eds.): DB&IS 2020, CCIS 1243, pp. 144–158, 2020.
https://doi.org/10.1007/978-3-030-57672-1_12

Customs agents use the product's origin and value together with the HS code to derive the tariff to be assessed. However, the correct classification of HS codes remains a challenging task [10]. Misclassification of products can have several reasons as listed in [8]. First, the HS nomenclature and the rules governing the classification process are very complex. Second, there is a terminological and the semantic gap between product descriptions in the HS nomenclature and goods descriptions in trade (i.e. commercial terms). This leads to the problem that simple text search that is currently used by many HS code databases and lookup systems cannot help traders to locate the relevant HS codes because of the difference and semantic disambiguation between the structured descriptions of the HS nomenclature and the text descriptions used during the trade process.

Misclassification is common and incorrect HS codes create a huge additional cost for retailers and e-marketplaces. In addition, misclassification of goods leads to duty underpayments. In 2017, the European Court of Auditors has reported that widely applied forms of evasion of customs duty payment are undervaluation, misclassification by shifting to a product classification with a lower duty rate and the wrong description of the origin of imported goods [3]. For example, the potential losses of customs duties were calculated to be close to 2 billion euro for the period 2013–2016 due to undervaluation of imports of textiles and footwear from China into the UK [3].

In order to cope with growing fraud, automated solutions for a product classification as well as an assessment of the correctness of HS codes for fraud detection become extremely important.

For solving the problem of misclassification of products many researchers propose automated systems for the classification of HS codes, considering this as a multiclass classification problem and using several machine learning approaches [2,10,17] or provide expert systems like 3CE HS code verification system [6] or automated neural network based tools for product categorization and mapping to HS codes [14].

In contrast, we aim in this paper at an automated assessment of the correctness of HS codes that are already classified and received from e-marketplaces or retailers to customs or logistic companies. In addition to assessment, we also provide some recommendations for corrections of HS codes in the cases of low assessment scores.

The main contribution of the paper is a new method for automated assessment of misclassification of HS codes based on machine learning (Doc2Vec [9]) and the combination of textual and semantic similarity measures. Provided combined similarity measure shows how good the textual description of the given HS code matches with the HS code's position in the HS code taxonomy (classification). The major advantage of our approach compared to pure text based learning approaches is that we may derive additional knowledge from HS code structure (taxonomy) in order to complement short textual descriptions of goods that alone provide insufficient knowledge for automated HS code correctness assessment for fraud detection.

The method is evaluated on the real open source data set of Bill of Lading Summary 2017 [1] that after filtering contains approximately 1.2 million rows with product descriptions and their corresponding HS codes. Gensim Python library [4] is used for the implementation of the method.

The paper is structured as follows. In Sect. 2 a review of related approaches is presented. Section 3 is devoted to an overview of our method and its components. In Sect. 4, we provide an evaluation of our method and descriptions of experiments. Section 5 concludes the paper.

2   Related Works

Most of the related work is devoted to automated commodity classification from the seller's perspective by using different machine learning approaches [2,10,17]. Our work has a perspective on fraud detection as a part of risk management systems.

Fusing textual descriptions of goods and visual data about products in order to automatically classify and recommend HS codes is another approach found in the literature [10,17]. Li and Li propose text–image dual convolutional neural network model for automated customs classification. The experiments of this work have been conducted on a limited manually tagged dataset of 10000 records including data only for four classes showing that fusion model works better than non-fusion model.

Another work [17] that combines topic maps and visual feature extraction and matching is evaluated on 4494 records. However, their result for combined recommendations of HS codes has an accuracy rate of about 78%.

In contrast to the works above, we do not use visual information but the structure of HS code taxonomy (ontology) as complementary knowledge to pure text.

In [20], a HS code recommendation approach to a product is presented. Their system is based on three types of ontologies: the HS code ontology, the product classification ontology and domain ontology. This is only related work where the HS code ontology is used. However, their HS code ontology is different from our HS code ontology in two aspects: we do not use any textual descriptions of ontology concepts as they are already available in the HS code nomenclature and in addition, we capture also sections in our HS code ontology.

To the best of our knowledge, no research has been published that covers all HS code chapters, as we do. Existing works focus on some chapters and/or 2 to 4 first digits of HS code for classification.

3   The Method Architecture

3.1   Preliminaries: HS Code Definition and Classification Taxonomy

HS code is a 6-digit standardized international numerical code to represent and identify the goods for worldwide trade. HS code digits are divided to three pairs, where the pairs of digits are referred to as Chapter, Heading and Subheading respectively. The HS code nomenclature can be represented as an ontology that includes only taxonomic (is-a) relationships and can be seen as a directed acyclic graph (DAG) (it is a tree as one HS code cannot belong to many headings at the same time) as shown in Fig. 1. In addition to the classes mentioned above, we add also classes that denote sections to our HS code taxonomy (ontology). This is because of using this ontology for the calculation of semantic similarity of HS codes (see Sect. 3.4). More hierarchy levels give more fine grained values for semantic similarity measures.

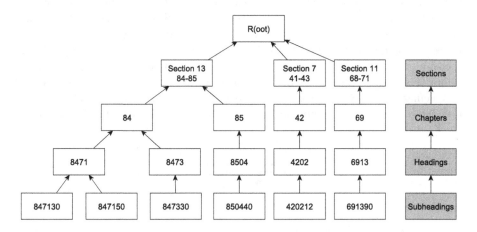

Fig. 1. An excerpt of HS code taxonomy.

The HS code classification is the process of finding the most specific description in the HS code taxonomy for the goods to be classified. For example, according to the taxonomy shown in Fig. 1, a product described as "laptop computer" is classified to have the HS code 847130 (i.e. belongs to the subheading 847130).

3.2   An Overview of the Method

As input to our method, we require that for each HS code to be assessed the corresponding product description (in trade) is made available. These data come from external systems or sources. The hypothesis for machine learning for prediction of HS codes is defined as follows:

Hypothesis I: *Similar textual descriptions of products are related to similar HS codes.*

For testing this hypothesis we use Doc2Vec [9] model that is based on Word2Vec [11,12] modeled according to the distributional hypothesis that words occurring in similar context tend to have similar meanings. We use Doc2Vec for the calculation of textual (cosine) similarities of documents (e.g. product descriptions) and predicting as well as recommending HS codes. However, application of Doc2Vec model has shown us that not always similar descriptions are related to the same or similar HS code meaning that the first hypothesis does not always hold (see Sect. 4). One reason is that texts of product descriptions are too short.

Therefore, in order to understand how good is the matching between the given HS code and the text of the description of the corresponding product we set up the second hypothesis as follows:

Hypothesis II: *Predicted HS codes and an original HS code are close to each other in HS code taxonomy.*

In order to test this hypothesis, we propose in addition to text similarity of descriptions to calculate the semantic similarity of HS code and use combined similarity measure for the overall assessment of HS code correctness. For that, we separate the HS code of the product for calculation its semantic similarity with respect to predicted HS code values and the HS code taxonomy. On the basis of cosine similarity of descriptions and semantic similarity, we propose a new similarity measure called combined similarity measure. This, in turn, is used for the calculation of HS code assessment scores. A general scheme of our method is provided in Fig. 2 and the explanation of its components in the following sections.

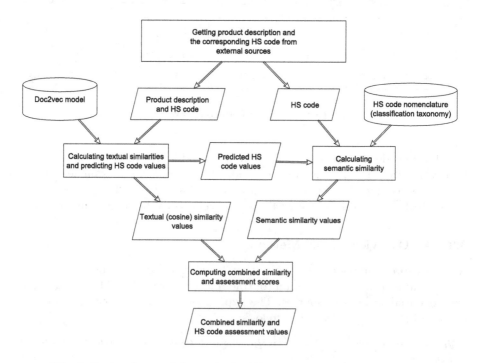

Fig. 2. Basic scheme of the method of HS code correctness assessment.

3.3 Textual Similarity of Descriptions of Goods and Prediction of HS Codes

Descriptions of goods are short texts. The calculation of textual similarity of descriptions of goods and prediction of the corresponding HS code values are based on the usages of Doc2Vec model by Le and Mikolov [9] that enables to create a numeric representation of a document. In our case a document is a description of some product (commodity).

The Doc2Vec extends the idea of Word2Vec [11,12] that is used to generate representation vectors from words. A word vector is a representation of text in a form of numerical vector. Word2Vec model embeds words in a lower-dimensional vector space using a neural network. The result is a set of words and vectors where vectors close together in vector space have similar meanings based on context, and vectors distant to each other have differing meanings. The textual similarity of words is measured as cosine similarity that measures cosine of the angle between two word vectors or document vectors (i.e. orientation).

There are two versions of Word2Vec model as follows: skip-grams (SG) and continuous-bag-of-words (CBOW) [11,12]. In 2014 Le and Mikolov introduced the Doc2Vec algorithm [9], which usually outperforms Word2Vec models. There are two approaches of Doc2Vec: Paragraph Vector – Distributed Memory (PV-DM) and Paragraph Vector – Distributed Bag of Words (PV-DBOW). PV-DM is analogous to CBOW and PV-DBOW is analogous to SG version of Word2Vec model.

We use Doc2Vec PV-DBOW variant implemented in Gensim Python library [4] for testing of our hypothesis, calculating text similarities and predicting HS codes. PV-DBOW is more suitable for short texts and therefore applicable in our case.

3.4 Semantic Similarity of HS Codes

HS codes are arranged into taxonomy as we have seen above (see Fig. 1). This calls for applying a semantic distance method that is based on the structural knowledge in ontology (taxonomy). There are several measures developed for measuring semantic similarity of concepts in ontology. A good overview is provided in [13,15] on various approaches of calculating semantic similarity.

In this paper, we apply a method suggested by Wu and Palmer [19] that takes into account the relative depth in the taxonomy of the concepts. Accordingly, equally distant pairs of concepts belonging to an upper level of taxonomy should be considered less similar than those belonging to a lower level. Originally, Wu and Palmer used their method in the domain of machine translation but nowadays, their method is widely used in many cases, where taxonomy depth needs to be taken account. Their similarity computation is based on the edge counting method. Semantic similarity measure between ontology concepts C_1 and C_2 is based on the distance (D_1 and D_2 accordingly) which separates nodes C_1 and C_2 from the root node R and the distance (D) which separates the closest common ancestor (the least common subsumer) of C_1 and C_2 from the root node R. The similarity measure of Wu and Palmer is calculated by the following formula as in [15] that is equivalent to the original formula by Wu and Palmer:

$$WPSim = \frac{2 \cdot D}{D_1 + D_2} \tag{1}$$

A disadvantage of this measure is that all the semantic links have the same weight. On the other hand, according to [15] the measure is easy to calculate and remains as expressive, as the other methods. Therefore, we base our combined similarity measure on this. However, there are other options, for example, to take into count a number of children of a particular parent node. We may consider this in the future work.

According to the HS code taxonomy in Fig. 1 we may pre-calculate $WPSim$ values for each of the mismatching taxonomy levels of the given HS code and predicted ones as the taxonomy has the tree structure with fixed number of levels of 0 to 4.

For example, if C_1 is code 847130 and C_2 is code 850440, then

$$WPSim(C_1, C_2) = \frac{2 \cdot 1}{4 + 4} = 0.25 \tag{2}$$

This means that in this case section numbers on level one match but chapter numbers on level 2 mismatch. Higher is semantic similarity value closer are the given HS codes in the HS code taxonomy. All possible $WPSim$ values are provided in Sect. 3.6 in Table 1.

3.5 Proposed Combined Similarity Measure

We developed an original hybrid approach to similarity measure calculation for assessment of misclassification of HS codes that combines the knowledge derived from the textual description and the taxonomy of HS codes. Cosine similarity ($CosSim$) of phrases (e.g. textual descriptions of goods) is calculated using Doc2Vec model as described above. Wu and Palmer semantic similarity measure ($WPSim$) is calculated on the basis of HS codes assigned to the products and HS code classification taxonomy. The combined similarity ($CombSim$) is calculated according to the following formula:

$$CombSim = CosSim \cdot WPSim \tag{3}$$

Semantic similarity takes into account the HS code taxonomy (classification) while text similarity is calculated as cosine similarity of sentences describing a product. High $CombSim$ values indicate that the given HS code matches better with the given product description than those that have lower $CombSim$ values. This also means that $CosSim$ values can be high but $CombSim$ values for the same product maybe not as $WPSim$ values of HS codes can be low.

3.6 HS Code Assessment Score

As a result of previous steps, we get for each predicted HS code its cosine similarity related to the given product description ($CosSim$), its semantic similarity related to the given HS code according to HS code taxonomy ($WPSim$) and its combined similarity ($CombSim$). In order to produce HS code assessment scores we proceed as follows:

1. Sort a list of predicted HS codes in descending order of values of $CombSim$ and return $WPSim$ of the HS code which $CombSim$ is the best.
2. Convert returned $WPSim$ to the score as shown in Table 1. These scores can be easily interpreted also by humans.
3. Return the score as HS code assessment score ($HSScore$).

This scoring process assumes that non-existing HS codes (according to the HS code nomenclature) are detected before this procedure and removed from the input to this process.

Table 1. Interpretation of HS code assessment scores.

$WPSim$	$HSScore$	Interpretation
0	0	Incorrect HS code; mismatching section
0.25	1	Incorrect HS code; matching section but mismatching chapter
0.5	2	Incorrect HS code; matching section and chapter but mismatching heading
0.75	3	Incorrect HS code; matching section, chapter and heading but mismatching subheading
1	4	Possibly correct HS code

4 Method Evaluation and Experimental Results

4.1 Data Sources and Data Preprocessing

As a data source we used Bill of Lading Summary 2017 (Bol2017) data set [1] published under CC BY-NC 4.0, which allows non-commercial use. The data set contains Bills of lading header information for incoming shipments regulated by U.S. Customs and Border Protection's Automated Manifest System [1]. The schema of the data set includes more than 20 different fields from what we are interested in the following two fields: Item Description and Harmonized Tariff Code. The latter is the code located in the Harmonized Tariff Schedule of the United States Annotated that describes the tariff number or Harmonized Tariff Schedule B that represents the commodity export [1]. The data set contains the HTS code (Harmonized Tariff Schedule), which is used in the US. However, we are interested in the HS code, which is used by the WCO. HS code can be constructed as first 6 digits (out of 8–10 digits) of HTS code.

For data pre-processing, the Bol2017 data set was downloaded from the public data set collection [1] at 25.10.19.

After that first steps of pre-processing were performed as follows:

1. Filtering out only those records, where HTS is not null and selecting required fields: Item Description, HTS.
2. Removing any non-alphabetic characters from an item description and removing all records, where an item description is empty.
3. Removing all records, where HS code is not numerical or less than 6 characters long or HS code chapter is out of bound.
4. Removing all records, such that the texts are the same, but HS codes are different, leaving only one such pair.

As a result of data pre-processing, we received approximately 1.2 million rows containing HS codes and descriptions of items. We used this data set for machine learning tasks.

4.2   Training Doc2Vec Model

Data Preparation for Training. We used Gensim library [4] and Python programming language in order to implement our method. For training the Doc2Vec model we performed some data preparation steps and transformed texts to tagged documents as follows:

1. Transforming text to set of words, removing all the following words from the set $W = $ "hs", "hscode", "hts", "htscode", "tel", "code", "pcs", "kg" and common words (stop words), such as articles, "for", "and", etc. The exact list can be found in [16] and all words with length 2 or less.
2. Tagging documents with a unique tag (for differentiating them). We use as a tag the index number of the document in the data set.
3. Adding non-unique tags to documents according to the Gensim library [4]. In our case, the HS code, which comes together with the product description, will be considered as the second tag.

The result of data preparation is a collection of tagged documents in the following form: (words = [``adapter'', ``laptop'', ``battery'', ``mouse'', ``docks''], tags = [``1035312'', ``847180'']). As we see from the example above, the unique tag for the document is 1035312 and non-unique tag is the HS code 847180.

For testing our models, we use train–test method that requires two data sets. We split a collection of tagged documents with proportion 90/10, where 90% of documents go as a training set and 10% as a testing set.

Model Initialization. The initial learning rate – alpha is chosen to be 0.025 for Doc2Vec PV-DBOW implementation employed by us. We do not allow the learning rate to drop as training progresses (so, minimal alpha is the same). We take into vocabulary all words: so, we do not ignore words with a total frequency lower than some value. For training we use PV-DBOW as training algorithm and the number of iterations (epochs) over the corpus is 10.

Doc2Vec is an unsupervised machine learning algorithm. Therefore, if only texts are used, then it is hard to estimate the correctness of the model. However, the manual inspection of the results is applicable.

4.3   Using Doc2Vec Model

Calculating Text Similarities of Descriptions of Goods. The Doc2Vec model allows to find the most similar documents to the original text. Suppose we choose an original text as "laptop computer" and try to find the texts that are similar to the original one. First of all, we need to pre-process the original text and transform it to the vector using pre-trained Doc2Vec model. Secondly, we can find the closest texts, by measuring cosine vector similarities between the original text vector and texts in the vocabulary. As a result, we have cosine similarities between the given original text and the most similar documents. For example, in Table 2 (columns one and three) top 8 most similar documents to the original text "laptop computer" are provided. This result makes it possible to do some manual inspection in order to see the meaningfulness of provided similarities.

HS Code Prediction. We can apply the previously described text similarity approach for HS code prediction. As was mentioned in Sect. 4.2 we have a set of tagged documents and one of the tags is a HS code. We try to find the most similar documents to the original text document, for example, "laptop computer", but now we also take into account tags. Results including top 8 most similar documents to the text "laptop computer" together with predicted HS codes (i.e. tags) are shown in Table 2. We see from the table that high text similarity is not always related to the same values or similar values of predicted HS codes (our first hypothesis does not always hold).

Table 2. Eight most similar documents to the original text document "laptop computer" and their tags.

$CosSim$	Predicted HS code	Textual description
0.886	847150	Desktop laptop
0.886	847130	Laptop
0.882	847130	Laptop desktop
0.88	691390	Laptop sleevewacthband
0.879	420212	Laptop bag laptop bag laptop
0.873	847130	Laptop
0.871	847330	Laptop stand
0.864	420222	Laptop bag

4.4   HS Code Recommendation Based on Text Similarity

Recommending Several HS Codes. We can use the results of the most similar text search to recommend HS codes. Depending on how many similar texts we return we can recommend different number of HS codes. For example, if we take the similar tagged texts from the previous example, we can recommend to original text, which is "laptop computer", the following codes: 847150, 847130, 691390, 420212, 847330, and 420222. In this experiment we returned 8 similar texts, but as a result, we have only 6 different codes because of repetitions.

It is important to estimate the quality of HS code recommendations. Table 3 presents experimental results of one of the possible ways to evaluate recommendations. First of all, we choose the number of returned similar texts N_{texts}. Secondly, for every document in a sample set (samples of size $S = 5000$ and $S = 10000$) we find a vector representation for that document, return the required number of similar texts and infer the HS codes with respect to tags. Thirdly, we check if the correct HS code (which comes with test set document) is in the set of recommended codes. Let's denote the percentage of occurrences of the true value HS code in predicted codes as O_S, where S is a sample size. Table 3 shows the results. For example, if we return only 8 similar documents, for the sample with size 5000, in the 80% of the cases the true value HS code will be in the set of predicted codes, for the entire test set, this value is 79.6%.

Table 3. Evaluation of HS code recommendations.

N_{texts}	O_{5000}	O_{10000}
7	79.5%	79.1%
8	80.2%	79.8%
10	81.6%	81.0%
20	85.3%	84.6%
50	88.9%	88.2%
100	90.9%	90.5%
200	92.8%	92.4%
500	94.8%	94.7%
1000	96.3%	96.0%

Recommending the Unique HS Code. Recommending only one HS code is a more complex task. We need two main components as follows: a list of similar texts with predicted HS codes returned by Doc2Vec model and the algorithm (method) for choosing only one of HS codes out of the set.

The first, the most obvious option for the algorithm is to use the mode function that returns the most frequently used value that will be the recommended code. However, if we have multimode the algorithm will return only one of them.

For mode function, weight of each occurrence is one. In contrast, we may evaluate each occurrence with some weight function. Therefore, we use weighted mode function, where the weights are cosine similarities of documents. This approach can help to minimize the number of multimode cases and also takes into account distances between texts.

For example, according to Table 2, the most frequent value of HS code is 847130. Using weighted mode function its weighted modal value is 2.641 (using mode function its frequency is 3). Table 4 shows the results of the experiment for the test samples with sizes 5000 and 35000. The same experiment fulfilled on the entire test set with $N_{texts} = 8$ gives accuracy 0.613 and F-score 0.609.

Table 4. Recommending the unique HS-code: accuracy and F-Score values.

N_{texts}	Accuracy $S = 5000$	F-Score $S = 5000$	Accuracy $S = 35000$	F-Score $S = 35000$
7	0.619	0.672	0.612	0.617
8	**0.622**	**0.675**	**0.613**	**0.618**
9	0.614	0.667	0.608	0.613
100	0.501	0.565	0.500	0.509

As our experiments on smaller sample sets have shown (see Tables 3 and 4) that adding more returned texts does not improve the results and the optimal value is 8 similar documents to be returned for HS code correctness assessment. This optimal value is taken into account in finding semantic similarity and combined similarity as well as in computing HS code assessment score. According to that, these calculations (see below) are based on top 8 similar documents returned by Doc2Vec model.

4.5   Computing Semantic and Combined Similarity

According to the HS code taxonomy in Fig. 1 and cosine similarities of texts, combined similarities for some original HS codes compared to predicted HS codes are calculated and results are provided in Table 5. For example, let C_1 be the original HS code 847130 and C_2 the predicted HS code 847150 in the HS code taxonomy (see Fig. 1). The calculation of their semantic similarity is performed according to the $WPSim$ formula (Eq. 1) as follows:

$$WPSim(C_1, C_2) = \frac{2 \cdot 3}{4 + 4} = 0.75 \tag{4}$$

The corresponding combined similarity is as follows:

$$CombSim(C_1, C_2) = 0.886 \cdot 0.75 = 0.665 \tag{5}$$

Cosine similarities have been presented in Table 2. In Table 5 we use the average value of cosine similarities in the case if more than one similar HS codes are predicted. We see that combined similarity compensates shortage of using only cosine similarity of textual descriptions to decide about the correctness of the corresponding HS code as it takes into account the HS code structure i.e. its position in HS code taxonomy. For example, in the case of original HS code 420212 for what the $WPSim = 1$, combined similarity measure assigns the highest score however the other predicted HS codes, except code 420222, with a higher level of cosine similarity of the text gets the value of zero as they belong to other sections then chapter 42 belongs to. The HS code 420222 is the next candidate for the suitable HS code.

4.6   Computing HS Code Assessment Score

Computing HS codes assessment scores is performed using the method described in Sect. 3.6. For example, according to this method (see also data provided in Tables 1 and 5) the assessment score for the original HS code 847130 is 4 (the highest score), for code 420212 it is 4, and for code 850440 it is 1.

Table 5. Similarity measures.

C_1	C_2	Textual descriptions for C_2	$CosSim$	$WPSim$	$CombSim$
847130	847150	desktop laptop	0.886	0.75	0.665
	847130	laptop/laptop desktop	0.88	1	0.880
	691390	laptop sleevewacthband	0.88	0	0
	420212	laptop bag	0.879	0	0
	847330	laptop stand	0.871	0.5	0.436
	420222	laptop bag	0.864	0	0
420212	847150	desktop laptop	0.886	0	0
	847130	laptop/laptop desktop	0.88	0	0
	691390	laptop sleevewacthband	0.88	0	0
	420212	laptop bag	0.879	1	0.879
	847330	laptop stand	0.871	0	0
	420222	laptop bag	0.864	0.75	0.648
850440	847150	desktop laptop	0.886	0.25	0.222
	847130	laptop/laptop desktop	0.88	0.25	0,220
	691390	laptop sleevewacthband	0.88	0	0
	420212	laptop bag	0.879	0	0
	847330	laptop stand	0.871	0.25	0.218
	420222	laptop bag	0.864	0	0

5 Conclusion

In order to solve an actual misclassification problem of goods automated systems need to be built and employed. In this paper, we have proposed a novel method for automated assessment of misclassification of goods for customs fraud detection based on the Doc2Vec model for predicting HS codes on the basis of text similarity of product descriptions. The original feature of the method is that for performing assessment we introduce a novel combined similarity measure based on cosine similarity of texts and semantic similarity of HS codes based on the HS code taxonomy. The method uses the structure of the HS code taxonomy as complementary knowledge to pure textual descriptions of products. This compensates insufficient knowledge obtained from short texts and makes assessment rates of HS codes more correct comparing to pure text based approaches.

The comparison with other similar methods with respect to performance needs to be separately investigated as entirely similar methods do not exist by now. Other methods do not perform machine learning on all chapters of the HS code nomenclature and therefore are partial solutions.

Acknowledgments. This research was partially supported by the Institutional Research Grant IUT33-13 of the Estonian Research Council.

References

1. Data Set of Bill of Lading Summary 2017. https://public.enigma.com/datasets/bill-of-lading-summary-2017/0293cd20-8580-4d30-b173-2ac27952b74b. Accessed 10 Feb 2020
2. Ding, L., Fan, Z., Chen, D.: Auto-categorization of HS code using background net approach. Procedia Comput. Sci. **60**, 1462–1471 (2015)
3. European Court of Auditors: Special report no. 19, import procedures (2017)
4. Gensim Python Library. https://radimrehurek.com/gensim/. Accessed 10 Feb 2020
5. Harmonized System Codes. https://tradecouncil.org/harmonized-system-codes/. Accessed 10 Feb 2020
6. 3CE HS Classification and Verification Solution. https://www.3ce.com/solutions/. Accessed 10 Feb 2020
7. HS Nomenclature 2017 Edition. http://www.wcoomd.org/en/topics/nomenclature/instrument-and-tools/hs-nomenclature-2017-edition/hs-nomenclature-2017-edition.aspx. Accessed 10 Feb 2020
8. Kappler, H.: Reversing the trend: low cost and low risk methods for assuring proper duty payments. World Cust. J. **5**, 109–122 (2011)
9. Le, Q., Mikolov, T.: Distributed representations of sentences and documents. In: Xing, E.P., Jebara, T. (eds.) Proceedings of the 31st International Conference on Machine Learning. Proceedings of Machine Learning Research, PMLR, vol. 32, no. 2, pp. 1188–1196, Beijng, China (June 2014)
10. Li, G., Li, N.: Customs classification for cross-border e-commerce based on text-image adaptive convolutional neural network. Electron. Commer. Res. **19**(4), 779–800 (2019)
11. Mikolov, T., Chen, K., Corrado, G., Dean, J.: Efficient estimation of word representations in vector space. In: Proceedings of Workshop at ICLR (January 2013)

12. Mikolov, T., Sutskever, I., Chen, K., Corrado, G.S., Dean, J.: Distributed representations of words and phrases and their compositionality. In: NIPS (2013)

13. Sanchez, D., Batet, M., Isern, D., Valls, A.: Ontology-based semantic similarity: a new feature-based approach. Expert Syst. Appl. **39**, 7718–7728 (2012)

14. Semantics3. Categorization API. https://www.semantics3.com/products/ai-apis# categorization-api. Accessed 10 Feb 2020

15. Shenoy, M., Shet, K.C., Acharya, U.D.: A new similarity measure for taxonomy based on edge counting. CoRR abs/1211.4709 arxiv:1211.4709 (2012)

16. Stone, B., Dennis, S., Kwantes, P.J.: Comparing methods for single paragraph similarity analysis. Top. Cogn. Sci. **3**(1), 92–122 (2011)

17. Turhan, B., Akar, G.B., Turhan, C., Yukse, C.: Visual and textual feature fusion for automatic customs tariff classification. In: 2015 IEEE International Conference on Information Reuse and Integration, pp. 76–81 (August 2015)

18. World Customs Organization (WCO): What is the harmonized system (HS)?. http://www.wcoomd.org/en/topics/nomenclature/overview/what-is-the-harmonized-system.aspx. Accessed 10 Feb 2020

19. Wu, Z., Palmer, M.: Verbs semantics and lexical selection. In: Proceedings of the 32nd Annual Meeting on Association for Computational Linguistics, ACL 1994, pp. 133–138. Association for Computational Linguistics, USA (1994)

20. Yang, K., Kim, W.J., Yang, J., Kim, Y.: Ontology matching for recommendation of HS code. In: HKICEAS-773 (December 2013)

Data and Knowledge Engineering

A Little Bird Told Me: Discovering KPIs from Twitter Data

Janis Zemnickis$^{(\boxtimes)}$, Laila Niedrite, and Natalija Kozmina

Faculty of Computing, University of Latvia, Raina Blvd. 19, Riga, Latvia
janiszemnickis@gmail.com,
{laila.niedrite,natalija.kozmina}@lu.lv

Abstract. The goal of our research and experiments is to find the definitions and values of *key performance indicators* (KPIs) in unstructured text. The direct access to opinions of customers served as a motivating factor for us to choose Twitter data for our experiments. For our case study, we have chosen the restaurant business domain. As in the other business domains, KPIs often serve as a solution for identification of current problems. Therefore, it is essential to learn which criteria are important to restaurant guests. The mission of our Proof-of-Concept KPI discovery tool presented in this paper is to facilitate the explorative analysis taking Twitter user posts as a data source. After processing tweets with Stanford CoreNLP toolkit, aggregated values are computed and presented as visual graphs. We see our tool as an instrument for data discovery applicable, for example, to define new qualitative and quantitative KPIs based on the values found in the graph. The graph represents a complete view of aggregated data that corresponds to the search results according to the user-defined keywords, and gives easy access to detailed data (tweets) that, in its turn, leads to better understanding of the post context and its emotional coloring.

Keywords: Key Performance Indicators · Unstructured data · Twitter · Case study

1 Introduction

Twitter [1] is a well-known microblogging platform founded in 2006 that has not lost its popularity until now. According to the recent statistics, the number of tweets per day in 2019 [2] has reached over 500 million daily posts making it a rich source of information on any kind of topics. The distinguishing trait of tweets is their length that for a long time could not exceed 140 characters but was extended to 240 tree years ago. For research community, Twitter is a valuable source of unstructured data (i.e. the data without a predefined data model and/or not fitting into relational tables). Unstructured data, due to its nature, requires more complex approaches and methods to handle free-form text, dates, and numbers (e.g. text mining, Natural Language Processing – NLP) as opposed to the structured data sources.

Authors [3] state: "Since social media posts are often non-anonymous and directly linked to a person, firm, or brand, the content produced on social media platforms can be

T. Robal et al. (Eds.): DB&IS 2020, CCIS 1243, pp. 161–175, 2020.
https://doi.org/10.1007/978-3-030-57672-1_13

interpreted as an indicator of people's attitude towards a product or service or an event". In fact, we share this point of view as the direct access to opinions of customers served as a motivating factor for us to choose Twitter as a data source for our experiments. The goal of our research and experiments is to find the definitions and values of *key performance indicators* (KPIs) in unstructured text. We present the tool that supports our experiments as well as examples that illustrate our ideas and findings.

For our case study, we have chosen the restaurant business domain. Running a restaurant business is a very challenging activity, which needs constant attention. It is highly important to identify the right targets that should be monitored periodically to stay on the market, beat the competitors, and maintain or improve the quality of the service provided to the customers. As in the other business domains, KPIs are often a solution for identification of current problems. Therefore, it becomes essential to learn which criteria are important to restaurant guests.

When companies take a decision to define and apply the appropriate performance measures, they should continue doing it systematically using some of the known frameworks. According to [4], companies may use wrong measures or misunderstand definitions including those of the KPIs and other main concepts for measuring and evaluating performance. Many of the published research papers clarify and systematize the terminology used in this field [5, 6]. We have based our experiments on the KPI features defined in these studies.

The rest of the paper is organized as follows. Section 2 describes concepts of the performance measurement. Section 3 introduces the KPIs in the restaurant domain. Section 4 discusses the related work. Section 5 explains in detail and illustrates with running examples the tool for KPI discovery from Twitter data. Section 6 presents the conclusions and future work.

2   Performance Measurement Concepts

2.1   Main Concepts

Before starting a discussion about performance measurement and selection of the appropriate measurement indicators, let's define the main concepts. We'd like to recall different definitions of success factors and performance measures presented in [4]. *Success factors* (SF) are aspects of organizational performance characterizing companies' success in a given industry. *Performance measures* are used to measure the performance in an organization. Performance measures are classified as *result indicators* (RI) or *performance indicators* (PI). The name "Key" in combination with all of these indicator types refers to the most important ones of these lists, e.g. *Critical success factors* (CSFs) are the most important ones of the SF list.

In this paper, we will employ the concept of Key Performance Indicators (KPIs) and will not distinguish between SF, PI, and RI. As stated in [4], we will use the following interpretation of the KPIs: "KPIs tell you what to do to increase performance dramatically". KPIs focus on the most critical aspects of performance for the current and future success of the organization.

2.2 Main Features of the KPIs

Having an intension to extract KPI expressions and their evaluations from unstructured text, we continued the further investigation of different theoretical aspects of KPIs to understand better the feasibility of our approach and to explore the features of KPIs, which could have been helpful to fulfil our idea.

The research process was mainly based on two studies: our earlier work, in which we examined the KPI properties to formalize data warehouse information requirements [5] as well as on the taxonomy presented in the review article [6]. We paid particular attention to those KPI features in both studies that directly or indirectly could help us identify KPIs in the text. In [6] KPI properties are observed from five different perspectives. For our study dedicated to discovery of KPIs, we selected some useful features mainly from two of the five perspectives. Let's have a closer look at the selected KPI properties.

The 1st perspective clarifies what is measured by a KPI by identifying features as *Performance measurement perspectives* and *Scope*. The most well-known measurement framework is Balanced Scorecards [7]. It has four measurement perspectives: Financial, Customer, Internal Process, and Learning and Growth. We are interested mostly in Customer perspective. The *Scope* aspect of KPIs can vary a lot. In our study, the Scope aspect is "restaurant business".

The 2nd perspective clarifies the features considered in the specification of KPIs, and among others also the Calculation features. Calculation features are important for correct acquisition of KPI values. For example, *Hardness* depends on the KPI nature, e.g. objective KPIs are directly measurable, but subjective KPIs are not. *Calculation rule* defines a formula, but *Value type* specifies the data type of KPI values and the unit of measure. *Filter* expresses the conditions for KPI calculations, e.g. time period. *Frequency* means the period of calculations. *Target* relates the KPI with a target value. *Source* of a KPI links it with data necessary to compute a KPI.

In our previous work [5], we analyzed KPI features based mainly on [4, 8]. Some of these features correspond to the perspectives defined in [6], while others describe additional KPI properties such as *Time, Activities*, and *Reporting aspect*.

3 KPIs for Restaurant Evaluation

In this section, we discuss the KPIs in the restaurant domain and synthesize the potential KPIs, the values of which can be found in Twitter data. As suggested in [9], the most important KPIs in restaurant domain can be grouped into 6 macro-categories:

- Revenue (measured in local currency, e.g. revenue per table),
- Occupancy (expressed in percentage or as a number, e.g. cancelled reservations),
- Customer feedback (expressed in percentage, e.g. positive feedback from guests),
- Service (expressed in percentage or as a number, e.g. unavailability of menu items),
- Quality compliance (expressed in percentage, e.g. product quality uniformity),
- Cost management (expressed in percentage, e.g. food loss, beverage loss).

The study [10] is an explorative analysis dedicated to examination of the criteria that not only attract customers and helps them make a choice in favor of a particular restaurant, but also retain existing customers. The dataset for the analysis of restaurant selection criteria, which was collected in terms of the BIGresearch's CIA (Consumer Intentions and Actions) survey, includes opinions gathered from 8,127 customers from different socio-economic groups.

Table 1. Restaurant selection criteria and KPI examples

Criteria	KPI example from customer feedback	Type	Hardness	TW
Advertising	Number of clicks on the restaurant advertisement	QT	Hard	No
	Source of information of the restaurant advertisement	QL	Soft	No
Cleanliness	The level of cleanliness of the table/floor/bathroom	QL	Soft	Yes
	Frequency of cleaning sessions	QT	Hard	No
Fast service	Speed of service in minutes during restaurant peak activity hours	QT	Hard	Yes
	Waiting time in minutes before being seated	QT	Hard	Yes
	Table Turnover Rate: (Number of guests served in a restaurant)/(Total number of tables)	QT	Hard	No
	Time per Table Turn: (Time when the table cashes out)—(Time when an order is first inputted)	QT	Hard	No
Healthy menu option	Availability of the gluten-free/vegetarian menu	QL	Soft	Yes
	The number of menu items for each category	QT	Hard	Yes
Kids friendly	Availability of kid dining chair/playground zone/kid menu	QL	Soft	Yes
Location	Distance in meters/km from the public transport hubs/city center	QT	Hard	Yes
Menu selection	Number of items in the menu	QT	Hard	Yes
	Availability of the gluten-free/vegetarian menu	QL	Soft	Yes
Open late	Availability of taking late lunch/dinner	QL	Soft	Yes
Portion size	The level of customer satisfaction by the portion size of each meal	QL	Soft	Yes

(continued)

Table 1. (*continued*)

Criteria	KPI example from customer feedback	Type	Hardness	TW
Competitor meal prices	Prices of the same menu items are equal or lower to those of the competitor restaurants	QT	Hard	Yes
Quality of food	The level of freshness/intensity of food taste	QL	Soft	Yes
Value menu	The frequency of orders of the least expensive menu items	QT	Hard	No
Trustworthy establishment	Average review score of the restaurant (e.g. on TripAdvisor)	QT	Hard	Yes
Friendly service	The level of customer satisfaction by restaurant staff	QL	Soft	Yes
	The number of customer claims/complaints expressed by customers	QT	Hard	Yes
Reservations taken	Availability of making a reservation in advance	QL	Soft	Yes
	Number of reservations made on Fridays/Saturdays/Sundays	QT	Hard	No
	Number of cancelled reservations/reserved tables	QT	Hard	No
Special offer/discounts	Availability of special offers/discounts during working days/weekends	QL	Soft	Yes
	Number of meals ordered qualified as a special offer/discount	QT	Hard	No

We would like to concentrate our attention on the findings of this study regarding the motivation of restaurant customers to dine in a particular restaurant most often. The answers included such criteria as "advertising", "cleanliness", "fast service", "healthy menu option", "kid friendly", "location", "menu selection", "open late", "portion size", "price", "quality of food", "value menu", and "trustworthy establishment", "friendly service", "friendly wait staff", "reservations taken", "special offer/discounts" [10].

Our case study is focused around gathering and processing data that come straight from the potential or actual restaurant customers. We have expanded the restaurant selection criteria mentioned in [10] into qualitative and quantitative KPIs represented in Table 1. The column "Type" indicates the KPI nature – quantitative (QT) if it can be expressed and a number, and qualitative (QL) in case if it cannot. The column "Hardness" is an already mentioned KPI feature from [6] that indicates if the KPI is directly measurable (Hard) or not (Soft). The column "TW" indicates the potential derivability of the KPI values from Twitter posts of the restaurant customers (Yes/No).

As demonstrated in Table 1, not all KPIs can be calculated from user feedback. For instance, some quantitative indicators (e.g. Number of reservations made on Fridays/Saturdays/Sundays) are internal statistical data available to restaurant management, but not traceable by restaurant customers.

4 Related Work

We can classify the papers related to our study in two groups. The first group contains works on customer review analysis in the area of tourism and restaurant business. A wide range of text analysis methods is applied to discover practical findings for business including customer opinions that can be interpreted as indicators for business evaluation; however, these studies do not directly mention the notion of KPI. We summarize some of the recent typical research studies from the first group below.

In [11] TripAdvisor serves as a data source containing data on restaurant guest reviews. Authors apply text mining techniques for review processing. After data pre-processing with text tokenization, stemming, and Part-of-Speech (POS) tagging methods, the popularity of each noun is measured. Authors performed: 1) an exploratory data analysis to compare the popularity of restaurant cuisine between different user groups, and 2) an analysis to discover dish or meal preferences, restaurant feature preferences (e.g. service quality), and sentiments (employing SentiStrength).

The authors [12] present a tool for opinion mining and sentiment analysis, which supports review analysis from TripAdvisor focusing on the restaurant sector. It performs many textual data processing steps including text parsing, review tokenization in sentences, etc. Authors consider user ratings as a source for text evaluation (i.e. positive/negative). Sentiment analysis is performed using word lexicons, emoticons from reviews and emoticon corpus. Therefore, the final evaluation combines the sentiment analysis based on review text and direct feedback from people.

The second group of related studies covers the extraction or calculation of KPIs from textual data in different business fields.

The study [13] presents a tool for automatic extraction of KPIs from financial reports that are publicly available. The tool allows monitoring of companies' websites and downloading of the financial reports. After processing the report text, convolutional neural networks are used to determine the KPIs and collect their values into a database for further graphical representation. Comparing this approach with the extraction of meaningful information from social networks, this research exploits the structure of reports and it is worth to notice that financial reports by definition contain KPIs and their values. Nevertheless, these KPIs cover only one perspective of the KPI analysis.

The study on Cultural Heritage (CH) [3] proposes a synergy between a data-driven approach integrated with an ontology. First, the semantic analysis of textual data from Twitter posts published from four Italian cities and marked with a hashtag #cultural-heritage was performed. Then, terms and concepts from tweets were linked to some of the pre-defined CH-related categories (e.g. art, sculptor, museum), and distributions of CH-related terms calculated. Finally, the authors [3] took advantage of the tweet location and timestamp to establish the correlation between particular cultural events, their duration period, and the level of cultural sensitivity of tweets from the nearby areas. The main goal was to help BI services measure the responsiveness of social network users to a specific subject such as cultural heritage represented with geographical and temporal dimensions by means of defining some useful metrics (i.e. KPIs). Given the settings similar to those of our study (i.e. Twitter as a data source, NLP methods for text analysis), the key difference is that in [3] KPIs were defined beforehand, while we present a tool to leverage the process of KPI discovery.

While there is a vast variety of tools and approaches for analyzing social media, only some of them take advantage of NLP methods. For instance, studies collected in [14] provide an overview of existing NLP application opportunities for social media analysis, though the evaluation of experimentation results is missing. In [15] techniques for analyzing Twitter data with NLP tools are discussed, results of their application are compared, but it is not explained how this data could be used for analytical purposes to improve a company's performance. In [16] medical industry-specific tools (e.g. cTakes, MetaMap) are employed to analyze medical records. However, it remains unclear how these tools would perform in other industries.

5   The Tool for KPI Discovery from Twitter Data

In this section, we explain in detail and illustrate with running examples the working principles of the tool developed in terms of this study for discovery of potential restaurant KPIs derivable from customer feedback in Twitter.

5.1   Natural Language Processing (NLP) with Stanford CoreNLP Toolkit

Stanford CoreNLP Toolkit [17] provides most of the common core natural language processing (NLP) steps from tokenization to coreference resolution. The toolkit is developed in Java, it's easy to use and to integrate even in PHP projects. Stanford CoreNLP Toolkit supports text processing in various natural languages. The default language is English, which we are using in this study. We implemented Stanford CoreNLP Toolking by calling .jar files from PHP.

We exploited the Enhanced English Universal Dependencies parser [18] in our study. Stanford dependencies provide a representation of grammatical relations between words in a sentence [19]. For example, for a sentence "Waited 30 min no service", Stanford CoreNLP online tool [20] would produce dependencies as depicted in Fig. 1. We can note that the output of the Stanford CoreNLP Toolkit [14] is twofold: 1) the POS type for each word of the sentence, e.g. type "NNS" for the word "minutes", and 2) dependencies between words, e.g. the word "minutes" is related to the word "waited" with relationship type "dobj".

The POS tagging and their types are described in [21]. POS types in Fig. 1 mean: *NNS* – Noun (plural), *VBD* – Verb (past tense), *NN* – Noun (singular or mass), *DT* – Determiner, *CD* – Cardinal number. In [22], word dependency types are presented in detail. The dependencies in Fig. 1 mean: *nummod* – a numeric modifier of a noun, i.e. any number phrase that serves to modify the meaning of the noun with a quantity, *dobj*

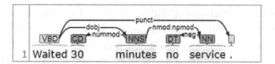

Fig. 1. Enhanced++ Dependencies example.

– the direct object of a VBD, e.g. the noun phrase which is the (accusative) object of the verb, and *neg* – the negation modifier, e.g. the relation between a negation word and the word that it modifies.

5.2 Technological Aspects of the KPI Discovery Tool

Our Proof-of-Concept tool for KPI discovery has been developed using web technologies. In this case, it has been a personal preference of the main tool developer, because of the high level of expertise and professional experience in these technologies. Currently, the functionality of the tool is developed using PHP 7.3.1 programming language and CodeIgniter 3.1.11 MVC framework. The data are stored in MariaDB 10.1.37. Client-side functionality is developed with jQuery v3.4.1, CSS, HTML, Bootstrap library v4.3.1. The graph is implemented with the D3.js v5.15.0 library and the example of "Language Network" [23]. Natural language text processing is performed with Stanford CoreNLP (stanford-parser-3.9.2).

5.3 Architectural Solution of the KPI Discovery Tool

We have chosen Twitter – one of the richest sources of real user feedbacks – as an open-access data source for our study. All principal components and data transformations in KPI discovery tool are depicted in Fig. 2.

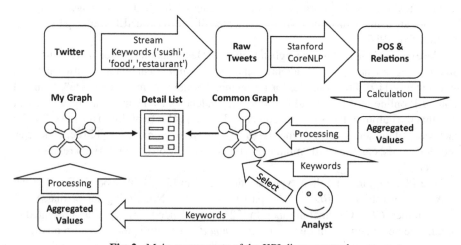

Fig. 2. Main components of the KPI discovery tool.

The Twitter data were fetched using an online stream [24] loading the data that contained such keywords as "restaurant", "food", or "sushi" (see "Twitter" and "Stream"), because the informational scope of the study is related to catering and restaurant business. The data from Twitter data stream was fed into the database tables without pre-processing resulting in 129046 tweets published from December 19, 2019 to January 14, 2020. We saved the following tweet data: tweet_id (tweet surrogate key in Twitter), user_id (user surrogate key in Twitter), text (tweet text), created_at (tweet creation timestamp), and name (name of the user who tweeted).

The next step was text processing with Stanford CoreNLP library (see "Stanford NLP"), where POS relations were being determined. After applying NLP techniques, we obtained 2 127 989 words. Each word in the tweet was assigned: its type [21], other words it was associated to, and the relationship type between these words. We have chosen to calculate aggregated values from raw relationship data to significantly improve performance and complexity of the graph generation. We calculated aggregated values (see "Calculation") for:

- The total number of occurrences of the word in various tweets and its type, e.g. "waiter NN 269";
- The number of occurrences of: 1) the word and its type, 2) the associated word and its type, and 3) relation of the two words (e.g. "waiter NN" and "bringing VBG 45 ACT" means that the total number of occurrences of the word "waiter" with type NN, the word "bringing" with type VBG, and relationship with type ACT is 45).

The KPI discovery tool user can take advantage of the aggregated values to build a graph. First, the user has to choose certain keywords based on the information of interest. For example, one may be interested in what people think about "spaghetti". The tool shows that there is a relationship in tweets between the word "spaghetti" of type NNS and the word "real" JJ. Nodes of the graph represent the words in user tweets and their POS types, while edges of the graph reflect the relationships between these words. The user can explore a word in detail, i.e. see all tweets containing that particular word with the corresponding POS type. The user can access the detailed view by clicking on one of the nodes. For example, one of the original tweets containing this relationship is: "Give me the real spaghetti please cause I eat that dog food over there".

Figure 3a demonstrates tweets that include the word "long". The user can add or remove this word from "My graph" (Fig. 2) by clicking on the "Add to graph" button or by clicking on the "Remove from graph" button respectively. "My graph" is visually the same as the "Common graph", but it displays only the user-selected elements, for instance, to observe the relationships in a particular element subset. A user can perform the same operations (i.e. add to/remove from "My Graph" and view details, see Fig. 3b) with the word relationships. For example, if the words "wait" and "hour" were added to "My Graph" already containing the word "long", the resulting graph would consist of 3 elements, where the nodes "wait" and "hour" would have been connected.

Unprocessed tweets are stored in the *tweets* table of the tool's database, while their relationships are stored in *relations* table after Standford CoreNLP processing. The *entity_clc* table stores the number of word occurrences and their POS types. The *rel_clc* table stores the number of word relationships and their types. The *exclusions* table stores

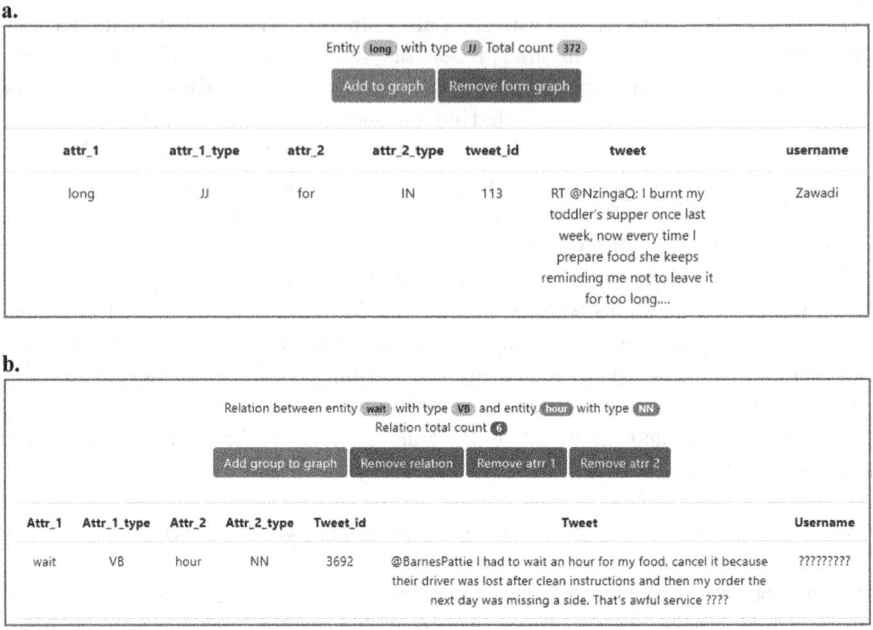

a.

			Entity `long` with type `JJ` Total count `372`				
			Add to graph Remove form graph				
attr_1	attr_1_type	attr_2	attr_2_type	tweet_id	tweet		username
long	JJ	for	IN	113	RT @NzingaQ: I burnt my toddler's supper once last week, now every time I prepare food she keeps reminding me not to leave it for too long....		Zawadi

b.

			Relation between entity `wait` with type `VB` and entity `hour` with type `NN`			
			Relation total count `6`			
			Add group to graph Remove relation Remove atrr 1 Remove atrr 2			
Attr_1	Attr_1_type	Attr_2	Attr_2_type	Tweet_id	Tweet	Username
wait	VB	hour	NN	3692	@BarnesPattie I had to wait an hour for my food, cancel it because their driver was lost after clean instructions and then my order the next day was missing a side. That's awful service ????	?????????

Fig. 3. Details of the tweet containing (a) the word "long", (b) the relation between the words "wait" and "hour".

words that are not included in the graph. The *users* table stores the registered users of the tool, whereas the *c_rel* and *c_entity* tables store the user-selected words and their relationships displayed in "My graph".

5.4 Case-Study Examples: Quantitative and Qualitative KPIs

In this section, we will consider two different KPI examples (KPI1 and KPI2).

KPI1: Quantitative/Hard KPI "Waiting time for a meal to be served should be less than N minutes". Though the KPI to evaluate such criteria as Fast service [10] can be precisely defined, it is not clear to the restaurant management, which KPI values would be optimal. Serving food quickly during peak hours could require a major investment such as hiring additional staff, who would have a lower workload during the rest of their working hours, or obtaining new equipment. The tool offers the ability to explore Twitter user feedback that could provide meaningful KPI values. Let us have a look at how one can discover values of the KPI1.

First, the user of the tool should choose to create a new graph by filling in the form in Fig. 4 (bottom-left) and stating the number of elements to display in the graph to adjust visibility ("Element count in graph"). The "Keyword" parameter is the most important one, because the graph will be generated based on its value. Theoretically, a graph may be composed of the unlimited number of keywords. In our example, the words in the graph are associated with the word "minutes". Since the dataset consists only of pre-filtered data on restaurant, food, and sushi, there is no need to add more keywords. The

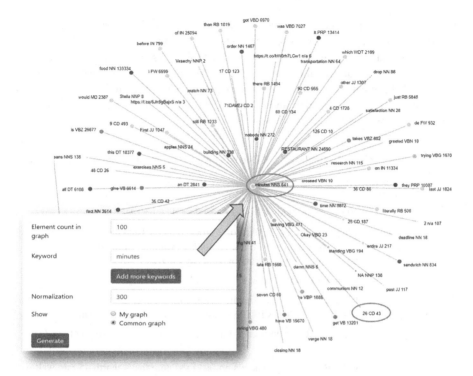

Fig. 4. Parameters for graph generation (bottom-left) and a resulting graph example (center) based on the keyword "minutes".

"Normalization" parameter served to improve visibility by regulating the maximum size of graph nodes. The "Show" parameter value indicates the type of the graph where to search for the keywords – "My graph" (user-defined) or "Common graph" (generic).The result of clicking "Generate" is the graph shown in Fig. 4 (center). In the graph, we can see that the keyword "minutes" is related to a set of other words in tweets. In this case, we are interested in numeric values, because the goal is to set a quantitative KPI value as, for instance, the relationship between "minutes" with type "NNS" (noun, plural) and the word "26" with type "CD" (cardinal number).

Attr_1	Attr_1_type	Attr_2	Attr_2_type	Tweet_id	Tweet	Username
minutes	NNS	26	CD	91631	ordered my food 26 minutes ago and still waiting. @tacobell staff needs to get their shit together.????	bre

Fig. 5. Details of the tweet containing the relation between the words "minutes" and "26".

When a user clicks on a relationship, the detailed list (see its fragment in Fig. 5) allows observing all the associated elements and reading the original tweets where the selected words are used. The number "26" refers to the time expressed in minutes that a restaurant guest has spent waiting for a meal. The customer is not satisfied with this fact. An analyst could conclude that waiting time longer than 26 min can cause negative emotions and the restaurant must pay more attention to the speed of service.

We collected several customer impressions in Table 2. As expected, the feedback was negative, when the waiting time was longer than 30 min, while customers gave positive feedback if the meal was served within 4 or 5 min. Thus, the analyst may deduce a potentially satisfying KPI value and set the KPI1 to *"Waiting time for a meal to be served should be less than 25 min"*.

Table 2. Examples of details containing the keyword *"minutes"*

Related attr. value	Tweet
30	30 min for a sandwich At a FAST FOOD RESTAURANT
30	Wings to go took 30 min for 2 orders of wings and a kids quesadilla just took forget our sides. It takes a lot for me to get irritated with a food establishment but I'm annoyed to say the least
30	Waited 30 min for food I've lost full…
36	It's been 36 min and I finally got my https://t.co/vnWU2ilDM7 PHONE IS ON 15 PERCENT. @PopeyesChicken thanks and no thanks?
35	@PopeyesChicken been waiting 35 min for my food. So much for fast food. Disappointing
45	RT @BostonJerry: There's no fast food item that's worth 45 min waiting in line
4	RT @DailyGuineaLips: It has been a whole 4 min since my face has been greeted with food… TOO LONG. Pic sent by @LeonardREW
5	Gluten-Free Vegan No-Cook Raw Cranberry Sauce…made with only 6 clean, real food ingredients and is ready in 5 min!

KPI2: Qualitative/Soft KPI "The level of customer satisfaction by restaurant staff". The KPI2 is an example of evaluation of the Friendly staff [10] criteria, which in this case is expressed by a qualitative (non-numeric) value.

To learn the potential characteristics of the restaurant staff, we can explore user feedback by creating a new graph setting the "Keyword" parameter equal to "staff". All other parameters are set in the same way as in the previous KPI example – see the form in Fig. 4. In the resulting graph in Fig. 6, we can observe that the words associated to "staff" are such as "great", "friendly", "poor", "rude", etc. We can inspect each of these relationships in the same way as demonstrated in the KPI1 example (see Fig. 5) by clicking on the edge of the graph (see some tweet details gathered in Table 3).

An analyst can conclude that Twitter users often discuss restaurant staff, which means that they pay close attention to the attitude of the staff towards guests. Restaurant staff characteristics discovered in tweets can indicate the low level of customer satisfaction when classified as "poor" or "rude", and high level – when classified as "great", "friendly", or "helpful". Hence, the analyst may set the KPI2 to *"The level of customer*

Fig. 6. A graph example based on the keyword "staff".

Table 3. Examples of details containing the keyword "*staff*"

Related attr. value	Tweet
friendly	Great little spot, friendly staff with delicious food and decent coffee, bit out of the way, but worth it
friendly	Great Food!!! Large portions Friendly staff
great	RT @johnbrewer168: @KitchenClonc @bigmoosecoffee for me, great staff, coffee and food always
great	Great party, great food, great people, great Chef, great staff, great Addo. Looking forward for a wonderful year of new experiences at Addo
poor	The food was really good, but the poor staff is way over worked. Those awesome waitresses need at least one more on deck
rude	@busabaeathai Westfield horrible food, extremely rude staff "Laura", use to be an amazing place to eat not anymore sadly.. shocked at the quality of food being served
friendly helpful	Jackson's have amazing food served by really helpful and friendly staff

satisfaction by restaurant staff should be high", which would imply that the restaurant staff should act friendly and be kind to the guests.

6   Conclusions and Future Work

The mission of our Proof-of-Concept KPI discovery tool presented in this paper is to facilitate the explorative analysis taking Twitter user posts as a data source. We see it as an instrument for data discovery applicable, for instance, to define new qualitative and quantitative KPIs based the values found in the graph as demonstrated in our case study. The graph represents a complete view of aggregated data that corresponds to the search results according to the user-defined keywords, and gives easy access to detailed data (tweets) that, in its turn, leads to better understanding of the post context and its emotional coloring. The most relevant elements of the graph can be stored in a separate graph that an analyst can consult later.

We would like to work on improving multiple aspects of the KPI discovery tool. One of the most significant improvements should be its integration with Big data technologies, which would allow processing significantly larger data volumes and applying more powerful algorithms for graph generation. Currently, we store only a few attributes from Twitter, since the tool is a prototype. However, we have noticed that it could be useful to collect other attributes too, for instance, geolocation data, which could provide new analysis perspectives such as searching and processing tweets from a certain country, city, or district. It might also be useful to implement tweet sentimental analysis to keep track of how many positive or negative tweets are associated with a particular word. We assume that it is possible to generate business intelligence requirements in an (semi-)automated way using the processed data.

References

1. Twitter Homepage. www.twitter.com. Accessed 27 Feb 2020
2. The Number of Tweets per Day in 2019. https://www.dsayce.com/social-media/tweets-day/. Accessed 27 Feb 2020
3. Chianese, A., Marulli, F., Piccialli, F.: Cultural heritage and social pulse: a semantic approach for CH sensitivity discovery in social media data. In: 2016 IEEE 10th International Conference on Semantic Computing (ICSC), Laguna Hills, CA, pp. 459–464 (2016)
4. Parmenter, D.: Key Performance Indicators: Developing, Implementing, and Using Winning KPIs. Wiley, New York, NY, USA (2007)
5. Niedritis, A., Niedrite, L., Kozmina, N.: Performance measurement framework with formal indicator definitions. In: Grabis, J., Kirikova, M. (eds.) BIR 2011. LNBIP, vol. 90, pp. 44–58. Springer, Heidelberg (2011). https://doi.org/10.1007/978-3-642-24511-4_4
6. Domínguez, E., et al.: A taxonomy for key performance indicators management. Comput. Stand. Interfaces **64**, 24–40 (2019)
7. Kaplan, R.S., Norton, D.P.: The Balanced Scorecard: Measures that Drive Performance. Harvard Business School Publishing, Cambridge (2005)
8. Muehlen, M.: Process-driven management informations systems – combining data warehouses and workflow technology. In: ICECR-4, pp. 550–566 (2001)
9. Measure It to Manage It – 25 Most Important Key Performance Indicators for All Restaurant Businesses. https://www.poshighway.com/blog/25-most-important-KPIs-metrics-for-restaurant-businesses. Accessed 27 Feb 2020
10. Kim, S., Chung, J.-E.: Restaurant Selection Criteria: Understanding the Roles of Restaurant Type and Customers' Sociodemographic Characteristics, Poster presented at Graduate Student Research Conference in Hospitality and Tourism. [Peer Reviewed] (2011)

11. Vu, H.Q., et al.: Exploring tourist dining preferences based on restaurant reviews. J. Travel Res. **58**(1), 149–167 (2019)
12. Agüero-Torales, M.M., et al.: A cloud-based tool for sentiment analysis in reviews about restaurants on TripAdvisor. Procedia Comput. Sci. **162**, 392–399 (2019)
13. Brito, E., et al.: A hybrid AI tool to extract key performance indicators from financial reports for benchmarking. In: Proceedings of the ACM Symposium on Document Engineering 2019, pp. 1–4 (2019)
14. Farzindar, A., Inkpen, D.: Natural language processing for social media. Synth. Lect. Hum. Lang. Technol. **8**(2), 1–166 (2015)
15. Pinto, A., Gonçalo Oliveira, H., Alves, A.: Comparing the performance of different NLP toolkits in formal and social media text. In: 5th Symposium on Languages, Applications and Technologies, SLATE'16, pp. 3:1–3:16 (2016)
16. Denecke K.: Extracting medical concepts from medical social media with clinical NLP tools: a qualitative study. In: Proceedings of the 4th Workshop on Building and Evaluation Resources for Health and Biomedical Text Processing (2014)
17. Manning, C.D., et al.: The stanford CoreNLP natural language processing toolkit. In: Proceedings of 52nd Annual Meeting of the Association for Computational Linguistics: System Demonstrations, pp. 55–60 (2014)
18. Schuster, S., Manning, C.D.: Enhanced English universal dependencies: an improved representation for natural language understanding tasks. In: LREC'16, pp. 2371–2378 (2016)
19. Stanford Dependencies. https://nlp.stanford.edu/software/stanford-dependencies.shtml. Accessed 27 Feb 2020
20. Stanford CoreNLP Online Tool. https://corenlp.run/. Accessed 27 Feb 2020
21. Toutanova, K., et al.: Feature-rich part-of-speech tagging with a cyclic dependency network. In: Proceedings of the 2003 conference of the North American chapter of the Association for Computational Linguistics on Human Language Technology, vol. 1. Association for Computational Linguistics, pp. 173–180 (2003)
22. De Marneffe, M.-C., Manning, C.D.: Stanford typed dependencies manual. Technical report, Stanford University (2008)
23. Language Network. http://www.cotrino.com/2012/11/language-network/. Accessed 27 Feb 2020
24. Consuming streaming data. https://developer.twitter.com/en/docs/tutorials/consuming-streaming-data. Accessed 27 Feb 2020

Automating Detection of Occurrences of PostgreSQL Database Design Problems

Erki Eessaar$^{(\boxtimes)}$ (iD)

Department of Software Science, Tallinn University of Technology, Tallinn, Estonia
erki.eessaar@taltech.ee

Abstract. SQL is a very resilient and widely used software language. In case of building a SQL database, one has to design schemas of the database so that the database management system (DBMS) can enforce these. The result of designing a database schema is a technical artifact, which may have technical debt. The debt makes it more difficult to understand, maintain, extend, and reuse the artifact. Smells are the signs of technical debt. Many database design smells manifest the same problems as code smells. It could also be that a database schema makes incorrect statements about the domain of the database or lacks necessary elements, i.e., is incomplete. Thus, database schemas can have numerous problems and finding these is a prerequisite of improving the schemas. The paper introduces a catalog of open-source SQL queries that have been designed for finding the occurrences of design problems in PostgreSQL databases (https://github.com/erk i77/database-design-queries). Most of the queries help us to detect the occurrences of database design smells. The queries are for a specific although popular DBMS. However, most of the problems that occurrences these help us to find can appear in any SQL database, regardless of the used DBMS.

Keywords: SQL · Database design · Technical debt · Design smell · Automated quality assessment

1 Introduction

A good database design and following standards/practices are important prerequisites of well-maintainable SQL database-driven software [1]. Like in case of any artificial artifacts, database designs can have problems with different scope and level of severity. The presence of these could be an explicit choice of developers or unintentional by-product of hurrying or lack of knowledge. Some of the problems will be fixed right away but others would linger in the database for a long time. The latter problems will constitute technical debt and like any debt, it usually has to be paid back with interest. In case of database design, paying interest means more difficulties in understanding, learning, using, extending, and maintaining the database and software that uses it. Many of these problems can be characterized as smells – quality-impacting issues, which may indicate deeper problems and that are caused by poor solutions to recurring problems or violations of best practices [2]. Developers need tools to quickly detect the problems.

© Springer Nature Switzerland AG 2020
T. Robal et al. (Eds.): DB&IS 2020, CCIS 1243, pp. 176–189, 2020.
https://doi.org/10.1007/978-3-030-57672-1_14

This is, for instance, a conclusion of a survey that investigated developers' opinion about code smells [3]. Tool support is a prerequisite of fixing the problems early. In case of smells the fixing process is called refactoring and it helps us to reduce the level of technical debt in the database.

In this paper, we present a set of PostgreSQL system catalog-based queries for getting an overview of the state of the database design or finding the occurrences of specific problems in it. All the queries have been published and the code is open-source.

Section 2 introduces some related work. Section 3 presents an example that illustrates a number of SQL database design problems. Section 4 introduces the catalog through its metadata and statistical values that describe the current state of the catalog. Section 5 explains the creation method of the queries as well as points to the strengths and weaknesses of our approach. Finally, we conclude and point to further work.

2   Related Works

There is an extensive body of knowledge about technical debt and smells in software systems in general [2, 4]. However, the corresponding research about a subdomain of software – databases – is not so extensive. For instance, Sharma and Spinellis [2] give a literature-based summary of research about software smells (445 primary studies) but in the context of database smells refer only to the book of Karwin [5]. Fernandes et al. [6] compare 29 tools for detecting bad smells in software but none of these is about detecting database design smells. At the same time, real databases have design problems as it is reported, for instance, in [7]. For example, Blaha [7] claims, based on the refactoring of a set of real-world databases, that about 75% of developers enforced primary keys (meaning 25% did not) and about 80% of databases were consistent in the use of data types (meaning 20% were not). Blaha [7] writes that only 10% of the investigated databases declared foreign keys. His findings are supported by Weber et al. [8], who propose using the lack of declared foreign key constraints as a basis to measure the level of technical debt in SQL databases. In the case study they consider OSCAR Electronic Medical Record system and notice the relative absence of foreign key constraints. Ambler [9] presents a catalog of database refactorings, i.e., actions. There can be more than one reason to carry out any such action. For instance, the reason to drop a column check constraint can be that it does not correspond to the rules of the database domain, it duplicates another constraint that is associated with the table (possibly though the SQL domain of the column), the constraint has multiple tasks and should be decomposed into smaller constraints according to the single-responsibility principle, or the constraint's Boolean expression has either a mistake or can be simplified.

We have written before about searching the occurrences of SQL database design problems by using queries based on the database system catalog [10, 11]. In [10], we presented 14 queries to search the occurrences of eleven database design antipatterns (presented in [5]) from PostgreSQL databases. In [11], we listed some additional questions about SQL database design that could be answered based on the database system catalog. The set of queries offered together with this paper allows us to get answers to all the questions and to many more. Thus, the current paper presents the results of the continuation of the research. Khumnin and Senivongse [12] present the most similar approach to ours. They implement SQL queries for detecting in MS SQL Server databases the occurrences of five database design antipatterns from [5]. They use improved heuristics compared to the queries in [10]. Sharma et al. [13] present a catalog of 13 SQL database design smells. They searched the occurrences of nine of theses smells from a large number of databases (both open-source and industrial projects) and created an open-source code analysis tool to automate the process.

Delplanque et al. [14] present a prototype tool (DbCritics) for analyzing SQL data definition statements (the result of dumping the schema definition) to find the occurrences of eleven design problems. Similarly to our work DbCritics supports PostgreSQL and it uses a design representation that has already been accepted by the DBMS, thus ensuring certain degree of syntactic quality. The result of dump presents the same information that is accessible by querying the system catalog.

Vial [15] writes about a refactoring project of a MS SQL Server database that used a custom stored procedure to check database schema against guidelines and standards. The author stresses the importance of automation in the refactoring process and using the information that is stored in the database system catalog.

Factor [16] presents a catalog of 150 SQL code smells of MS SQL Server databases. Similarly to our work some of the smells are specific to a particular DBMS but most are relevant in case of any SQL database, regardless of the used DBMS.

Program SonarQube [17] can be used to analyze the source code of programs in case of many programming languages, including some languages for writing user-defined routines in databases. Using queries to analyze database design is a variant of static code analysis where one reads information about the code after the DBMS has accepted it. Some of our queries about user-defined routines search similar things as SonarQube (for instance, find PL/pgSQL functions that do not have RETURN clause or functions that commit or rollback transactions). The queries take advantage that the source of routines is stored in the system catalog. The queries use regular expressions.

Another example of using queries to find information about a database is sp_Blitz® – Free SQL Server Health Check Script [18]. Our queries search mostly information about the design of database conceptual and external schemas whereas the sp_Blitz® queries search information about the internal schema and the status of the DBMS. Similarly, some modern DBMSs have built-in advisors that are able to suggest and even autonomously perform database schema changes, usually in the internal schema. These tools certainly must have access to information that is in the database system catalog.

3   An Example

We constructed the example to demonstrate a set of problems that SQL database designs can have. The problems include bad (not descriptive enough, inconsistent) naming, inconsistencies (naming, implementation of constraints, generating surrogate key values), duplication or lack of constraints as well as inadequate data types, field sizes, and compensating actions. There is a query for each of these problems (and many more queries for many more problems) in the proposed set of queries. Firstly, we present the database design in terms of SQL data definition statements. Next, we list the problems in the proposed database. Information about the required changes and improved code is at the project homepage (https://github.com/erki77/database-design-queries).

```
CREATE TABLE Person_state_type (
person_state_type_code INTEGER PRIMARY KEY,
name VARCHAR(50),
CONSTRAINT chk_person_state_type_name
CHECK(trim(name)<>''),
CONSTRAINT chk_code CHECK(person_state_type_code>0));

CREATE TABLE Public_person_data (id INTEGER GENERATED
ALWAYS AS IDENTITY,
first_name VARCHAR(50) NOT NULL,
last_name VARCHAR(50) NOT NULL,
persons_state_type_code SMALLINT NOT NULL,
registration_time TIMESTAMP WITH TIME ZONE NOT NULL,
CONSTRAINT pk_person PRIMARY KEY (id),
CONSTRAINT "FK_person person_state_type" FOREIGN KEY
(persons_state_type_code)
REFERENCES Person_state_type (person_state_type_code) ON
DELETE CASCADE,
CONSTRAINT chk_person_data_last_name
CHECK(trim(last_name) IS NOT NULL),
CONSTRAINT chk_person_data_last_name2 CHECK(last_name
!~'[[:digit:]]'),
CONSTRAINT chk_code CHECK(persons_state_type_code>0));

CREATE TABLE Comment (person_id INTEGER NOT NULL,
comment_text TEXT NOT NULL,
comment_registration_time TIMESTAMP DEFAULT
CURRENT_TIMESTAMP,
check_date TIMESTAMP,
active BOOLEAN,
comment_id SERIAL PRIMARY KEY,
CONSTRAINT comment_check
CHECK(comment_text!~'^[[:space:]]*$' AND
check_date>=CURRENT_TIMESTAMP));
```

- Some names have gratuitous context [4]. Table name **Public_person_data** starts with the schema name (default PostgreSQL user schema). Column names **comment_registration_time** and **comment_text** of table *Comment* start with the table name. Moreover, the style of using table names in column names is not consistent across tables.
- Table names **Comment** and *Public_person_data* are too generic. In case of the former, it is unclear what is the subject of comments (are these about persons?). In case of the latter, the word *data* is a noise because all tables contain data.
- Column name *id* is too generic. SQL antipattern *One Size Fits All* warns against using the name [5]. Moreover, another surrogate key column – **comment_id** – uses a different naming style. Thus, there is also a naming inconsistency.

- If a cultural tradition of database users is to present surname before given name, then the column names *first_name* and **last_name** will cause confusion.
- Column name *person_id* does not reveal the role of persons in terms of comments.
- Column *active* contains Boolean data but does not follow a naming convention to have prefix *is_* or *has_*.
- The one letter difference of the primary/foreign key column names (*person_state_type_code vs. persons_state_type_code*) makes writing join queries more difficult and error prone and prevents the use of USING syntax for the join operation.
- Constraint name *chk_code* is too generic and does not sufficiently explain the meaning and/or context of the constraint.
- Two tables have a directly attached check constraint with the same name (*chk_code*).
- Names of some table constraints (for instance, *chk_code*) do not contain the name of the table. It contributes towards having duplicate constraint names in a schema.
- Constrain name *"FK_person person_state_type"* is a delimited identifier. Thus, it is case sensitive, complicating schema maintenance and evolvement. Other identifiers are case insensitive regular identifiers. Hence, there is also a naming inconsistency.
- Constraint name *chk_person_data_last_name2* contains a sequence number instead of explaining more precisely the meaning of the constraint.
- Most of the constraint names are user-defined whereas the primary key constraints of tables *Comment* and *Person_state_type* would have system-generated names.
- The primary key column *comment_id* is not the first in table *Comment*.
- Table *Comment* does not have the foreign key constraint to enforce the relationship between tables *Comment* and *Public_person_data*.
- Textual non-foreign key column *first_name* does not have a check constraint to prevent the empty string or strings that consist of only whitespace characters.
- Columns with a timestamp type (*check_date, registration_time, comment_registration_time*) do not have a check constraint to prevent illogical values that are far back in time (for instance, 1200-12-22) or in the distant future (for instance, 4000-12-22). Such values belong to the type but are inappropriate to use in case of the domain.
- In table Comment there is no check constraint that connects columns *check_date* and *comment_registration_time*. In practice, temporal columns in a table correspond to events and quite often, there is a particular order of events in the domain.
- The check ensuring that last names cannot contain numerical digits is too restrictive.
- The check constraint of table *Comment* has multiple tasks (responsibilities).
- Duplication of parent table check constraint on the foreign key column (column *persons_state_type_code* of table *Public_person_data*).
- Check constraint (check_date >= **CURRENT_TIMESTAMP**) invokes a non-deterministic function in a manner that data that conforms to the constraint at the registration time does not necessarily conform to it later.
- Check constraint (trim(last_name) IS NOT NULL) implements incorrectly the rule that last name cannot be the empty string or a string that consists of only spaces. PostgreSQL does not automatically replace the empty string with NULL.
- In case of columns *name* and *last_name* the intent is to prevent strings that consist of only spaces, not strings that consist of only whitespace like in case of column *comment_text*. The inconsistency could be intentional or a mistake.

- Column *comment_registration_time* has a default value but the column is optional, raising the question as to whether the column should have NOT NULL constraint.
- Column *active* of *Comment* is optional. It leads to the use of three-valued logic.
- In table *Person_state_type* all the non-primary key columns are optional raising the question as to whether the columns should have NOT NULL constraint.
- Columns for registering personal names (*first_name*, *last_name*) do not take into account the possibility of long names (longer than 50 characters) and the existence of mononymous persons, i.e., persons who have a single name.
- Column *persons_state_type_code* of table *Person_data* does not have a default value. The value should be the code of the first state that a person gets according to the state machine model of entity type *Person*.
- Boolean column *active* of table *Comment* does not have a default value.
- In table *Comment* the registration time column has a default value whereas in table *Public_person_data* it does not (lack of a default value; inconsistency).
- The default value and type of column *comment_registration_time* are inconsistent. It leads to the question as to whether the registration of time zone is needed or not.
- Tables *Public_person_data* and *Comment* use an internal and an external sequence generator, respectively, to generate surrogate key values (inconsistency).
- In one table, column *person_state_type_code* has type SMALLINT and in another type INTEGER (inconsistency). Thus, certain state codes that one could register in table *Person_state_type* cannot be used in table *Public_person_data*.
- In table *Public_person_data* registration time value must contain time zone whereas in table *Comment* it cannot (inconsistency).
- Column name *check_date* is not consistent with the datatype, leading to the question as to what should be the precision of data (date or timestamp) in this column.
- Comments have a simplistic state machine (active/inactive). The task to register the current state is implemented differently in case of different tables (inconsistency).
- The foreign key constraint that refers to *Person_state_type* does not have ON UPDATE CASCADE compensating action although the classifier codes could change over time. Moreover, having ON DELETE CASCADE there is reckless.
- The default FILLFACTOR parameter value of base tables has not been changed.
- Foreign key columns are not indexed.

4   Introduction of the Catalog

The catalog is available through https://github.com/erki77/database-design-queries The catalog is too large for publishing it within a paper. The numeric values describe the state of the catalog *at the time of the paper submission* and *are subject to change* due to continuous changes in it. The catalog homepage has a link to the latest statistics.

In total, there are 535 queries (SELECT statements) in the catalog. Each query belongs to zero or more categories, which classify the queries and each category contains zero or more queries. There are 47 categories with at least one query. The most popular categories (topics) are (number of queries is in the brackets) naming (107), user-defined routines (106), validity and completeness (105), comfortability of database evolution (86), and CHECK constraints (75). Most of the categories (for instance, naming, user-defined routines, and CHECK constraints) are artifact characteristics-based classifiers [2]. Categories like comfortability of database evolution, comfortability of data management, and duplication of implementation elements are effect-based classifiers [2].

Each query is classified either as a problem detection query (72% of the queries), a software measure query (7%), or a general query (21%). Problem detection queries are meant for directly finding problems in the database design. Each row that such query returns refers to a possible occurrence of a problem in the database. An example of such query is to find base tables that have neither a unique constraint nor the primary key. Software measure queries produce numeric information about database schemas. An example of such query is to find the referential degree of each base table. Some of the queries calculate software measures that are proposed in [19] but there are more queries. General queries find information about certain aspects of the database and report it together with the contextual information. For instance, an overview of all table check constraints returns for each constraint its schema name, table name, table type (base or foreign), column name, constraint name, constraint expression, and whether the constraint is associated to the table directly or through a domain. The results of the software measure and general queries do not necessarily point to the presence of design problems but nevertheless examining these can help inspectors to find problem occurrences. The occurrences of all the design problems in Sect. 3 can be found from query results. There is a problem detection query for most of these problems.

Some of the queries search problems from the database structure or from the properties of behavioral elements (constraints, triggers, and routines) whereas others check SQL data manipulation statements in database routines or subqueries of derived tables and try to find problems from there. The latter is similar to the static code analysis of application source code that tries to identify problematic SQL statements. The difference is that the queries analyze database access code that is inside the database.

According to the classification of [2] the method of detecting the occurrences of database design problems by using the problem detection and general queries belongs to the class of rules/heuristic-based smell detection whereas using the results of the software measure queries belongs to the class of metrics-based smell detection.

All the problem detection queries have a classification (based on the opinion of the author) as to whether the reliability of the query results is low (12% of the queries), medium (49%), or high (39%). The higher the reliability, the less false positive (correct design is reported as problematic) and false negative (problematic design is considered to be correct and data about it is not returned) results the query produces.

Each query belongs to zero or more collections (tests) and each collection contains zero or more queries. The collections are used to group together queries that may be executed together for one purpose. One collection contains problem detection queries, which results, according to the assessment of the author, point to the problems in the evaluated database with high probability. In the context of teaching databases, the author suggests students to regularly execute the queries. Because of the relatively high reliability of the results, students can inspect the results and use these in their design process even without the help of the lecturer. Another collection contains less reliable problem detection queries as well as software measure and general queries. The results of the queries potentially point to the design problems. However, a human expert has to interpret the results and make decisions. In the teaching context, this set of queries is the best suited to execute when the lecturer and students can together look the results.

Some of the queries need user-defined functions. In some cases, this is an aggregate function to calculate the median. In other cases, the functions search certain values from base tables that contain user data. All these queries are accompanied with statements for creating and dropping the functions.

To support changing the database, some of the problem detection queries are accompanied with the queries that generate statements for making the changes in the database structure or behavior. The queries get identifiers of database objects from the database system catalog and use the system-defined *format* function to produce correctly formatted SQL statements. Due to the possibility of false-positive results, the designer must make sure that the changes are actually needed. There could be multiple ways to fix a problem. For instance, there could be a duplication of implementation elements in a database. The fixing queries could return statements for dropping all these elements but the database designer has to decide which elements to keep and which elements to drop.

The database system catalog can also have design problems. We have found possible occurrences of six antipatterns in PostgreSQL 9.2 system catalog [11]. We assume that the queries will be mostly used to check the user-defined part of the database. Information about the catalog would reduce the comprehensibility of the results. Thus, the queries eliminate results about the system catalog, objects belonging to PostgreSQL extensions, and user-defined functions that the queries themselves need.

5 Discussion

A semiotic quality framework of conceptual modelling [20] defines three quality aspects – syntactic, semantic, and pragmatic. Only a few queries (13) detect syntactic mistakes because in most part the DBMS has already checked the syntax. Examples of mistakes include incorrect regular expressions that the system checks at runtime instead of creation time. Another example is using 'NULL' (a textual value) instead of NULL. There are more queries (105) about semantic quality problems. The framework describes two semantic quality goals – validity and completeness. Validity means in this context that the statements that the database design states about the database domain are correct and relevant. Completeness means that the database design incorporates all the correct and relevant statements about the domain. Many of these queries give information about declared constraints (including data types of columns) or point to potentially missing, incorrect, or redundant constraints. Most of the proposed queries are about the pragmatic quality aspect and help us to find out how comprehensible the database design is. All such queries are about detecting design smells, which are the signs of technical debt. The debt means that there are things in the database design that make its understanding, learning, maintenance, and extension more difficult.

5.1 The Method of Creating and Improving the Queries

The development process was action design research [21]. As a lecturer of university database courses the author has to quickly and thoroughly give feedback to and assess many database design projects. The author created additional queries to the initial set of queries [10, 11] based on different sources that described good and bad practices of software design in general [2, 4] and database design in particular [13, 14, 16, 17, 19].

For instance, our queries implement almost all the rules of DbCritics [14] either exactly or with some variation or extensions. For example, in case of DbCritics rule 6 (stubs) we have a query to find user-defined routines that invoke certain system-defined functions without providing any arguments just like [14] suggests. Moreover, we have queries to find enumeration types with zero or one value, user-defined routines with no action, user-defined routines that only return a value or NULL, check constraints that do not refer to any column, user-defined routines with no parameters, and tables with no columns. All these database objects may be intended to be stubs (placeholders). The results of the first four queries point with high probability to the occurrences of design problems. In case of the latter two queries the probability of a real problem is lower. For instance, in PostgresSQL, one can create base tables with no columns and use these to record truth-values (see TABLE_DEE and TABLE_DUM [22]). Thus, results of the queries need human review. We do not implement rule 8 from DbCritics (unused functions) because we assume that user-defined non-trigger routines are invoked by applications and our queries do not analyze application code. On the other hand, we have queries for finding other unused database objects – schemas, domains, enumerated types, sequence generators, named parameters of routines, trigger functions, foreign data wrappers, and foreign servers. There are also queries for finding disabled triggers and rules. In case of rule 10 (View using only one table) we improved the heuristics and search derived tables (both views and materialized views) that present data from one base table without adding columns, renaming columns, changing the order of columns, removing columns, and restricting rows. Similarly, all the smells in [13] have one or more corresponding queries in our catalog.

Our view of design smells is similar with [4, 16] in the sense that the smells are not limited with "severe" (that is a subjective concept) design issues but include also, for instance, naming issues. Thus our catalog is much bigger than for instance in [13, 14].

As a part of the query development process, one has to find out as to what checks the DBMS performs at the time of modifying the database schemas. For instance, in PostgreSQL, one cannot create trigger functions with parameters and thus there is no need for a query to find trigger functions that have one or more parameters.

The author checked the queries right away based on the project databases of students. Starting from the end of 2014, the author has checked more than 350 different databases with the queries, in most cases repeatedly. The variability of the quality of the checked designs was very useful in evaluating the queries and finding necessary changes to minimize the number of false positive and false negative results. Using many different databases was also useful for determining the best order of columns and rows and additionally needed contextual information in the query results. All this facilitates finding the occurrences of a problem by using an inspection and deciding as to whether the result of a problem detection query refers to a real problem occurrence. The designs of student databases gave many ideas of new queries, which were immediately implemented and tested based on the databases.

5.2 Strengths

The main advantage of the queries is that these make possible to quickly check database design and receive instant feedback. This is important in any context, not only learning to design. For instance, execution of a set of more than 300 queries (without generating fixing statements), which results quite probably point to the problems, and generating the report of results takes about 30 s based on a database of approximately 200 tables. Developers could use the queries while working to try to avoid the problems in the first place instead of fixing these later. In case of legacy systems, one can use the queries to get an overview of the technical debt level in the database and identify concrete problem occurrences that should be fixed by refactoring. The bigger number of database objects there is, the bigger advantage it offers. Another advantage of using the queries is that due to the big number of possible problems (see Sect. 3 as an example) it is easy to forget checking something. Automated tests never fail in terms of that.

The author regularly uses the queries in the teaching process and has made the execution of query collections (see Sect. 4) available to all the students who participate in a database course. For instance, during the 2018/2019 fall semester 141 different students executed the collections based on 159 different databases more than six thousand times that resulted with almost 1.5 million executions of individual queries. The median number of collection executions among students who initiated at least one execution was 22. A group of lecturers (let alone one lecturer) cannot give so much feedback over the same period. Although the author has not formally investigated how the use of the queries influences the results of students, he claims, based on the first-hand experience, that the quality of database designs that students present for the grading has significantly improved since the introduction of queries to the learning process.

The query execution software has simple core functionality. The queries are registered in a database with metadata that facilitates searching the queries and understanding their results. The software gets information that is needed to connect the checked database and query collection identifier as an input. It has to read the queries from the collection, execute these against the checked database, and present the results. The user could choose the amount of reported metadata, whether to present the queries that do not return any rows, and whether to let the system generate fixing SQL statements. Another possible set of functionalities is about logging the query executions, execution speeds, and the number or even details of detected problem occurrences.

The use of student databases during the query development process (see Sect. 5.1) was a strength because in the learning context students can naturally make mistakes and thus their designed databases offer a good condensed source of possible problems that could also appear in the databases designed by more experienced people.

For the users of other DBMSs than PostgreSQL the catalog is relevant because it is essentially *a catalog of design problems* that can appear in any SQL database and thus the checks could be implemented in their respective systems. Problem detection queries codify the problems. It is similar to test-based development where tests constitute specification of the functionality that the tested system must have. Only a small number of queries are about features that are specific to PostgreSQL (for instance, exclude constraints). However, only about 25% of all the queries are completely based on the standardized *information_schema* views. Moreover, some DBMSs do not implement the *information_schema*. Thus, the code is mostly not directly usable in other DBMSs.

Yamashita and Moonen [3] found that a large portion (32%) of surveyed professional developers did not know about code smells. Thus, teaching students about smells and technical debt is certainly relevant. Doing it in different contexts (application design, database design, modeling [23]) would enforce their understanding that many problems (for instance, inconsistency and unnecessary duplication) are universal and can appear in different types of technical artifacts. Having a tool that allows learners to quickly find possible occurrences of smells is very helpful in this regard. Yamashita and Moonen [3] also found that those developers who are interested in code smells want to have possibility to check the code in real time as well as customizable and domain-specific detection of smells. The proposed queries implement domain-specific detection of smells. Additional customization can be achieved by putting together query collections with a specific task or changing the order of queries in collections. Our experience with students shows that the queries can be used in real time to check the database design after changes have been made in it. According to the survey [3] the developers were most concerned about duplicate code and in lesser extent about the size and complexity of the code. We have queries that deal with the problems. For instance, the category of duplication of implementation elements currently contains 37 queries.

Some of our queries have associated queries that generate SQL statements that help us to fix the problem. At the same time the tools [13, 14] do not fix the found problems.

Eessaar and Käosaar [23] concluded that many code smells are variants of generic problems that can also appear in system analysis models. The current work showed that many of the generic problems (for instance, inconsistency, duplication, unused elements, bad names, and not separating concerns) can also appear in the database design.

5.3 Weaknesses

A weakness of using system-catalog based queries about database design is that one cannot get feedback about the database design while modeling the database.

The queries have been designed for and have been tested against the latest version of the DBMS and some of these do not work in some earlier system versions.

The query creation process was influenced by the same forces (lack of time, continuous appearance of new requirements, etc.) that influence any software development task. The desire to quickly get a working version lead to the technical debt in the queries regardless that the queries were created only by one person. The author continuously improves the queries. However, it is an elusive goal to get completely debt-free. Trying the best not to have too much debt in the first place is an important strategy to have the debt under control. Examples of technical debt in the queries are the following.

- Inconsistent use of uppercase and lowercase. Not writing keywords in uppercase.
- Inconsistencies of using newlines and writing logical operator at the beginning or end of a line in case of search conditions.
- The use of short and often meaningless aliases in the queries.

- Inconsistencies of solving the same sub-problems in different queries. For instance, in different queries the same sub-problem may be solved by querying *information_schema* views or by directly querying the system catalog base tables.
- Inconsistent naming of columns in the results of different queries.
- Inconsistent output of the context in case of queries about related problems.

PostgreSQL allows multiple check and foreign key constraints with the same name in the same schema. Thus, queries based on the *information_schema* views about a constraint based on its name could return rows about multiple constraints. Therefore, in many (but currently not all) queries about constraints we use system catalog base tables instead. Queries about constraints based on the *information_schema* views have a risk to return false positive results if the names of constraints are not unique. To see the extent of the problem there is a query for finding repeating constraint names.

5.4 On Fixing the Identified Problem Occurrences

Whether or not to make changes in the database depends on the severity of the problem. A small number of queries (currently 8) are about problems that prevent the correct use of the database and thus are categorized as fatal. An example of such problem is to have on the same set of columns multiple foreign key constraints that point to different tables. Other examples include syntax errors, for instance in regular expressions, that the system detects at runtime not at the compile (creation) time. One should fix such problems immediately. In case of most of the problems their severity estimate depends on the context. If someone executes the queries based on a database, then one should also think through what would be the importance of each problem by taking into account the particular context. For instance, in the teaching context from where this set of queries originates there is a grading model that assigns different number of minus points to different problems. The grading model depends on the objectives of the course.

In addition to changing database schemas, one may have to change the artifacts that depend on the database (applications, tests) as well as models of the database.

Fixing a problem could solve other problems. For instance, dropping a constraint could fix a problem of inconsistent naming of constraints. On the other hand, solving one problem could lead to new problems or to finding previously undetected problems. For instance, one could declare a previously missing foreign key constraint with an unsuitable compensating action. After declaring the constraint the queries are also able to find that the foreign key column has an unsuitable data type or a duplicated check constraint. The queries did not find it before due to the lack of declared constraint. Renaming a database object may require renaming other database objects or their components depending on the used database naming conventions. For instance, renaming a base table may lead to renaming of constraints and indexes of the table and foreign key constraints that refer to the table. To summarize, it is important to be able to execute the checks continuously. It is a variant of regression testing. The queries get most of the information about the meaning of data from the names of database objects and declared constraints. Improving these aspects may gradually reveal bigger structural problems in the database. Small incremental changes in the database design will lead over time to the improvement of the general quality of the database design.

6 Conclusion

The paper is about the automation of finding occurrences of database design problems in PostgreSQL database schemas by querying database system catalog. At the time of submitting the paper, the published catalog contained 535 queries. The queries are written in SQL and use base tables and views of the PostgreSQL system catalog. The full catalog is available through https://github.com/erki77/database-design-queries

Some of the queries give an overview of a specific database aspect to facilitate manual search of problem occurrences whereas others produce results that directly point towards possible problem occurrences. Still, a human inspector has to review the results because false positive results are possible, although their probability varies between different queries. The problem detection queries codify possible database design problems. Many database design problems have the same underlying problems as code smells (duplication, having multiple responsibilities, bad naming, etc.). The queries can be used to get a quick overview of the level of technical debt in a database, find potentially missing or incorrect constraints, find concrete places in a database that need refactoring, and evaluate the result of changing database schemas. The queries have been originally created to support learning but we are convinced in wider usefulness of these.

Future work includes identifying additional design problems, writing queries based on these, refactoring the existing queries, and using the queries to evaluate larger databases. A line of work is to translate the queries for some other DBMS. Because NoSQL DBMSs increasingly make it possible to specify explicit schema-on-write in databases it is relevant to research the potential design problems in these schemas.

References

1. Riaz, M., Mendes, E., Tempero, E.D.: Maintainability predictors for relational database-driven software applications: results from a survey. In: SEKE, pp. 420–425 (2011)
2. Sharma, T., Spinellis, D.: A survey on software smells. J. Syst. Softw. **138**, 158–173 (2018). https://doi.org/10.1016/j.jss.2017.12.034
3. Yamashita, A., Moonen, L.: Do developers care about code smells? An exploratory survey. In: 20th Working Conference on Reverse Engineering, pp. 242–251. IEEE (2013). https://doi.org/10.1109/WCRE.2013.6671299
4. Martin, R.C.: Clean Code. A Handbook of Agile Software Craftsmanship. Pearson Education, London (2009)
5. Karwin, B.: SQL Antipatterns. Avoiding the Pitfalls of Database Programming. The Pragmatic Bookshelf (2010)
6. Fernandes, E., Oliveira, J., Vale, G., Paiva, T., Figueiredo, E.: A review-based comparative study of bad smell detection tools. In: Proceedings of the 20th International Conference on Evaluation and Assessment in Software Engineering, pp. 1–12. ACM (2016). https://doi.org/10.1145/2915970.2915984
7. Blaha, M.: A retrospective on industrial database reverse engineering projects - part 2. In: Proceedings Eighth Working Conference on Reverse Engineering, pp. 147–153. IEEE (2001). https://doi.org/10.1109/WCRE.2001.957818
8. Weber, J.H., Cleve, A., Meurice, L., Ruiz, F.J.B.: Managing technical debt in database schemas of critical software. In: Sixth International Workshop on Managing Technical Debt, pp. 43–46. IEEE (2014). https://doi.org/10.1109/MTD.2014.17

9. Catalog of Database Refactorings. http://www.agiledata.org/essays/databaseRefactoringCatalog.html. Accessed 21 Dec 2019

10. Eessaar, E.: On query-based search of possible design flaws of SQL databases. In: Sobh, T., Elleithy, K. (eds.) Innovations and Advances in Computing, Informatics, Systems Sciences, Networking and Engineering. LNEE, vol. 313, pp. 53–60. Springer, Cham (2015). https://doi.org/10.1007/978-3-319-06773-5_8

11. Eessaar, E., Voronova, J.: Using SQL queries to evaluate the design of SQL databases. In: Elleithy, K., Sobh, T. (eds.) New Trends in Networking, Computing, E-learning, Systems Sciences, and Engineering. Lecture Notes in Electrical Engineering, vol. 312, pp. 179–186. Springer, Cham (2015). https://doi.org/10.1007/978-3-319-06764-3_23

12. Khumnin, P., Senivongse, T.: SQL antipatterns detection and database refactoring process. In: 18th IEEE/ACIS International Conference on Software Engineering, Artificial Intelligence, Networking and Parallel/Distributed Computing (SNPD), pp. 199–205. IEEE (2017). https://doi.org/10.1109/SNPD.2017.8022723

13. Sharma, T., Fragkoulis, M., Rizou, S., Bruntink, M., Spinellis, D.: Smelly relations: measuring and understanding database schema quality. In: Proceedings of the 40th International Conference on Software Engineering: Software Engineering in Practice, pp. 55–64. ACM (2018). https://doi.org/10.1145/3183519.3183529

14. Delplanque, J., Etien, A., Auverlot, O., Mens, T., Anquetil, N., Ducasse, S.: CodeCritics applied to database schema: Challenges and first results. In: 2017 IEEE 24th International Conference on Software Analysis, Evolution and Reengineering (SANER), pp. 432–436. IEEE (2017). https://doi.org/10.1109/SANER.2017.7884648

15. Vial, G.: Database refactoring: lessons from the trenches. IEEE Softw. **32**(6), 71–79 (2015). https://doi.org/10.1109/MS.2015.131

16. Factor, P.: SQL Code Smells. Redgate. http://assets.red-gate.com/community/books/sql-code-smells.pdf. Accessed 29 Dec 2019

17. Sonarsource PL/SQL rules. https://rules.sonarsource.com/plsql. Accessed 21 Dec 2019

18. sp_Blitz® – SQL Server Takeover Script. https://www.brentozar.com/blitz/. Accessed 21 Dec 2019

19. Piattini, M., Calero, C., Sahraoui, H.A., Lounis, H.: Object-relational database metrics. L'Objet **7**(4), 477–496 (2001)

20. Lindland, O.I., Sindre, G., Solvberg, A.: Understanding quality in conceptual modeling. IEEE Softw. **11**, 42–49 (1994). https://doi.org/10.1109/52.268955

21. Sein, M.K., Henfridsson, O., Purao, S., Rossi, M., Lindgren, R.: Action design research. MIS Q. **35**, 37–56 (2011). https://doi.org/10.2307/23043488

22. Date, C.J.: SQL and Relational Theory. How to Write Accurate SQL Code, 2nd edn. O'Reilly, Sebastopol (2011)

23. Eessaar, E., Käosaar, E.: On finding model smells based on code smells. In: Silhavy, R. (ed.) CSOC2018 2018. AISC, vol. 763, pp. 269–281. Springer, Cham (2019). https://doi.org/10.1007/978-3-319-91186-1_28

Complexity Issues in Data-Driven Fuzzy Inference Systems: Systematic Literature Review

Jolanta Miliauskaitė[1] and Diana Kalibatienė[2(✉)]

[1] Institute of Data Science and Digital Technologies, Vilnius University,
08663 Vilnius, Lithuania
jolanta.miliauskaite@mif.vu.lt
[2] Vilnius Gediminas Technical University, 10223 Vilnius, Lithuania
diana.kalibatiene@vgtu.lt

Abstract. The development of a data-driven fuzzy inference system (FIS) involves the automatic generation of membership functions and fuzzy if-then rules and choosing a particular defuzzification approach. The literature presents different techniques for automatic FIS development and highlights different challenges and issues of its automatic development because of its complexity. However, those complexity issues are not investigated sufficiently in a comprehensive way. Therefore, in this paper, we present a systematic literature review (SLR) of journal and conference papers on the topic of FIS *complexity issues*. We review 1 340 papers published between 1991 and 2019, systematize and classify them into categories according to the complexity issues. The results show that FIS complexity issues are classified as follows: computational complexity, fuzzy rules complexity, membership functions complexity, input data complexity, complexity of fuzzy rules interpretability, knowledge inferencing complexity and representation complexity, accuracy and interpretability complexity. The results of this study can help researchers and practitioners become familiar with existing FIS complexity issues, the extent of a particular complexity issue and to decide for future development.

Keywords: Membership function · FIS · Issue · Limitation · Complexity

1 Introduction

Development of a data-driven fuzzy inference system (FIS) involves automatic generation of membership functions (MFs), which reflect what is known about linguistic variables in application domains, and fuzzy if-then rules, used for inferencing or assessment, and choosing a particular defuzzification approach to determine the output variables in interpretable and understandable way for the end-user.

The literature presents different techniques for automatic FIS development [1–3], and highlights different challenges and issues, because of its complexity, like the rule base (RB) complexity [4], data complexity [5], a number of linguistic terms [1, 6]. However, those complexity issues are not investigated sufficiently in a comprehensive way. In the

© Springer Nature Switzerland AG 2020
T. Robal et al. (Eds.): DB&IS 2020, CCIS 1243, pp. 190–204, 2020.
https://doi.org/10.1007/978-3-030-57672-1_15

analyzed papers, authors have focused on a particular one or two issues separately, like computational complexity [2, 7], MF complexity [8, 9], fuzzy rules complexity [10, 11], etc. This lack of understanding of a general situation hampers progress in the field since academics are offering limited approach [12].

The question arises – *What are the complexity issues in FIS?* In order to answer the question raised, a systematic literature review (SLR) is presented in this paper. SLR has two purposes and contributions. It is used to determine, first, the possible set of complexity issues, and, second, the extent of a particular complexity issue in FIS area. The rest of this paper is structured as follows. Section 2 introduces complexity in the context of FIS and explains the use of this concept in this paper. Section 3 presents the review methodology. Section 4 shows the obtained results of SLR. Section 5 discusses the obtained results and concludes the paper.

2   Background and Related Work

FIS consists of four main components [1, 13, 14] (Fig. 1). *Data Collection and Pre-Processing* is responsible for crisp or linguistic stream collecting from one or multiple sources and its cleaning, organization and integration [15] for future data exploitation in the Fuzzification Mechanism. *Fuzzification Mechanism* transforms the data stream into MFs using fuzzy set theory. *Fuzzy Inference* uses MFs and applies a particular fuzzy reasoning mechanism to obtain a fuzzy output. *Knowledge base* is responsible for the definition and management of fuzzy rules, used by the Fuzzy Inference component for inferencing. *Output Processing* performs approximation, defuzzification and type reduction to convert the results of inferencing into output data (i.e., crisp or linguistic values), which should be understandable to a Stakeholder or a System.

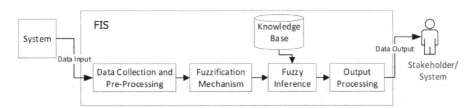

Fig. 1. The reference schema of a data-driven Fuzzy Inference System (FIS).

The distinctive feature of FIS is that it is data-driven, i.e., MFs and fuzzy rules are generated from synthetic or real data streams automatically, but not defined by an expert. In FIS knowledge is represented through two levels [1]. First, in the *semantic level* knowledge is expressed as fuzzy sets and MFs. Second, in the *syntactic level* knowledge is represented in a form of fuzzy rules. This understanding of FIS and its complexity are used in this paper.

The concept of complexity in FIS can be viewed from different perspectives as the primary analysis shows. In [4], *the rule base (RB) complexity* is measured as the total number of conditions in the antecedents of the rules. Authors of [16] understand complexity as interpretability of RB, and interpretability of fuzzy partitions as integrity of the database (DB). A *data complexity* is measured in terms of the average number of patterns per variable (i.e., data density) for pattern recognition in [5].

A data-driven Fuzzy Inference System suffers from exponential complexity, which is manifested through a *number of linguistic terms* (number of subspaces on the universe of discourse of input variables) and a *number of input variables* [1]. Complexity is also measured by *counting the number of operations* [6] or *number of elements in RB* including the number of MFs, rules, premises, linguistic terms, etc. [1]. Selecting a small number of linguistic terms and the right linguistic terms is essential for *better interpretability*. Total number of parameters of the fuzzy RB is also a measure of interpretability. A system with less number of *parameters* is more interpretable and less complex [17]. In [1, 18], authors suggest reducing the exponential complexity of FIS be reducing the number of fuzzy (linguistic) terms or the number of fuzzy (linguistic) variables or both. According to [19], the *model interpretability* is measured in terms of complexity: *"Complexity is affected by the number of features used for generating the model: the lower the number of features, the lower the complexity"*.

Summing up, based on system thinking, the definition of system complexity depends on the complexity of its components and a complexity of combination of those components as a whole. Therefore, in the next section we describe main components of a data-driven fuzzy inference system (FIS).

3   Review Methodology

The review methodology was developed and executed according to the guidelines and hints provided by [20, 21]. The structure of the methodology is adapted from [22] and presented in Table 1 as a review protocol [23].

Table 1. Review protocol.

Question Formulation
Question Focus: Membership function, development, generation, construction, issue, limit, complex, fuzzy inference system
Question (Q): "What are the complexity issues in FIS?"
Keywords and Synonyms: membership function, develop*, generat*, construct*, issue*, limit*, complex*
Effect: Description of different FIS development complexity issues; visualisation of statistics by diagrams, view integration
Field/Scope/Confines: Publications regarding MF and FIS issues
Application: Computer Science (CS), Information Systems (IS), Software Engineering (SE)
Sources Selection

(continued)

Table 1. (*continued*)

Question Formulation
Search string: (fuzzy) AND ("membership function*") AND ("develop*" OR "generat*" OR "construct*") AND ("issue*" OR "limit*" OR "complex*")
Studies Language: English
Sources list: Web of Science (WoS), https://apps.webofknowledge.com/ (see below)
Studies Selection
Studies Inclusion Criteria (IC): **IC1**: Universally accepted relevant fundamental works on MF development, MF generation, MF construction, FIS and issues, limitations or complexity. **IC2**: Papers must be available to download. **Studies Exclusion Criteria (EC)**: **EC1**: Exclude papers, which contain relevant keywords, but MF and FIS issues, limitations or complexity are not the main topic of the paper. **EC2**: Exclude relevant sources that repeat ideas described in earlier works. **EC3**: Exclude papers, whose length is less than 8 pages, since such short papers can present only a general idea, but not describe overall approach. **EC4**: If there are several papers of the same authors with the similar abstract, i.e., one paper is an extension of another, the less extended (i.e., containing less pages) paper is excluded.
Studies Type Definition: Journal publications (research papers) and proceeding papers.
Procedures for Papers Selection (PPS): **PPS-1.** Run the search strings at the selected source ➜ A primary set of papers is obtained. **PPS-2.** Extract the title, abstract and keywords of papers for the primary set. **PPS-3.** Evaluate a primary set of papers (the title, abstract and keywords) according to IC and EC ➜ A secondary set of paper is obtained.
Selection execution: See Table 2.
Information Extraction
Information Inclusion and Exclusion Criteria Definition: The extracted information from papers must contain definition or analysis of the MF and FIS issues
Synthesis of findings: The information extracted from the papers was tabulated and plotted to present basic information about the research process

Table 2. Number of papers (Articles (A) or Proceedings Papers (PP)) for each PPS.

Years	PPS-1			PPS-3		
	A	PP	All	A	PP	All
1991–2019	864	476	1 340	78	23	101

In Fig. 2, the trend of the research on the topic is illustrated. The number of papers on fuzzy theory application to solve different complex domain problems has raised. This increase of papers can be attributed to technological development. However, the issues

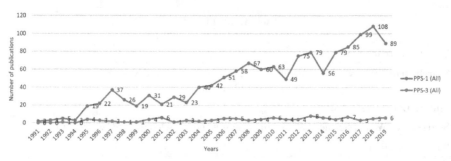

Fig. 2. Number of papers after PPS-1 and PPS-3.

related to the usage of fuzzy theory are analyzed insufficiently. Issues related to the usage of fuzzy theory are analyzed more in _A_ comparing to _PP_ (Table 2).

Sources Evaluation: The Web of Science (WoS) database was chosen for the analysis, since it covers a wider range of refined and not duplicating researches. WoS and Scopus databases are not overlapping only 12,2% of documents in Engineering and Computer Science [114]. WoS has an Impact Factor (IF), which is calculated to assess the quality of publications and the level of scientific research in close fields of knowledge. More-over, WoS presents an easy mechanism to export the search results in different formats, supported by various reference management software, like Mendeley[1], EndNote[2], etc., and bibliometric tools, like VOSviewer[3], CiteSpace[4], etc.

Threats to Validity: For the analysis, papers were chosen based on the searching strategy in Table 1. Validity of the results was performed applying the following measures. Reading the abstract and the title of the papers introduces a threat, because the abstract and the title allows excluding not relevant from the first glance papers [12]. Moreover, both authors of this paper have assessed the obtained results (primary and secondary sets of papers) independently and combined the results. Finally, to minimize the threat associated with inaccurate extraction of data, only papers describing complexity issues were selected.

4   Results

The main results of our SLR are presented in Table 3. It consists of eleven columns, nine of which present the complexity issues found. They are as the following: References (R); Year of publication (Year); computational complexity (CC) (1) (i.e., the huge number of calculations in all FIS components); complexity of fuzzy rules (CFR) (2) (i.e., extraction, modification and optimization of fuzzy rules); complexity of MF (CMF) (3) (i.e., MF development, optimization, simplification); data complexity (DC) (4) (i.e., related to big

---

[1] https://www.mendeley.com/?interaction_required=true.

[2] https://endnote.com/.

[3] https://www.vosviewer.com/.

[4] http://cluster.cis.drexel.edu/~ cchen/citespace/.

data issues); complexity of fuzzy rules interpretability (CFRI) (5); complexity of inferencing (CI) (6); complexity of knowledge representation (CKR) (7) (i.e., development of MF and RB issues); accuracy (ACC) (8) (i.e., the ability to approximate the output of the system accurately); interpretability (I) (9) (i.e., ability to describe the behavior of the system in an interpretable way). Temporal distribution of nine complexity issues found in the papers included in the review, are given in Fig. 3. The size of the bubbles indicates the number of papers analyzing each complexity issue.

Table 3. The secondary set of papers (1 – analyzed in the paper, 0 – not analyzed).

R	Year	(1)	(2)	(3)	(4)	(5)	(6)	(7)	(8)	(9)
[2, 3, 25]	2019	1	0	0	0	0	0	0	0	0
[8]		0	0	1	0	0	0	0	0	0
[24]		1	1	0	0	0	0	0	0	0
[26]		0	1	1	0	0	0	1	1	0
[27]	2018	0	0	1	0	0	0	0	0	0
[28, 29]		0	1	1	0	0	0	0	0	0
[30]		1	1	0	0	0	0	0	1	0
[7]		1	0	0	0	0	0	0	0	0
[1]	2017	0	1	1	0	0	0	0	0	1
[19, 31]		0	0	0	1	0	0	0	0	0
[32]		0	1	1	1	0	0	1	0	0
[33, 35, 36]	2016	1	0	0	0	0	0	0	0	0
[10, 34]		0	1	0	0	0	0	0	0	0
[37]		0	0	1	0	0	0	0	0	0
[9, 40]	2015	0	0	1	0	0	0	0	0	0
[38]		0	1	0	0	0	0	0	0	0
[39]		1	0	0	0	0	0	0	0	0
[41]	2014	0	0	1	0	0	0	0	0	0
[11]		0	1	0	0	0	0	0	0	0
[42]		0	1	1	0	0	0	1	0	0
[43]		0	1	0	0	1	0	0	0	0
[44]		0	0	0	1	0	0	0	0	0
[45]		1	0	0	0	0	0	0	0	0
[46]	2013	1	0	0	0	0	0	0	0	0
[48]		0	1	0	0	0	0	0	0	1
[49]		0	1	1	0	0	0	0	0	0

(continued)

Table 3. (*continued*)

R	Year	(1)	(2)	(3)	(4)	(5)	(6)	(7)	(8)	(9)
[50]		0	0	1	0	0	0	0	0	0
[51–53]		0	1	0	0	0	0	0	0	0
[54]	2012	1	0	0	0	0	0	1	0	0
[47]		1	1	0	0	0	0	0	0	0
[55]		0	0	0	1	0	0	0	0	0
[56]		1	0	0	0	0	0	0	0	0
[57]		0	1	0	0	0	0	0	0	0
[16]	2011	0	0	1	0	0	0	0	0	1
[58]		0	1	1	0	0	0	0	0	0
[59]		0	0	1	0	0	0	0	0	0
[60]		0	0	0	1	0	0	0	0	0
[61]	2010	0	0	1	0	0	0	1	0	0
[4, 62, 64]		0	1	1	0	0	0	0	0	0
[63]		0	1	0	0	0	0	0	0	0
[65]		0	0	1	0	0	0	0	0	0
[66]	2009	0	1	0	0	0	0	0	0	0
[67–69]		1	0	0	0	0	0	0	0	0
[70]	2008	0	1	0	0	0	1	0	0	0
[71]		1	0	0	0	0	0	0	0	0
[72]		0	1	0	0	0	0	0	0	0
[73]	2007	1	0	0	0	0	0	0	0	0
[74]		0	1	0	0	0	0	0	1	1
[75]		0	1	0	0	0	0	0	0	0
[76]		0	1	0	0	0	0	0	1	0
[77]		1	0	0	0	0	0	0	1	0
[78, 80–82]	2006	0	1	0	0	0	0	0	0	0
[79]		0	1	0	0	0	1	0	0	0
[83, 84]	2005	0	1	0	0	0	0	0	0	0
[85]		1	1	0	0	0	0	0	0	0
[86, 87]	2004	0	1	0	0	0	0	0	0	0
[88, 90]	2003	1	0	0	0	0	0	0	0	0
[89]		0	0	0	0	0	0	1	0	0

(*continued*)

Table 3. (*continued*)

R	Year	(1)	(2)	(3)	(4)	(5)	(6)	(7)	(8)	(9)
[91]	2002	0	1	0	0	0	0	0	0	0
[92, 95]	2001	0	1	0	0	0	0	1	0	0
[93]		1	1	0	0	0	0	1	0	0
[94]		0	1	0	0	1	0	0	0	0
[96]		0	0	0	0	0	0	1	0	0
[97]		0	0	0	0	0	0	0	1	0
[98]	2000	1	0	0	0	0	0	0	0	0
[99]		0	1	0	0	0	0	1	0	0
[100]		0	1	0	0	0	0	0	0	0
[101]		1	1	0	0	0	0	1	0	0
[102]	1999	0	1	0	1	0	0	0	0	0
[103]	1998	0	1	0	0	0	0	0	0	0
[104]	1997	1	0	0	0	0	0	0	0	0
[105]		1	1	0	0	0	0	0	0	0
[106]	1996	1	0	0	0	0	0	0	0	0
[107, 108]		0	1	0	0	0	0	0	0	0
[109, 111]	1995	0	0	0	0	0	0	1	0	0
[110]		0	0	1	0	0	0	0	0	0
[112]		0	1	0	0	0	0	0	0	0
[113]	1993	0	1	0	0	0	0	0	0	0

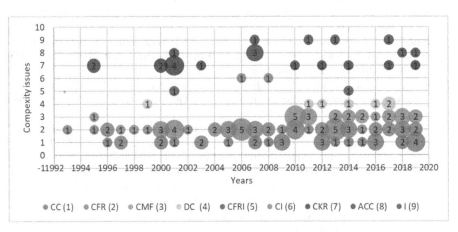

Fig. 3. Found complexity issues according to years.

5 Discussion and Conclusions

Finally, we can summarise the obtained results and answer to the research question "*What are the complexity issues in FIS?*". Based on Table 3, nine main issues are extracted from the analysed papers. Figure 3 shows that the computational complexity (CC) (1) and complexity of fuzzy rules (CFR) (2) remained relevant throughout the analysed years (1991–2019). The complexity of MF (CMF) (3) issue becomes relevant since 2010. Such relevance of the issue can be explained by the growth of technologies that generate increasing amounts of data. Therefore, the need to develop MFs from large data strings that requires high computational power is raised. The data complexity (DC) (4) issue becomes relevant since 2011. Its relevance can be explained by the emergence of big data and unstructured data and their usage in FIS. The issues related to complexity of fuzzy rules interpretability (CFRI) (5), complexity of inferencing (CI) (6), accuracy (ACC) (8) and interpretability (I) (9) are weakly expressed directly because they are analysed in tandem with other issues.

The correlation analysis of complexity issues shows that in 67,33% (68 papers of 101) of papers authors consider only one particular complexity issue. In 24,75% (25) – two complexity issues, in 5,94% (6) – three complexity issues, and in 1,98% (2) – four complexity issues are analysed in tandem. Summing up, it shows that FIS complexity issue is characterized by complexity issues related to its components and a complexity of combination of those components as a whole (see Sect. 2). Therefore, the FIS complexity issue should be analysed as an ensemble of components complexity issues. In the future research, we are going to do the following: 1) to extend our SLR to several sources; 2) to offer a decision tree of complexity issue solutions existing in the literature now.

References

1. Askari, S.: A novel and fast MIMO fuzzy inference system based on a class of fuzzy clustering algorithms with interpretability and complexity analysis. Expert Syst. Appl. **84**, 301–322 (2017). https://doi.org/10.1016/j.eswa.2017.04.045
2. Ruiz-Garcia, G., Hagras, H., Pomares, H., Rojas, I.: Towards a fuzzy logic system based on general forms of interval type-2 fuzzy sets. IEEE Trans. Fuzzy Syst. **27**(12), 2381–2395 (2019). https://doi.org/10.1109/tfuzz.2019.2898582
3. Lee, R.S.: Chaotic Interval Type-2 Fuzzy Neuro-oscillatory Network (CIT2-FNON) for worldwide 129 financial products prediction. Int. J. Fuzzy Syst. **21**(7), 2223–2244 (2019). https://doi.org/10.1007/s40815-019-00688-w
4. Antonelli, M., Ducange, P., Lazzerini, B., Marcelloni, F.: Exploiting a three-objective evolutionary algorithm for generating Mamdani fuzzy rule-based systems. In: FUZZ-IEEE 2010, pp. 1–8. IEEE, Barcelona, Spain (2010). https://doi.org/10.1109/fuzzy.2010.5583965
5. Alcalá, R., Ducange, P., Herrera, F., Lazzerini, B., Marcelloni, F.: A multiobjective evolutionary approach to concurrently learn rule and data bases of linguistic fuzzy-rule-based systems. IEEE Trans. Fuzzy Syst. **17**(5), 1106–1122 (2009)
6. Ephzibah, E.P.: Time complexity analysis of genetic- fuzzy system for disease diagnosis. ACIJ **2**(4), 23–31 (2011). https://doi.org/10.5121/acij.2011.2403
7. Zhu, X., Pedrycz, W., Li, Z.: Granular representation of data: A design of families of ϵ-information granules. IEEE Trans. Fuzzy Syst. **26**(4), 2107–2119 (2017)

8. Fan, X., Li, C., Wang, Y.: Strict intuitionistic fuzzy entropy and application in network vulnerability evaluation. Soft. Comput. **23**(18), 8741–8752 (2019)
9. Ibarra, L., Rojas, M., Ponce, P., Molina, A.: Type-2 Fuzzy membership function design method through a piecewise-linear approach. Expert Syst. Appl. **42**(21), 7530–7540 (2015). https://doi.org/10.1016/j.eswa.2015.05.029
10. Harandi, F.A., Derhami, V.: A reinforcement learning algorithm for adjusting antecedent parameters and weights of fuzzy rules in a fuzzy classifie. J. Intell. Fuzzy Syst. **30**(4), 2339–2347 (2016). https://doi.org/10.3233/ifs-152004
11. Bouchachia, A., Vanaret, C.: GT2FC: An online growing interval type-2 self-learning fuzzy classifier. IEEE Trans. Fuzzy Syst. **22**(4), 999–1018 (2013)
12. Ivarsson, M., Gorschek, T.: A method for evaluating rigor and industrial relevance of technology evaluations. Empir. Softw. Eng. **16**(3), 365–395 (2011)
13. Takagi, T., Sugeno, M.: Fuzzy identification of systems and its applications to modeling and control. IEEE Trans. Syst. Man Cybern. Syst. **SMC-15**(1), 116–132 (1985). https://doi.org/10.1109/tsmc.1985.6313399
14. Mamdani, E.H.: Application of fuzzy algorithms for control of simple dynamic plant. In: IEE 1974, vol. 121, No. 12, pp. 1585–1588. IET (1974)
15. Wang, H., Xu, Z., Pedrycz, W.: An overview on the roles of fuzzy set techniques in big data processing: Trends, challenges and opportunities. Knowl. Based Syst. **118**, 15–30 (2017). https://doi.org/10.1016/j.knosys.2016.11.008
16. Antonelli, M., Ducange, P., Lazzerini, B., Marcelloni, F.: Learning knowledge bases of multi-objective evolutionary fuzzy systems by simultaneously optimizing accuracy, complexity and partition integrity. Soft. Comput. **15**, 2335–2354 (2011). https://doi.org/10.1007/s00500-010-0665-0
17. Ishibuchi, H., Nojima, Y.: Discussions on interpretability of fuzzy systems using simple examples. In: IFSA/EUSFLAT 2009, pp. 1649–1654 (2009)
18. Kaynak, O., Jezernik, K., Szeghegyi, A.: Complexity reduction of rule based models: a survey. In: FUZZ-IEEE'02, vol. 2, pp. 1216–1221. IEEE (2002)
19. Antonelli, M., Ducange, P., Marcelloni, F., Segatori, A.: On the influence of feature selection in fuzzy rule-based regression model generation. Inform. Sci. **329**, 649–669 (2016). https://doi.org/10.1016/j.ins.2015.09.045
20. Kitchenham, B., Charters, S.: Guidelines for performing systematic literature reviews in software engineering. Technical report. Keele University (2007)
21. Kitchenham, B., Brereton, O.P., Budgen, D., Turner, M., Bailey, J., Linkman, S.: Systematic literature reviews in software engineering – A systematic literature review. Inf. Softw. Technol. **51**(1), 7–15 (2009). https://doi.org/10.1016/j.infsof.2008.09.009
22. Dybå, T., Dingsøyr, T.: Empirical studies of agile software development: A systematic review. Inform. Softw. Tech. **50**(9–10), 833–859 (2008). https://doi.org/10.1016/j.infsof.2008.01.006
23. Miliauskaitė, J.: A fuzzy inference-based approach to planning quality of enterprise business services. Doctoral dissertation. Vilnius University (2015)
24. Marimuthu, P., Perumal, V., Vijayakumar, V.: OAFPM: optimized ANFIS using frequent pattern mining for activity recognition. J. Supercomput. **75**, 1–20 (2019). https://doi.org/10.1007/s11227-019-02802-z
25. Melin, P., Ontiveros-Robles, E., Gonzalez, C.I., Castro, J.R., Castillo, O.: An approach for parameterized shadowed type-2 fuzzy membership functions applied in control applications. Soft. Comput. **23**(11), 3887–3901 (2019). https://doi.org/10.1007/s00500-018-3503-4
26. Rajeswari, A.M., Deisy, C.: Fuzzy logic based associative classifier for slow learners prediction. J. Intell. Fuzzy Syst. **36**(3), 2691–2704 (2019). https://doi.org/10.3233/jifs-18748

27. Elkano, M., Uriz, M., Bustince, H., Galar, M.: On the usage of the probability integral transform to reduce the complexity of multi-way fuzzy decision trees in Big Data classification problems. In: IEEE BigData Congress 2018, pp. 25–32. IEEE (2018)

28. Altilio, R., Rosato, A., Panella, M.: A sparse bayesian model for random weight fuzzy neural networks. In: FUZZ-IEEE, pp. 1–7. IEEE (2018)

29. Ravi, C., Khare, N.: BGFS: Design and development of brain genetic fuzzy system for data classification. Int. J. Intell. Syst. 27(2), 231–247 (2018). https://doi.org/10.1515/jisys-2016-0034

30. Golestaneh, P., Zekri, M., Sheikholeslam, F.: Fuzzy wavelet extreme learning machine. Fuzzy Set Syst. 342, 90–108 (2018). https://doi.org/10.1016/j.fss.2017.12.006

31. Ge, X., Wang, P., Yun, Z.: The rough membership functions on four types of covering-based rough sets and their applications. Inform. Sci. 390, 1–14 (2017). https://doi.org/10.1016/j.ins.2017.01.032

32. Dineva, A., Várkonyi-Kóczy, A., Tar, J.K., Piuri, V.: Performance enhancement of fuzzy logic controller using robust fixed point transformation. In: Jabłoński, R., Szewczyk, R. (eds.) Recent Global Research and Education: Technological Challenges. AISC, vol. 519, pp. 411–418. Springer, Cham (2017). https://doi.org/10.1007/978-3-319-46490-9_55

33. Ananthi, V.P., Balasubramaniam, P., Kalaiselvi, T.: A new fuzzy clustering algorithm for the segmentation of brain tumor. Soft. Comput. 20(12), 4859–4879 (2016). https://doi.org/10.1007/s00500-015-1775-5

34. Tan, Y., Li, J., Wonders, M., Chao, F., Shum, H.P., Yang, L.: Towards sparse rule base generation for fuzzy rule interpolation. In: FUZZ-IEEE 2016, pp. 110–117. IEEE (2016)

35. Chen, S.Y., Lee, C.Y., Wu, C.H., Hung, Y.H.: Intelligent motion control of voice coil motor using PID-based fuzzy neural network with optimized membership function. Eng. Comput. 33(8), 2302–2319 (2016). https://doi.org/10.1108/ec-08-2015-0250

36. Ren, P., Xu, Z., Lei, Q.: Simplified interval-valued intuitionistic fuzzy sets with intuitionistic fuzzy numbers. J. Intell. Fuzzy Syst. 30(5), 2871–2882 (2016). https://doi.org/10.3233/ifs-151735

37. Almasi, O.N., Rouhani, M.: A new fuzzy membership assignment and model selection approach based on dynamic class centers for fuzzy SVM family using the firefly algorithm. Turk. J Elec. Eng. Comp. Sci. 24, 1797–1814 (2016). https://doi.org/10.3906/elk-1310-253

38. Shill, P.C., Akhand, M.A.H., Asaduzzaman, M.D., Murase, K.: Optimization of fuzzy logic controllers with rule base size reduction using genetic algorithms. Int. J. Inf. Tech. Decis. 14(05), 1063–1092 (2015). https://doi.org/10.1109/cica.2013.6611664

39. Kumbasar, T., Hagras, H. (2015). A self-tuning zSlices-based general type-2 fuzzy PI controller. IEEE Trans. Fuzzy Syst. 23(4), 991–1013 (2015). https://doi.org/10.1109/tfuzz.2014.2336267

40. Kaur, P., Kumar, S., Singh, A.P.: Nature inspired approaches for identification of optimized fuzzy model: a comparative study. MVLSC 25(6), 555–587 (2015)

41. Deng, X., Yao, Y.: Decision-theoretic three-way approximations of fuzzy sets. Inform. Sci. 279, 702–715 (2014). https://doi.org/10.1016/j.ins.2014.04.022

42. Sami, M., Shiekhdavoodi, M.J., Pazhohanniya, M., Pazhohanniya, F.: Environmental comprehensive assessment of agricultural systems at the farm level using fuzzy logic: a case study in cane farms in Iran. Environ. Model Softw. 58, 95–108 (2014). https://doi.org/10.1016/j.envsoft.2014.02.014

43. GaneshKumar, P., Rani, C., Devaraj, D., Victoire, T.A.A.: Hybrid ant bee algorithm for fuzzy expert system based sample classification. TCBB 11(2), 347–360 (2014). https://doi.org/10.1109/tcbb.2014.2307325

44. Chaudhuri, A.: Modified fuzzy support vector machine for credit approval classification. AI Commun. 27(2), 189–211 (2014). https://doi.org/10.3233/aic-140597

45. Ramathilaga, S., Jiunn-Yin Leu, J., Huang, K.K., Huang, Y.M.: Two novel fuzzy clustering methods for solving data clustering problems. J. Intell. Fuzzy Syst. **26**(2), 705–719 (2014). https://doi.org/10.3233/ifs-120761

46. Zhu, X.-L., Chen, B., Wang, Y., Yue, D.: H∞ stabilization criterion with less complexity for nonuniform sampling fuzzy systems. Fuzzy Sets Syst. **225**, 58–73 (2013). https://doi.org/10.1016/j.fss.2012.12.011

47. Chakraborty, A., Konar, A., Pal, N.R., Jain, L.C.: Extending the contraposition property of propositional logic for fuzzy abduction. IEEE Trans. Fuzzy Syst. **21**(4), 719–734 (2012). https://doi.org/10.1109/tfuzz.2012.2230006

48. Soua, B., Borgi, A., Tagina, M.: An ensemble method for fuzzy rule-based classification systems. Knowl. Inf. Syst. **36**(2), 385–410 (2013). https://doi.org/10.1007/s10115-012-0532-7

49. Pratama, M., Er, M.J., Li, X., Oentaryo, R.J., Lughofer, E., Arifin, I.: Data driven modeling based on dynamic parsimonious fuzzy neural network. Neurocomputing **110**, 18–28 (2013). https://doi.org/10.1016/j.neucom.2012.11.013

50. Alaei, H.K., Salahshoor, K., Alaei, H.K.: A new integrated on-line fuzzy clustering and segmentation methodology with adaptive PCA approach for process monitoring and fault detection and diagnosis. Soft. Comput. **17**(3), 345–362 (2013). https://doi.org/10.1007/s00500-012-0910-9

51. Samantaray, S.R.: A systematic fuzzy rule based approach for fault classification in transmission lines. Appl. Soft Comput. **13**(2), 928–938 (2013). https://doi.org/10.1016/j.asoc.2012.09.010

52. Kumar, P.G., Vijay, S.A.A., Devaraj, D.: A hybrid colony fuzzy system for analyzing diabetes microarray data. In: IEEE CIBCB 2013, pp. 104–111. IEEE (2013)

53. Ansari, A.Q., Biswas, R., Aggarwal, S.: Neutrosophic classifier: an extension of fuzzy classifer. Appl. Soft Comput. **13**(1), 563–573 (2013). https://doi.org/10.1016/j.asoc.2012.08.002

54. Lou, C.W., Dong, M.C.: Modeling data uncertainty on electric load forecasting based on Type-2 fuzzy logic set theory. Eng. Appl. Artif. Intell. **25**(8), 1567–1576 (2012). https://doi.org/10.1016/j.engappai.2012.07.006

55. Sanz, J., Bustince, H., Fernández, A., Herrera, F.: IIVFDT: Ignorance functions based interval-valued fuzzy decision tree with genetic tuning. Int. J. Uncertain. Fuzz. **20**(supp02), 1–30 (2012). https://doi.org/10.1142/s0218488512400132

56. Murshid, A.M., Loan, S.A., Abbasi, S.A., Alamoud, A.R.M.: A novel VLSI architecture for a fuzzy inference processor using triangular-shaped membership function. Int. J. Fuzzy Syst. **14**(3), 345–360 (2012)

57. Chiu, H.-P., Tang, Y.-T., Hsieh, K.-L.: Applying cluster-based fuzzy association rules mining framework into EC environment. Appl. Soft Comput. **12**(8), 2114–2122 (2012). https://doi.org/10.1016/j.asoc.2011.08.010

58. Antonelli, M., Ducange, P., Lazzerini, B., Marcelloni, F.: Learning concurrently data and rule bases of Mamdani fuzzy rule-based systems by exploiting a novel interpretability index. Soft. Comput. **15**(10), 1981–1998 (2011). https://doi.org/10.1007/s00500-010-0629-4

59. Tamir, D.E., Kandel, A.: Axiomatic theory of complex fuzzy logic and complex fuzzy classes. IJCCC, **6**(3), 562–576 (2011). https://doi.org/10.15837/ijccc.2011.3.2135

60. Shill, P.C., Hossain, M.A., Amin, M.F., Murase, K.: An adaptive fuzzy logic controller based on real coded quantum-inspired evolutionary algorithm. FUZZ-IEEE **2011**, 614–621 (2011)

61. Al-Mamun, A., Zhu, Z.: PSO-optimized fuzzy logic controller for a single wheel robot. In: Vadakkepat, P., Kim, J.-H., Jesse, N., Mamun, A.A., Kiong, T.K., Baltes, J., Anderson, J., Verner, I., Ahlgren, D. (eds.) FIRA 2010. CCIS, vol. 103, pp. 330–337. Springer, Heidelberg (2010). https://doi.org/10.1007/978-3-642-15810-0_42

62. Rania, C., Deepa, S.N.: PSO with mutation for fuzzy classifier design. Procedia Comput. Sci. **2**, 307–313 (2010). https://doi.org/10.1016/j.procs.2010.11.040

63. Kim, D.W., de Silva, C.W., Park, G.T.: Evolutionary design of Sugeno-type fuzzy systems for modelling humanoid robots. Int. J. Syst. Sci. **41**(7), 875–888 (2010). https://doi.org/10.1080/00207720903474314

64. Beldjehem, M.: A unified granular fuzzy-neuro min-max relational framework for medical diagnosis. Int. J. Adv. Intell. Paradig. **3**(2), 122–144 (2010). https://doi.org/10.1504/ijaip.2011.039745

65. Fateh, M.-M.: Robust fuzzy control of electrical manipulators. J. Intell. Robot. Syst. **60**(3–4), 415–434 (2010). https://doi.org/10.1007/s10846-010-9430-y

66. Leng, G., Zeng, X.J., Keane, J.A.: A hybrid learning algorithm with a similarity-based pruning strategy for self-adaptive neuro-fuzzy systems. Appl. Soft Comput. **9**(4), 1354–1366 (2009). https://doi.org/10.1016/j.asoc.2009.05.006

67. Choi, B.-I., Rhee, F.C.-H.: Interval type-2 fuzzy membership function generation methods for pattern recognition. Inf. Sci. **179**(13), 2102–2122 (2009). https://doi.org/10.1016/j.ins.2008.04.009

68. Starczewski, J.T.: Efficient triangular type-2 fuzzy logic systems. Int. J. Approx. Reason. **50**(5), 799–811 (2009). https://doi.org/10.1016/j.ijar.2009.03.001

69. Lee, C.-H., Pan, H.-Y.: Performance enhancement for neural fuzzy systems using asymmetric membership functions. Fuzzy Sets Syst. **160**(7), 949–971 (2009). https://doi.org/10.1016/j.fss.2008.09.007

70. Huang, Z., Shen, Q.: Fuzzy interpolation and extrapolation: A practical approach. IEEE Trans. Fuzzy Syst. **16**(1), 13–28 (2008). https://doi.org/10.1109/tfuzz.2007.902038

71. Nie, M., Tan, W.W.: Towards an efficient type-reduction method for interval type-2 fuzzy logic systems. In: 2008 IEEE International Conference on Fuzzy Systems (IEEE World Congress on Computational Intelligence), pp. 1425–1432. IEEE, Hong Kong (2008)

72. Feng, H.-M., Wong, C.-C.: Fewer hyper-ellipsoids fuzzy rules generation using evolutional learning scheme. Cybernet Syst. **39**(1), 19–44 (2008). https://doi.org/10.1080/01969720701710022

73. Modi, P.K., Singh, S.P., Sharma, J.D.: Voltage stability evaluation of power system with FACTS devices using fuzzy neural network. Eng. Appl. Artif. Intell. **20**(4), 481–491 (2007). https://doi.org/10.1016/j.engappai.2006.08.003

74. Liu, F., Quek, C., Ng, G.S.: A novel generic hebbian ordering-based fuzzy rule base reduction approach to Mamdani neuro-fuzzy system. Neural Comput. **19**(6), 1656–1680 (2007). https://doi.org/10.1162/neco.2007.19.6.1656

75. Kenesei, T., Roubos, J.A., Abonyi, J.: A Combination-of-tools method for learning interpretable fuzzy rule-based classifiers from support vector machines. In: Yin, H., Tino, P., Corchado, E., Byrne, W., Yao, X. (eds.) IDEAL 2007. LNCS, vol. 4881, pp. 477–486. Springer, Heidelberg (2007). https://doi.org/10.1007/978-3-540-77226-2_49

76. González, J., Rojas, I., Pomares, H., Herrera, L.J., Guillén, A., Palomares, J.M., Rojas, F.: Improving the accuracy while preserving the interpretability of fuzzy function approximators by means of multi-objective evolutionary algorithms. Int. J. Approx Reason. **44**(1), 32–44 (2007). https://doi.org/10.1016/j.ijar.2006.02.006

77. Pan, H.Y., Lee, C.H., Chang, F.K., Chang, S.K.: Construction of asymmetric type-2 fuzzy membership functions and application in time series prediction. In: ICMLC 2007, vol. 4, pp. 2024–2030. IEEE, Hong Kong (2007). https://doi.org/10.1109/icmlc.2007.4370479

78. Xiong, N., Funk, P.: Construction of fuzzy knowledge bases incorporating feature selection. Soft. Comput. **10**(9), 796–804 (2006). https://doi.org/10.1007/s00500-005-0009-7

79. Huang, Z., Shen, Q.: Fuzzy interpolative reasoning via scale and move transformations. IEEE Trans. Fuzzy Syst. **14**(2), 340–359 (2006). https://doi.org/10.1109/tfuzz.2005.859324

80. Kim, M.W., Khil, A., Ryu, J.W.: Efficient fuzzy rules for classification. In: AIDM 2006, pp. 50–57. IEEE (2006)

81. Zanganeh, M., Mousavi, S.J., Etemad-Shahidi, A.: A genetic algorithm-based fuzzy inference system in prediction of wave parameters. In: Reusch, B. (ed.) 9th Fuzzy Days in Dortmund International Conference, pp. 741–750. Springer, Berlin, Heidelberg (2006). Int. J. Comput. Intell. Appl.

82. Kim, M.W., Ryu, J.W.: Optimized fuzzy decision tree using genetic algorithm. In: King, I., Wang, J., Chan, L.-W., Wang, D. (eds.) ICONIP 2006. LNCS, vol. 4234, pp. 797–806. Springer, Heidelberg (2006). https://doi.org/10.1007/11893295_88

83. Casillas, J., Cordón, O., del Jesus, M.J., Herrera, F.: Genetic tuning of fuzzy rule deep structures preserving interpretability and its interaction with fuzzy rule set reduction. IEEE Trans. Fuzzy Syst. **13**(1), 13–29 (2005). https://doi.org/10.1109/tfuzz.2004.839670

84. Kim, M.W., Ryu, J.W.: Optimized Fuzzy Classification Using Genetic Algorithm. In: Wang, L., Jin, Y. (eds.) FSKD 2005. LNCS (LNAI), vol. 3613, pp. 392–401. Springer, Heidelberg (2005). https://doi.org/10.1007/11539506_51

85. Kóczy, L.T., Botzheim, J.: Fuzzy models, identification and applications. In: IEEE ICCC 2005, pp. 13–19. IEEE (2005)

86. Baranyi, P., Kóczy, L.T., Gedeon, T.D.: A generalized concept for fuzzy rule interpolation. IEEE Trans. Fuzzy Syst. **12**(6), 820–837 (2004). https://doi.org/10.1109/tfuzz.2004.836085

87. Kim, M.W., Ryu, J.W.: Optimized fuzzy classification for data mining. In: Lee, Y., Li, J., Whang, K.-Y., Lee, D. (eds.) DASFAA 2004. LNCS, vol. 2973, pp. 582–593. Springer, Heidelberg (2004). https://doi.org/10.1007/978-3-540-24571-1_53

88. Hong, T.P., Lin, K.Y., Chien, B.C.: Mining fuzzy multiple-level association rules from quantitative data. Appl. Intell. **18**(1), 79–90 (2003). https://doi.org/10.1023/a:1020991105855

89. Makrehchi, M., Basir, O., Kamel, M.: Generation of fuzzy membership function using information theory measures and genetic algorithm. In: Bilgiç, T., De Baets, B., Kaynak, O. (eds.) IFSA 2003. LNCS, vol. 2715, pp. 603–610. Springer, Heidelberg (2003). https://doi.org/10.1007/3-540-44967-1_72

90. Hsu, C.C., Szu, H.H.: Chaotic neural network for learnable associative memory recall. In: Independent Component Analyses, Wavelets, and Neural Networks, vol. 5102, pp. 258–266. SPIE (2003). https://doi.org/10.1117/12.502480

91. Xiong, N., Litz, L.: Reduction of fuzzy control rules by means of premise learning–method and case study. Fuzzy Sets Syst. **132**(2), 217–231 (2002). https://doi.org/10.1016/s0165-0114(02)00112-4

92. Xiong, N.: Evolutionary learning of rule premises for fuzzy modelling. Int. J. Syst. Sci. **32**(9), 1109–1118 (2001). https://doi.org/10.1080/00207720010015735

93. Mitaim, S., Kosko, B.: The shape of fuzzy sets in adaptive function approximation. IEEE Trans. Fuzzy Syst. **9**(4), 637–656 (2001). https://doi.org/10.1109/91.940974

94. Guillaume, S.: Designing fuzzy inference systems from data: An interpretability-oriented review. IEEE Trans. Fuzzy Syst. **9**(3), 426–443 (2001). https://doi.org/10.1109/91.928739

95. Di, L., Srikanthan, T., Chandel, R.S., Katsunori, I.: Neural-network-based self-organized fuzzy logic control for arc welding. Eng. Appl. Artif. Intell. **14**(2), 115–124 (2001). https://doi.org/10.1016/s0952-1976(00)00057-9

96. Matarazzo, B., Munda, G.: New approaches for the comparison of LR fuzzy numbers: a theoretical and operational analysis. Fuzzy Sets Syst. **118**(3), 407–418 (2001). https://doi.org/10.1016/s0165-0114(98)00425-4

97. Alcalá, R., Casillas, J., Cordón, O., Herrera, F.: Building fuzzy graphs: features and taxonomy of learning for non-grid-oriented fuzzy rule-based systems. J. Intell. Fuzzy Syst. **11**(3–4), 99–119 (2001)

98. Yao, J., Dash, M., Tan, S.T., Liu, H.: Entropy-based fuzzy clustering and fuzzy modeling. Fuzzy Sets Syst. **113**(3), 381–388 (2000). https://doi.org/10.1016/s0165-0114(98)00038-4

99. Hsu, Y.T., Chen, C.M.: A novel fuzzy logic system based on N-version programming. IEEE Trans. Fuzzy Syst. **8**(2), 155–170 (2000). https://doi.org/10.1109/91.842150

100. Rojas, I., Pomares, H., Ortega, J., Prieto, A.: Self-organized fuzzy system generation from training examples. IEEE Trans. Fuzzy Syst. **8**(1), 23–36 (2000). https://doi.org/10.1109/91.824763

101. Gil, J., Hwang, C.-S.: A Design of Genetic-Fuzzy Systems Using Grammatical Encoding and Its Applications. In: Mohammadian, M. (ed.) New Frontiers in Computational Intelligence and Its Applications, vol. 57, pp. 178–196. IOS Press, Amsterdam (2000)

102. Hong, T.P., Chen, J.B.: Finding relevant attributes and membership functions. Fuzzy Sets Syst. **103**(3), 389–404 (1999). https://doi.org/10.1016/s0165-0114(97)00187-5

103. Lu, P.C.: The application of fuzzy neural network techniques in constructing an adaptive car-following indicator. AI EDAM **12**(3), 231–241 (1998). https://doi.org/10.1017/s0890060498123028

104. Giachetti, R.E., Young, R.E.: Analysis of the error in the standard approximation used for multiplication of triangular and trapezoidal fuzzy numbers and the development of a new approximation. Fuzzy Sets Syst. **91**(1), 1–13 (1997). https://doi.org/10.1016/s0165-0114(96)00118-2

105. Marinelli, C., Castellano, G., Attolico, G., Distante, A.: Optimization of a fuzzy controller by genetic algorithms. In: Applications of Soft Computing, vol. 3165, pp. 153–160. SPIE (1997)

106. KóczY, L.T., Sugeno, M.: Explicit functions of fuzzy control systems. Int. J. Uncertain Fuzz. Knowl. Based Syst. **04**(06), 515–535 (1996). https://doi.org/10.1142/s0218488596000287

107. Wang, L., Langari, R.: Sugeno model, fuzzy discretization, and the EM algorithm. Fuzzy Sets Syst. **82**(3), 279–288 (1996). https://doi.org/10.1016/0165-0114(95)00228-6

108. Castellano, G., Fanelli, A.M.: Pruning in fuzzy-neural systems. In: Javor, A., et al. (eds.) ESM 1996, pp. 673–677. Soc. for Computer Simulation International, Budapest (1996)

109. Laukonen, E.G., Passino, K.M.: Training fuzzy systems to perform estimation and identification. Eng. Appl. Artif. Intell. **8**(5), 499–514 (1995). https://doi.org/10.1016/0952-1976(95)00029-z

110. Bridges, S.M., Higginbotham, C., McKinion, J.M., Hodges, J.E.: Fuzzy descriptors of time-varying data: theory and application. AI Appl. **9**(2), 1–14 (1995)

111. Takagi, T., Imura, A., Ushida, H., Yamaguchi, T.: Conceptual fuzzy sets as a meaning representation and their inductive construction. Int. J. Intell. Syst. **10**(11), 929–945 (1995). https://doi.org/10.1002/int.4550101102

112. Wang, F.Y., Kim, H.M.: Implementing adaptive fuzzy logic controllers with neural networks: A design paradigm. J. Intell. Fuzzy Syst. **3**(2), 165–180 (1995). https://doi.org/10.3233/ifs-1995-3206

113. Rhee, F.C.H., Krishnapuram, R.: Fuzzy rule generation methods for high-level computer vision. Fuzzy Sets Syst. **60**(3), 245–258 (1993). https://doi.org/10.1016/0165-0114(93)90436-1

114. Martín-Martín, A., Orduna-Malea, E., Thelwall, M., López-Cózar, E.D.: Google Scholar, Web of Science, and Scopus: A systematic comparison of citations in 252 subject categories. J. Inf. **12**(4), 1160–1177 (2018)

Towards DSL for DL Lifecycle Data Management

Edgars Celms[1(✉)], Janis Barzdins[1], Audris Kalnins[1], Arturs Sprogis[1],
Mikus Grasmanis[2], Sergejs Rikacovs[2], and Paulis Barzdins[1]

[1] Institute of Mathematics and Computer Science, University of Latvia, Riga, Latvia
{edgars.celms,janis.barzdins,audris.kalnins,arturs.sprogis,
paulis.barzdins}@lumii.lv
[2] Innovation Labs LETA, Riga, Latvia
{mikus.grasmanis,sergejs.rikacovs}@leta.lv

Abstract. A new method based on Domain Specific Language (DSL) approach to Deep Learning (DL) lifecycle data management tool support is presented: a very simple DL lifecycle data management tool, which however is usable in practice (it will be called Core tool) and a very advanced extension mechanism which in fact converts the Core tool into domain specific tool (DSL tool) building framework for DL lifecycle data management tasks. The extension mechanism will be based on the metamodel specialization approach to DSL modeling tools introduced by authors. The main idea of metamodel specialization is that we, at first, define the Universal Metamodel (UMM) for a domain and then for each use case define a Specialized Metamodel. But for use in our new domain the specialization concept will be extended: we add a functional specialization where invoking an additional custom program at appropriate points of Core tool is supported.

Keywords: DSL · DL · Metamodel specialization · DL lifecycle data management

1 Introduction

The Deep Learning (DL) process (i.e., training of neural networks) for specific domains is long and complicated. It usually consists of a large number of DL program runs, during which training parameters, training data sets and even the DL program itself are modified. All this actualizes the issue of effective training lifecycle data management. At this moment there already are several systems supporting this process. A more detailed view on them will be given in the next section. Here we only note that for different DL tasks requirements for support may vary greatly. Due to this aspect the existing DL lifecycle data management systems either cover a small part of these requirements or become excessively complicated in order to cover as large as possible part of the requirements. This situation becomes very similar to the one in the system modeling area. There the Universal Modeling Language (UML) was developed and naturally this language was very complicated. Typically for any real tasks a very small subset of these

T. Robal et al. (Eds.): DB&IS 2020, CCIS 1243, pp. 205–218, 2020.
https://doi.org/10.1007/978-3-030-57672-1_16

many possibilities was applicable, while at the same time something was missing for tasks in the given domain. Besides that, in real application domains there is a desire to obtain software implementation from the chosen language automatically. As a result, the idea of Domain Specific Languages (DSL) and tools developed rapidly. Required was not a single universal tool, but a DSL tool building framework. By using such a platform an expert of the given problem domain could relatively easily build the required tool himself. This is the area where the authors of this paper have also given their investment [1–4].

A natural question appears, whether the DSL approach could not be applied to the DL lifecycle data management area as well? In other words, whether instead of a complicated universal tool, a DSL tool building framework could be built, by means of which a DL domain expert himself could relatively easily build a tool for his domain and training methodology. We note that for the DL lifecycle data management area the situation is more complicated since e.g. here we have to provide easy simultaneous collaboration for several human actors (see Sect. 5).

The goal of this paper is to deeper investigate the DSL approach for the DL lifecycle data management area and offer one possible solution for this problem:

1. Very simple DL lifecycle data management tool, which however is usable in practice (in what follows it will be called Core tool);
2. Advanced extension mechanism for this Core tool which in fact converts the Core tool into a DSL tool building framework for DL lifecycle data management tasks.

The proposed extension mechanism to a great degree will be based on the metamodel specialization approach for DSL modeling tools introduced by authors [1–4]. The main idea of metamodel specialization is that we at first define the Universal Metamodel (UMM) for a domain and then for each use case in this domain define a Specialized Metamodel (SMM). SMM contains a set of subclasses of UMM classes, as many as we need. The subclasses are defined according to UML rules, but with some restrictions. Class attributes may be assigned with new fixed values, but new attributes may not be added. Similarly, for associations the role names may be redefined (subset) and multiplicities may be changed (shrunk). In our new domain we also allow attribute names and types to be redefined. We illustrate all this on a very simple example from a workflow domain. This example is taken from our paper [4], but slightly extended to also show our new specialization features. Figure 1 shows the UMM for this workflow.

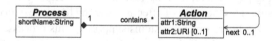

Fig. 1. UMM for simple workflow.

Figure 2 shows a specialization of this UMM for business trip workflow in an enterprise in a standard UML notation. Similarly to [4], in order to make diagrams more compact and readable, we use here a custom notation for specialization (only slightly extended with respect to [4]). This notation uses the super-object (class, attribute or association) name in braces to reference it in the sub-object. See this notation for business trip in Fig. 3. In the general case not all UMM classes may be specialized. In order to define which UMM classes may be specialized, we show their class names in italic (in our example these classes are *Process* and *Action*).

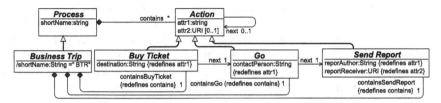

Fig. 2. Workflow specialization in standard UML notation.

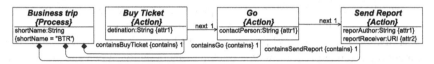

Fig. 3. Custom notation for Business Trip specialization.

Now the main new idea in this paper. In comparison with the paper [4] the specialization concept itself will be extended. In [4] it was assumed that the semantics of specialized classes are directly determined by their attribute values or a default attribute values set. We will call such specialization a simple specialization. But in this paper, we need a broader specialization concept where the semantics are determined by some additional information as well. Such specialization will be called functional specialization. In our domain we will use true custom extension of the Core tool functionality specially adapted for the given DL use case by means of invoking an additional custom program at appropriate points of the Core tool functioning. The functional specialization defines how such custom programs can be found. Both simple and functional specialization will be used in this paper.

2   Related Work

Some related works were already mentioned in the previous section. In this section we will present works which directly refer to DL lifecycle data management.

Machine learning (ML) has a complex lifecycle consisting of many phases and steps, from the preparation of the training and test data via model development and model training, to testing and deployment. Although the ML libraries themselves (Scikit-Learn, Tensorflow, PyTorch, Keras, etc.) have already matured in the last few years, the pipeline around them and the corresponding tool landscape is still in development and is very fragmented. Each of the tools covers one or several aspects of model development, and for a complete pipeline you may need to select a set of several tools which work together in a pipeline.

There are tools in the landscape which orchestrate ML workflows in the cloud [5–7]. Other tools like [8] extend the workflow orchestration with data warehouse integration, state transfer and meta-training. However, they do not provide any means for monitoring the training and propose to use Jupyter notebooks for this purpose.

Some tools like DVC [9] focus on version and dependency management for the data artefacts and models, but they do not track the experiments themselves.

One of the most important phases in ML is model development and training. Some tools (e.g. AutoKeras [10]) try to automate this phase providing means for automatic exploration of hyperparameter space and selection of the best parameter values for the given problem and training data as well as with selecting the best architecture for the model, making the ML available for non-ML experts. In some cases these tools abstract the developer from directly running the ML experiments.

However, these techniques are not mature enough yet, and in many cases, developers still have to run the ML experiments manually. This involves iterative running of experiments in search for the best model architecture and for the best hyperparameters. Natural requirements here are the ability to track, compare and reproduce the experiments. Good tool support is essential for development productivity.

Typically, these tools [11–17] provide a set of library functions which can be used to augment the training program with a tracking functionality. When such augmented program is run, the tracking information is recorded in some sort of a database, either locally or on a remote server. The tracking part of these tools has a natural counterpart, a tool for visualization and comparison of the experiment results.

Some of the tools concentrate on the tracking functionality, and their support for visualization of ML experiments is limited [11, 12], or they provide a command line interface for experiment comparison [18]. Other tools [17] rely on complementary tools (e.g. [19]) for experiment visualization.

However, most tools have been built with support for visualization and comparison of experiment metrics, usually as a dashboard containing tables and sometimes charts.

There are cloud-based solutions [13, 14] which have many dashboard options built in, but they are commercially closed projects, and their users are limited to the visualization options provided by the platform and cannot extend the tool with their own.

Some projects like [15, 16] which are the closest to our approach do support both experiment tracking and visualization dashboards and are open source, but you have to dive into the programming if the prebuilt visualizations are not sufficient.

The most important feature missing in all these tools is an easily usable extension possibility for adapting to a specific DL task domain, e.g. tasks required for news agencies as in this paper. Open source tools like [15] can be extended, but such an extension besides direct development of the required software requires deep understanding of the existing software and, especially, the data structures used in it. Therefore, our proposed extension mechanism described in Sect. 5 can be used also by domain experts (not only DL experts).

3   DL Lifecycle Data Management Framework: General Structure

The general structure of our DL Lifecycle Data Management Framework (LDM framework) is presented in Fig. 4. The LDM framework consists of two components:

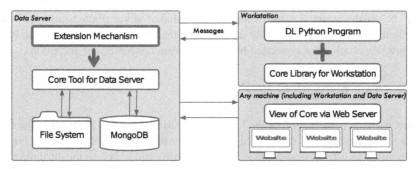

Fig. 4. General structure of LDM framework.

1. Core platform, which includes:

   a. Core tool which works on Data Server.
   b. Core library which is placed on Workstation.

2. Core extension mechanism which in fact ensures the development of the DSL tool for the given DL lifecycle data management.

The Core tool and extension mechanisms will be presented in a greater detail in the next sections. Here we note only that the Core extension mechanism refers only to Core data which is stored on Data server and does not affect the interaction mechanism between Workstation and Data server. In other words, the Core library for Workstation is universal, i.e. it does not depend on Core extension (the usage of role_name ensures the universality of this library). The only information the DL Python programmer should know about this library is that the following functions can be called:

login(user_id, psw): a trial to authorize the user with user_ID using the password psw, in case of success returns the token_id

startRun(project_name): start new run in the project project_name

log(msg,role_name): store on DS the message msg and the corresponding role_name in the current run

uploadFile(file_name, role_name): upload the file file_name and the corresponding role_name in the current run

finishRun(): finish the current run

From a higher abstraction level we can say that by means of these functions Workstation sends the following messages (shown in Fig. 5) to Data server.

Login	StartRun	Log	UploadFile	FinishRun
dataServerIP:string	projectName:string	roleName:string	roleName:string	//token :jwtToken
userName:string	//token :jwtToken	msg:string	fileName:lstring	//runID:string
password:string	/runID:string	//token :jwtToken	//token :jwtToken	/endTime:string
/userIP	/startTime:string	//runID:string	//runID:string	
			/uploadTime:string	

Fig. 5. Class diagram of messages.

"//" before the attribute name means that the value of this attribute is inserted by the Core library. "/" before the attribute name means that the value of this attribute is not sent from Workstation but generated by Core platform upon message reception.

4   Core Tool for Data Server

We start with the presentation of the Logical Data Model for this platform in the form of a class diagram (see Fig. 6). In what follows we will call this model the Core Logical MM. In this MM (and in next MMs as well) the slash symbol before the attribute name will mark those attributes whose values are set by the Core platform itself. The values of other attributes come from the messages sent by the Workstation (or are directly entered via the relevant web page, e.g. the project Name for a new Project).

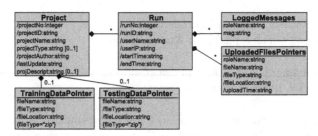

Fig. 6. The Core Logical MM.

Now about the semantics of this MM. Class and attribute names already explain the semantics to a great degree. We only note that instances of the *Run* class (together with classes *LoggedMessage* and *UploadedFile*) mean the information sent to the Data server from Workstation during the training run.

Here we assume that the neural network training process consists of many runs. In addition, the network itself may be modified between two consecutive runs. In order to clarify this situation, Fig. 7 presents an instance of this MM which corresponds to two training runs. Figure 8 shows the same instance in the form of web pages, which should be built by our offered Core platform.

Here we have to add a couple of words on entering the Training and Testing Data: the page Project Details contains the Upload button which is used for this goal. This data is meant to always be entered as zip files and will be stored in the repository visible in Fig. 10 in the folder TrainTestData. The unzipped folders are meant to be stored in the same repository and will have the same names as the corresponding zip file. In the case where Training and/or Testing data required for the given project are already stored in the folder (i.e. they were entered before) the Upload button should not be used and in the corresponding Training and/or Testing field the corresponding file name should simply be entered.

In the conclusion of this section we note that the information already presented is more or less adequate for a simple Workstation user to start using the Core platform seriously: to extend their DL program in Python with Core library function calls for

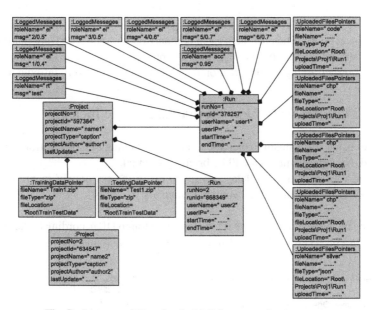

Fig. 7. Instance of Core Logical MM representing two runs.

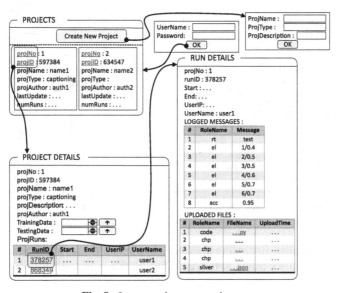

Fig. 8. Instance shown as web pages.

sending data to Data Server as well as for downloading files from Data Server to their Workstation, e.g. Code or Checkpoint from an earlier Run. Such file download is planned to be done via the web page (see Fig. 8) using the traditional web browser facilities – open the web page on their Workstation and download the reachable from this page files via the Save As option.

The next section will explain the Core platform extension facilities which open significant new possibilities for the user in comparison with the bare Core platform.

Let us remind that the time-consuming DL process occurs on Workstation and on Data Server only training results are stored and this occurs relatively infrequently.

5 Core Platform Extension Mechanism: Basic Ideas

For the extension mechanism explanation, a deeper opening of Core platform internals is required. Now these internals will be briefly presented.

Physical representation of data corresponding to the previously mentioned Core Logical MM (Fig. 6) is done via two complementary facilities:

a. The Logical MM and its instances are stored in Mongo DB according to the structure shown in Fig. 9 (ProjectID and RunID are generated automatically),

```
db.createCollection("project")
db.project.insertOne({projectId:597384, projectNo:1,
    projectName:"name1", ... })
db.project.insertOne({projectId:634547, projectNo:2,
    projectName:"name2", ... })
db.createCollection("run")
db.run.insertOne({runId:378257, projectId:597384,
    runNo:1, ... })
db.run.insertOne({runId:868349, projectId:597384,
    runNo:2, ... })
db.createCollection("loggedMessages")
db.loggedMessages.insertOne({runId:378257,
    roleName:"rt", msg:"test"})
db.loggedMessages.insertOne({runId: 378257,
    roleName: "el", msg:"1/0.4"})
db.createCollection("uploadedFilesPoint")
db.uploadedFilesPoint.insertOne({runId: 378257,
    roleName:"code", fileName:"..." ...}) ... ... ...
db.createCollection("trainingDataPoint")
db.trainingDataPoint.insertOne({projectId:597384,
    filename:"Train1.zip", fileType:"zip", fileLocation:
    "ROOT\TrainTestData"}) ... ... ...
```

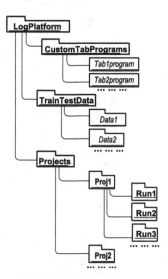

Fig. 9. Mongo DB presentation of the given instance.   **Fig. 10.** Repository structure

b. The files themselves (including the Core platform software) are stored in the Data server file system according to the repository shown in Fig. 10.

Now some comments on this structure. LogPlatform is the root folder of this structure. In this folder the Core platform software is stored. For instance, the full address of this folder could be C:\Programs\LogPlatform. This address will be denoted by ROOT.As a result the full name of folder Proj1 would be ROOT\Projects\Proj1.

The opening of Core platform internals mentioned above is sufficient for our offered extension mechanism. We start the definition of this mechanism by extending the Core Logical MM with new classes called extension classes (their names are shown in italic font). The extended MM is shown in Fig. 11, further on we will call it the Universal Meta-model (UMM). As Fig. 11 shows, there are two kinds of extension classes corresponding to two kinds of extensions supported by our LDM framework:

a. Sense classes: *LiteralWithGeneralSense, LiteralWithSlashPairSense, FileWithSense-Pointer*
b. Custom tab classes: *CustomProjectTab* and *CustomRunTab*

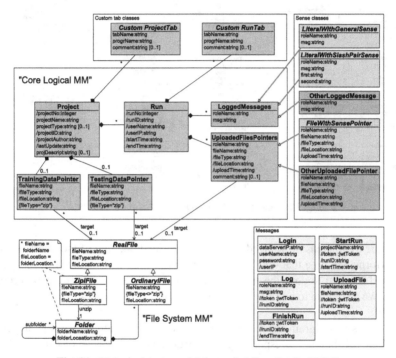

Fig. 11. Universal metamodel (extended Core Logical MM).

The LDM framework we offer is based on the idea that by means of specialization of the mentioned extension classes we will define concrete DL lifecycle data management tools (called DL DSL tools) which provide new additional possibilities in comparison with the Core platform.

Now let us explain this idea in a greater detail. For sense classes we will apply simple specialization, its result is illustrated in Fig. 12.

However, the main heavyweight DL DSL tool building facility is the specialization of custom tab classes. For these classes we will apply the functional specialization. These classes have an attribute progrName, which after specialization must point to an independent executable program, also called an Extension program. This program should be inserted in the repository, shown in Fig. 10. This means that simultaneously with defining a specialized tab class we have to build the corresponding extension program.

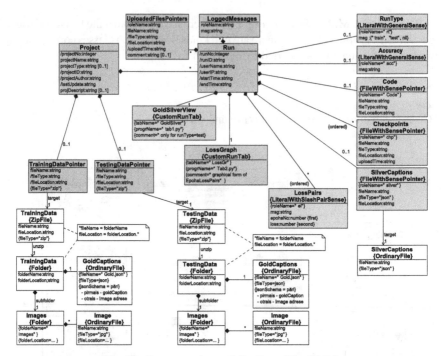

Fig. 12. One concrete specialization of the UMM.

Namely due to this reason we need the above described opening of the internals of the Core platform. We note that our UMM also includes the File system MM. Its specialization will be used to describe more precisely the source data for extension program building. We also have to add two more details on extension programs:

a. Any extension program has just one parameter. Its value in the corresponding extension call will be the corresponding projectID value (in the case of *Custom Project Tab*) or the corresponding runID value (in the case of *Custom Run Tab*).
b. Any extension program call will open a new web page presenting the result of this program execution (e.g. Loss graph).

Before proceeding we want to stress the following aspect: our DL DSL framework is related to the following 4 human actors:

1. Framework developer
2. DSL tool configurator/developer
3. DSL tool user, i.e. DL programmer at a Workstation
4. End user, e.g. LETA data expert

The DSL tool developer is the actor who performs the corresponding UMM class specialization and, if required, develops the corresponding extension programs and places these programs in executable form on Data Server in the repository shown in Fig. 10.

Beforehand however the tool developer has to perform one more job – together with the DSL tool users fix the list of permitted role names and the semantics of these roles for messages to be sent from a Workstation to the Data server. Together with the role list it is also necessary to agree on the structure of messages corresponding to these roles, including the files to be uploaded. The agreement on the file structure should be sufficient for developing the corresponding extension programs. Such an agreement for a DSL will be called a DSL memorandum. Let us stress once more that such a memorandum stands outside of the formalism used by us (the above-mentioned file structure MM only helps in writing such a memorandum). In fact, there is a need for such a memorandum for the development of any DSL tool, e.g. to explain in natural language the semantics of used DSL symbols (but it is not referred to so formally). In our case the agreement covers a wider area and therefore we use such a term.

Now let us go to the explanation of Fig. 12 presenting one concrete specialization of the UMM. In a sense it will be the memorandum for the DSL tool defined by this specialization. First, let us stress that our extension mechanism (via the extension class specialization) refers only to additional features of Data Server (DS) which permit to view in a more understandable way the information sent by Workstation to Data Server (in comparison with the bare Core platform). The custom tabs permit to view this information in a completely new format, e.g. in the form of various graphs. For this explanation we assume that from a Workstation to Data Server the same messages have been sent as in the example mentioned in Sect. 4 (see the Fig. 7). According to the Fig. 7 the following message roles are used: acc, rt, lp for ordinary messages; and code, chp, silver for files. The semantics of these roles to a great degree is explained by sufficiently expressive names of specialized classes used in the example: *Accuracy*, *RunType*, *LossPairs*, *Code*, *Checkpoint* and *SilverCaptions*. Some words are needed for the class *LossPairs* and its parent class *LiteralWithSlashPairsSense*: the attribute msg of this class is used to code message pairs (first, second) separated by the slash character. For example, if msg="25/0.95", then first = 25 and second = 0.95. At defining the class *LossPairs*, the first is renamed to epochNo and second to loss (such a redefinition is permitted at class specialization).

The results of this specialization are illustrated in Fig. 13 where the Run Details web page is presented. The first difference from Fig. 8 where the corresponding web page is also visible is such that the messages sent to DS are grouped according to the specialized classes and thus have become more understandable (in addition also the possibilities related to *LiteralWithSlashPairSense*).

Now let us discuss the Custom tabs. Figure 12 shows two Custom tabs: LossGr and GoldSilver, they both are specializations of *CustomRunTab*. As already mentioned, the feature there is the extension program: in the case of *LossGr* it is a program with the name tab2.py, but in the case of *GoldSilver* it is a program with name tab1.py.

Now let us explain what these programs are doing. The program tab2.py for the given *Run* instance (when invoked with the parameter value equal to the runID of this instance) generates a web page with a Loss graph from the *LossPairs* instances related to the given *Run* instance. In this graph epochNO is mapped on the x-axis, but lossValue on the y-axis. The program tab1.py performs a slightly more complicated action. This program (invoked with runID value of a *Run* instance) finds the corresponding *RunType*

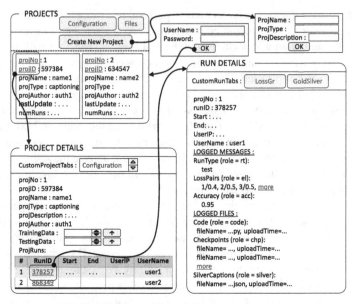

Fig. 13. The result of specialization as a web page.

instance and if its msg attribute value is equal to "test", generates a web page which for the corresponding *TestingData* contains the table visualized in Fig. 14. For this purpose this program first uses the folder *TestingData* visible in Fig. 12. This folder in turn contains the Images folder and the *GoldCaptions* file. Secondly, this program finds the *SilverCaptions* file corresponding to this Run instance.

IMAGE		GOLD	SILVER
		three men fishing	a man is riding a boat
		Riga city skyline	a city filled with lots of buildings
		cars standing in traffic	a car is parked on a street
... ...		... ...	... ...

Fig. 14. Results of the GoldSilver extension program execution.

Had our example more Custom tabs, they should be explained as well and our Memorandum would be longer. Now on the topic where these Custom tabs are visible in the Data Server website and how to invoke them. Let us look at Fig. 13. There we see that Custom Run tabs are visible in the Run Details web page, but Custom Project tabs in the Project Details web page. By clicking on these tabs, the following Core platform action occurs: the corresponding ID value is found (in the case of *Run* it is runID, in the case of *Project* it is projectID). Then the extension program corresponding to this tab is invoked with the selected ID value as the input parameter. As it was mentioned above, program execution result is to show the corresponding web page.

Finally, how the Core platform knows which tabs must be shown in the given web page and what values must be passed as parameters. For this purpose a special configuration tab named Configuration is in the Project Details page. By clicking on the Configuration tab, the page visible in Fig. 15 is opened. By executing the actions visible in this page (i.e. by filling in the corresponding tables) we pass to the Core platform all the required information – both for sense class specialization and custom tab definition.

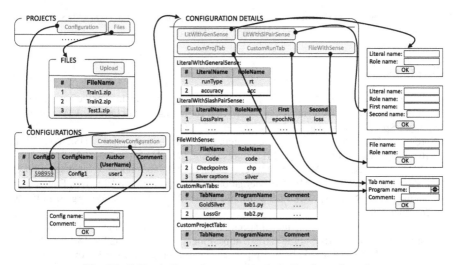

Fig. 15. Tables in the web page opened via Configuration tab.

Now briefly about the Core platform implementation. The implementation of the "bare" Core platform is quite straightforward: the Core Logical MM is stored in the Mongo DB (see Fig. 9), but the corresponding files are stored in the file system according to Fig. 10. Then follows a resource demanding, but quite simple from the logical point of view programming of the used web pages. Certain comments are required on the Extended Core platform implementation, which ensures the described Extension mechanism. In order to make the use of the Extension mechanism simpler, we will use not the code generation method (as it is typically done for building traditional DSL tools), but an interpretation method. Namely the information entered via the Configuration tool (the tables visible in Fig. 15) is directly stored in the Mongo DB and further, when a request for a web view appears, this view is generated from the "bare" Core information and modified in the interpretation mode according to the entered configuration information.

6 Conclusions

The paper provides both new theoretical and practical results for the DL lifecycle data management area. The main theoretical result is a significant extension of the metamodel specialization approach for DSL development. But the practical aspects are related to the ERDF project 1.1.1.1/18/A/045, where an easily usable system for DL lifecycle data management framework covering all phases of DL must be developed. A special orientation there is towards tasks for news agencies, including the Latvian News Agency LETA (it is a partner in the project). That is namely why the task of image captioning is chosen as a specialization example in the paper. We also have to note that a preliminary version of such system is already developed (available at https://github.com/IMCS-DL4 media/LDM), this version served as a source for details of the Core tool in the paper.

Acknowledgements. The research was supported by ERDF project 1.1.1.1/18/A/045 at Institute of Mathematics and Computer Science, University of Latvia.

References

1. Barzdins, J., Cerans, K., Grasmanis, M., Kalnins A., et al.: Domain specific languages for business process management: A case study. In: Proceedings of 9th OOPSLA Workshop on Domain-Specific Modeling, pp. 34–40 (2009)
2. Sprogis, A., Barzdins, J.: Specification, configuration and implementation of DSL tools. Front. Artif. Intell. Appl. **249**, 330–343 (2012). https://doi.org/10.3233/978-1-61499-161-8-330
3. Kalnins, A., Barzdins, J.: Metamodel specialization for graphical modeling language support. In: Proceedings of 19th ACM/IEEE International Conference on Model Driven Engineering Languages and Systems, MODELS 2016, pp. 103–112 (2016). https://doi.org/10.1145/297 6767.2976779
4. Kalnins, A., Barzdins, J.: Metamodel specialization for graphical language support. Softw. Syst. Model. J. **18**(3), 1699–1735 (2019). https://doi.org/10.1007/s10270-018-0668-3
5. Bisong, E.: Kubeflow and kubeflow pipelines. In: Building Machine Learning and Deep Learning Models on Google Cloud Platform, pp. 671–685. Apress (2019). https://doi.org/10. 1007/978-1-4842-4470-8_46
6. Flyte: Cloud Native Machine Learning and Data Processing Platform. https://flyte.org
7. Dagster: System for building modern data applications. https://github.com/dagster-io/dagster
8. Metaflow: Framework for real-life data science. https://metaflow.org
9. DVC: Open-source Version Control System for Machine Learning Projects. https://dvc.org
10. Haifeng, J., Qingquan. S., Xia, H.: Auto-Keras: An efficient neural architecture search system. In: Proceedings of 25th ACM SIGKDD International Conference on Knowledge Discovery and Data Mining, pp. 1946–1956 (2019). https://doi.org/10.1145/3292500.3330648
11. Observatory: Solution for tracking machine learning models. https://github.com/wmeints/obs ervatory
12. lab: MLearning Lab. https://github.com/beringresearch/lab
13. Weights&Biases. https://www.wandb.com
14. comet. https://www.comet.ml
15. mlflow: An open source platform for the machine learning lifecycle. https://mlflow.org
16. FGLab: ML Dashboard. https://kaixhin.github.io/FGLab
17. Sacred. https://github.com/IDSIA/sacred
18. guild.ai: The ML Engineering Platform. https://guild.ai
19. Sacredboard: Web dashboard for the Sacred machine learning experiment management tool. https://github.com/chovanecm/sacredboard

A Method of Comparative Spatial Analysis of a Digitized (LiDAR) Point Cloud and the Corresponding GIS Database

Riina Maigre[1]([📧]) [ID], Hele-Mai Haav[1] [ID], Rauni Lillemets[1], Kalev Julge[1], and Gaspar Anton[2]

[1] Tallinn University of Technology, Akadeemia tee 15a, 12618 Tallinn, Estonia
riina@ioc.ee, helemai@cs.ioc.ee,
{Rauni.Lillemets,Kalev.Julge}@taltech.ee
[2] Reach-U Ltd., Tartu, Estonia
Gaspar.Anton@reach-u.com

Abstract. Creation of a consistent 3D model of a city requires accurate data. Usually, accuracy assurance problems of data are solved by time consuming and expensive process of collecting and aligning with ground control points (GCP). Therefore, alternative methods become important. Using existing Geographic Information Systems (GIS) databases may decrease the time and cost of creating a reference dataset by reducing the number of GCPs required for producing high quality 3D data or GIS databases can serve as reference data. For this purpose, new spatial data analysis methods are needed to assure that GIS databases are of high-quality. In this paper, we propose a novel methodology and its sample development for comparative spatial analysis of digitized point cloud and the corresponding GIS database in order to statistically assess opportunities to align Mobile Mapping Systems (MMS) data with existing GIS databases or to improve involved datasets. The method is evaluated using LiDAR data provided by Estonian company Reach-U Ltd. and GIS database layers from different Estonian open and closed databases.

Keywords: Spatial data analysis · Clustering · LiDAR point cloud · MMS · GIS

1 Introduction

Nowadays, many cities all over the world (e.g., New York, London, Singapore, Helsinki, and Tallinn) create 3D models of their environments in order to provide data for various applications in the fields of mapping, urban planning, tourism, security, emergency and disaster analysis as well as commerce. Data for 3D models can be acquired from GIS databases (e.g., NYC [1]), using Light Detection and Ranging (LiDAR) data from scanners mounted on cars driving in cities (e.g., Google Street View) or on airborne drones. Data collected by LiDAR scanner systems are point clouds that are large collections of data points defined by a given coordinates system. In a 3D coordinates system, a point cloud may define the shape of different spatial features like curbstones, poles, buildings,

© Springer Nature Switzerland AG 2020
T. Robal et al. (Eds.): DB&IS 2020, CCIS 1243, pp. 219–232, 2020.
https://doi.org/10.1007/978-3-030-57672-1_17

trees, etc. Geographic LiDAR point cloud data are most commonly available in LiDAR Aerial Survey (LAS) or ASCII formats.

Most of the applications require that the 3D model must be detailed, up-to-date, and globally consistent. In order to create a consistent 3D model, 3D data accuracy assurance becomes extremely important. To improve the accuracy of Mobile Mapping Systems (MMS) (or airborne drone) point cloud data, ground control points (GCP) with known coordinates are commonly used. These points form a reference dataset with respect to which the other datasets are relatively evaluated. However, collecting GCPs is a time-consuming and expensive process. The collection of GCPs can be reduced or skipped by using existing GIS databases as a reference dataset. To use existing GIS databases, the quality/accuracy of the data must be evaluated to confirm that data are suitable for this task.

The main contribution of this paper is the methodology and its sample development for comparative spatial analysis of digitized point cloud and the corresponding GIS database in order to assess the quality of data of the GIS database or LiDAR point cloud.

The main research question answered by the method is how to identify points (or other geometries) from digitized (LiDAR) point cloud and the corresponding GIS databases that can be matched indicating that they denote the same real-world spatial feature. In addition, the goal is not only to find matching spatial features but also to identify other types of correspondences among features from both datasets as well as to detect missing features in GIS database or in LiDAR dataset within the given area.

The proposed method uses positional data of spatial features and DBSCAN clustering [2] extended with categorization and analysis of clusters in order to find different types of correspondences of features in both datasets. The choice of DBSCAN algorithm is justified by the goal of the method to find also missing features in addition to matching ones. This makes K-nearest neighbours analysis not suitable.

The novelty of our method lies in combining clustering, database technology, and statistical analysis for comparative spatial analysis of features of any geometry. In this paper, we consider only geometries of point and line as the paper is devoted to LiDAR data collected using MMS that does not allow getting point cloud data covering the entire shape of buildings having the geometry of polygon.

In order to automate the workflow of the method, the corresponding sample is developed on the basis of PostgreSQL database system using PostGIS spatial extension. The method has been evaluated using LiDAR data provided by Estonian company Reach-U and GIS database layers from different Estonian GIS databases. In this paper, the case study based on the Tallinn Spatial Database (TAR)[1] is presented.

The rest of the paper is organized as follows. In Sect. 2, related work is reviewed. Section 3 gives an overall picture of the proposed method. Section 4 is devoted to data pre-processing and Sect. 5 provides a detailed presentation of clustering, categorization of clusters and analysis of resulting clusters. In Sect. 6 we present statistical metrics. Section 7 is devoted to the evaluation of the method by the case study related to the TalTech test area in Tallinn. Section 8 concludes the work.

---

[1] https://www.tallinn.ee/est/geoportaal/Andmed.

2   Related Work

In general, our work is related to the works in the field of spatial feature matching that is a part of more general research on spatial data conflation involving the matching and merging of counterpart features in multiple datasets [3]. The goal of the spatial data conflation is to merge the geometry and attribute data of matched features in order to get more accurate dataset. Our approach in this paper has different goals and wider scope as we analyse besides matching also other relationships between features.

Most tightly related work to our approach is provided by Helbich et al. [4], where a comparative spatial analysis is performed as the statistical analysis of the positional accuracy of different data sources including OpenStreetMap[2] (OSM) and survey data from GIS databases. Their study considered only roads (streets), basically road junctions. The deviation of the junction point coordinates from the corresponding points in the defined reference dataset was used as a measure of positional accuracy. As a method of analysis, their research uses bi-dimensional regression models as descriptive statistics to determine the correspondence between datasets and the G*-statistic to explore spatial heterogeneity in the positional errors. Our method principally differs from their method. First, our method is general and not dependent on the geometry of spatial features to be studied e.g. points. Second, we combine clustering, database technology and statistical analysis.

GIS databases can be used to validate LiDAR data as shown by Webster [5], where the GIS database was used as a source for independent validation data for determining the accuracy of the different LiDAR data acquisition systems and the occurrence of a systematic range bias for one of the LiDAR methods proposed.

Haklay [6] provides OSM data quality analysis that is based on a comparison of voluntarily collected OSM data with Ordnance Survey (OS) datasets in order to assess how good is OSM data. The method used for OSM data accuracy assessment evaluated positional and attribute accuracy, completeness, and consistency of data. As for positional accuracy, the study concentrated to the calculation of overlap of motorway features (multiline objects) between the two datasets in several areas of London and England.

In [7] a method for quantitative assessments of spatial accuracy and completeness for features with line geometry is proposed. The paper also evaluates several other spatial accuracy assessment methods for lines including buffer overlay statistics (BOS) method. This method of assessment of positional accuracy is related to our work as we applied the same method for evaluating positional accuracy of multiline features like curbstones in a GIS database and in the corresponding LiDAR dataset.

3   An Overview of the Proposed Method

The main goal of the method of comparative spatial analysis is to find a set of matching spatial features of the given geometry from a digitized sample area of (LiDAR) point cloud and the corresponding area from the GIS database. The method seeks for database features that have exactly one LiDAR feature within a distance given by distance threshold value. These features can be matched according to the hypothesis of the research.

---

[2] http://www.openstreetmap.org.

In addition to finding matching spatial features, the method identifies other types of correspondences among features from both datasets as well as detects missing features in GIS database or in LiDAR dataset within the given area. In Fig. 1, overall workflow of the method is presented.

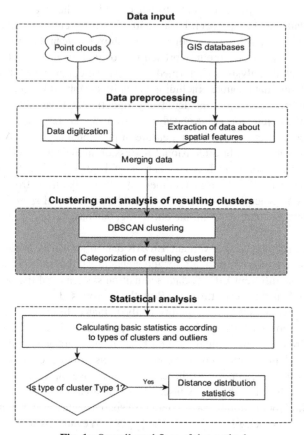

Fig. 1. Overall workflow of the method

We see that the method of comparative spatial analysis is based on manual digitization of (LiDAR) point cloud, extraction of spatial features from GIS databases and application of DBSCAN clustering algorithm [2]. An original feature of the method is a categorization of clusters calculated by DBSCAN clustering and providing statistical analysis of clusters and matching features. In Fig. 1, the following steps of the method are presented: data input, data pre-processing, clustering and analysis of resulting clusters, and statistical analysis. Clustering and analysis of resulting clusters are automated. All other steps have a semi-automated process.

4   Data Sampling, Input and Pre-processing

Two types of data are considered as input to the method: GIS databases and point cloud data that are collected using MMS or airborne drones. In experiments presented in this paper, we have used TAR as an open GIS database.

By now, the method was applied only on MMS LiDAR point cloud data. LiDAR data collection was performed by Reach-U Ltd. who has developed its own (portable) MMS that is based on Velodyne VLP-16 LiDAR and SBG Systems Ellipse-D dual antenna GNSS/INS system [8]. The main limitation of MMS is that it can collect data only within the areas that are connected with some road network.

We have set some principles of selection of sample data (area) from GIS database layers as follows. The area must be covered with LiDAR data and LiDAR's range of detection has to be taken into account. We use a buffer of 20 m from both sides of the road for point objects and 5 m for line objects. A road is chosen randomly from the area of interest in a city or from a set of roads that have around them big enough number of interesting spatial features to be included in the study. For line objects (e.g., curbstones) we used a sample of 6300 m that included 130 curbstones. We did not use polygon objects as MMS does not capture entire buildings.

Observed spatial features in the GIS database are usually given in shapefile format (SHP) or have to be converted to SHP file format that is a digital vector storage format for storing geometric location and associated attribute information. In the corresponding point cloud, observed spatial features located within the chosen sample area are digitized manually on the basis of the given area and number of features in this area according to the GIS database. The SHP file of digitized spatial data contains values of x and y coordinates of features.

In the data pre-processing step, data of the corresponding layers of the GIS database, LiDAR data and a sample area are loaded to a PostgreSQL/PostGIS database. In case of point objects, ST_Within function is used to ensure that the points are within the given sample area. In case of line objects, only parts of the line within the area are used, which means, that lines intersecting with the border of the area have to be split at the point(s) of the intersection. Since one multiline can intersect with the border of the area multiple times, if as the result of the split the multiline has parts within the area that are not connected anymore, we handle its parts as separate lines. Once the sample data only contains data within the sample area for both GIS and LiDAR layers, we use PostgreSQL to merge both layers into one. In this step, we keep the original identifiers of features in different columns of the table of the merged layer so that their origin could easily be determined later. Pre-processed data from both layers are also saved as SHP files.

5   Clustering and Analysis of Resulting Clusters

In order to obtain a set of matching objects from both datasets (our main goal), we first apply density-based spatial clustering of applications with noise (DBSCAN) algorithm to the features of merged layer and then additionally analyse different types of resulting clusters using PostgreSQL/PostGIS queries. DBSCAN algorithm was firstly published in [2] and later revisited by its authors [9] and by others [10]. DBSCAN algorithm has many implementations and modifications [11, 12]; however, in our method, we use PostGIS 2.5.3 implementation of the algorithm in the form of ST_ClusterDBSCAN function.[3]

5.1   Clustering with DBSCAN

DBSCAN algorithm [9] uses minimum density estimation (minPts) that defines a threshold for the number of neighbours within the radius epsilon (EPS) that is a local radius for expanding clusters. In our case, the distance metric for EPS is Euclidean distance. Objects with more than minPts neighbours within this radius (including the query point) are considered to be a core point. All neighbours within the EPS radius of a core point are considered to be a part of the same cluster as the core point. If any of these points is again a core point, the neighbours of these points are transitively included. Points which are not density reachable from any core point are considered outliers and do not belong to any cluster.

According to our method, features of the merged layer (LiDAR and GIS database layers) are clustered by a PostGIS query using the ST_ClusterDBSCAN function that is a 2D implementation of the DBSCAN algorithm. The ST_ClusterDBSCAN function has three parameters: input geometry, density (i.e., minPts value) and maximum distance between clustered points EPS. The function returns cluster number for each input geometry according to the given minPts and EPS parameters.

It should be noticed that we do not apply DBSCAN in a traditional way, where it is used on one GIS database layer that collects spatial data about certain features. Our spatial data come from different sources (LiDAR and GIS database) representing data about the same spatial features. We preserve the identification numbers for both layers at different columns on the merged layer. When these layers are merged we get one layer to run the algorithm but still know to what data source a clustered point belongs to. We are also interested in very tense clusters with minPts = 2 in order to be able to detect matching points or correspondences among points from different sources forming the same cluster. Therefore, the value of the density parameter is set to 2 for ST_ClusterDBSCAN.

It is not so easy to set radius parameter EPS. As also mentioned by the authors of the DBSCAN algorithm, in general, some heuristics for choosing appropriate EPS parameter value is needed [9] or some automated EPS estimation should be developed [12].

In principle, DBSCAN is designed so that EPS value should be as small as possible [6]. In GIS applications and in particular, in the application domain of our method, the value of EPS depends on domain knowledge. For example, a domain expert may decide that objects within 100 cm are considered as neighbours (or matching) and EPS value is chosen accordingly.

However, in our method, we propose to vary EPS parameter value in order to provide domain experts with different insights into collected data. We use the calculation of some basic statistical metrics (see Sect. 6.1, Fig. 3) after clustering with different EPS radius values in order to give a domain expert data for making the decision of suitable EPS radius values. The flexibility of choosing the EPS value is important as features from

---

[3] PostGIS 2.5.3dev Manual, https://postgis.net/docs/manual-dev/ST_ClusterDBSCAN.html.

different datasets are not considered matching if they are farther apart than a given value of the radius EPS.

5.2   Categorization of Resulting Clusters and Basic Statistical Metrics

Clustering alone does not give an answer to research questions of our methodology. We need to analyse the content of the resulting clusters in order to decide what objects can be matched, what cannot and what are reasons for mismatch. For that purpose, we categorize clusters to different types using the corresponding database queries.

Clustering results contain several types of clusters and outlier features (i.e. objects that do not belong to any cluster) as depicted in Fig. 2. There can be many clusters of the same type. For each type of clusters, the corresponding basic statistical metrics are developed and applied. The number of clusters of different types depends on the particular input to the method e.g., datasets to be processed and analysed.

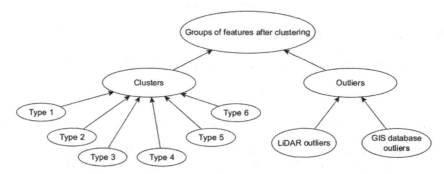

Fig. 2. The taxonomy of groups of features after DBSCAN clustering

The Cluster of Type 1. It contains exactly one digitized (LiDAR) point cloud feature and one GIS database feature (i.e. relationship 1:1) indicating that features that are included to this cluster are matching. For this cluster, a number of matching features is calculated. It is equal to the number of clusters of type 1 (due to minPTS $= 2$).

The Cluster of Type 2. This cluster contains one GIS database feature and more than one digitized LiDAR features (i.e. relationship 1:n). Numbers of LiDAR features and database features in these clusters are calculated. The number of database features in these clusters is denoted by $DT2$ that is equal to the number of such clusters denoted by n. The number of LiDAR features is denoted by $LT2$ and is calculated according to the following formula:

$$LT2 = \sum_{i=1}^{n} Li, \tag{1}$$

where Li denotes the number of LiDAR features in the cluster i.

The Cluster of Type 3. It contains one digitized LiDAR point and more than one GIS database features (i.e. relationship n:1). Numbers of LiDAR features and database features in these clusters are calculated. The number of LiDAR features denoted by *LT3* is equal to the number of such clusters denoted by *m* (i.e. *LT3* = *m*). The number of database features is calculated according to the following formula:

$$DT3 = \sum_{j=1}^{m} Dj, \tag{2}$$

where *Dj* is the number of database features in the cluster *j*.

The Cluster of Type 4. It contains more than one GIS database features and more than one digitized LiDAR features (i.e. relationship n:m). The number of these clusters is denoted by *p*. The number of LiDAR features in these clusters denoted by *LT4* is calculated by the following formula:

$$LT4 = \sum_{i=1}^{p} Li, \tag{3}$$

where *Li* is the number of LiDAR features in the cluster *i*.

The number of database features denoted as *DT4* is calculated as follows:

$$DT4 = \sum_{i=1}^{p} Di, \tag{4}$$

where *Di* is the number of database features in the cluster *i*.

The Cluster of Type 5. This cluster contains only digitized LiDAR features. The number of such clusters is denoted by *r*. The number of LiDAR features in these clusters is denoted by *LT5* and is calculated as follows:

$$LT5 = \sum_{i=1}^{r} Li, \tag{5}$$

where *Li* is the number of LiDAR features in the cluster *i*.

The Cluster of Type 6. It contains only GIS database features. The number of such clusters is denoted by *s*. The number of database features in these clusters is denoted by *DT6* and is calculated as follows:

$$DT6 = \sum_{j=1}^{s} Dj, \tag{6}$$

where *Dj* is the number of database features in the cluster *j*.

Lidar and GIS Database Outliers. In addition to clusters of types 1–6, we analyse outlier (or noise) features. These are GIS database features and digitized LiDAR features that are not included in any cluster.

Numbers of outlier LiDAR features and GIS database features are calculated and denoted correspondingly by *Lo* and *Do*. For the calculation of these basic statistics, the corresponding database queries were developed and applied.

6 Analysis of Categorization Results of Clusters

6.1 Relative Distribution Metrics

In addition to basic statistical metrics given above, relative distribution metrics are calculated using database queries and Excel. The following relative distribution metrics are calculated:

- Percentage of matching features out of the number of the given GIS database features in the sample area.
- Percentage of features in clusters of type 2–4 out of the number of corresponding features in the GIS database and in LiDAR dataset.
- Percentage of GIS database features that are not recognized in LiDAR data (i.e. *DT5* + *Do*) out of the number of the given GIS database features.
- Percentage of LiDAR dataset features that are not within the given EPS radius value of any GIS database point (i.e. *LT5* + *Lo*) out of the number of digitized LiDAR dataset features.

After automated calculations based on the formulas above, the following chart (see Fig. 3) is presented to a domain expert to decide suitable EPS radius values.

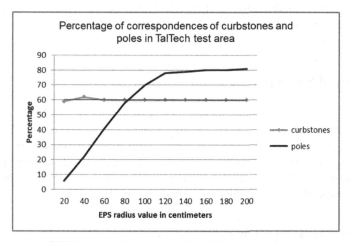

Fig. 3. Percentage of GIS database features out of all GIS database features in the test area that had exactly one feature from LiDAR dataset within different EPS radius values

According to the chart in Fig. 3, we may see that the ratio of matching poles is starting to become high within a distance of 100 cm. For 140, 160, 180 cm distance this ratio is high too. However, domain experts are interested in smaller distances (better accuracy). For curbstones the EPS radius value of 40 cm is optimal.

6.2   Assessment of Distance of Matching Features

For *matching point objects* (clusters of type 1), Euclidean distances of corresponding objects are calculated using a database query. On the basis of the results of the query, some descriptive and distribution statistics are calculated over the distances of corresponding objects from the GIS database and LiDAR data within the chosen EPS radius value. The following descriptive statistical metrics are calculated on the basis of distance of corresponding point objects (e.g., poles, trees) for the cluster of matching points: count, MAX, MIN, 1. quartile, 2. quartile, 3. quartile as well as the difference between 3 and 1 quartile.

For *matching multi-line or line objects* we need another method for analysis of distance of matching objects. Using just minimum distance function ST_distance for calculation of the distance of matching lines and distribution statistics do not give much information about positional accuracy of lines as the minimum distance of lines can be zero meaning that lines intersect.

There are several methods available to conduct an assessment of deviation of line objects based on the notion of epsilon band that defines a fixed zone of uncertainty around the measured line, within which the considered line exists with some probability [6, 7, 13]. One of the methods based on epsilon band concept is buffer overlay statistics (BOS) method [7] that we use in this paper to find approximations for the epsilon band for LiDAR dataset relative to GIS database.

In the sample implementation of the method, different statistical metrics are calculated and the corresponding query results are imported to MS Excel, where all needed charts are created.

7   Results of Experiments

We have performed experiments in many areas of Tallinn on the basis of different databases. In this paper, we analyse only experiments performed in TalTech test area. We consider features like poles and curbstones as they are represented using two different geometries; points and (multi)lines. Our method is applicable to features having the geometry of polygon too. However, we did not conduct any studies on this as MMS is not capable to produce LiDAR data covering the entire shape of buildings.

7.1   The Test Area and Set-up of Experiments

The considered TalTech test area covers parts of Akadeemia tee, Tehnopol and Tallinn University of Technology inside which the poles and curbstones were digitized by Reach-U team. The buffer size around roads was 20 m from edges of roads for poles and 5 m for curbstones because MMS can capture low features better if they are near to roads.

As a result of the digitization process performed by Reach-U, totally 132 poles were digitized in the given test area that contains 139 poles in t02_71_post layer in TAR (Tallinn Basemap: Tallinn Urban Planning Department July 2019). Some poles present in the database were not digitized.

The test area contained 102 curbstones in the GIS database. As a result of the digitization process performed by Reach-U, totally 106 edge lines with curbstones that were located in the given test area were digitized. It is more than the number of curbstones in TAR in this area. This indicates that digitizers have split long curbstones into smaller lines or the corresponding part of the line was not visible for MMS.

7.2   Categories of Clusters and Their Distribution

Some of the statistical results concerning the percentage of corresponding objects have been provided already in Fig. 3 together with EPS radius value estimation. In Fig. 4, we provide some basic statistical metrics about the results of clustering features from LiDAR and TAR datasets into the groups (cluster types) defined above (see Sect. 5.2 and 6). A number of poles and curbstones falling into different types of clusters are shown. We used for poles clustering EPS radius value of 100 cm and for curbstones, EPS radius value of 40 cm was chosen. Although numbers of considered poles and curbstones were different we may see that poles clustering created only the cluster of matching objects and LiDAR and database outliers. In contrast, curbstones belong to all clusters except types of 5 and 6.

In Fig. 4, we see that quite many curbstones belong to the cluster of type 2 that contains one feature of database and more than one from LiDAR dataset or vice versa. The first case indicates that curbstones of TAR were digitized in LiDAR dataset as consisting of many separate lines.

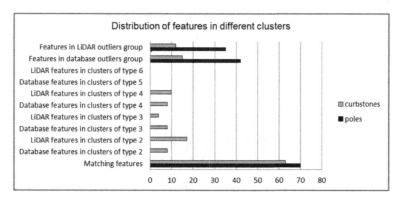

Fig. 4.   Distribution of features in different types of clusters (the number of curbstones and poles)

Relative distribution of poles was as follows:

- Ratio of GIS database poles that matched LiDAR poles was 70% in GIS database.
- Poles of GIS database noise constituted 30% of GIS database poles.
- LiDAR noise constituted 27% from LiDAR dataset poles.

Relative distribution of curbstones is provided in Fig. 5.

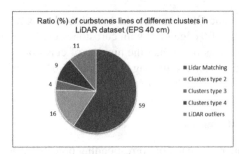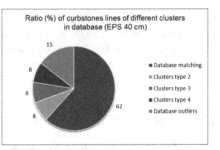

Fig. 5. Relative distribution of curbstones in clusters for the EPS radius value of 40 cm

We may see from Fig. 5 that ratio of matching curbstones is smaller (62%) than matching poles (70%) provided above.

7.3 Statistics for Matching Features

For *matching point objects* we calculate frequency distribution and relative frequency distribution of distances between objects locations given in the GIS database and in LiDAR point cloud within the chosen maximum distance. For example, calculation of frequency distribution of distances between street poles locations given in the TAR database and in LiDAR point cloud for distances within 100 cm is shown in Fig. 6.

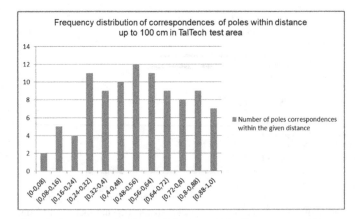

Fig. 6. Frequency distribution of poles within distance up to 100 cm

For *matching line objects* we use BOS method [7] as mentioned above.

For each intersection, $A \cap B$ and difference values $A \backslash B$ and $B \backslash A$ we calculated the percentage from the union $A \cup B$ with the corresponding buffer radius.

A represents a set of all buffers with the corresponding buffer radius around the matching lines in the GIS database and B represents all buffers with the corresponding buffer radius around the matching lines in LiDAR dataset. If the lines are very similar, the area of the intersection will dominate, but as the lines become more different, the area of the other two will increase as a function of the size of the displacements. The area of intersection compared to the total area that is inside A or B could, therefore, be used as a measure for the line dataset accuracy [7].

The corresponding values are shown in Fig. 7. The graph shows two crossing points. The buffer radius for these crossing points will give an indication of the relative spatial accuracy of the two lines. The chart in Fig. 7 indicates that curbstones in TalTech area are quite accurate as the curves of the accuracy cross at buffer radius of 12 cm (LiDAR) and 13 cm (TAR database).

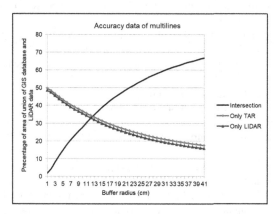

Fig. 7. Data of accuracy analysis of curbstone lines in GIS database and LiDAR dataset

8   Conclusion

In this paper, a novel methodology of comparative spatial analysis of digitized point cloud and the corresponding GIS database was provided. The proposed method makes it possible to statistically assess opportunities to align MMS LiDAR data with existing GIS databases or to improve involved datasets. The method finds matching spatial features within the given maximum distance between clustered points and identifies other types of correspondences among features from both datasets as well as detects missing features in GIS database or in LiDAR dataset within the given area.

The method uses positional data of spatial features and DBSCAN clustering extended with categorization and analysis of clusters in order to find correspondences and other relationships between features in both datasets. A sample implementation of the method is based on the PostgreSQL database system using PostGIS spatial extension. The method is evaluated on the basis of different case studies in Tallinn.

Acknowledgements. This research was partially supported by the Archimedes Foundation in the scope of the smart specialization research and development project #LEP19022 "Applied research for creating a cost-effective interchangeable 3D spatial data infrastructure with survey-grade accuracy". The work of Hele-Mai Haav was also supported by the Institutional Research Grant IUT33-13 of the Estonian Research Council. Last but not least, we thank Marta Olvet and Kristiina Kindel for their work related to data pre-processing.

References

1. Kolbe, T.H., Burger, B., Cantzler, B.: CityGML goes to Broadway. In: The Proceedings of Photogrammetric Week 2015, pp 343–355. Wichmann/VDE Verlag, Belin & Offenbach (2015)
2. Martin, E., Kriegel, H-P., Sander, J., Xu, X.: A density-based algorithm for discovering clusters in large spatial databases with noise. In: The Proceedings of the Second International Conference on Knowledge Discovery and Data Mining (KDD 1996), pp. 226–231. AAAI Press (1996)
3. Lei, T., Lei, Z.: Optimal spatial data matching for conflation: a network flow based approach. Trans. GIS **23**, 1152–1176 (2019)
4. Helbich, M., Amelunxen, C., Neis, P., Zipf, A.: A comparative spatial analysis of positional accuracy of OpenStreetMap and proprietary geodata. In: The Proceedings of GI_Forum 2012: Geovizualisation, Society and Learning, pp. 24–33. Wichmann/VDE Verlag, Belin&Offenbach (2012)
5. Webster, T.L.: LIDAR validation using GIS: a case study comparison between two LIDAR collection methods. Geocarto Int. **20**(4), 1–9 (2005)
6. Haklay, M.: How good is volunteered geographical information? A comparative study of OpenStreetMap and ordnance survey datasets. Environ. Plann. B: Plann. Des. **37**(4), 682–703 (2010)
7. Tveite, H.: An accuracy assessment method for geographical line data sets based on buffering. Int. J. Geograph. Inf. Sci. **13**(1), 27–47 (1999)
8. Julge, K., Vajakas, T., Ellmann, A.: Performance analysis of a compact and low-cost mapping-grade mobile laser scanning system. J. Appl. Remote Sens. **11**(4), 044003 (2017)
9. Schubert, E., Sander, J., Ester, M., Kriegel, H.-P., Xu, X.: DBSCAN revisited, revisited: why and how you should (Still) use DBSCAN. ACM Trans. Database Syst. **42**(3), 1–21 (2017)
10. Gan, J., Tao., Y.: DBSCAN revisited: mis-claim, un-fixability, and approximation. In: The Proceedings of the ACM International Conference on Management of Data (SIGMOD), pp. 519–530. ACM Press (2015)
11. Campello, R.J.G.B., Moulavi, D., Sander, J.: Density-based clustering based on hierarchical density estimates. In: Pei, J., Tseng, V.S., Cao, L., Motoda, H., Xu, G. (eds.) PAKDD 2013. LNCS (LNAI), vol. 7819, pp. 160–172. Springer, Heidelberg (2013). https://doi.org/10.1007/978-3-642-37456-2_14
12. Wang, C., Ji, M., Wang, J., Wen, W., Li, T., Sun, Y.: An improved DBSCAN method for LiDAR data segmentation with automatic eps estimation. Sensors **19**(1), 172–198 (2019)
13. Goodchild, M.F., Hunter, G.J.: A simple positional accuracy measure for linear features. Int. J. Geograph. Inf. Sci. **11**, 299–306 (1997)

Enterprise and Information Systems Engineering

On Case-Based Reasoning for ETL Process Repairs: Making Cases Fine-Grained

Artur Wojciechowski and Robert Wrembel[(✉)] ⓘ

Poznan University of Technology, Poznań, Poland
{artur.wojciechowski,robert.wrembel}@cs.put.poznan.pl

Abstract. Data sources (DSs) being integrated in a data warehouse frequently change their structures. As a consequence, in many cases, an already deployed ETL process stops its execution, generating errors. Since the number of deployed ETL processes may reach dozens of thousands and structural changes in DSs are frequent, being able to (semi-)automatically repair an ETL process after DS changes, would decrease ETL maintenance costs. In our approach, we developed the *E-ETL* framework, for ETL process repairs. In *E-ETL*, an ETL process is semi-automatically or automatically (depending on a case) repaired, so that it works with the changed DS. *E-ETL* supports two different repair methods: (1) user defined rules, (2) and Case-Based Reasoning (CBR). Having experimented with CBR, we learned that large cases do not frequently fit a given DS change, even though they include elements that could be applied to repair a given ETL process, and vice-versa - more complex DS changes cannot be handled by small cases. To solve this problem, in this paper, we contribute algorithms for decomposing detected structural changes in DSs. The purpose of the decomposition is to divide a set of detected structural DSs changes into smaller sets, to increase the probability of finding a suitable case by the CBR method.

Keywords: Data source evolution · ETL process repair · Case-based reasoning

1 Introduction

A data warehouse (DW) architecture is used for the integration of heterogeneous, distributed, and autonomous data storage systems, further called data sources (DSs), deployed in a company. In the DW architecture, DSs are integrated by the so-called Extract-Transform-Load (ETL) layer. It is responsible for extracting data from DSs, transforming and cleaning data, removing missing, inconsistent, and redundant values, integrating data, and loading them into a DW. An ETL layer, is implemented as a *workflow* of tasks managed by an ETL engine. An ETL workflow will interchangeably be called an ETL *process*. A task in an ETL workflow will interchangeably called an *activity*.

© Springer Nature Switzerland AG 2020
T. Robal et al. (Eds.): DB&IS 2020, CCIS 1243, pp. 235–249, 2020.
https://doi.org/10.1007/978-3-030-57672-1_18

An inherent feature of DSs is their evolution in time w.r.t. their structures (schemas) [18]. As reported in [9,14,15], in practice, DSs change their structures frequently. As a consequence of DSs changes, in many cases, an already deployed ETL process stops its execution with errors. Such a process will further be called *non-functioning*. As a consequence, a non-functioning ETL process must be redesigned and redeployed to work on a modified DS. We call this activity an ETL process *repair*.

In practice, in large companies the number of different ETL workflows reaches dozens of thousands. Thus, a manual repair of ETL workflows is complex, time-consuming, and prone-to-fail. Since structural changes in DSs are frequent, being able to use a technique of an automatic or semi-automatic repair of an ETL workflow after such changes would decrease ETL maintenance costs. However, handling and incorporating structural changes to the ETL layer received so far little attention from the research community, cf., Sect. 5. None of the commercial or open-source ETL tools existing on the market [6] supports this functionality either.

In our research, we have designed and developed an ETL framework, called *E-ETL* that is able to repair workflows (semi-)automatically [16,17], based on Case-Based Reasoning (CBR) (cf. Sect. 2 for an overview). Having experimented with *E-ETL*, we figured out that while applying the state-of-the art CBR method, it was difficult to find a case, say C_i, that would be applicable to a given ETL repair problem, say P_i. First, often C_i included multiple elements inapplicable to repair P_i. Second, P_i was only partially covered by C_i. In this context, we posed a **research question** whether it will be possible to decompose a large repair problem into smaller ones, so that existing cases can cover the smaller problems.

In this paper we **contribute** three algorithms: *Single Case*, *Full Search*, and *Greedy*, for the decomposition of a large repair problem into smaller ones, cf. Sect. 4. The contributed algorithms find a set of cases that handle all detected data source changes. The *Single Case* algorithm finds one case the most suitable to solve a given problem. The *Full Search* algorithm finds an optimal set of cases that are the most similar to a given repair problem. A drawback of this algorithm is its low search performance. For this reason, we developed the *Greedy* algorithm that is much faster but it finds a sub-optimal set of cases. This way, we extend not only the ETL repair method but also improve the CBR method.

2   Case-Based Reasoning for ETL Repair

Case-Based Reasoning solves a new problem, say P_i, by adapting and applying to P_i solutions previously applied to problems that were similar to P_i [1]. CBR is inspired by human reasoning and the fact that people commonly solve problems by remembering how they solved similar problems in the past. In the context of the CBR on an ETL process repair, we define two notions, namely: a *problem*, *solution*, and *case*, as follows.

Definition 1. *Problem and Solution. Let us assume data source DS_i from which ETL process E_i ingests data. problem P_i is a sequence of modifications applied to DS_i that make E_i non-functioning. A solution to P_i is a recipe explaining how to repair E_i. In the CBR method, in order to find the solution, a similar case should be found and adapted to solve P_i.*

Definition 2. *Case. A case is a pair: (1) a sequence of changes in DSs and (2) a sequence of modifications of a non-functioning ETL process that adjust the process to the new state, so that it works without errors on the modified DSs. Cases helping to solve a new problem can be found in two dimensions of an ETL project: (1) fragments of the ETL process and (2) time. The first dimension means that a case represents either same change in the same DS or a similar change in different part of the ETL process that uses a similar DS. The time dimension allows to look for cases in the whole evolution history of the ETL process. Therefore, if there was a change in the past and now a different part of the same ETL process changes in the same way, then the previously repaired change can be a case for the ETL process repair algorithm.*

Example 1. Let us assume an ETL process that loads data from a few instances of a customer-relationship-management system. Every instance can use a different version of the system, hence each instance (treated as a DS) is similar to the other instances but, not necessarily the same. For each instance, there can be a dedicated ETL sub-process. Let us assume some updates of the structures of the DSs that result in repairs of the relevant ETL sub-processes. Changes in one DS and a manual repair of the associated ETL sub-process may be used as a case for a repair algorithm to fix other ETL sub-processes associated with the updated DSs.

Example 2. Let us assume that in a DS three physical tables are partitions of the same logical table, i.e.: (1) individual customers, (2) corporate customers, and (3) institutional customers. Each of these tables may include some specific columns, which are important only for one type of a customer but, all of them have also a common set of columns. If there is a change in DSs that modifies the common set of columns (e.g., adding a rating to all three types of customers), then the change of one of these tables and the repair of the ETL process associated with this table can be used as a case for a repair algorithm to fix other ETL parts associated with the other two tables.

Structural changes in DSs may be handled in multiple ways. Required modifications of a non-functioning ETL process may vary on many elements i.e., the design of the ETL process, the domain of the processed data, the quality of data. Even the same problem in the same process may need different solution due to new circumstances i.e., new company guidelines, new functionality available in an ETL tool. Therefore, we cannot guarantee that the solution delivered by means of the CBR method is always correct. Nevertheless, we can propose to the user a solution, which was applicable in the past, and let the user decide if it is correct. In companies where dozens of thousands of ETL processes are maintained in parallel, the probability that there are several similar processes using similar DSs may be reasonably high. Therefore, the more ETL processes exists, the more feasible is the CBR method for the ETL repair.

3   E-ETL Framework

E-ETL allows to detect structural changes in DSs and handle the changes in the ETL layer. Changes are detected either by means of event-condition-action mechanism (triggers) or by comparing two consecutive DS metadata snapshots. The detection of a DS schema change causes a repair of the ETL process that interacts with the changed DS. The repair of the ETL process is guided by a few customizable repair algorithms.

One of the key features of the *E-ETL* framework is that it stores the whole history of all changes in the ETL process. This history is the source for building the *Library of Repair Cases* (LRC). After every modification of the ETL process, a new case is added to the *LRC*. Thus, whenever a DS change is detected, the procedure of evolving the ETL process repairs it by using one of the supported repair methods. As the result of this repair, new cases are generated and stored in the *LRC*. The repair methods are based on the *User Defined Rules*, and the CBR method.

The *E-ETL* framework is not supposed to be a fully functional ETL designing tool but an external extension to commercial ETL tools available on the market. Therefore, the proposed framework was developed as a module external to an ETL engine. Communication between *E-ETL* and an ETL engine is realized by means of an API provided by the ETL engine. When the user introduces manually some modifications in an ETL process using a proprietary ETL tool, then *E-ETL* ingests the new definition of the ETL process and compares it with the previous version stored in *E-ETL*. The result of this comparison is a set of all modifications made manually by the user. Those modifications together with detected DS changes are considered as repair cases.

3.1   Case Detection Algorithm

Within the *E-ETL* framework we provide the *Case Detection Algorithm* (CDA) [17] that detects and builds cases for the ETL repair algorithm, based on CBR. The *CDA* requires as an input: (1) a set of all detected DSs that have been changed and (2) an ETL process with all modifications of the ETL process activities that handle the detected changes of a modified DS.

Every modification, say M_i of an ETL process activity, say A_i consists of a set of changes AC_i. Every change AC_i^n was applied in order to adjust the activity A_i to some detected changes of a modified DS. An example of change AC_i^n may be renaming a column that is processed by activity A_i. Modification M_i may consist of multiple changes, e.g., renaming multiple columns. There is a one-to-one relationship between A_i and M_i.

The *CDA* algorithm consists of two main steps.

- Step 1: initiate a new case for each DS that was modified. Every newly initiated case consist of: (1) a set of DS changes that change a single DS (e.g., single table in database), and (2) a set of modifications that concern ETL activities processing data that originate from the changed DS.
- Step 2: merge all cases that have at least one common modification. A final merged case consists of a set of DS changes that modigy multiple DSs and a set of modifications that is a union of modifications from the merged cases.

The *CDA* may detect multiple cases and return a set of them, every returned case consists of different set of DS changes, i.e., changes of different data sources and different data structures.

3.2   Choosing the Right Case

One of the key points in CBR is to choose the most appropriate case for solving a new problem. In an ETL environment, a new problem includes changes in DSs. Therefore, to solve a problem it is crucial to find such a case whose set of DS changes is similar to the problem. Moreover, the set of modifications in the case must be applicable to the ETL process where the problem is meant to be solved.

The similarity of sets of DS changes is based on the assumption that types of DS changes have to be the same (e.g., changing a domain of an attribute, renaming an attribute, removing or adding an attribute) but the changes may apply to non-identical DS elements. For example, if a new DS change is an addition of attribute *Contact* to table *EnterpriseClients*, then a similar change can be an addition of attribute *ContactPerson* to table *InstitutionClients*. Both changes represent attribute addition, but the names of the attributes and the names of the tables are different. Therefore, a procedure that compares changes not only has to consider element names but also their types and sub-elements (notice that if an element is an ETL task, then its sub-elements are attributes; an ETL activity attribute does not have sub-elements).

Measuring Similarity of Cases. As mentioned before, repair case C_i is similar to a new problem P_i if: (1) the set of DS changes is similar to P_i and (2) modification in C_i can be applied to P_i in order to repair a non-functioning ETL process. It is possible that more than one case is similar to P_i. Therefore, it is necessary to be able to assess how similar is a given repair case C_i to P_i. The more similar C_i to P_i is, the more probable is the application of C_i to solve P_i, i.e., to repair a non-functioning ETL process. Therefore, the case that is the most similar to a new problem should be chosen.

In order to assess the similarity of C_i to P_i, we proposed a measure called *Factor of Similarity and Applicability* (FSA) [17]. *FSA* takes into account: (1) features of modified data sources (column names, column types, column type lengths, table names), (2) attributes (a set of input columns, a set of output columns, parameters) of a non-functioning ETL process activities, (3) a number of case usages, and (4) a scope of a case.

Informally, a *scope* of a case reflects how strongly a given case is related to an ETL process that has to be repaired. We distinguished two types of a scope, namely: (1) a process scope and (2) a global scope. A *process scope* is assigned to cases that originate from the same ETL process as P_i. In other words, cases with *process scope* were detected in the same ETL process that has to be repaired. A *global scope* is assigned to cases that do not originate from previous repairs of P_i. Notice that cases from the global scope can also be used for repairs of P_i.

The more common features of: (1) a modified data source and (2) attributes of activities, between a non-functioning ETL process and a case, the higher *FSA* is. Cases form the process scope have higher values of *FSA*, whereas cases form the global scope have lower values of *FSA*. If there are two cases with the same value of *FSA*, the case that has been already used more times is probably the more appropriate one. For this reason, the next component used to compute a value of *FSA* is the number of usages of the case that were previously accepted and verified by the user. The higher the value of *FSA*, the more appropriate is the case for solving a given problem.

In order to calculate a value of *FSA*, common features of DSs and common elements in an ETL process have to be obtained. To this end, a case has to be mapped into a new problem. DS changes defined in the case have to be mapped into DS changes defined in a new problem. Analogically, activities modified by the set of case modifications have to be mapped into new problem activities.

Searching Algorithm. In *E-ETL*, finding the best case in the *Library of Repair Cases* is executed by the *Best Case Searching Algorithm* (BCSA). In an unsupervised execution of *E-ETL*, a case with the highest value of *FSA* is chosen as the best one and is used for a repair. In a supervised execution, *E-ETL* presents to the user n best cases, out of which one is finally selected by the user.

Finding a suitable case for a new problem requires a calculation of *FSA* for every case in *LRC*. To this end, a case has to be mapped into a new problem in order to calculate the similarity and applicability. Defining the similarity of sets of DS changes requires the comparison of every DS change in one set of DS changes with every DS change in another set of DS changes, in order to map equivalent DS changes. Analogically, defining the applicability requires mapping between modifications sets. These two operations cause that every iteration might be computationally expensive. For this reason, it is crucial to limit the set of potential cases in *LRC* for a new problem.

4   Decomposing ETL Repair Problem

BCSA finds one single case that has the highest value of *FSA* for a given problem. Nevertheless, *BCSA* does not guarantee that the found case handles all DS changes in a given problem P_i. Therefore, there is a need for decomposing P_i into smaller problems, P_i^m, ..., P_i^q. The decomposition of P_i allows to solve the problem using more than one case. Each case is used for handling a subset of the detected DS changes. On the one hand, the smaller a subset of DS changes, the higher is the probability of finding a case that handles all DSCs in a given subset. On the other hand, the higher number of DS changes in a subset, the higher is the probability of finding a problem that is similar to a given problem.

Example 3. Let us consider new problem *Prob_AB* consisting of two DS changes, namely *DSC_A* and *DSC_B*. Let us assume that in *LRC* there are three cases, namely *Case_A*, *Case_B*, and *Case_ABC* such that:

- *Case_A* has one DS change called *DSC_A* and one modification called *Mod_A*, which handle *DSC_A*; *Mod_A* is dependent on *DSC_A*;
- *Case_B* has one DS change - *DSC_B* and one modification - *Mod_B*, which handles *DSC_B*; *Mod_B* is dependent on *DSC_B*;
- *Case_ABC* has three DS changes, namely *DSC_A*, *DSC_B*, and *DSC_C*; these three chanes are handled by two modifications, namely *Mod_AC* and *Mod_BC*;
- *Mod_AC* is dependent on *DSC_A* and *DSC_C*;
- *Mod_BC* is dependent on *DSC_B* and *DSC_C*.

The aforementioned dependencies are visualized in Fig. 1.

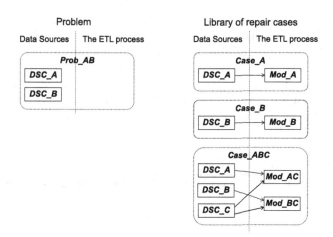

Fig. 1. Example of a problem decomposition

The most desired case for *Prob_AB* has two DS changes, namely *DSC_A* and *DSC_B*, but it is not present in the example *LRC*. *Case_ABC* has *DSC_A* and *DSC_B*, but *Case_ABC* modifications depend on *DSC_C*, which is not present in *Prob_AB*. Therefore, *Case_ABC* modifications can not be applied in order to solve *Prob_AB*.

Let us assume that *Prob_AB* is decomposed into two problems, namely *Prob_A* and *Prob_B*. *Prob_A* consists of *DSC_A* and *Prob_B* consists of *DSC_B*. *Prob_A* can be solved using *Case_A* (applying modification *Mod_A*). *Prob_B* can be solved using *Case_B* (applying modification *Mod_B*). After decomposing, DS changes of *Prob_AB* are handled by modifications included in *Case_A* and *Case_B*.

Within the *E-ETL* framework we have designed three approaches for the problem decomposition, namely: *Single Case*, *Greedy*, and *Full Search* (cf., the following sections).

4.1   *Single Case* Algorithm

In the first approach, a single case is being used during a repair. In order to get the best case, the *BCSA* algorithm is executed once. This execution returns a single case with the highest value of *FSA*. When a repair in *E-ETL* is supervised by the user, *BCSA* may return n best cases so he/she can choose one of them. The *Single Case* algorithm is the fastest, but as mention before, a single case may not handle all DS changes. Changes that are not handled by the algorithm, have to be handled manually by the user. The *Single Case* algorithm is suitable only for handling problems with very low number of DS changes that can be solved with a single case.

4.2   *Greedy* Algorithm

In the second approach, *BCSA* is executed iteratively, cf. Algorithm 1. In every iteration, *BCSA* returns the best case for the current set of DS changes. After every iteration, the changes that are handled by the found case are removed from the current set of DS changes. The iterations are executed as long as there exists at least one DS change. Therefore, the *Greedy* algorithm handles all DS changes in a given problem. When a repair in *E-ETL* is supervised by the user, *BCSA* may return n best cases so he/she can choose one of them.

ALGORITHM 1: *Greedy*

1: n {A maximum number of cases that should be found, and presented to the user}
2: $prob \leftarrow problem$
3: $DSCs\_toSolve \leftarrow prob.DSCs$
4: $solving\_cases \leftarrow [\ ]$
5: **while** $DSCs\_toSolve \neq \emptyset$ **do**
6:     $bestCases \leftarrow findBestCases(DSCs\_toSolve, n)$ {Find n best cases for not handled DS changes ($DSCs$)}
7:     $bestCase \leftarrow userChoice(bestCases)$ {The case chosen from $bestCases$ by the user}
8:     $DSCs\_toSolve.Remove(bestCase.DSCs)$ {Remove DSCs that are solved by the best case from the set of DSCs to solve}
9:     $solving\_cases.Add(bestCase)$ {Add the best case to the set of solving cases}
10: **end while**
11: **return** $solving\_cases$

Since the *Greedy* algorithm executes *BCSA* several times, it is slower than *Single Case*. Every subsequent iteration is executed with smaller set of DS changes, therefore such iterations are faster. In practice, the *Greedy* algorithm requires a few iterations. In the worst scenario, it requires n executions of *BCSA* in order to solve a given problem P_i that consists of n DS changes. The worst scenario occurs when every DS change has to be solved with a single case.

Although the *Greedy* algorithm handles all DS changes in the problem, the set of cases may be not optimal. For problems with multiple DS changes it is possible to handle them with many alternative sets of cases. Therefore, there is a need for comparing which set of cases is more appropriate for solving a given problem. Comparing sets of cases can be done using *FSA*. One of the features of *FSA* is that it is additive. Thus, it is possible to sum up values of *FSA*s for multiple cases in order to calculate the value of *FSA* for the whole set of cases, which is defined by Formula 1.

$$FSA(Case\_1 + Case\_2) = FSA(Case\_1) + FSA(Case\_2) \tag{1}$$

The higher the sum of *FSA* for a set of cases, the more appropriate is that set for solving a given problem. The following example clarifies why a particular set of cases may be not optimal.

Example. Let us consider a new problem that consist of four DS changes: (1) *DSC_A*, (2) *DSC_B*, (3) *DSC_C*, and (4) *DSC_D*. Let us assume that *LRC* includes four cases: *Case_ABC*, *Case_AB*, *Case_CD*, and *Case_D*, such that:

- *Case_ABC* handles *DSC_A*, *DSC_B* and *DSC_C*
- *Case_AB* handles *DSC_A* and *DSC_B*
- *Case_CD* handles *DSC_C* and *DSC_D*
- *Case_D* handles *DSC_D*
- $FSA(Case\_D) < FSA(Case\_CD) < FSA(Case\_BC) < FSA(Case\_ABC) < FSA(Case\_ABC + Case\_D) < FSA(Case\_AB + Case\_CD)$

In such a scenario, the *Greedy* algorithm returns two cases: *Case_ABC* (the best single case) and *Case_D* (the best case that handles the rest of the DS changes). However, the value of *FSA(Case_ABC + Case_D)* is lower than the value of *FSA(Case_AB + Case_CD)*. Therefore, the optimal result includes: { *Case_AB*, *Case_CD* }.

4.3 *Full Search* Algorithm

This approach finds an optimal set of cases, cf. Algorithm 2. To this end, all combinations of sets of cases are analyzed. In the first step, all subsets of the set of DS changes contained in a given problem P_i are generated. Next, for every generated subset A_i, *BCSA* is executed. During the full search, *BCSA* finds only these cases that solve all DS changes in subset A_i.

The result of *BCSA* is compared with the result of the best combination of subsets A_i^m of subset A_i. The result (i.e., a single case returned by *BCSA* or a set of cases assigned as solutions of subsets A_i^m) with higher FSA is assigned as a solution for a given subset A_i. In order to reduce search time, subsets are sorted by theirs numbers of elements. Therefore, searching for the best combinations of subsets A_i^m can use results assigned to previous subsets. The last subset contains all DS changes and its assigned solutions of problem P_i.

The *Full Search* algorithm requires 2^n executions of *BCSA* in order to solve a given problem P_i that consists of n DS changes. Therefore, the performance of *Full Search* is low and therefore, inappropriate for large problems.

ALGORITHM 2: *Full Search*

1: $prob \leftarrow problem$
2: $DSCs\_toSolve \leftarrow prob.DSCs$
3: $solving\_cases \leftarrow [\ ]$
   {Step 1 - prepare DSCs subsets }
4: $DSCs\_subsets \leftarrow generateAllSubsets(DSCs\_toSolve)$ {Generate all subsets of the set of DS changes (*DSCs*). The generated collection of subsets is ordered by a number of a subset items.}
   {Step 2 - calculate FSA for subsets}
5: **for all** $DSCs\_subset$ in $DSCs\_subsets$ **do**
6:     $currentSubsetsPairs \leftarrow getAllSubsetPairs(DSCs\_subset)$ {Get all possible divisions of $DSCs\_subset$ into two subset}
7:     $currentBestSubsets \leftarrow getPairWithMaxFsa(currentSubsetsPairs)$ {Get a pair of subsets with the highest sum of FSA}
8:     $currentMaxFSA \leftarrow currentBestSubsets.FSA$ {Get FSA of the best subsets pair}
9:     $currentBestCase \leftarrow findBestCase(DSCs\_subset, currentMaxFSA)$ {Find the best single case solving all DSCs in DSCs_subset}
10:    **if** $currentBestCase.FSA > currentMaxFSA$ **then**
11:        {A case for the given subset is more appropriate than the set of cases for subsets of the given subset}
12:        $DSCs\_subset.solution \leftarrow currentBestCase$ {Assign the best case for a given subset}
13:    **else**
14:        {A case for the given subset is less appropriate than the set of cases for subsets of the given subset}
15:        $DSCs\_subset.solution \leftarrow currentBestSubsets$ {Assign a set of subsets solutions for the given subset}
16:    **end if**
17: **end for**
   {Step 3 - choose the best subsets}
18: $solving\_cases \leftarrow DSCs\_subsets.lastSubset.solution$ {The solution of the last subset in the ordered collection of subsets is the solution of the problem}
19: **return** $solving\_cases$

4.4 Preliminary Experimental Evaluation

The three aforementioned algorithms were evaluated experimentally on *LRC* that included 108000 synthetically generated cases. Figure 2 shows the value of *FSA* computed by the *Single Case*, *Greedy*, and *Full Search* algorithm, for different number of cases. Figure 3 shows computational time of these algorithms w.r.t. the number of cases. From the charts we clearly observe that: (1) *Full Search* returns cases with higher values of *FSA* at much higher computational costs, (2) the value of *FSA* does not increase much for more than about 50000 cases analyzed, and (3) computational time depends linearly on the number of cases.

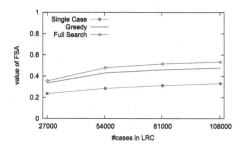
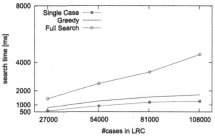

Fig. 2. *FSA* w.r.t. no. cases   **Fig. 3.** Search time w.r.t. no. cases

5 Related Work

Detecting structural changes in DSs and propagating them into the ETL layer, so far has not received much attention from the research community. One of the first solution of this problem is *Evolvable View Environment* (EVE) [12,13]. EVE is an environment that allows to repair at some extent an ETL workflow that is implemented by means of views. For every view, the user can: (1) specify which elements of the view may change and (2) determine whether a particular attribute both, in the *select* and *where* clauses, can be omitted, or replaced by another attribute. Moreover, for every table, which is referred by a given view, the user can define whether, in the process or repairing the view, this table can be omitted or replaced by another table.

Recent development in the field of evolving ETL workflows includes a framework called *Hecataeus* [10,11]. In Hecataeus, all ETL workflows and DSs are modeled as a graph whose nodes are relations, attributes, queries, conditions, views, functions, and ETL tasks. Nodes are connected by edges that represent relationships between different nodes. The graph is annotated with rules that define the behavior of an ETL workflow in response to a certain DS change event. In a response to an event, Hecataeus can either propagate the event, i.e., modify the graph according to a predefined policy, prompt the user, or block the event propagation.

Based on these ideas, another approach, called *MAIME* was proposed. In MAIME [5], a graph representing an ETL process has associated an altering algorithm that uses policies to block, propagate, or manually modify the ETL process. The policies must be explicitly defined for each graph element and the user must determine each policy in advance, like in Hecataeus. MAIME can handle only four operations of DS schema changes, i.e., adding, renaming, deleting of an attribute, and changing its data type. The set of ETL tasks that can be used in a repaired ETL process is limited to: source, destination, aggregate, split, data conversion, derived column, lookup, sort, and union all.

In [7,8], the authors proposed a method for the adaptation of *Evolving Data-Intensive Ecosystems* (EDIE), built on top of *Hecataeus*. The key idea of the method is to maintain alternative variants (old versions) of DSs and ETL processes. ETL operations can be annotated with policies that instruct whether they should be adapted to an evolved DS or should use the old version of the DS. Since DSs are typically external and independent systems, it is difficult or impossible to maintain alternative versions of such systems for the purpose of using them in the ETL layer, which is the strongest limitation of EDIE.

Finally, [2–4] proposed *Extended Evolving ETL* (E3TL). It models an ETL process by means of BPMN and then transforms it into a workflow of tasks expressed in relational algebra. The evolution of the workflow is managed by predefined rules that guide the repairs of their components. E3TL tacitly assumes the existence of a repository of cases (exactly as in CBR), from which new repair rules are mined. However, the construction and maintenance of this repository has not been discussed.

Table 1 compares the aforementioned approaches with respect to their basic functionality. In all the approaches discussed in this section, it is the user who has to define how each element of an ETL process should behave in response to a DS change. To this end, he/she has define explicit *rules* for each element or a group of elements in the ETL process, or apply a set of default rules. Even if the user decides to apply only the default rules, he/she needs to consider if there exist exceptions for each element. *E3TL* also uses CBR but only as a mean to automatically discover new rules to augment the set of initial rules. Thus, the main repair mechanism in *E3TL* are rules. On the contrary, *E-ETL* mainly uses CBR to repair processes, whereas the predefined repair rules are used as an auxiliary mechanism. For this reason, *manual effort* for *E-ETL* is lower than for the alternative approaches.

An ETL processes often contains user defined functions *UDFs and complex activities*. Such elements are often treated as black boxes without any information about their possible repairs. From what we have understand from the available papers, EVE, Hecataeus, MAIME, EDIE, E3TL could theoretically support UDFs and complex activities at a limited extent, but this problem has not been addressed in these papers (thus marked '?' in Table 1. On the con-

Table 1. The comparison of the *E-ETL* framework with alternative approaches

Approach Feature	EVE	Hecataeus	MAIME	EDIE	E3TL	E-ETL
Repair by means of	rules	rules	rules	rules	rules + CBR	CBR + rules
Manual effort	higher	higher	higher	higher	medium	lower
UDFs and complex tasks	?	?	?	?	?	at some extent
Cooper. with ETL tools	no	no	no	no	no	yes
Repair correctness	yes	yes	yes	yes	yes (rules)	yes (rules) + no (CBR)

trary, if cases in *LRC* contain modifications of UDFs or complex activities, then *E-ETL* is able to apply repairs from these cases to an ETL process.

E-ETL was designed from scratch as an independent software module. It allows to *cooperate with external ETL tools* that provide API to access ETL designs. All the other approaches developed stand-alone tools (environments) that can repair only these ETL processes that were previously designed in these environments.

The *repair correctness* of an ETL process means that the process has been repaired in a proper way and it fulfills user requirements. The competitors can prove the correctness of a process repair, according to rules defined by the user. Since, a repair in *E-ETL* is mainly based on repairs from the past (from *LRC*), we cannot guarantee, that a new problem at hand will be solved in the same way as a problem from the past. Therefore, it is impossible to prove the correctness of an ETL process repair done by means of CBR.

6 Summary

The problem of repairing an ETL process after a DS change received so far little attention from the research community (only 6 solutions proposed). The solutions are limited to simple DS changes and require defining (for each DS change) explicit repair rules by the user. Neither the commercial nor open-source ETL tools offer such a functionality.

Our solution is unlike the ones discussed in Sect. 5, as we propose to use Case Based Reasoning. To this end, we developed the *E-ETL* framework that allows to repair semi-automatically a non-functioning ETL process. However, having experimented with CBR for the repair algorithms, we figured out that: (1) cases were often too large for a given repair problem and (2) cases covered only partially a large problem. In order to solve this issue, in this paper we **contribute** three algorithms: *Single Case*, *Full Search*, and *Greedy*, for the decomposition of a large repair problem into smaller ones. This way, **we extend not only our ETL repair method but also improved the general CBR method**.

While experimentally evaluating *E-ETL* we experienced a problem of **missing real datasets** on data sources, detailed history of their evolution, and deployed ETL processes (this problem has been faced also by most of the alternative approaches). In spite of the fact that there exist a few ETL benchmarks, they focus on ETL performance, but not on ETL repairs. For this reason, we can experimentally evaluate our CBR-based ETL repair method using only synthetic data (what we have done in [17]). Currently, we are extending our *LRC* to include new synthetic cases, to further evaluate *E-ETL*, in particular the three algorithms proposed in this paper.

Next, we will improve the *FSA* computation algorithm, as in the current version, *FSA* takes into account only structural properties of DSs and an ETL process (e.g. table names, column names, data types). In the next version of the *FSA* computation algorithm, we will exploit also the semantics of DSs, DS changes, cases, and ETL processes, by using metadata and ontologies.

References

1. Aamodt, A., Plaza, E.: Case-based reasoning: foundational issues, methodological variations, and system approaches. AI Commun. **7**(1), 39–59 (1994)
2. Awiti, J.: Algorithms and architecture for managing evolving ETL workflows. In: Welzer, T., et al. (eds.) ADBIS 2019. CCIS, vol. 1064, pp. 539–545. Springer, Cham (2019). https://doi.org/10.1007/978-3-030-30278-8_51
3. Awiti, J., Vaisman, A., Zimányi, E.: From conceptual to logical ETL design using BPMN and relational algebra. In: Ordonez, C., Song, I.-Y., Anderst-Kotsis, G., Tjoa, A.M., Khalil, I. (eds.) DaWaK 2019. LNCS, vol. 11708, pp. 299–309. Springer, Cham (2019). https://doi.org/10.1007/978-3-030-27520-4_21
4. Awiti, J., Zimányi, E.: An XML interchange format for ETL models. In: Welzer, T., et al. (eds.) ADBIS 2019. CCIS, vol. 1064, pp. 427–439. Springer, Cham (2019). https://doi.org/10.1007/978-3-030-30278-8_42
5. Butkevicius, D., Freiberger, P.D., Halberg, F.M.: MAIME: a maintenance manager for ETL processes. In: EDBT/ICDT Workshops (2017)
6. Gartner: Data integration tools Marketcs. https://www.gartner.com/reviews/market/data-integration-tools
7. Manousis, P., Vassiliadis, P., Papastefanatos, G.: Automating the adaptation of evolving data-intensive ecosystems. In: Ng, W., Storey, V.C., Trujillo, J.C. (eds.) ER 2013. LNCS, vol. 8217, pp. 182–196. Springer, Heidelberg (2013). https://doi.org/10.1007/978-3-642-41924-9_17
8. Manousis, P., Vassiliadis, P., Papastefanatos, G.: Impact analysis and policy-conforming rewriting of evolving data-intensive ecosystems. J. Data Semant. **4**(4), 231–267 (2015). https://doi.org/10.1007/s13740-015-0050-3
9. Moon, H.J., Curino, C.A., Deutsch, A., Hou, C., Zaniolo, C.: Managing and querying transaction-time databases under schema evolution. VLDB **1**, 882–895 (2008)
10. Papastefanatos, G., Vassiliadis, P., Simitsis, A., Sellis, T., Vassiliou, Y.: Rule-based management of schema changes at ETL sources. In: Grundspenkis, J., Kirikova, M., Manolopoulos, Y., Novickis, L. (eds.) ADBIS 2009. LNCS, vol. 5968, pp. 55–62. Springer, Heidelberg (2010). https://doi.org/10.1007/978-3-642-12082-4_8
11. Papastefanatos, G., Vassiliadis, P., Simitsis, A., Vassiliou, Y.: Policy-regulated management of ETL evolution. JoDS **13**, 147–177 (2009)

12. Rundensteiner, E.A., Koeller, A., Zhang, X.: Maintaining data warehouses over changing information sources. CACM **43**(6), 57–62 (2000)
13. Rundensteiner, E.A., et al.: Evolvable View Environment (EVE): non-equivalent view maintenance under schema changes. In: SIGMOD, pp. 553–555 (1999)
14. Vassiliadis, P., Zarras, A.V.: Schema evolution survival guide for tables: avoid rigid childhood and you're EN route to a quiet life. JoDS **6**(4), 221–241 (2017)
15. Vassiliadis, P., Zarras, A.V., Skoulis, I.: Gravitating to rigidity: patterns of schema evolution - and its absence - in the lives of tables. IS **63**, 24–46 (2017)
16. Wojciechowski, A.: E-ETL framework: ETL process reparation algorithms using case-based reasoning. In: Morzy, T., Valduriez, P., Bellatreche, L. (eds.) ADBIS 2015. CCIS, vol. 539, pp. 321–333. Springer, Cham (2015). https://doi.org/10.1007/978-3-319-23201-0_34
17. Wojciechowski, A.: ETL workflow reparation by means of case-based reasoning. Inf. Syst. Front. **20**(1), 21–43 (2017). https://doi.org/10.1007/s10796-016-9732-0
18. Wrembel, R.: A survey on managing the evolution of data warehouses. Int. J. Data Warehous. Min. **5**(2), 24–56 (2009)

Rule Discovery for (Semi-)automatic Repairs of ETL Processes

Judith Awiti[1][(✉)] and Robert Wrembel[2]

[1] Université Libre de Bruxelles, Brussels, Belgium
judith.awiti@ulb.ac.be
[2] Poznan University of Technology, Poznań, Poland
robert.wrembel@cs.put.poznan.pl

Abstract. A data source integration layer, commonly called extract-transform-load (ETL), is one of the core components of information systems. It is applicable to standard data warehouse (DW) architectures as well as to data lake (DL) architectures. The ETL layer runs processes that ingest, transform, integrate, and upload data into a DW or DL. The ETL layer is not static, since the data sources being integrated by this layer change their structures. As a consequence, an already deployed ETL process stops working and needs to be re-designed (repaired). Companies typically have deployed from thousands to hundreds of thousands of ETL processes. For this reason, a technique and software support for repairing semi-automatically a failed ETL processes is of vital practical importance. This problem has been only partially solved by technology or research, but the solutions still require an immense work of an ETL administrator. Our solution is based on a case-based-reasoning combined with repair rules. In this paper, we contribute a method for automatic discovery of repair rules from a stored history of repair cases.

Keywords: Data source evolution · ETL process repair · Case-Based-Reasoning · Rule discovery from cases

1 Introduction

Data source integration is one of the major issues in building an information system, like a data warehouse (DW) or a data lake (DL). Such systems, typically are composed of: (1) a data source (DS) layer, (2) an integration layer - commonly called extract-transform-load (ETL), (3) a repository layer - a DW or DL, and (4) an analytical layer. The ETL layer is responsible for extracting data from DSs, transforming data into a common model, cleaning data, removing missing, inconsistent, and redundant records, integrating data, and loading them into a DW. This layer, is implemented as a workflow of tasks (a.k.a. a process), managed by a dedicated software, called an ETL engine.

In practice, the structures of data sources evolve in time frequently, cf. [9, 14,22,23]. For example, the Wikipedia schema has changed on average every

© Springer Nature Switzerland AG 2020
T. Robal et al. (Eds.): DB&IS 2020, CCIS 1243, pp. 250–264, 2020.
https://doi.org/10.1007/978-3-030-57672-1_19

9–10 days in years 2003–2008. As shown in [20, 22], the most frequent changes in structures of DSs include: (1) creating or dropping a table, (2) creating or dropping an attribute of a table, and (3) changing the definition of an attribute.

Such structural changes in DSs impact the ETL and other layers of an information system. As the first consequence, a previously deployed ETL process stops its execution with errors and must be re-designed and re-deployed. Following [25], further in this paper we will call this activity an ETL process *repair*. In practice, such repairs have to be done manually by an ETL designer, as neither commercial nor open source ETL tools support (semi-)automatic repairs of such processes. Having in mind that large companies have from thousands to hundreds of thousands ETL processes deployed in their infrastructures, manual repairs are very costly.

A workaround to this problem applied by some companies is: (1) a deployment of generic ELT processes whose inputs include fully described structures of data to be processed or (2) screening the changes by designing views. However, these approaches do not solve the problem, as an ETL designer must either manually provide new (changed) structures to an ETL process or design a new set of screening views (i.e, repairs are done manually).

Handling and incorporating DS structural changes at the ETL layer have received so far little attention from the research community. To the best of our knowledge, only five approaches have been proposed (excluding our approach), namely: *EVE, Hecataeus, Maime, EDIE*, and *E-ETL*, cf. Sect. 2. The first four approaches propose to manually annotate ETL processes with repair policies, whereas *E-ETL* applies case-based-reasoning to find and apply the most similar case to a given repair problem at hand. Each of them proposes only a partial solution to this extremely difficult problem.

Previously, we have proposed the Extended Evolving ETL (*E3TL*) approach [3]. It models ETL processes by means of BPMN and then transforms them to workflows of tasks expressed by relational algebra [4] by means of an XML interchange format [5]. The workflows then are managed by rules and cases that guide the repairs of their components.

In this paper, we extend the concept and architecture of *E3TL* and propose to **combine ETL processes repairs based on rule-based reasoning (RBR) and case-based-reasoning (CBR)**. In particular, we propose **a method for discovering new repair rules from previous repair cases**. This way, predefined rules in *E3TL* are extended with the discovered rules.

This paper is organized as follows. Section 2 discusses the related research approaches to handling the evolution and repairs of ETL processes. Section 3 outlines basic concepts of ETL used in this paper. Section 4 discusses the *E3TL* workflow reparation framework. In Sect. 5 we contribute the rule discovery mechanism which infers rules from cases in the *E3TL* framework and a preliminary experimental evaluation of the rule discovery mechanism. Finally, Sect. 6 summarizes and concludes the paper.

2   Related Work

A complementary work towards handling evolving ETL processes was presented in [16,18] where the authors presented a method for assessing the design quality of an ETL process wrt. its vulnerability to DS changes and drew conclusions on how the vulnerability depends on a design of an ETL process. The approaches to handling the evolution and repairs of ETL processes can be divided into two main categories, namely: (1) repairs by means of pre-defined rules (further called the *rule repairs* approach) and (2) repairs by means of case-based-reasoning mechanisms (further called the *CBR* approach).

The *rule repairs* approach includes the following contributions: *EVE* [21], *Hecataeus* [15,17], *EDIE* [12,13], and *MAIME* [7].

Evolvable View Environment (EVE) contributes the first solution to ETL repairs. In *EVE* and ETL process is not typical, since it is implemented by means of views. For every view, user-defined rules guide its evolution.

In *Hecataeus*, an ETL process is represented as a graph, where nodes represent relations, attributes, queries, conditions, views, functions, and DSs, whereas edges represent relationships between nodes. The graph is annotated with policies that define how to evolve given parts of the graph in response to data source changes, i.e., whether to propagate a change, block it, or ask a designer for a decision. The policies can handle attribute changes (rename, type change, length change, deletion) and table changes (rename, deletion). The limitations of *Hecataeus* are that: (1) the policies must be explicitly defined for each graph element, (2) a user must determine a policy in advance, before changes to a DS were applied, (3) ETL tasks are limited to steps expressed by SQL, and (4) the supported ETL evolution operations do not include column addition, table addition, table split, and table merge.

EDIE builds on the concept proposed in *Hecataeus*. The main idea of *EDIE* is to maintain alternative variants (old versions) of data sources and ETL processes to use them when needed. To this end, ETL tasks are annotated with policies that instruct whether a given ETL process should be adapted to an evolved DS or should use an old version of the DS. This approach is difficult to be applied in practice, as DSs typically do not maintain versions.

MAIME builds also on the concept of *Hecataeus*. A graph representing an ETL process has associated an altering algorithm that is configurable to block, propagate, or manually modify an ETL process. The set of changes in *MAIME* is limited only to adding, renaming, deleting of a property, and changing its data type. The set of ETL steps is limited to: source, destination, aggregate, split, data conversion, derived column, lookup, sort, union all. Moreover, the policies must be explicitly defined for each graph element and a user must determine a policy in advance, like in *Hecataeus*.

To the best of our knowledge, a unique and the only approach to applying *CBR* to ETL process repairs was proposed in [24,25]. In this approach, called *E-ETL*, in order to repair a given ETL workflow, a base of historical cases is searched to find a similar case. If the case is found, then it can be tailored to a given repair problem at hand or applied directly (if possible). To this end, the author proposed a metamodel, case base search algorithm, and a similarity measure to compare cases. However, the disadvantage or *E-ETL* is that to be able to repair an ETL process, it needs a large base of adequate cases adequate for repairing a problem at hand.

3   Preliminaries

3.1   Common ETL Tasks

In this section, we review the extended relational algebra (RA) operators for ETL processes as discussed in [4]. The left-hand side of Table 1 shows the standard RA operators which is described in classic database literature like [10]. The extended RA operators found on the right-hand side of Table 1 have been developed to suit common ETL tasks. Both the standard and extended RA operators are used to automatically generate SQL queries to be executed in any relational database.

Table 1. Standard relational algebra operators and extended relational operators

Standard operator	Notation	Extended operator	Notation
Selection	$\sigma_C(R)$	Aggregate	$\mathcal{A}_{A_1,...,A_m \mid C_1=\mathsf{F}_1(B_1),...,C_n=\mathsf{F}_n(B_n),D_1,...,D_n}(R)$
Projection	$\pi_{A_1,...,A_n}(R)$	Delete Data	$R - \sigma_C(R)$
Cartesian Product	$R_1 \times R_2$	Derived Column	$\mathcal{E}_{A_1=\mathsf{Expr}_1,...,A_n=\mathsf{Expr}_n}(R)$
Union	$R_1 \cup R_2$	Input Data	$\mathcal{I}_{A_1,...,A_n}(F)$
Intersection	$R_1 \cap R_2$	Insert Data	$R \cup S$ or $R \leftarrow S$
Difference	$R_1 - R_2$	Lookup	$\pi_{A_1,...,A_n}(R_1 \bowtie_C R_2)$
Join	$R_1 \bowtie_C R_2$	Rename	$\rho_{A_1 \leftarrow B_1,...,A_n \leftarrow B_n}(R)$ or $\rho_S(R)$
Natural Join	$R_1 * R_2$	Sort	$\tau_{A_1...,A_n}(R)$
Left Outer Join	$R_1 ⟕_C R_2$	Update Column	$\mathcal{U}_{A_1=\mathsf{Expr}_1,...,A_n=\mathsf{Expr}_n \mid C}(R)$
Right Outer Join	$R_1 ⟖_C R_2$	Update Set	$\mathcal{U}(R)_{A_1=\mathsf{Expr}_1,...,A_n=\mathsf{Expr}_n \mid C}(S)$
Full Outer Join	$R_1 ⟗_C R_2$		
Semijoin	$R_1 ⋉_C R_2$		
Division	$R_1 \div R_2$		

The semantics of the extended operators is as follows.

- **Aggregate:** Let F be an aggregate function such as Count, Min, Max, Sum, or Avg. The aggregate operator $\mathcal{A}_{A_1,...,A_m \mid C_1=\mathsf{F}_1(B_1),...,C_n=\mathsf{F}_n(B_n)}(R)$ partitions the tuples of relation R into groups that have the same values of attributes A_i and for each group it selects attributes D_i and computes new values of attributes C_i by applying aggregate function F_i to the values of attribute B_i in the group, or the cardinality of the group if $F_i(B_i)$ is Count($*$). If no grouping attributes are given (i.e., $m = 0$), the aggregate functions are applied to the whole relation R. The schema of the resulting relation has the attributes $(A_1, \ldots, A_m, C_1, \ldots, C_n)$.
- **Delete Data:** Denoted as $R - \sigma_C(R)$, removes from relation R the tuples that satisfy the Boolean condition C.
- **Derived Column:** Given a relation R, the Derived Column operation $\mathcal{E}_{A_1=Exp_1,..., A_n=Exp_n}(R)$ extends each tuple in relation R with new attributes A_i obtained by computing the expression Exp_i.

- **Input Data:** Denoted as $\mathcal{I}_{A_1,\ldots,A_n}(F)$, inputs a set of tuples constructed from the content of the file F into an ETL workflow. Note that file F could be replaced a relation from an operational database.
- **Insert Data:** Given two relations R and S, this operation, denoted as $R \cup S$, adds to R the tuples from S. When a new relation R is created with the contents of S, the operation is denoted $R \leftarrow S$. Also if the two relations have different arity, the attributes of the second relation must be explicitly stated as, e.g., $R \cup \pi_{B_1,\ldots,B_n} S$.
- **Lookup:** The lookup operation is denoted as $\pi_{A_1,\ldots A_n}(R_1 \bowtie_C R_2)$, projects attributes $(A_1,\ldots,A_n)$ from relations R_1 and R_2 where the join operation can be any of the six types in Table 1.
- **Rename:** This operation is applied over relation names or over attribute names. For the former, the operation is denoted as $\rho_S(R)$, where the input relation R is renamed to S. For attributes, $\rho_{A_1 \leftarrow B_1,\ldots,A_n \leftarrow B_n}(R)$, renames the attributes A_i in relation R to B_i, respectively.
- **Sort:** Denoted as $\tau_{A_1\ldots,A_n}(R)$, sorts the tuples of a relation R by the attribute A_i depending on the order of the attributes.
- **Update Column:** denoted as $\mathcal{U}_{A_1=Expr_1,\ldots,A_n=Expr_n|C}(R)$, replaces the value of the attribute A_i with the value of Expr_i for each tuple in relation R that satisfies the Boolean condition C.
- **Update Set:** denoted as $\mathcal{U}(R)_{A_1=\mathsf{Expr}_1,\ldots,A_n=\mathsf{Expr}_n|C}(S)$, replaces the value of the attribute A_i with the value of Expr_i for tuples in relation R that correspond to tuples in relation S and satisfy the Boolean condition C. Unlike the *Update Column* operation, the condition of the *Update Set* operation includes matching the corresponding tuples of the two relations, R and S.

3.2   Running Example

To explain our ETL process repair method, we describe below an ETL scenario from the *TPC-DI* benchmark [19] for loading a Slowly Changing Dimension table called DimBroker (for details, a reader is referred to the TPC-DI specification document). We adapted this scenario to simulate DS changes in our approach.

As shown in Table 2, the ETL process that loads DimBroker starts with an input data task which inputs records from an HR.csv file (a DS file) (Eq. 1). A select task filters only records with EmployeeJobCode value of 314 (Eq. 2). After that, a lookup task retrieves the Salary column of the SALARY table by joining corresponding EmployeeID columns (Eq. 3). The resultant records are aggregated to obtain the sum of Salary of each employee (Eq. 4). A surrogate key column with the value of the row number is added the ETL flow (Eq. 5) and finally, an insert data task inserts the records into DimBroker (Eq. 6). At each stage of the ETL, intermediate data are stored in temporary tables (Temp1, ..., Temp5).

4   ETL Workflow Reparation in *E3TL*

Our approach to ETL workflow reparation upon DS schema changes is based on the following concepts: (1) Rule-Based-Reasoning, (2) Case-Based-Reasoning,

Table 2. RA expressions to model the ETL process for DimBroker

Temp1 ← $\mathcal{I}$_{EmployeeID,ManagerID,FirstName,LastName,EmployeeJobCode,Phone1,Phone2,...} (HR.csv)	(1)
Temp2 ← σ_{EmployeeJobCode = '314'} (Temp1)	(2)
Temp3 ← π_{EmployeeID,ManagerID,FirstName,...,Salary} (Temp2 ⋈ SALARY)	(3)
Temp4 ← $\mathcal{A}$_{EmployeeID	Total_Salary=SUM(Salary),EmployeeID,ManagerID,FirstName...} (Temp3)	(4)
Temp5 ← $\mathcal{E}$_{SK_BrokerID = rownumber()} (Temp4)	(5)
DimBroker ← DimBroker ∪ (π_{SK_BrokerID, EmployeeID,ManagerID,FirstName,...} (Temp5))	(6)

and (3) Automatic Discovery of Rules from cases. Rule-Based-Reasoning (RBR) is a type of reasoning that uses (if-then-else) rule statements [6]. In Case-Based-Reasoning (CBR), a given problem (e.g., repair) is solved by applying a solution that was applied to a similar problem in the past [1]. A problem and its solution is called a *case*. Automatic Discovery of Rules (ADR) applies data mining techniques to discover rules from cases collected and stored as part of CBR. The three aforementioned concepts have been incorporated into the *E3TL* framework that we are developing.

In this section we present a prototype *E3TL* system, RBR, an CBR, whereas in Sect. 5 we present ADR.

4.1 *E3TL* Prototype

The main components of the prototype *E3TL* system [3], which is currently being built, are shown in Fig. 1. The *ETL Parser* parses relational algebra statements, which are used to implement an ETL process. *ETL Manager* assesses the impact of DS changes on each ETL task. For DS changes that can be handled by applying pre-defined repair rules (stored in *Rule Base*), the *ETL Rewriter* component rewrites the commands in the ETL workflow by applying recommendations from *ETL Manager*. *ETL Rewriter* iterates through the ETL commands and makes changes to them. It also stores the history of versions of the ETL process being repaired.

If adequate rules cannot be applied, then *ETL Rewriter* rewrites the ETL commands by applying the user's decision. The *Case Base* is searched to find the most suitable case to repair the ETL workflow. If the case is found, it is displayed to the user and he/she either applies it directly to repair the process or modify it to adjust to the repair scenario. In any case, the user's decision and the DS change are stored together in the *Case Base* as a new case.

Right after deploying *E3TL*, only pre-defined rules are available in *Rule Base*. The set of rules are constantly discovered from cases, by the *Translator*. As the prototype works, the *Rule Base* is augmented with discovered rules. *E3TL* supports two types of rules, namely *predefined rules* and *inferred rules*, cf. Sect. 4.2.

Changes to data sources schemas include (cf., [22]): (1) adding, deleting, renaming a column, (2) merging two columns, (3) splitting a column, (4) changing a data type of a column, (5) adding, deleting, renaming a table. However, in this paper, we focus on the deleting, renaming, merging, and splitting of columns.

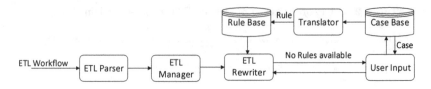

Fig. 1. Components of the *E3TL* prototype system

In a step-by-step manner we will extend the functionality of *E3TL* to handle the remaining changes.

4.2   RBR: Pre-defined Rules in *E3TL*

Predefined rules are default and unambiguous rules present in *Rule Base* at the start of the ETL workflow reparation. These rules are applied in scenarios where only one solution is possible to repair the ETL workflow. Note that, predefined rules in *Rule Base* must not make any changes to a DW schema. This is because the ETL workflow might not be the only application that is dependent on the DW. Other business analysis applications may be dependent on the DW. Hence, we do not alter the DW schema unless the user allows that in *Case Base*.

In Table 3, as values of column *Parts of Expression* we show separate parts of each of the extended ETL operators (ETL tasks), from Table 1. Six types of parts are distinguished, namely: Expression, Condition, Group By, Rename, Selection, and Sort. These parts are the possible places a column can reside in an ETL task. Since predefined rules must be unambiguous, we explicitly state the part of an ETL task where a changed DS column exists and appropriate actions to be taken to repair the ETL process.

Table 3. Parts of an ETL tasks where a column may be used

ETL task	Parts of Expression
Aggregate	$\mathcal{A}_{GroupBy|Expression,Selection}(R)$
Delete Data	$R - \sigma_{Condition}(R)$
Derived Column	$\mathcal{E}_{Expression}(R)$
Input Data	$\mathcal{I}_{Selection}(F)$
Insert Data	$R \cup \pi_{Selection}S$
Lookup	$\pi_{Selection}(R_1 \bowtie_{Condition} R_2)$
Rename	$\rho_{Rename}(R)$
Sort	$\tau_{Sort}(R)$
Update Column	$\mathcal{U}_{Expression|Condition}(R)$
Update Data	$\mathcal{U}(R)_{Expression|Condition}(S)$

With regards to column changes, we state the part of the ETL task where the changed column resides in the *if* part of the rule. In the *then* part, we describe the repair action to be taken by the *E3TL* framework. The set of pre-defined rules for column changes in the current version of the *E3TL* framework includes:

1. *If* a DS column is renamed, *then* rename that column in all ETL tasks, but not in a DW table.
2. *If* a deleted DS column exists only in the Selection part of ETL tasks and it does not exist in a DW table, *then* remove this column from the ETL tasks.
3. *If* a deleted DS column is the only column in a Sort task, *then* delete the Sort task.
4. *If* a deleted DS column is not the only column in a Sort task, *then* delete that column from the Sort task.
5. *If* a deleted DS column is the only column in the Condition part of the Select task, *then* change the Select task into the Project task or delete the Select task.
6. *If* a deleted DS column is one of the columns in the Group By part but not in the Expression part of an Aggregate task, *then* delete that column from the Aggregate task.
7. *If* merged DS columns exist only in a Selection part of ETL tasks and they do not exist in a DW table, *then* replace them with the newly merged column.
8. *If* all merged DS column(s) are found in a Sort task, *then* replace the merged columns with the new column.
9. If one or all merged DS column(s) is/are the only column(s) in the Condition parte of the Select task, *then* replace the merged columns with the new column.
10. *If* all merged DS columns exist in a Group By part of an Aggregate task, but not in an Expression part, *then* replace them with the new column.
11. *If* a column is split into two or more columns, and it exists in a Selection part of ETL tasks and it does not exist in a DW table, *then* replace it with the split columns.
12. *If* a split DS column is the only column in a Sort task, *then* replace it with the split columns in any order.

4.3   Case-Based-Reasoning in *E3TL*

In this section we give an overview of applying CBR to ETL workflow repairs, in order to provide a basis for discussion on how rules are inferred from CBR cases in Sect. 5. This discussion is inspired by [25].

In cases where pre-defined rules cannot be applied to repair a given ETL process, i.e., a repair initiated by a DS change was not described by the existing rules, then the CBR is used. To this end, the *Case Base* is searched to find the most suitable case to repair a given ETL process. If the case is found, it can be applied to repair the ETL process. The found case can also be manually adjusted by a user to the repair scenario. In any case, a new case is created and stored in *Case Base*.

To illustrate how the case-based repair works, let us consider a case of column deletion in our running example. For example, if column EmployeeJobCode is deleted in file HR.csv, there are several ways an ETL designer might want to repair an ETL workflow, i.e.:

- to delete EmployeeJobCode from Eqs. 1, 3, 4 and 6, delete the entire Select task of Eq. 2 and delete EmployeeJobCode from DimBroker; this option may be applicable if the deleted column is not needed anymore in the DW table;
- to delete EmployeeJobCode from Eqs. 1, 3, 4 and 6 as well as to replace EmployeeJobCode in Eq. 2 with another column; this option may be applicable if a user still wants to filter some of the records based on another column of his/her choice;
- to delete EmployeeJobCode from wherever it appears in the ETL flow and store a null value in the corresponding EmployeeJobCode column of DimBroker; this option may be applicable if a user does not want to make any changes to the DW and wants to keep the deleted DS column in the DW table.

As a summary, Table 4 lists some ETL tasks, DS changes, actions taken by a user, and parts of an ETL task a column can reside in. Each element of this table has its identifier and name. For instance, D1 = Delete Column means that the ID of Delete Column (i.e., a DS change) is D1; A1 = Delete Column means that the ID of Delete Column (i.e., user action) is A1; P1 = Selection means that the ID of a column residing in the Selection part of an ETL task is P1; T1 = Input Data means that the ID of an Input Data task is T1.

Table 4. The description of an example content of *Case Base*

DS changes	Actions taken by user
D1 = Delete Column	A1 = Delete Column
D2 = Merge Columns	A2 = Replace Column
D3 = Split Column	A3 = Rename Column
D4 = Rename Column	A4 = Delete Table
D5 = Delete Table	A5 = Replace Table
D6 = Rename Table	A6 = Delete Task
D7 = Change Data Type	A7 = Replace and Create Column in DW
	A8 = Delete Column in task and in DW
	A9 = Replace with NULL
Part of ETL Task	ETL Task
P1 = Selection	T1 = Input Data
P2 = Expression	T2 = Select
P3 = Group By	T3 = Lookup
P4 = Condition	T4 = Aggregate
P5 = Match	T5 = Derived Column
P6 = Rename	T6 = Insert Data

In *E3TL, Case Base* is implemented in a relational database. Its simplified schema is shown in Fig. 2. The Project, Cases, DSC, Task, Action, Part tables contain all possible data source changes, ETL task, actions taken by a user, and parts of ETL tasks affected by a data source change. The Project table stores information about ETL workflow reparation project. A project can include several cases. Each case is stored in the Cases table with an identity value (CaseID). The DSC, Task, Action, and Part tables store the DS changes, ETL tasks, user action, parts of ETL tasks, respectively.

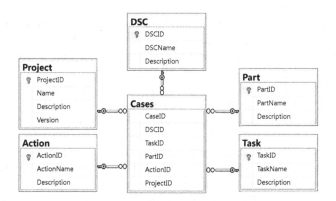

Fig. 2. The schema of Case Base

As an example, let us consider three cases from three different modifications to the ETL workflow discussed above:

Case1: D1, T1P1A1, T2P4A6, T3P1A1, T4PIA1, T5, T6P1A8
Case2: D1, T1P1A2, T2P4A2, T3P1A3, T4PIA1, T5, T6P1A7
Case3: D1, T1P1A1, T2P4A2, T3P1A1, T4PIA1, T5, T6P1A9

In this example, (Case1) represents a column deletion (D1), T1P1A2 means that: (1) the deleted column is in the Selection part P1 of the Input task T1 and (2) the user applied a delete column action A1 to that task. T2P4A6 implies that (1) the deleted column is in the Condition part P4 of the Select task T2 and (2), the user applied action A6 (i.e., delete task) to that task. T3P1A1, T4PIA1 and T6P1A8 follow the same principle as described above. T5 indicates that the Derived Column task is present, but an ETL developer does not apply any action or change to it.

5   RBR: Automatic Rule Discovery in *E3TL*

As mentioned earlier, after deploying *E3TL*, only the set of pre-defined rules is available. These rules are used to repair ETL processes. While *E3TL* works, new cases are constantly created by an ETL developer - as the result of manual repairs. All these cases are stored in *Case Base*.

Inferred rules are derived by applying an algorithm to translate cases in *Case Base* into new rules. Only if *Case Base* includes cases, new rules can be inferred from these cases. It is possible that an inferred rule contradicts with a pre-defined one. In such a case, the inferred rule takes precedence (this behaviour is the subject of further investigation).

5.1 Rule Discovery Technique

In order to discover new rules from cases, we use frequent item set mining and association rule learning [2]. In particular, we use the Apriori algorithm [2] to discover frequent patterns in *Case Base*. It is a standard algorithm for finding frequent patterns in a dataset for association rule. It identifies frequent items in a database and iteratively extends them to larger itemsets, as long as these itemsets appear sufficiently often in the database. Further in this paper we use standard definitions of *support* and *confidence* [11]. We applied *Apriori* as: (1) it is intuitive and (2) discovered rules are intuitive and easy to understand. Notice that this is a pilot work and we have chosen a simple to implement algorithm to quickly test the feasibility of our approach. In the future, we plan to apply more advanced machine learning techniques for rule discovery.

We discover strong association rules from the discovered frequent patterns by pruning cases, which have the support and confidence lower than a user-defined minimum support (min_sup) and minimum confidence (min_conf) thresholds. Higher values of min_sup and min_conf imply that some rules may not be detected, and lower values imply that unfitting rules may be detected.

For all cases in the *Case Base*, we apply the *Apriori* algorithm to find frequent patterns/itemsets. Note that, each case is made up of a list of items. An item could be a data source change, an ETL task, or a combination of an ETL task, a part of the ETL task, and an action applied to an ETL task, as discussed in Sect. 4.3.

The *Apriori* algorithm comprises of two main processes namely: (1) the candidate itemset generation, in which the *Case Base* is scanned to get the count of the number of occurrences, called support, of each item separately, and (2) the large itemset L generation, which is done by pruning items from the candidate itemset with support values lower than the user-defined min_sup value. Next, a list of all pairs from L is generated. Step 1 is done by scanning newly generated itemset pairs and obtaining the support count of the occurrence of each itemset pair in the *Case Base*. Step 2 is done by pruning the candidate itemset pairs to obtain large itemset pairs. Steps 1 and 2 are repeated iteratively, each time increasing the size of the itemsets. The algorithm ends when L becomes empty. The large itemsets of the iteration before the empty set was obtained are considered as the frequent itemsets.

After that, we generate association rules from the frequent itemsets obtained by the *Apriori* algorithm. For each frequent itemset, we generate all of their nonempty subsets. We calculate the confidence of each of the subsets and compare it with a user-defined min_conf. We prune subsets with confidence < min_conf. Strong rules are written from subsets with confidence ≥ min_conf.

Figure 3 summarizes an extension of the rule discovery part of the *E3TL* framework (from Fig. 1). The *Apriori* algorithm and rule discovery procedure are run in *Translator*. The inferred rules are stored in the rule base and are used to handle similar DS changes in the future.

5.2   Preliminary Experimental Evaluation

Our rule discovery approach was evaluated by preliminary experiments. Their goal was to discover rules from cases stored in *Case Base*. First, we mined frequent patterns and second, we found strong rules from these frequent patterns. In order to discover rules, we used *Case Base* with 60 cases, generated manually as follows. In the running example (cf., Sect. 3.2, we describe a scenario where the EmployeeJobCode is deleted. We provide three different ways a user may handle that situation. So we create *Case Base* that contains these three different cases replicated 20 times each. In this scenario the cases are applied at equal times to show that association rule mining can generate rules from a *Case Base* where all cases are equally represented (no case skew exists).

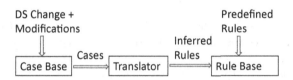

Fig. 3. Rule discovery framework

The patterns were discovered by the Apriori algorithm, implemented in C#, based on the source code obtained from [8]. The input of the algorithm is the list of cases in the Case Base and a pre-defined min_sup value. Given a min_sup threshold of 60%, the algorithm discovered 19 frequent patterns.

Next, we create rules by combining the subsets of each frequent pattern. The size of possible subsets of each frequent pattern is $2^n - 1$ (excluding the empty set), where n is the number of items in a frequent pattern. The *confidence* value of each subset is computed in a standard way. The *confidence* value of each subset is compared with the user-defined min_conf threshold. A subset with confidence value greater than min_conf became a strong association rule.

Out of the 19 patterns, we discovered 40 rules with confidence of 100%, e.g., T4P1A1, T3P1A1, T1P1A1, T5 (support: 66,67%, confidence: 100%). This implies that in another ETL scenario with tasks T1, T3, T4 and T5, if a column is deleted from the DS, then the modifications of T4P1A1, T3P1A1, T1P1A1, T5 will be automatically applied. In the 40 rules the order of their items is important. For

Table 5. An example rule that items T4P1A1, T3P1A1, T1P1A1, T5

$T1P1A1 \Rightarrow T4P1A1, T3P1A1, T5$
$T1P1A1, T5 \Rightarrow T4P1A1, T3P1A1$
$T3P1A1 \Rightarrow T4P1A1, T1P1A1, T5$
$T3P1A1, T5 \Rightarrow T4P1A1, T1P1A1$
$T3P1A1, T1P1A1 \Rightarrow T4P1A1, T5$
$T3P1A1, T1P1A1, T5 \Rightarrow T4P1A1$
$T4P1A1, T1P1A1 \Rightarrow T3P1A1, T5$
$T4P1A1, T1P1A1, T5 \Rightarrow T3P1A1$
$T4P1A1, T3P1A1 \Rightarrow T1P1A1, T5$
$T4P1A1, T3P1A1, T5 \Rightarrow T1P1A1$
$T4P1A1, T3P1A1, T1P1A1 \Rightarrow T5$

example, the rule which contains items T4P1A1, T3P1A1, T1P1A1, T5 has 11 different arrangements, as shown in Table 5.

In our implementation, we have not considered sequences of tasks (i.e., with the order implied), as ETL tasks can be rearranged in different orders to produce the same results. As a consequence, the presented 11 arrangements are treated as a single rule, meaning: *if* a deleted DS column exists in the Selection part $P1$ of ETL tasks $T1$, $T3$, $T4$ and ETL task $T5$ is present, *then* action $A1$ is applied to $T1$, $T3$ and $T4$.

6   Summary

In this paper, we presented the *E3TL* framework for (semi-)automatic repairs of evolving ETL processes. *E3TL* is based on the three following concepts: (1) Rule-Based-Reasoning, (2) Case-Based-Reasoning, and (3) Automatic Discovery of Rules from cases. In order to discover rules from cases stored in a repository, we used association rule mining (the *Apriori* algorithm). A limitation of the rule discovery approach is that it needs a large repository of repair cases.

This paper presents a preliminary work that opens the following new research problems: (1) how to integrate the discovered rules with the pre-defined ones in a consistent way, i.e., without creating duplicate rules or contradictory rules, (2) how to manage rule subsumptions, (3) how to prioritize rules, and (4) how to construct efficient and consistent sequences of repair tasks. These problems will be investigated in the nearest future.

Acknowledgements. The authors express their gratitude to Prof. Patrick Marcel (Université de Tours) for his comments on the rule discovery approach. The work of Judith Awiti is supported by the European Commission through the Erasmus Mundus Joint Doctorate project *Information Technologies for Business Intelligence-Doctoral College* (IT4BI-DC). The work of Robert Wrembel is supported by the grant of the Polish National Agency for Academic Exchange, within the Bekker Programme.

References

1. Aamodt, A., Plaza, E.: Case-based reasoning: foundational issues, methodological variations, and system approaches. AI Commun. **7**(1), 39–59 (1994)

2. Agrawal, R., Imielinski, T., Swami, A.N.: Mining association rules between sets of items in large databases. In: Proceedings of SIGMOD, pp. 207–216. ACM (1993)

3. Awiti, J.: Algorithms and architecture for managing evolving ETL workflows. In: Welzer, T., et al. (eds.) ADBIS 2019. CCIS, vol. 1064, pp. 539–545. Springer, Cham (2019). https://doi.org/10.1007/978-3-030-30278-8_51

4. Awiti, J., Vaisman, A., Zimányi, E.: From conceptual to logical ETL design using BPMN and relational algebra. In: Ordonez, C., Song, I.-Y., Anderst-Kotsis, G., Tjoa, A.M., Khalil, I. (eds.) DaWaK 2019. LNCS, vol. 11708, pp. 299–309. Springer, Cham (2019). https://doi.org/10.1007/978-3-030-27520-4_21

5. Awiti, J., Zimányi, E.: An XML interchange format for ETL models. In: Welzer, T., et al. (eds.) ADBIS 2019. CCIS, vol. 1064, pp. 427–439. Springer, Cham (2019). https://doi.org/10.1007/978-3-030-30278-8_42

6. Bassiliades, N., Governatori, G., Paschke, A.: Rule-Based Reasoning, Programming, and Applications. LNCS, vol. 6826. Springer, Heidelberg (2011). https://doi.org/10.1007/978-3-642-22546-8

7. Butkevicius, D., Freiberger, P.D., Halberg, F.M.: MAIME: a maintenance manager for ETL processes. In: Proceedings of EDBT/ICDT Workshops (2017)

8. Codeding: Apriori algorithm. http://codeding.com/?article=13. Accessed Oct 2019

9. Curino, C., Moon, H.J., Tanca, L., Zaniolo, C.: Schema evolution in Wikipedia - toward a web information system benchmark. In: Proceedings of ICEIS, pp. 323–332 (2008)

10. Garcia-Molina, H., Ullman, J.D., Widom, J.: Database Systems - The Complete Book, 2nd edn. Pearson Education, London (2009)

11. Bayardo, R.J., Agrawal, R., Gunopulos, D.: Constraint-based rule mining in large, dense databases. Data Min. Knowl. Discov. 4(2/3), 217–240 (2000). https://doi.org/10.1023/A:1009895914772

12. Manousis, P., Vassiliadis, P., Papastefanatos, G.: Automating the adaptation of evolving data-intensive ecosystems. In: Ng, W., Storey, V.C., Trujillo, J.C. (eds.) ER 2013. LNCS, vol. 8217, pp. 182–196. Springer, Heidelberg (2013). https://doi.org/10.1007/978-3-642-41924-9_17

13. Manousis, P., Vassiliadis, P., Papastefanatos, G.: Impact analysis and policy-conforming rewriting of evolving data-intensive ecosystems. J. Data Semant. 4(4), 231–267 (2015). https://doi.org/10.1007/s13740-015-0050-3

14. Moon, H.J., Curino, C.A., Deutsch, A., Hou, C.Y., Zaniolo, C.: Managing and querying transaction-time databases under schema evolution. Proc. VLDB 1, 882–895 (2008)

15. Papastefanatos, G., Vassiliadis, P., Simitsis, A., Sellis, T., Vassiliou, Y.: Rule-based management of schema changes at ETL sources. In: Grundspenkis, J., Kirikova, M., Manolopoulos, Y., Novickis, L. (eds.) ADBIS 2009. LNCS, vol. 5968, pp. 55–62. Springer, Heidelberg (2010). https://doi.org/10.1007/978-3-642-12082-4_8

16. Papastefanatos, G., Vassiliadis, P., Simitsis, A., Vassiliou, Y.: Design metrics for data warehouse evolution. In: Li, Q., Spaccapietra, S., Yu, E., Olivé, A. (eds.) ER 2008. LNCS, vol. 5231, pp. 440–454. Springer, Heidelberg (2008). https://doi.org/10.1007/978-3-540-87877-3_32

17. Papastefanatos, G., Vassiliadis, P., Simitsis, A., Vassiliou, Y.: Policy-regulated management of ETL evolution. J. Data Semant. 13, 147–177 (2009). https://doi.org/10.1007/978-3-642-03098-7_6

18. Papastefanatos, G., Vassiliadis, P., Simitsis, A., Vassiliou, Y.: Metrics for the prediction of evolution impact in ETL ecosystems: a case study. J. Data Semant. 1(2), 75–97 (2012). https://doi.org/10.1007/s13740-012-0006-9

19. Poess, M., Rabl, T., Jacobsen, H., Caufield, B.: TPC-DI: the first industry benchmark for data integration. PVLDB **7**(13), 1367–1378 (2014)
20. Qiu, D., Li, B., Su, Z.: An empirical analysis of the co-evolution of schema and code in database applications. In: European Software Engineering Conference and ACM SIGSOFT Symposium on the Foundations of Software Engineering, pp. 125–135 (2013)
21. Rundensteiner, E.A., et al.: Evolvable view environment (EVE): non-equivalent view maintenance under schema changes. In: SIGMOD, pp. 553–555 (1999)
22. Vassiliadis, P., Zarras, A.V.: Schema evolution survival guide for tables: avoid rigid childhood and you're en route to a quiet life. J. Data Semant. **6**(4), 221–241 (2017). https://doi.org/10.1007/s13740-017-0083-x
23. Vassiliadis, P., Zarras, A.V., Skoulis, I.: Gravitating to rigidity: patterns of schema evolution - and its absence - in the lives of tables. Inf. Syst. **63**, 24–46 (2017)
24. Wojciechowski, A.: E-ETL framework: ETL process reparation algorithms using case-based reasoning. In: Morzy, T., Valduriez, P., Bellatreche, L. (eds.) ADBIS 2015. CCIS, vol. 539, pp. 321–333. Springer, Cham (2015). https://doi.org/10.1007/978-3-319-23201-0_34
25. Wojciechowski, A.: ETL workflow reparation by means of case-based reasoning. Inf. Syst. Front. **20**(1), 21–43 (2018). https://doi.org/10.1007/s10796-016-9732-0

Testing of Execution of Concurrent Processes

Janis Bicevskis and Girts Karnitis[✉]

University of Latvia, Riga, Latvia
{janis.bicevskis,girts.karnitis}@lu.lv

Abstract. Authors propose an algorithm for analysis of business processes to detect potentially incorrect results of concurrent processes execution. Our novel approach is to conclude necessary database isolation level from business process description. If traditional languages with loops and arithmetic operations (two-way counters) are used for business process descriptions, the problem of detecting incorrect execution of concurrent processes cannot be algorithmically solved. This paper introduces a simplified business processes description language CPL-1, a transaction mechanism and an algorithm that supports detection of incorrect results during the concurrent execution of business processes. Business processes are often run concurrently in real world tasks like billing systems, ticket distribution, hotel reservations, etc. Currently there are some popular solutions preventing incorrect execution of concurrent business processes by using built-in transaction mechanisms and/or resource reservations in database management systems (DBMS). The proposed solution is an alternative, which can be used when resource locking or DBMS transaction mechanisms cannot be applied.

Keywords: Concurrent transactions · Symbolic execution · Transaction execution state

1 Introduction

Many modern data processing systems support very complex business processes; many information systems are in use with one or more databases. Usually multiple processes are run concurrently, and without a proper control, concurrent processes may interleave and corrupt data used by other processes.

These problems are well-known in the DBMS world and they are addressed through the ACID (Atomicity, Consistency, Isolation, Durability) transactions. The transaction management algorithms used in different DBMS have proven their practical applicability; unfortunately, there are cases when they are not applied properly due to programmers' errors or for objective reasons. When developing software, programmers must specify the beginning and the end of each transaction, and it may be done incorrectly. If complex business processes involving multiple organizations, each with its own IS, are run, it is not possible to create one single transaction for such complex processes.

Our novel approach is to conclude necessary database isolation level from business process description. This paper describes testing of such complex, concurrent processes. As we know, full testing of Turing-complete language is not possible; so, authors have

© Springer Nature Switzerland AG 2020
T. Robal et al. (Eds.): DB&IS 2020, CCIS 1243, pp. 265–279, 2020.
https://doi.org/10.1007/978-3-030-57672-1_20

created the process definition language CPL-1 and an algorithm for testing of proceses written in CPL-1. The developed algorithm uses symbolic execution of processes and is suitable for finding cases of incorrect concurrent process execution.

The paper is structured as follows: Sect. 2 is devoted to refining concepts and identifying problems. Section 3 describes the transaction concurrency execution algorithm, which identifies the possible execution errors for CPL-1. Section 4 gives an overview of similar studies by other authors and compares them with the solution proposed in this paper. Section 5 contains conclusions and future study.

2 Problem Identification

2.1 Concurrent Process Execution

In the real world, many processes are run concurrently, i.e. multiple instances of processes are executed simultaneously using different input data and sharing resources (such as data in a database). A transaction is a set of actions, which are either executed by the end of the transaction, or are reversed, thereby returning the system to the its initial state it was before the transaction was started. If the multiple transactions do not share information, they can be executed correctly in a single computing system at the same time. The computing system itself (usually the operating system and information system) ensures that the execution of one transaction does not affect the execution of others, even though the transactions use the same resources of the computing system - processor, RAM, etc.

By the concurrent execution in a situation where the multiple processes use shared information resources, we will realize that one process can be terminated after the completion of some of its transactions, then another process (or its transaction) is executed, and then the first process is restored from the state it was interrupted. Such an organization of execution is useful if some process steps are executed autonomously and on a long-term basis; for example, writing or reading from a database or finding out additional information outside the process require time that could be used for execution of other processes. Formally, the concurrent execution will be defined in CPL-1 using the concept of breakpoints. The breakpoint is a command in the program that, when reached, can interrupt a process; after a specified time, the process will be restored to the state of the local variables it was before the break and will be continued to run. It should be noted that the value of the global information resource may be altered during the interruption by another process. If multiple concurrent processes access the same global data, some problems may arise because the global data used by one process may be modified by another process during the interruption of the first one.

In the DBMS world, these problems are well known and are addressed through ACID transactions. Usually transactions are based on locking algorithms - a transaction locks the data used in the transaction depending on the level of access required (Read/Write), another transaction is allowed or denied the access to this data respectively. Locked data is released at the end of a transaction by COMMIT or ROLLBACK and may be fully accessed by other transactions. If the simultaneous use of any data in two transactions can lead to erroneous results, the ACID mechanism ensures that a later transaction must wait while the locking transaction will finish its work.

The transaction management algorithms used by the DBMS have proven their practical applicability; unfortunately, there are situations when they are not provided due to programmers errors or for objective reasons. When developing software, programmers must specify the beginning and the end of each transaction, which may be incorrectly specified due to a programmers' error.

Worse is the case if some data processing process Pi consists of several transactions t1, t2 ... tn, where each transaction is independent and has its own BEGIN TRANSACTION... COMMIT TRANSACTION block. In this case the ACID transaction properties are executed in every transaction, but the process Pi contain multiple steps, each containing one or more transaction calls and not containing common BEGIN TRANSACTION... COMMIT TRANSACTION block. Therefore, the transaction management algorithms used by DBMS will not help because during the process Pi between calls of transactions ti and ti + 1, another process Pm may modify the database data used by process Pi or read and use intermediate results which may lead to incorrect results. This is possible due to the specificity of the process - the process is so long that it is unreasonable to keep the shared resource locked during all the process, so there are breakpoints in the process where the shared resource is unlocked.

Even worse is the complex data processing processes that occur between multiple systems that are not even able to create a common transaction. For example, at a municipal meeting it is decided that addresses of existing buildings will be changed to a new street name and new address. Along with the creation of the addresses, the people who live there are assigned to their new addresses. Information about new addresses is sent to the addresses register, while information about the people's registered addresses is sent to the population register. Attempt to change a person's record in the Population Register prior to registering his new address in the Address Register will be unsuccessful because any individual can be registered only in some address existing in the Address Register.

2.2   Correct and Incorrect Execution of Processes

In this article, we look at the concurrent processes Pi, Pj, Pk ... Pm and define the execution correctness according to the DBMS ACID transaction correctness. It is assumed that the database is in correct state before the processes are executed. Then after a single transaction will be executed, the database will be in the correct state. If several transactions are executed serially (one after another without parallelism), the result also will be correct; here and thereafter, we will understand the correct result in relation to the database. It means that if some process will be executed without concurrent execution of other processes, the result will be correct. Thus, if several processes will be executed serially, the result also will be correct.

In serial execution of multiple processes, the different sequence of process execution is possible, which can lead to different results; it is called as nondeterministic behavior [1, 2]. We will consider the result of any such serial process to be correct. So we have an exact criterion for any concurrent process and any input – the correct result can be only the result of one of the serial execution of processes. If the result of the concurrent execution of processes does not match any of the serial execution results at this input, the concurrent execution of these processes are considered incorrect. In addition, it must be correct for all possible input data.

2.3 Analysis of Concurrent Execution of Processes

The programmer must foresee and eliminate the possibility of incorrect execution of processes when he/she creates an information system. Often, to prevent the incorrect concurrent execution of processes, the concurrent execution of processes is not allowed at all. This reduces productivity of information processing. Sometimes shared resource reservation is used. Using a transaction mechanism, the DBMSs do not allow writing in or reading from a shared resource, if it has already been done by another process that has not yet validated transaction. Unfortunately, it is not always possible to use the ACID transaction mechanisms of the database, for example, if the locking shared resources for whole process time is not business-friendly, or the process uses multiple information systems that do not provide common transactions.

In this paper, we will offer another mechanism - the symbolic execution of processes. Doing so, we will create execution conditions - linear inequality systems to compare concurrent process execution results with serial process execution conditions; it will provide information on equivalence of results.

3 Algorithm for Concurrent Processes Execution Analysis

3.1 Process Description Language CPL-1

We will use a simplified hypothetical computational system consisting of:

- processes - programs in the process definition language CPL-1; the process consists of several successive transactions, the transactions are fully executed, they are not interrupted during the execution of the transactions and no other process is executed at that time; local variables can be used in the programs; you can assign a real number to the variable; the variables can form numeric and logical expressions; numeric expressions include only addition and subtraction operations, there are operators to assign values to variables in the programs;
- input data - parameters and global resources (global variables); parameter values are passed to the transaction by calling it, parameters can contain real numbers; a global resource is a variable, which is available for multiple transactions that can run concurrently and whose values can be read and written by multiple transactions;
- execution configurations that specifies which transactions with which parameters can be executed concurrently and what will be the value of the global resource at the start of execution;
- executor - a processor that is capable to execute commands specified in processes, whereby concurrent execution of transactions is possible; execution configuration is transmited to the executor to complete it.

The language of the above processes, hereafter referred to as CPL-1, contains the following commands:

```
START PROCESS – start process
END PROCESS – finish process
BEGIN TRANSACTION – start transaction
COMMIT TRANSACTION – commit/finish transaction
READ (x,r) – read the value of the global resource r and write it into variable x.
WRITE (x,r) – write the value of the variable x into global resource r.
```

Logical constructions:

```
IF L THEN
  BLOCK1
ELSE
  BLOCK2
ENDIF
```

If the logical expression L is true, then the BLOCK1 is executed and execution continues with the command after ENDIF; if not, the BLOCK2 is executed. BLOCK1 and BLOCK2 - one or more commands.

$y = \text{EXPR}(x1, x2, ..., xn)$ – expression calculation. y, x1, x2, ... xn - local variables. EXPR is a linear expression for which x1, x2, ... xn are parameters and y is the result.

The concurrent execution of one or more processes is a session. The global resource value r is defined at the beginning of the session. Processes are called by passing parameters to them. The process may contain multiple transaction calls. After each transaction call, an external interruption is possible, which should be followed by the next transaction call.

Execution result is final value(s) of the global resource(s).

Obviously, there are no loops in CPL-1. Thus, the program contains only finite length paths and the concurrent execution path of several processes is also finite. The problem lies in the fact that in order to prevent an incorrect execution of transactions, the results of serial and concurrent execution must coincide for all parameter values.

3.2 Correctness of Execution of Concurrent Processes in Language CPL-1

In this section, the main result for CPL-1 will be demonstrated through an example. Authors have created the algorithm which for any 2 processes written in CPL-1:

- finds out whether incorrect concurrent execution of these processes is possible,
- finds all possible scenarios for incorrect concurrent execution of both processes.

The algorithm will be demonstrated according to the following plan. First, process breakpoints where process breaks are possible will be defined. Next, using symbolic execution, we will show an algorithm for constructing a process concurrent execution tree, which will contain all possible process concurrent execution scenarios. Comparing the tree branches of the scenario tree, which corresponds to the serial execution, to the branches corresponding to the concurrent execution, reveals all possible concurrent execution inaccurate situations that give an incorrect result.

3.3   An Example of Incorrect Concurrent Process Execution

Let's look at a simple example of concurrent processes execution. This example will illustrate the idea of the proposed solution, which will be generalized in the following sections. Suppose that payments p1 and p2 are debited from the bank account r (resource r). It is executed by two processes Payment(p1) and Payment(p2), where the Payment program is as follows:

```
START PROCESS Payment(p, global(r))

  BEGIN TRANSACTIONT1
2    READ (x,r)
  COMMIT TRANSACTION T1

  BEGIN TRANSACTIONT2
3    IF p<=x THEN
4      WRITE (x-p,r)
5    ENDIF
  COMMIT   TRANSACTION T2

END PROCESS
```

In the following, we will use the abbreviation Payment(p)

Consider the execution of two processes with the parameter values $p1 = 2$ and $p2 = 5$ at the resource value $r = 17$, denoted by Payment(2) and Payment(5) (full syntax would be Payment(2, global(r))). The serial execution of processes starting with Payment(2), during which both transactions T1 and T2 of that Payment process will be executed serially, followed by Payment(5), during which transactions T1 and T2 of the second process also will be executed serially, yields $r = 10$. Also the second serial execution started by Payment(5) and followed by Payment(2) gives the same result.

A completely different situation arises when both processes are executed concurrently. In our example, let's define one breakpoint - after the first transaction T1 is executed (after the COMMIT TRANSACTION T1 command is executed). After the T1 execution, both the same process transaction T2 and the second process transaction T1 can be executed. Note that reading from the global r esource r is located in transaction T1, while writing into the global resource r is the essence of the transaction T2.

Two concurrent execution scenarios:

Payment(2) => T1; Payment(5) => T1; Payment(2) => T2; Payment(5) => T2
Payment(5) => T1; Payment(2) => T1; Payment(5) => T2; Payment(2) => T2

provide results 12 and 15. Such a result is impossible using the serial execution of the processes. The result of the execution is thus considered to be incorrect.

In addition, this simple example shows that concurrent execution will provide different results using various payment parameters and we cannot exclude the possibility of the correct result for some couple of parameters. It means that analyzing concurrent execution of processes one has to look at a set of all possible parameters and resource values. This is the condition that most seriously complicates the solution algorithm and removes the trivial impression on the finite set of options. The essence of the problem - is it possible to predict the incorrect result of the simultaneous execution of two processes using only the code of the payment process program?

3.4 Process Concurrency Analysis Algorithm

Let us demonstrate the algorithm using the example already described but with all possible parameter values and execution scenarious.

Construction of the Tree of Possible Scenarios. Our example scenario tree is given in Table 1. The tree consists of 16 branches. Each branch represents one scenario of the proceses execution that is written in one row of the table. For example, in the first row of the table, the path column depicts the execution scenario for the processes P1 and P2, which begins with the execution of transaction T1 for process P1, followed by execution of transaction T2 commands (3,5) for the same process P1. In the next step process P2 transaction T1 commands, followed by process P2 transaction T2 commands (3,5) are executed. It is easy to make sure that the execution of the processes P1 and P2 is possible in 16 different scenarios, both serial and concurrent ones.

Conditions of Scenario Execution. For each scenario, we create the path execution conditions by symbolical executing the corresponding set of commands. For example, for scenario #2: P1(T1 > T2 (3,4,5)) => P2(T1 > T2 (3,5)):

- after executing transaction T1 of process P1, the symbolic value of variable x is r;
- execution of process P1 transaction T2 commands (3,4,5) is possible if condition $v1 <= r$ is TRUE, where v1 is symbolic value of process P1 parameter p1;
- after execution transaction T2 commands (3,4,5) of process P1, the symbolic value of the global resource is $r - v1$;
- after executing transaction T1 of process P2, the symbolic value of the its variable x is $r - v1$;
- execution of process P2 transaction T2 commands (3,5) is possible at condition $v2 > r - v1$, where v2 is symbolic value of process P2 parameter p2;
- after the execution of process P2 transaction T2 commands (3,5), the symbolic value of the resource does not change – it is $r - v1$ (scenario execution result is $r - v1$).

That is, such a path is possible if the system of conditional inequalities ($v1 <= r$) & ($v2 > r - v1$) is satisfied. Since the system of conditions ($v1 <= r$) & ($v2 > r - v1$) has a solution, the scenario under consideration is executable because the parameter and resource values can be chosen so that the system of inequalities is true. The values of the resource r and the parameters $v1$ and $v2$, which are the system solution, for example $r = 17$, $v1 = 2$, $v2 = 16$, will allow respective scenario to be executed. In our example the conditions of execution are given in column *condition* of the Table 1. If the inequality system has no solution, the path is unexecutable and the branch is excluded from further analysis. There are no unexecutable scenarios in our example.

Conditions for Incorrect Concurrent Execution. Let's compare all execution scenarios of the concurrent processes P1 and P2 (scenarios #9 to #16 in this example) with the serial execution scenarios (scenarios #1 to #8 in this example). Note that the solutions for the execution conditions for the concurrent scenario #12 ($v1 <= r$)&($v2 <= r$) are partly the same as the execution conditions for the serial execution scenario #4 and #8, but the outcome of the scenarios are different. This means that we can choose the values of $v1$, $v2$ and r (e.g., $v1 = 2$, $v2 = 5$, $r = 17$) so that the result of the concurrent execution will not be equal to any serial execution result at this configuration. For these values, serial executions #4 and #8 produces value 10, while concurrent execution #12 produces value 12, which is incorrect.

This proves the possibility of incorrect concurrent execution of processes. Similar result show comparison of concurrent scenario #16 and serial scenarious #4 and #8.

The algorithm shown is capable of constructing an executable tree for any two programs written in the process language CPL-1. Chapter 3.4.1 illustrates determination whether an incorrect execution of processes can occur; if it does, chapter 3.4.2 shows development of the process execution scenario, inputs values of parameters and resources that will lead to incorrect execution of processes.

3.5   Concurrent Process Execution Analysis for Processes with Resource Reservation

The previous chapter showed an example where the incorrect execution of processes can occur. In this chapter, let's look at another example related to resource reservation, which is a very popular procedure which contains concurrent processes on a daily basis that would not lead to incorrect results.

In this process, the Payment (p) parameter p contains the amount due; r represents the amount in the bank account, q represents the reserved amount.

Table 1. Execution paths of concurrent execution of proceses P1 and P2

#	Path	Condition	Result r
1	P1(T1 > T2(3,5)) => P2(T1 > T2(3,5))	(v1 > r) & (v2 > r)	r
2	P1(T1 > T2(3,4,5)) => P2(T1 > T2(3,5))	(v1 <= r) & (v2 > r − v1)	r − v1
3	P1(T1 > T2(3,5)) => P2(T1 > T2(3,4,5))	(v1 > r) & (v2 <= r)	r − v2
4	P1(T1 > T2(3,4,5)) => P2(T1 > T2(3,4,5))	(v1 <= r) & (v2 <= r − v1)	r − v1 − v2
5	P2(T1 > T2(3,5)) => P1(T1 > T2(3,5))	(v1 > r) & (v2 > r)	r
6	P2(T1 > T2(3,4,5)) => P1(T1 > T2(3,5))	(v1 > r − v2) & (v2 <= r)	r − v2
7	P2(T1 > T2(3,5)) => P1(T1 > T2(3,4,5))	(v1 <= r) & (v2 > r)	r − v1
8	P2(T1 > T2(3,4,5)) => P1(T1 > T2(3,4,5))	(v1 <= r − v2) & (v2 <= r)	r − v1 − v2
9	P1(T1) > P2(T1) => P1(T2(3,5)) > P2(T2(3,5))	(v1 > r) & (v2 > r)	r
10	P1(T1) > P2(T1) => P1(T2(3,4,5)) > P2(T2(3,5))	(v1 <= r) & (v2 > r)	r − v1
11	P1(T1) > P2(T1) => P1(T2(3,5)) > P2(T2(3, 4,5))	(v1 > r) & (v2 <= r)	r − v2
12	**P1(T1) > P2(T1) => P1(T2(3,4,5)) > P2(T2(3, 4,5))**	**(v1 <= r) & (v2 <= r)**	**r − v2**
13	P2(T1) > P1(T1) =>P2(T2(3,5)) > P1(T2(3,5))	(v1 > r) & (v2 > r)	r
14	P2(T1) > P1(T1) =>P2(T2(3,4,5)) > P1(T2(3,5))	(v1 > r) & (v2 <= r)	r − v2
15	P2(T1) > P1(T1) =>P2(T2(3,5)) > P1(T2(3, 4,5))	(v1 <= r) & (v2 > r)	r − v1
16	**P2(T1) > P1(T1) =>P2(T2(3,4,5)) > P1(T2(3, 4,5))**	**(v1 <= r) & (v2 <= r)**	**r − v1**

```
START PROCESS PaymentWithReservation (p, global(r, q))
     reserved=FALSE
   BEGIN TRANSACTIONT1
1    READ(x,r)
     READ(y,q)
2    IF p<=x-y THEN
3       WRITE(y+p,q)
        reserved=TRUE
4    ENDIF
   COMMIT TRANSACTION T1

   BEGIN TRANSACTION T2
5    READ(x,r)
     READ(y,q)
6    IF reserved=TRUE THEN
7       WRITE(x-p,r)
        WRITE(y-p,q)
8    ENDIF
   COMMIT TRANSACTION T2
END PROCESS
```

Table 2 shows all possible process concurrency execution scenarios as in the previous example - scenarios #1 to #8 represent the serial execution scenarios and scenarios #9 to #16 represent the concurrent execution scenarios.

The column *condition* shows the scenarios execution conditions and the *result* column - the scenarios execution results. It can be seen from the table that serial and concurrent scenarios (e.g., scenarios #4 and #12) under the same scenario conditions give the same results in all cases. This proves that the incorrect cocnsurrent execution of scenarios is not possible for these two processes that are implemented by analyzed process. Resource reservation systems are often used by practitioners in payment systems because correctly implemented resource reservation prevents the incorrect concurrently execution of processes.

Table 2. Execution paths of concurrent execution of two processes with resource reservation

#	Path	Condition	Result r
1	P1(T1(1,2,4) > T2(5,6,8)) => P2(T1(1,2,4) > T2(5,6,8))	$(v1 > r - q)$ & $(v2 > r\,q)$	r
2	P1(T1(1,2,3,4) > T2(5,6,7,8)) => P2(T1(1,2,4) > T2(5,6,8))	$(v1 <=r - q)$ & $(v2 > r - q)$	$r - v1$
3	P1(T1(1,2,4) > T2(5,6,8)) => P2(T1(1,2,3,4) > T2(5,6,7,8))	$(v1 > r - q)$ & $(v2 <=r - q)$	$r - v2$

(continued)

Table 2. (*continued*)

#	Path	Condition	Result r
4	P1(T1(1,2,3,4) > T2(5,6,7,8)) => P2(T1(1,2,3,4) > T2(5,6,7,8))	$(v1 <= r - q)$ & $(v2 <= r - q - v1)$	$r - v1 - v2$
5	P2(T1(1,2,4) > T2(5,6,8)) => P1(T1(1,2,4) > T2(5,6,8))	$(v1 > r - q)$ & $(v2 > r - q)$	r
6	P2(T1(1,2,3,4) > T2(5,6,7,8)) => P1(T1(1,2,4) > T2(5,6,8))	$(v1 > r - v2)$ & $(v2 <= r)$	$r - v2$
7	P2(T1(1,2,4) > T2(5,6,8)) => P1(T1(1,2,3,4) > T2(5,6,7,8))	$(v1 <= r)$ & $(v2 > r)$	$r - v1$
8	P2(T1(1,2,3,4) > T2(5,6,7,8)) => P1(T1(1,2,3,4) > T2(5,6,7,8))	$(v1 <= r - q - v2)$ & $(v2 <= r - q)$	$r - v2 - v1$
9	P1(T1(1,2,4)) > P2(T1(1,2,4)) => P1(T2(5,6,8)) > P2(T2(5,6,8))	$(v1 > r - q)$ & $(v2 > r - q)$	r
10	P1(T1(1,2,3,4)) > P2(T1(1,2,4)) => P1(T2(5,6,7,8)) > P2(T2(5,6,8))	$(v1 <= r - q)$ & $(v2 > r - q)$	$r - v1$
11	P1(T1(1,2,4)) > P2(T1(1,2,3,4)) => P1(T2(5,6,8)) > P2(T2(5,6,7,8))	$(v1 > r - q)$ & $(v2 <= r - q)$	$r - v2$
12	P1(T1(1,2,3,4)) > P2(T1(1,2,3,4)) => P1(T2(5,6,7,8)) > P2(T2(5,6,7,8))	$(v1 <= r - q)$ & $(v2 <= r - q - v1)$	$r - v1 - v2$
13	P2(T1(1,2,4)) => P1(T1(1,2,4)) = > P2(T2(5,6,8)) => P1(T2(5,6,8))	$(v1 > r - q)$ & $(v2 > r - q)$	r
14	P2(T1(1,2,4)) => P1(T1(1,2,3,4)) => P2(T2(5,6,8)) => P1(T2(5,6,7,8))	$(v1 <= r - q)$ & $(v2 > r - q)$	$r - v1$
15	P2(T1(1,2,3,4)) => P1(T1(1,2,4)) => P2(T2(5,6,7,8)) => P1(T2(5,6,8))	$(v1 > r - q)$ & $(v2 <= r - q)$	$r - v2$
16	P2(T1(1,2,3,4)) => P1(T1(1,2,3,4)) = > P2(T2(5,6,7,8)) => P1(T2(5,6,7,8))	$(v2 <= r - q)$ & $(v1 <= r - q - v2)$	$r - v1 - v2$

3.6 Result

For each program written in Process Language CPL-1 with given break points, a final scenarious tree can be constructed. The assertion is obvious because the proposed transaction language does not offer the ability to create cycles. The feasibility of verifying the executability of scenarios is also obvious, since the systems of linear equatations of scenarious executability are used. The next steps of the algorithm also use the linear equatation systems. Similar constructions with symbolic execution have been used many times, for example in Intelly Test, CTS theory [3]. Thus, it is shown that the algorithm described above for any two processes in CPL-1 with the fixed breakpoints finds all concurrent transaction execution scenarios and parameter value conditions that will lead to the incorrect transaction execution.

3.7 Generalisations of CPL-1

It is easy to make sure that by performing concurrently more than two processes, the development of the proposed algorithm is executable. Thus, it is reasonable to say that the proposed algorithm is adaptable for arbitrary number of processes to analyse all concurrent execution scenarios and find parameter value conditions that lead to incorrect execution of transactions. Of course, the volume of the scenarious tree, depending on the number of processes and transactions and the complexity of the programs, can increase rapidly. This assures that the tools for supporting concurrent performance analysis are needed for practical application of the method.

The proposed process and transaction definition language CPL-1 is very simple because the program does not allow loops. The CTS (Complete Test systems) theory [4] has proved that by allowing programs with cycles as well as addition and subtraction operations to be used in programs, the complete execution tree problem is algorithmically insolvable. A similar result applies for the language CPL-1 with cycles - there is no algorithm that finds all scenarios and parameter conditions that lead to incorrect transaction execution. The proofis reduced to the possibility of simulating the operation of the Turing machine in by language of transactions. There is a known result - the stopping problem for Turing machines is not algorithmically solvable. The operation of the Turing machine can be simulated with a program that allows cycles and at least two bidirectional counters, called the Turing-complete programming languages. If we would able to build a definitive scenario tree for that language, then we would be able to solve the Turing machine stopping problem, which cannot be solved. Therefore, it is not possible to create such a definitive scenario tree.

4 Current Situation and Studies of Other Authors

The problem has been investigated to create an algorithm for determining whether a program follows all possible paths, or more precisely, whether a set of tests can be created to execute each command in the program at least once [3]. A set of commands that can and cannot be executed has been proven, and an algorithm and a prototype to do it have been created. If we have a set of information system transactions, we can create an algorithm that in number of cases can tell, whether these transactions will work correctly also in a concurrent mode. This cannot be done for any transaction, since the transactions can contain complex constructions that in principle prevent the creation of such algorithm. Nevertheless, in practice mostly simple transactions are used that do not contain complex and long code. Our experience shows that the most computer programs do not contain complex code; we assume that the most transactions are also simple enough to test the concurrent operation of multiple transactions automatically.

Although the idea of symbolic execution in software testing emerged years ago, only recently symbolic execution algorithms are applied in industry tools [5].

There are several surveys whose authors have done a comprehensive compilation and analysis of different concurrent process testing methods [5, 6]. A widely developed approach is to operate with different input data, or so-called mutation testing [7] in the hope that an incorrect test example would be found. Because the different execution sequences could provide different results, a number of methods recommend testing of concurrent processes many times using the same data – to find some sequence in which system is not working properly [8]. To improve the methodology, it is proposed to include random delays, hoping for more different execution order [9, 10], or to try to construct delays based on execution sequences [11].

There are tools to help build test cases that test certain aspects of the correctness of database transactions. Research is done either by generating different execution sequences based on the commands accessing shared resources (datatabase data) or executing logs.

The authors of the study [11] test distributed systems by creating the system model and implementing random delays between different operations, thereby simulating communication delays in distributed systems.

The authors of the article [9] study execution of concurrent transactions. Authors generate the "interesting" execution paths, execute transactions concurrently and analyse results. The interesting paths are generated using the transaction control flow graph (TCFG) based on the application source code, viewing only transactions that run on the same data. For each transaction all the data elements it reads and /or writes are written down. There is a list for each database cell and memory variable made that shows, which database cells and memory variables are used to calculate it (the transitive graph is calculated). The authors have created a SQL query testing tool AGENDA [12]. In this tool, firstly, the tester selects how the transactions will behave, and then the tool generates input data, executes the transactions and checks certain aspects of correctness. Unfortunately, the tool is only able to control a few simple aspects of correctness and requires the use of a domain-specific tester to participate in the testing process. A lot of attention is paid to ensuring the external integrity of the database. Tester mustcreate a pre-condition and a post-condition for each transaction. Based on the source code, the (TCFG) is created; the authors develop their approach in [12]. The research ideas are close to our ideas.

Several studies investigate how to generate all concurrently executing trees for specific test cases. It is up to testers to choose good test cases that will show if the execution sequences generated are likely to produce incorrect results. The first article investigates only linear processes; the second article is supplemented by cycles [13, 14]. Other studies take a similar approach - generates all (or at least large numbers) of possible execution trees by symbolic execution [15].

Our approach is the best defined in [16] – model-based testing, where test creation and execution can be automated, using an abstract system model as the input.

5   Conclusions

Authors have offered an algorithm for business process concurrent execution analysis, which can detect incorrect executions of these processes. In general, when traditional business-oriented modelling and programming languages are used, which include cycle and arithmetic operations (bidirectional counters), incorrect executions of business processes cannot be detected. Our study offers:

- An algorithm that detects the possibility of errorneos concurrent execution of business processes using the simplified business process description language CPL-1, which contains a transaction mechanism;
- the proposed algorithm is based on symbolic execution of the program, which enables to create conditions of process execution scenarios, to execute them and to produce symbolic values of expected execution results;
- if symbolic values for serial and concurrent execution of processes differ for the same argument values, then potentially incorrect concurrent execution cases are detected;
- the solution can be used when database transaction mechanisms cannot be used due to lomg process, or the process uses multiple systems and it is not possible to create a common transaction, or when locking a shared resource is not possible due to business process specifics;
- application of the algorithm for two concurrent business processes execution cases shows: (1) the concurrent execution of payment processes without reservation of a common resource could lead to incorrect execution of processes; (2) a payment process with correct reservation of a common resource cannot lead to incorrect concurrent execution of processes.

The research is continued by analyzing other concurrent execution cases that will allow developing the proposed algorithm for a wider range of tasks.

Acknowledgments. The research leading to these results has received funding from the research project "Competence Centre of Information and Communication Technologies" of EU Structural funds, contract No. 1.2.1.1/18/A/003 signed between IT Competence Centre and Central Finance and Contracting Agency, Research No. 1.6 "Concurrence analysis in business process models".

References

1. Mcdowell, C., Helmold, D.: Debugging concurrent programs. ACM Comput. Surv. **21**(4), 593–622 (1989)
2. Tai, K., Carver, R.: Testing of distributed programs (chap. 33). In: Zomaya, A. (ed.) Parallel and Distributed Computing Handbook. McGraw-Hill, New York (1996)
3. Auziņš, A., Bārzdiņš, J., Bičevskis, J., Čerāns, K., Kalniņš, A.: Automatic construction of test sets: theoretical approach. In: Bārzdiņš, J., Bjørner, D. (eds.) Baltic Computer Science. LNCS, vol. 502, pp. 286–359. Springer, Heidelberg (1991). https://doi.org/10.1007/BFb001 9362
4. Barzdin, J.M., Bičevskis, J.J., Kalninsh, A.A.: Construction of complete sample system for correctness testing. In: Bečvář, J. (ed.) MFCS 1975. LNCS, vol. 32, pp. 1–12. Springer, Heidelberg (1975). https://doi.org/10.1007/3-540-07389-2_178
5. Cadar, C., Koushnik, S.: Symbolic execution for software testing: three decades later. Commun. ACM **56**, 82–90 (2013)
6. Bianchi, F., Margara, A., Pezz, M.: A survey of recent trends in testing concurrent software systems. IEEE Trans. Softw. Eng. **44**(8), 747–783 (2018)
7. Jia, Y., Harman, M.: An analysis and survey of the development of mutation testing. IEEE Trans. Softw. Eng. **37**(5), 649–678 (2011)
8. Musuvathi, M., Qadeer, C., Ball, T.: CHESS: a systematic testing tool for concurrent software. In: Microsoft Research Technical Report MSR-TR-2007-149 (2007)

9. Deng, Y., Frankl, P., Chen, Z.: Testing database transaction concurrency. In: Automated Software Engineering. Proceedings of the 18th IEEE International Conference, pp. 184–193. IEEE (2003)

10. Fu, H., Wang, Z., Chen, X., Fan, X.: A systematic survey on automated concurrency bug detection, exposing, avoidance, and fixing techniques. Softw. Qual. J. **26**, 855–889 (2017). https://doi.org/10.1007/s11219-017-9385-3

11. Cai, S., Gallina, B., Nyström, D., Seceleanu, C.: Effective test suite design for detecting concurrency control faults in distributed transaction systems. In: Margaria, T., Steffen, B. (eds.) ISoLA 2018. LNCS, vol. 11246, pp. 355–374. Springer, Cham (2018). https://doi.org/10.1007/978-3-030-03424-5_24

12. Chays, D., Deng, Y., Frankl, P.G., Dan, S., Vokolos, F., Weyuker, E.: An AGENDA for testing relational database applications. J. Softw.: Test. Verif. Reliab. **14**, 17–44 (2004)

13. Hwang, G.H., Chang, S.J., Chu, H.D.: Technology for testing nondeterministic client/server database applications. IEEE Trans. Software Eng. **30**(1), 2004 (2004)

14. Lin, C.S., Hwang, G.H.: State-cover testing for nondeterministic terminating concurrent programs with an infinite number of synchronization sequences. Sci. Comput. Program. **78**, 1294–1323 (2013)

15. Li, C., Csallner, C.: Dynamic symbolic database application testing. In: DBTest 2010, 7 June 2010 (2010)

16. Marinescu, R., Seceleanu, C., Le Guen, H., Pettersson, P.: A research overview of tool supported model-based testing of requirements-based designs. In: Advances in Computers, vol. 98, pp 89–140 (2015)

The Use of the Recommended Learning Path in the Personalized Adaptive E-Learning System

Vija Vagale[1,2]($\boxtimes$) , Laila Niedrite[1] , and Svetlana Ignatjeva[2]

[1] Faculty of Computing, University of Latvia, Raina boulv.19, Riga, Latvia
vija.vagale@gmail.com, laila.niedrite@lu.lv
[2] Daugavpils University, Vienibas 13 Street, Daugavpils, Latvia
svetlana.ignatjeva@du.lv

Abstract. This paper promotes the idea of the learning process management in the e-learning system. A personalized adaptive e-learning system is used in this research that comprises three developed topic acquisition sequences: teacher, learner or optimal topic sequences. The learner has the ability to switch between the aforementioned topic sequences. The system stores data about the course acquisition process. The analysis of the stored data demonstrated that a bit more than half of the students used the teacher topic sequence; higher grades in topics got those students who chose the learner or optimal topic sequence; the grades of the half of the students who used the optimal and teacher topic sequences were in the same level. The obtained results were used as the justification for the improvement of the existing optimal topic sequence development method. As a result, an algorithm for the recommended learning path development is proposed in this paper. The topics of the course and links in between are described using a weighted directed graph. The weight of every edge and vertex of the graph is calculated based on the parameter values describing the topic. Afterwards, the recommended learning path is assumed to be the path with the lowest weight that is found in the weighted oriented graph using a search.

Keywords: Personalized adaptive system · E-Learning · Recommended learning path

1 Introduction

Nowadays a variety of different information technologies, including personalised adaptive e-learning systems [1, 3, 12], are widely used in the education. The main role of the learning process has been granted to the learner aiding the learner-/student-centered e-learning [5]. The personalized adaptive e-learning system provides learners with the opportunity to take control over the own learning process and offers the individually adjusted content based on the characteristics describing the learner, and his needs [1]. The emphasis of the learner-centered approach is transferred from teaching to learning. In this approach, the teacher is the "mediator" between the learner and the acquired knowledge. The main task of the learner-centered approach is to help the learner to acquire

T. Robal et al. (Eds.): DB&IS 2020, CCIS 1243, pp. 280–294, 2020.
https://doi.org/10.1007/978-3-030-57672-1_21

the learning skill [5]. Some of the features of the learner-centered learning approach are [2, 6]: (a) reliance on the active work of the learner; (b) the emphasis on deep learning and understanding; (c) higher responsibility and accountability of the learner; (d) increased sense of autonomy in the learner; (e) participation of the learner in the planning of the own learning process. The aforementioned features indicate that the learner-centered learning approach can be successfully realized in the personalized adaptive system. The use of such a learning approach raises up the question about the management of the learning process of the learner and the use of the recommended learning path within the personalised adaptive e-learning system.

In the experiment, a learner model based personalized adaptive e-learning system (LMPAELS) [12] developed by the authors was used. In the LMPAELS, three course topic sequences (TS) have been realized: the learner topic sequence (LTS), the teacher topic sequence (TTS) and optimal topic sequence (OTS) [10]. By default, the system has a TTS, but the learner is able to change the selected TS several times. The experiment consisted of two stages. In the first stage of the experiment, data was gathered and analysed, explaining how the learners used the three TS for the course acquisition that are realised in the system and the grades of every topic depending on the chosen TS. The results of this experiment stage demonstrated that, regards the use of TS, firstly, (a) learners are passive in the choice of topics and in more cases are using the default TS (i.e. TTS). 64,1% of all students used TTS, 20,3% of students used OTS and 15,6% - LTS. The analysis of the data obtained in the first stage of the experiment regards the used TS and grades in topics, the results showed that, (b) in 80% of the cases, higher topic grades were of those students who used LTS and 20% - OTS; (c) the grades of the half of the students who used OTS were in the same level as of those using TTS. The conclusions of the first stage of the experiment promoted the idea of improving the optimal topic sequence method (OTSM) used in LMPAELS. In the second stage of the experiment, the topic acquisition influential parameters were obtained and analysed with a goal to improve the existing OTSM and propose a recommended learning path (RLP) development algorithm. The chosen parameters characterising topics were grade, complexity and importance. The topic grade describes the level of the topic acquisition and it is acquired by testing the learner. The topic complexity characterises the level of the topic acquisition difficulty. The topic importance describes the location of the topic in the course.

In the literature review various personalized and/or adaptive systems that are employing a learning path are analysed. To our knowledge, no previous research has investigated methods of searching the learning path that are based on the graph theory and are using the following topic characterizing parameters: topic grade, complexity and importance. We found a graph to be a promising tool for the search of the RLP on the grounds that a graph is a mathematical structure consisting of elements with reciprocal relationships or link [3]. In the graph we are proposing, vertices represent learning objects/topics whereas edges between them are the existing paths between topics. The weights are calculated both for the vertices and edges of the graph. First of all, the weights of the graph vertices are calculated based on the values of three object/topic characterizing parameters: topic grade, complexity (from the learner's and teacher's perspective), and importance (from the learner's and teacher's perspective) ratings. Secondly, the weights of the edges are calculated based on the weights of the adjacent vertices. Finally, the RLP is modelled based on the weights of the graph vertices and edges. The RLP in this paper represents the sequence of all the learning elements (topics) that gains the best course acquisition results.

The key contribution of this work is the developed algorithm for the recommended learning path development that was used for the "Programming Foundations I" course, described in this paper. A significant benefit of the method is the provisional "independence from the teacher" for the learner, at the same time, offering the path for achieving good results and not letting the learner in the self-flow.

The paper is organised as follows: Sect. 2 reviews related works. Section 3 describes the development of the optimal topic sequence method and the personalized adaptive system used in the experiment. In Sect. 4, the algorithm for the RLP development is explained. Section 5 discusses the evaluation of the experiment results. Finally, concluding remarks and future work are drawn in Sect. 6.

2 Related Work

Numerous computing techniques such as neural networks, fuzzy systems and genetic algorithms are used to create learning paths [7]. A learning path (LP) is used not only in traditional learning systems with a limited number of learners and learning objects (LOs), but also in systems with a large number of learners, courses and LOs [3, 4].

Heberle et al. [4] is using LP to address the problems of high dropout rate in the Massive Open Online Course (MOOC) system. Considering the learner's didactic factors (e.g. age, difficulty level), an individualized ontology is created, with the help of which the most suitable LOs and LPs are identified. Based on the obtained ontology, a semantic query is generated, in which the corresponding small open educational resources are selected.

Aeiad and Meziane [1] describe a personalized adaptive system consisting of three models: the learner model, the knowledge extraction model, and the content delivery model. The modelling of the content of a specific learning subject is done using ontology. Learners are provided with freely accessible online learning resources. The content is adapted using a learning style of learner (visual, auditory, reading/writing, kinaesthetic) and prior knowledge (beginner, intermediate, advanced). Two vectors are used to create the learning content: the learning concept vector and the vector of the XHTML network elements. Then a program is developed for the learner to learn a specific module. The program consists of topics, web links, hours needed to learn each topic, exercises and evaluation. Content adaptation is based on learner feedback - learner responses (5 questions) on satisfaction with the proposed learning process (content offered, learning experience, etc.) and the quality of the content delivered.

Patel et al. [8] analyses the LPs commonly used by students. The analysis uses sequence clustering and graph-based process mining on educational data. All student activities are recorded in the event log. The events are selected that tell about the student's interaction with the digital assets and the platform. From the obtained events, Student ID, Activity ID, and Timestamp are selected. Next, a matrix $n \times n$ is created, where n is the number of activities the student performed. The matrix records how many times students performed actions *i* and *j*. The resulting matrix was used to construct a directed graph. Using cluster analysis, the most commonly used LPs were identified in the graph.

Durand et al. [3] describes a learning design recommendation system that uses a directed graph for a personalized LP search. The vertices of the graph describe the LOs and the edges indicate the links between these objects. For each vertex, a pair of competencies is defined - the competencies needed to master the specific LO (prerequisite competencies) and the competencies acquired after the acquisition of the particular LO. The learning system operates with a large amount of the LOs stored in the distributed database Cassandra. The learning path search is based on the competences that the learner is expected to acquire.

The LP described in [3] is based on prerequisite and acquired competencies. In our algorithm for development of a recommended learning path (RLP), competencies are implicitly identified through links between topics. Our proposed algorithm for developing RLP operates on any number of LO descriptive parameters.

3   Background

3.1   Personalized Adaptive E-Learning System

A learner model-based personalised adaptive e-learning system LMPAELS, that is based on the open source content management system Moodle, has been used in the research. Three models are used in the system: a learner model, a content model and an adaptation model. The learner model describes an adult learner and is used for lifelong learning. This model includes following data categories: personal data, personality data, pedagogical data, preference data, device data, system experience, current moment's knowledge, and history data about learning process. A complete description of the learner model is given in the article [9].

The content model represents the learning course structure and the variety of the resources used in the course. A learning course consists of topics, where each topic consists of LOs (e.g. a specific concept from the topic to be learned). Each LO has four parts: topic summary, theory, practice, and evaluation. The evaluation part includes the developed tests based on varying course difficulty level (chosen by the learner). The learning content of varying resource formats depends on the learning style chosen by the learner. A complete description of the content model can be found in [9].

The LMPAELS system is used for adaptation of (i) the course structure, (ii) the course content, and (iii) the course TS. The course structure in the system adapts depending on the course type (theoretical or practical). The theoretical courses do not anticipate exercises; therefore, the structure of the LO excludes the practical part. The content adaptation occurs based on the learner's pre-knowledge (yes, no) in the specific course, as well as learning style (visual, aural, read, kinaesthetic, the combination of visual and aural) and the chosen course difficulty level (low, middle, high) [12].

Three kinds of TSs have been realised in the system: teacher, learner and optimal [10]. TS is a selection of topics arranged based on specified feature. TTS is based on the teacher's experience. The topics in it are arranged corresponding to their order numbers. LTS is created by the learner and his choice of studied topics. After the acquisition of the specific topic, the system offers the next topics based on the teacher's indicated links between topics. If the topic T_j can be studied after the topic T_i, then there exists a directed link from topic T_i to topic T_j. OTS is developed using the optimal topic sequence method (see Sect. 3.2). The management of course TS in the system is described in the previous article [11]. A complete description of the architecture of personalised adaptive system is given in paper [12].

3.2 Optimal Topic Sequence Method

The optimal topic sequence method (OTSM) is based on learners' achievements (grades) in the course, topic sequences used by the learner for course acquisition and links between the topics of the course. The principle of the method is following: in the acquisition of a specific course, all the TSs used by learners are divided into groups where each group includes equal TS. Then, the mean course acquisition grade is calculated for each TS group. The TS with the highest mean grade is assumed to be the optimal topic sequence of the specific course. In case of multiple TS groups with equal mean grades, the OTS is searched within these TS based on the highest topic repetition frequency in the specific TS position and links between topics. When developing OTS, the existence of links between the last chosen OTS topic and the selected following topic is checked. Next check searches that the selected topic is not included in the OTS before. The complete OTS development algorithm is give in the article [10].

In the both experiment stages the learners studied "Programming Foundations I" course. The course consists of the following ten topics: (1) "C++ program structure. Data output", (2) "Data types. Data input", (3) "Mathematical functions", (4) "Conditional constructions", (5) "User-defined functions", (6) "Parametric functions", (7) "Cyclic constructions", (8) "One-dimensional numeric arrays", (9) "Multi-dimensional numeric arrays", and (10) "Symbolic arrays". The numbers in the brackets represent the topic sequence number and matches the topic sequence offered by the teacher. There are links defined between the topics that indicate which topics can be studied after finishing the selected topic. Figure 1 represents links between the topics, where the vertices of the graph, represented by numbers, are the topics and edges between them indicate the link using directed arrows. For example, topic "4" can be followed by topics "5" or "7".

In the both experiment stages, OTS = {1,3,5,7,8,9,10,2,4,6} was used and it acquisition is described more in the paper [10]. In the case of a large number of learners, the OTSM is working correctly. However, when the number of learners is small, this method does not help creating a better TS. That was proven by the results of the experiment (see Subsect. 5.2). The described OTSM is using topic grades and links between topics. The improved method proposed in this paper suggests including additional parameters characterising each topic, like, the complexity and importance. The use of several characterising parameters allows to evaluate the location of each topic within the course in a more objective way.

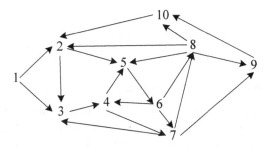

Fig. 1. The interconnected course topics graph [10].

4   Improving the Optimal Topic Sequence Method

4.1   Definitions and Assumptions

A directed graph is used for the deeper examination of the course topics and links between them. A directed graph $G = (V, E)$ consists of a non-empty finite set V of elements called vertices and a finite set E of distinct ordered pairs of vertices called directed edges. We assume that course topics are vertices of the graph and the links between topics are the edges of the graph. Topics are described by a finite set $V = \{V_1, V_2, ..., V_k, ..., V_n\}$, where n is the number of topics in the course and the graph vertex index represents the order number of the topic in the course. For example, the vertex V_1 represents the first topic. Vertices V_i and V_j are connected using a directed edge where V_j is the head and V_i is the tail. This directed edge means that after finishing to study topic V_i, it is allowed to study topic V_j. The links between topic are defined by the developer of the course based on the acquired knowledge and competencies. Links between topics of the "Programming Foundations I" course that was used in the experiment are represented in Fig. 1.

For getting a better description of the order of the topic in the course, each topic gets assigned parameters describing the topic, i.e. each vertex of the graph is described using a finite set of parameters. In the general case, $V_k = \{p_1, p_2, ..., p_m\}$, where V_k is the graph vertex, $p_1, p_2, ..., p_m$ are the parameters and m is the number of parameters. Every vertex is described using the same parameters. The weight of the vertex V_k is WV_k and it is the total sum of the vertex parameter values pv. See Formula 1, where pv_i ($1 \leq i \leq m$) is the value of parameter and m is the number of parameters.

$$WV_k = pv_1 + pv_2 + ... + pv_m \tag{1}$$

The edge weight WE_{ij} between two vertices V_i and V_j is the absolute difference of the weights of the both vertices (see Formula 2).

$$WE_{ij} = |WV_j - WV_i| \tag{2}$$

Smaller absolute difference between weights of two vertices indicates the smaller edge weight between the vertices. The edge weight describes how similar the two vertices are according to their parameter values. The development of the course recommended learning path is based on the search of the edge with the lowest weight. The direction of the edges between vertices are defined using adjacency vertices matrix. Adjacency vertices matrix *A is* created as follows: if there is an edge from node *i* to node *j*, then value "1" is entered in the corresponding row *i*, column *j* of the matrix *A*.

4.2 Algorithm of Recommended Learning Path

Finding a recommended learning path (RLP) is described using an algorithm. The following conditions were considered in the development of the RLP algorithm: (a) the course should always start with the first topic and (b) the course should include all the topics included in the course description (document describing the course requirements). The algorithm is based on 13 steps shown in the activity diagram in Fig. 2. Initially (step 1–3), three arrays are initialised: adjacency vertices matrix *A* (see Subsect. 4.1), vertices weight array *WV* (see Formula 1), and edges weight matrix *WE* (see Formula 2). Next, the *RLP* development begins. The first vertex is recorded at the beginning of the *RLP* (step 4).

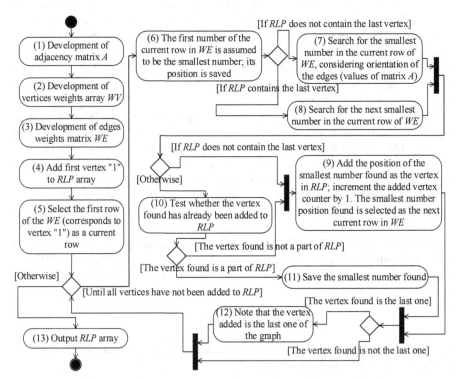

Fig. 2. An activity diagram of the recommended learning path creation.

In the weights matrix WE, the first (current) row that corresponds to the vertex recorded in the RLP is selected (step 5). The lowest number in the current row is searched next. The current row assumes the first number as the smallest (step 6). If the *RLP* has not yet recorded a vertex with the last sequence number, then the current row is searched for the smallest number given the existence of the edge between vertices (i.e. the values of matrix A) (step 7). If the *RLP* already has a vertex with the last sequence number, then the next smallest number is searched in the current row without considering the values of matrix A (step 8). This is possible because in *RLP* there is always a written topic with the number "1", which means that there will always be a path from the first vertex to a vertex that is smaller than the last vertex. If the vertex with the last sequence number has not yet been recorded in the *RLP*, the position of the lowest number found (the vertex found) is recorded in the *RLP* (step 9), otherwise it is checked whether the vertex found is already in the *RLP* (step 10). If the found vertex is already written in the *RLP*, the smallest number found is saved (step 11) so that in step 8 the next smallest number can be searched for. If a vertex with the last sequence number was added, this event is saved (step 12). The algorithm stops working when all vertices of the graph have been added to the *RLP*. In step 13, the developed *RLP* is returned as a result.

4.3   Example of the Recommended Learning Path Search

Using the algorithm described in Subsect. 4.2, the RLP for the "Programming Foundations I" course used in the experiment was searched. The structure of the course is described in Subsect. 3.2. The links between the topics are shown in Fig. 1. Each topic is described with the following five parameters:

- p1 – the grade in the topic;
- p2 – the rating of the topic complexity according to the learner;
- p3 – the rating of the topic complexity according to the teacher;
- p4 – the rating of the topic importance according to the learner;
- p5 – the rating of the topic importance according to the teacher.

The acquisition of these parameter values is described in Sect. 5. The arithmetic mean values of the parameters obtained in the experiment are summarised in Table 2. The sum of the parameter values describing topics (using Formula 1) were assumed to be the weights of the graph (see Fig. 1) vertices used in the RLP search. Differences between the weights of each vertex were calculated (using Formula 2), i.e. edge weights with values summarized in Table 1, where $V_1, V_2, ..., V_{10}$ are graph vertices.

Figure 3 shows a directed weighted graph where the numbers on edges represent the edge weight, or the absolute difference between vertex weights. The vertices of the graph are represented as numbers that correspond to the course topic sequence numbers. While the vertex with the last sequence number has not been added to the RLP yet, the least weighted edges are searched starting from the first vertex, and the vertex number of the head of the directed edge is added to the RLP. The path from the first topic to the last (tenth) with the smallest edge weight is shown in Fig. 3 with bold lines. This means that RLP = {1,2,3,4,7,8,10}. Some vertices were not considered along this path. Since the RLP contains the vertex with the last number, i.e. "10", then the next searched vertex is the vertex that has the smallest weight difference with the vertex "10" (see Table 1). Such a vertex is vertex "4". However, this vertex is already added to the RLP.

Table 1. Weights of the course topic graph edges.

Weight of edges	V_1	V_2	V_3	V_4	V_5	V_6	V_7	V_8	V_9	V_{10}
V_1	0	4.39	8.23	15.48	12.03	16.56	16.8	15.89	13.26	14.51
V_2	4.39	0	3.84	11.09	7.64	12.17	12.41	11.5	8.87	10.12
V_3	8.23	3.84	0	7.25	3.8	8.33	8.57	7.66	5.03	6.28
V_4	15.48	11.09	7.25	0	3.45	1.08	1.32	0.41	2.22	0.97
V_5	12.03	7.64	3.8	3.45	0	4.53	4.77	3.86	1.23	2.48
V_6	16.56	12.17	8.33	1.08	4.53	0	0.24	0.67	3.3	2.05
V_7	16.8	12.41	8.57	1.32	4.77	0.24	0	0.91	3.54	2.29
V_8	15.89	11.5	7.66	0.41	3.86	0.67	0.91	0	2.63	1.38
V_9	13.26	8.87	5.03	2.22	1.23	3.3	3.54	2.63	0	1.25
V_{10}	14.51	10.12	6.28	0.97	2.48	2.05	2.29	1.38	1.25	0

Then the vertex with the next smallest weight difference is taken. It is the vertex "9". The vertex found is added to the RLP, now RLP = {1,2,3,4,7,8,10,9}. Next, we search for the vertex with the smallest weight difference with vertex "9". Such a vertex is the vertex "5". Since this vertex is not yet added to the RLP, it is added now, so RLP = {1,2,3,4,7,8,10,9,5}. Next, we search for the vertex with the smallest weight difference with the vertex "5". Such a vertex is the vertex "7". However, it is already included in RLP. It is similar to the vertices "4", "3" and "8". Then the next vertex taken is "6". It has not been added to the RLP yet, so it is added now. As the result, RLP = {1,2,3,4,7,8,10,9,5,6} and it includes all 10 vertices of the graph.

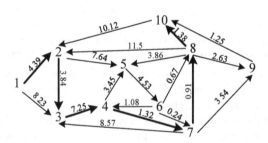

Fig. 3. The graph of the course topic acquisition with weights on edges.

5 Experiment and the Results

An experiment was organised in Daugavpils University (Latvia). The experiment involved first-year students of the professional bachelor study program "Information Technologies". During the study process, students were given the opportunity to study a practical course "Programming Foundations I" in the learner based personalised adaptive e-learning system LMPAELS. The course includes ten mandatory topics (see Sect. 3.2) in accordance with the study program accredited by the university. Each topic of the course consists of one learning object.

The experiment was organised in two stages. In the first stage of the experiment, data on the use of topic sequences (teacher, learner and optimal TS), implemented in the LMPAELS, and the grades of learners in each TS were obtained. In the second stage of the experiment, data describing the course topics (parameters' values), such as topic grade, topic complexity, and topic importance, were obtained.

The first phase of the experiment took place in 2015/2016 and 2016/2017 with 47 students participating. The second phase of the experiment took place in 2019/2020 with 25 students participating. As some students did not complete the course due to personal reasons, only the data of 17 student learning process remained valid. As a result, the study used (a) learning process data of 64 students, such as the topic sequences used in the learning process, the choice of topic sequences, the position of each topic in the learning path, and grades obtained in each topic and (b) the complexity and importance rating for topics by 17 students.

The topic grades are on a scale of 1 to 10. Learners were tested after finishing each topic. A topic is considered passed if the grade in the test is higher than 4 (including). In the second phase of the experiment, after each topic, the learners rated the complexity and importance of the topic on a scale from 1 (lowest) to 10 (highest). The teacher also evaluated the complexity and importance of each topic in order to gain an objective opinion. Table 2 summarizes the arithmetic mean grades of learners, as well as, the arithmetic means of the complexity and importance of each topic from the perspective of the learners, and the teacher. "T" stands for topics, where the index indicates the topic number.

Table 2. Parameters describing the course topic and their arithmetic mean values.

Parameters of topic	T_1	T_2	T_3	T_4	T_5	T_6	T_7	T_8	T_9	T_{10}
Grade	8.11	6.59	6.89	7.05	7.04	6.44	7.23	6.91	7.14	5.98
Complexity (learner)	2.77	4.59	4.77	5.18	5.05	6.09	5.59	5.91	5.05	6.18
Complexity (teacher)	1.00	2.00	4.00	6.00	5.00	7.00	8.00	9.00	10.00	7.00
Importance (learner)	8.82	7.91	8.27	8.95	8.64	8.73	8.68	8.77	8.77	9.05
Importance (teacher)	1.00	5.00	6.00	10.00	8.00	10.00	9.00	7.00	4.00	8.00
Total	21.7	26.09	29.93	37.18	33.73	38.26	38.5	37.59	34.96	36.21

5.1 Analysis of the Topic Sequence

During the course acquisition, learners were given the opportunity to use three topic sequences (TS): teacher (TTS), learner (LTS), and optimal topic sequence (OTS), with the ability to change them after each topic. The results showed that 41 students, or 64.1%, used the TS offered by the teacher. Only 23 students, or 35.9% of students, took the opportunity to choose a different TS. Of these, 13 learners (20.3%) used the OTS and 10 students, (15.6%) created their own learning path (LTS). The results show that most of the learners are passive in managing their own learning process or rely on the experience of the teacher in the sequence of topic acquisition and use the system's default TS, i.e. TTS.

5.2 Relationship Between Topic Grades and Topic Sequence Choice

Mean grades of each topic were calculated depending on the topic sequence used (see Fig. 4). The use of the learner topic sequence in the course is justified, as the learners who used LTS have high grades in the topics (8 highest and 2 middle). Learners using OTS also earned high grades in topics (2 highest, 3 middle and 5 lowest). Learners using TTS users have 5 middle and 5 lowest grades in topics. The analysis of results show that topic grades are better for LTS students rather than OTS students, as expected. That has led to a decision to improve the OTS development algorithm by including other parameters characterising the topic (like complexity and importance) additionally to the learner grades to develop a new recommended learning path.

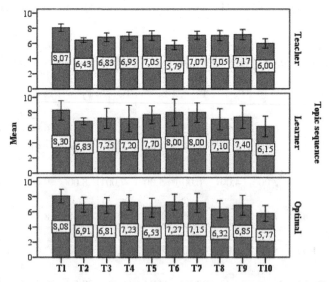

Fig. 4. Arithmetic mean grades of each topic of the course "Programming Foundations I" depending on the selected course topic sequence.

5.3 Relationship Between Topic Grades, Importance and Complexity

Arithmetic mean rating for the complexity and importance were calculated for each topic. The learner arithmetic mean grades in topics were analysed depending on the complexity of each topic (see Fig. 5). Learners consider the topics number "4", "6", "7", "8" and "10" to be the most complex topics (with ratings above mean). In Fig. 5 the mean value in the figure is represented using a dashed line. The results are very close to the teacher's rating of complexity (see Table 2). The differences between the learners' and the teacher's complexity ratings for each topic are as follows (the position of each number corresponds to the topic number): 1.77, 2.59, 0.77, 0.82, 0.05, 0.91, 2.41, 3.09, 4.95, 0.82. The largest difference in rating is for a topic number "9" (the difference is 4.95). The complexity ratings for 5 topics similar (with a difference less than 1).

The first topic is considered simple by the learners and the mean grade of this topic is the highest compared to the other topics (see Fig. 5). The teacher also rated this topic the least complex. The lowest grade is for topic number "10", which students also find the most difficult. Grades higher than mean are for topics number "4", "5", "7" un "9". To conclude, learners assess the topic complexity in a similar way as a teacher.

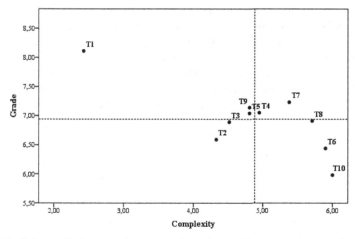

Fig. 5. Relationship between the complexity rating and learner grades in each topic.

Analysing the importance and arithmetic mean grade of each topic (see Fig. 6), it is concluded that students consider topics "2" and "3" less important than others. Other topics are considered more important by learners.

The differences between the learners' and the teacher's importance rating for each topic (see Table 2) are as follows (the position of each number corresponds to the topic number): 7.82, 2.91, 2.27, 1.05, 0.64, 1.27, 0.32, 1.77, 4.77, 1.05. The calculated differences show that the importance rating of the learners and the teacher are similar only for two topics. Small differences (less than 1) have topics number "5" and "7". The largest difference is for the topic "1" (the difference is 7.82). The topic importance rating of student and teacher differ much more than their complexity ratings. This can

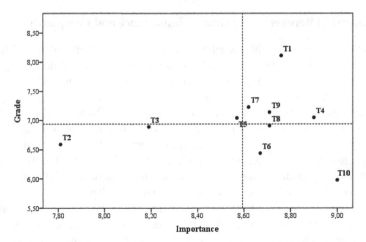

Fig. 6. Relationship between the importance rating and learner grades in each topic.

be explained by the lack of experience of the learner in the programming field. Out of the most important topics, the highest grades received topics "1", "4", "7", "8", and "9".

The analysis of the relationship between the arithmetic mean rating of complexity and importance of the topics showed how the learners perceive each topic of the course (see Fig. 7). Students find topic "1" non-complex and important. Topics number "2" and "3" are non-complex and non-important. Topics number "5" and "9" have mean complexity ratings (the mean value is represented by a dashed line in the figure). Topic number "9" is considered important. The other topics are both important and complex.

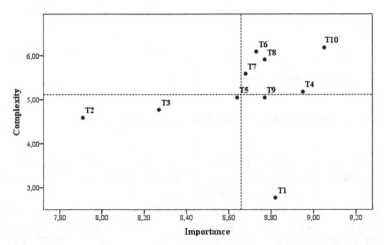

Fig. 7. Relationship between the importance and complexity rating for each topic

6   Conclusions

The data obtained during the first phase of the experiment showed that, in general, learners are passive in organising their own learning process. Only 23 students, or 35.9% of the learners, took advantage of the system's option to use a topic sequence that is different from the teacher topic sequence. A small part of students, only 10 students (15.6%), developed their own course topic sequence based on the links between the topics. These learners received the highest grades in eight topics. The obtained results could be explained both by the chosen topic sequence and the attitude of students towards the learning process. This assumption might be addressed in future studies.

The course used in the experiment was "Programming Foundations I" with OTS = {1,3,5,7,8,9,10,2,4,6}. This topic sequence was used by 13 students (20.3%). Grades of students using OTS, in the topics, were lower than grades of students using LTS and higher than grades of students using TTS.

In this study, an algorithm for the development of a recommended learning path was developed that considers the characteristics of the topic. Additionally, the number of these parameters can be arbitrary. Using the developed algorithm for the "Programming Foundations I" course, the recommended learning path was created, RLP = {1,2,3,4,7,8,10,9,5,6}. Parameters such as topic grades, complexity, and importance ratings were considered when designing the path. Future research will focus on testing the resulting recommended learning path.

References

1. Aeiad, E., Meziane, F.: An adaptable and personalised E-learning system applied to computer science programmes design. Educ. Inf. Technol. **24**(2), 1485–1509 (2018). https://doi.org/10.1007/s10639-018-9836-x
2. Attard, A., Di Iorio, E., Geven, K., Santa, R.: Student-centred learning: toolkit for students, staff and higher education institutions. European Students' Union (NJ1). Laserline, Berlin (2010)
3. Durand, G., Belacel, N., LaPlante, F.: Graph theory based model for learning path recommendation. Inf. Sci. **251**, 10–21 (2013)
4. Heberle, F., Henning, P.A., Streicher, A., Swertz, C., Bock, J., Zander, S.: Advancement of MOOCs with learning pathways. Int. J. Excell. Educ. **184**(1792), 1–9 (2014)
5. Jurane-Bremane, A.: Formative assessment in the study process. The doctoral thesis. Riga, University of Latvia (2018)
6. Lea, S.J., Stephenson, D., Troy, J.: Higher Education Students' Attitudes to Student-centred learning: beyond 'educational bulimia'? Stud. Higher Educ. **28**(3), 321–334 (2003)
7. Niknam, M.: LPR: an adaptive learning path recommendation system using ACO and meaningful learning theory. The doctoral thesis. The University of Manitoba, Canada (2017)
8. Patel, N., Sellman C., Lomas, D.: Mining frequent learning pathways from a large educational dataset. arXiv preprint arXiv:1705.11125 (2017)
9. Vagale, V., Niedrite, L.: Learner classification for providing adaptability of E-Learning systems. In: Haav, H.-M., Kalja, A., Robal, T. (eds.) Baltic DB&IS 2014, pp. 181–192. TUT Press, Tallin (2014)
10. Vagale, V., Niedrite, L.: The application of optimal topic sequence in adaptive e-learning systems. In: Arnicans, G., Arnicane, V., Borzovs, J., Niedrite, L. (eds.) DB&IS 2016. CCIS, vol. 615, pp. 352–365. Springer, Cham (2016). https://doi.org/10.1007/978-3-319-40180-5_24

11. Vagale, V., Niedrite, L.: The organization of topics sequence in adaptive e-Learning systems. Front. Artif. Intell. Appl. Databases Inf. Syst. X, **291**, 327–340 (2016). IOS Press
12. Vagale, V., Niedrite, L., Ignatjeva, S.: The architecture of the personalized adaptive E-learning system. In: Lupeikiene, A., Matulevičius, R., Vasilecas., O. (eds) Baltic DB&IS 2018, CEUR Workshop Proceedings, vol. 2158, p. 114–123 (2018)

Security of Information Systems

Composition of Ensembles of Recurrent Neural Networks for Phishing Websites Detection

Paulius Vaitkevicius[(✉)] and Virginijus Marcinkevicius

Vilnius University Institute of Data Science and Digital Technologies,
Vilnius, Lithuania
{paulius.vaitkevicius,
virginijus.marcinkevicius}@mif.vu.lt
http://dmsti.vu.lt/

Abstract. Phishing remains a continual security threat, causing global losses exceeding 3.5 billion USD in 2019, according to the FBI's Internet Crime Complaint Center. The Anti-Phishing Working Group (APWG) reported as many as 2,172 unique phishing websites detected per day in 2019. Most of the methods to solve the phishing websites' detection problem proposed by the scientific community are based on classical classification algorithms on phishing datasets with hand-extracted features. Although these methods demonstrate high accuracies, unfortunately, they are sensitive to changing environment: phishers can learn the most relevant URL features and adapt their attacks to overcome the security check. Therefore, in search of less sensitive methods, deep neural networks were started to employ, as they do not require manual feature extraction and can directly learn a representation from the URL's sequence of characters. The purpose of this research is to propose a new method for phishing websites' URL detection based on ensembles of Recurrent neural networks and other types of deep neural networks. The results of our approach are presented in this paper and compared with the performance of other Recurrent neural networks. These results are additionally compared with the performance of classical classification algorithms on the same dataset with 48 features extracted. Our method with no manually extracted feature gives a significant increase in classification accuracy, compared with single Recurrent neural networks, and matches the accuracy of classical classification ensembles with manually extracted features.

Keywords: Phishing · Classification · Ensembles · Recurrent neural networks

1 Introduction

Phishing is a cybercrime built on social engineering which employs technical trickery and masking as a trustworthy entity to steal sensitive user data, such

© Springer Nature Switzerland AG 2020
T. Robal et al. (Eds.): DB&IS 2020, CCIS 1243, pp. 297–310, 2020.
https://doi.org/10.1007/978-3-030-57672-1_22

as passwords, credit card details, digital identity data from unsuspecting users. Phishers usually lure victims into entering a fraudulent website by impersonating legitimate URL and sending it to the victim by email or SMS along with a threatening message, like notice of account termination or illegal transaction [14]. Phishing attacks are still very successful nowadays, despite many existing anti-phishing solutions. The Anti-Phishing Working Group (APWG) reported as many as 2,172 unique phishing websites detected per day in 2019 with a 71.0% increase during the last six years of monitoring [2]. Global losses from phishing activities exceeded 3.5 billion USD in 2019, with a 29.6% annual increase and total global losses of 10.2 billion USD in the last five years, according to the FBI's Internet Crime Complaint Center [11]. This success is determined by the fact that phishers are professional adversaries who: (i) have the financial motivation, (ii) exploit computer illiteracy of ordinary Internet users [1], and (iii) manage to learn from their previous experience and improve their future attacks.

The scientific community has put much effort into solving the phishing websites' URL detection problem during the last decade, seeing the ability to determine the maliciousness of a website by evaluating its URL as a significant advantage. The number of victims can be reduced, minimizing operational efforts by avoiding extensive use of more complex methods such as content analysis of a website [3]. Many proposed methods attempted to solve phishing websites detection as a supervised machine learning problem on different phishing datasets with predefined features [5,22]. These methods work well on predefined dataset design but are sensitive to changing environment: phishers can learn the most relevant URL features these methods employ and adapt their behavior to avoid being detected [16]. In search of methods resilient to the changing environment, the scientific community started to explore deep learning techniques with automatic feature detection to identify complicated behaviors with new patterns of attack. Deep learning algorithms developed rapidly in recent years and found many applications for problem solving in different areas. Therefore, the hope of creating a resilient phishing websites' URL detection method lies with these algorithms [3,16].

To our best knowledge, no previous research involved methods, employing the ensembles constructed of RNN and CNN algorithms. The results of the literature review and the well-known fact that ensembles of classification algorithms usually produce better results than single algorithms, motivate us to go one step further and propose a new method, based on the ensembles of RNNs, which would improve classification accuracy.

In this paper, we present the results of our experiment and answer these research questions:

1. Do methods, composed of RNN ensembles, show significantly better classification results in comparison with single RNN methods?
2. Do methods, composed of RNN ensembles, show significantly better results on raw URL dataset in comparison with classical classification algorithms on the same dataset with manually designed features? To answer this question, we compare achieved results with the results of classical classification algorithms on the same dataset from the authors' previous paper [22].

The rest of the paper is organized as follows: In Sect. 2 we give a review of related works. In Sect. 3 we describe our research methodology. In Sect. 4 we report our experiment results. We conclude the paper in Sect. 5.

2   Related Works

The first methods for phishing websites' URL detection were created more than a decade ago and included blacklisting techniques and heuristic approaches. There still are a few initiatives to use a centralized phishing websites' URLs blacklisting solutions (e.g., PhishTank[1], Google Safe Browsing API [2]). Although these methods were proven unavailing because phishing websites have a very short lifespan (usually not more than a day) and it takes time to detect, report, confirm, and publish a malicious URL in a blacklisting database [24].

Later, as an improvement on blacklisting methods, the heuristic methods were implemented where the signatures of frequent attacks were identified and blacklisted for the future use of Intrusion Detection Systems, giving these methods better generalization capabilities and the ability to detect threats in previously unseen URLs [19]. Although heuristic methods superseded simple blacklisting methods, they could not generalize to all types of new threats [24].

More recent methods for phishing websites' URL detection were based on the application of classical supervised machine learning algorithms on phishing datasets with predefined features. Best performing methods are enlisted in the Table 1. These methods scored above 99.49% and were implemented using different types of classifiers: neural networks, regression, decision trees, ensembles, and probabilistic. Although these methods work well on predefined dataset design but they are sensitive to changing environment: phishers can learn the most relevant URL features these methods employ and adapt their behavior to avoid being detected [16]. It should be stated that methods enlisted in the Table 1 measure accuracy and use highly unbalanced datasets, therefore, evaluating performance by accuracy does not reveal how these methods would perform on more balanced datasets.

Table 1. Accuracy of classical classification methods with predefined features.

Year	Authors	Classifier	Phishing URLs	Legitimate URLs	Accuracy
2017	Marchal et al. [15]	Gradient Boosting	100,000	1,000	99.90%
2010	Whittaker et al. [26]	Logistic Regression	16,967	1,499,109	99.90%
2011	Xiang et al. [27]	Bayesian Network	8,118	4,780	99.60%
2018	Cui et al. [7]	C4.5	24,520	138,925	99.78%
2013	Zhao et al. [30]	Perceptron	990,000	10,000	99.49%

---

[1] https://www.phishtank.com/.

[2] https://developers.google.com/safe-browsing/.

Most recent approaches use deep learning techniques, including Recurrent neural networks like Long Short-Term Memory networks (LSTM) or Gated Recurrent Unit (GRU). The results of the best methods on balanced datasets are enlisted in Table 2. Authors of these papers built their work on the premise that deep learning methods can automatically learn the feature representation from URL's character sequence, without using any predefined features. Additionally, Vazhayil et al. [23] have shown, that adding CNN layers to the LSTM improves classification accuracy.

Table 2. Deep learning based classification methods accuracy.

Year	Authors	Classifier	Phishing URLs	Legitimate URLs	Accuracy
2017	Saxe and Berlin [18]	CNN	9,533,939	9,533,939	99.30%
2018	Vazhayil et al. [23]	CNN-LSTM	58,050	58,050	98.90%
2018	Vazhayil et al. [23]	CNN	58,050	58,050	98.70%
2017	Bahnsen et al. [3]	LSTM	1,000,000	1,000,000	98.70%
2019	Yang et al. [28]	CNN-LSTM	1,021,758	989,021	98.50%
2019	Zhao et al. [29]	GRU	240,000	150,000	98.50%

From the literature review, we can ascertain that blacklisting, heuristic, and classical classification methods on datasets with predefined features are prone to learn a specific dataset design and are not capable of safeguarding internet users from "zero-hour" attacks. We can also see the potential of deep learning-based methods with automatic feature detection to achieve accuracies close to classical classification methods while having the quality of being resilient to the changing environment and cope with "zero-hour" attacks. Furthermore, we can see that the scientific community focuses on RNN and CNN based methods for the qualities like having internal memory, the ability to find patterns in raw data, and automatically learning the essential features from the data.

To our best knowledge, no previous research involved methods, employing the ensembles constructed of RNN and CNN algorithms. The results of the literature review and the well-known fact that ensembles of classification algorithms usually produce better results than single algorithms, motivate us to go one step further and propose a new method, based on the ensembles of RNNs, which would improve classification accuracy.

3   Research Methodology

In this section, we describe our research methodology. We start by defining algorithms used in the experiment and reasons for the algorithm selections (Subsect. 3.1), later we describe the dataset (Subsect. 3.2), metrics and methods (Subsect. 3.3) used in the experiment. We finish this section by explaining how all previous sections are composed to set up the experimental design for our research (Subsect. 3.4). The results of our experiment, designed according to this experimental design, are presented in Sect. 4.

3.1 Algorithms Used in the Experiments

In this subsection, we present the algorithms we used and explain in detail the configuration of methods we composed and tested in our experiment.

We have chosen to employ RNN and CNN algorithms for the construction of our method in order to utilize RNN's properties of having a memory and CNN's properties of recognizing data patterns. Combined properties of these algorithms allow our method to automatically learn the feature representation from URL's character sequence, without using any manually predefined features, thus increasing our method's flexibility, as well as resilience to the changing environment and "zero-hour" attacks.

Figure 1 provides a formal description of the architecture of our RNN-based methods as well as CNN-RNN hybrid methods [23,28]. Each method consists of three main parts: (i) input and embedding layers, (ii) different RNN (and in some methods additional CNN) layers, and (iii) a dense layer for making a final prediction. We will describe all parts in more detail in the following subsections.

Character Embedding. Instead of extracting URL features manually, we aim to learn a representation directly from the sequence of URL characters, building our methods on the premise that RNNs can learn essential features and sequential dependencies of the data automatically [3,18,28]. First, we encode each URL character in its ASCII code and set the URL size to 256 characters. If the URL is shorter than 256 characters, we pad it with zeroes in the front, and if it is longer, we cut off characters from the beginning of the URL. Later, character encoded URL vectors are provided as inputs to the embedding layer, which optimizes character vectors to better reflect their semantic meaning, by being optimized jointly with the rest of the model during the learning process [25]. The embedding layer parameters are described in Table 3.

Recurrent Neural Network Layers. In our experiment, we use four different recurrent neural networks:

- Long Short-Term Memory network (LSTM), which is a well-known implementation of RNN with a designated memory, widely used by the scientific community in various fields. LSTM overcomes a well known long-term dependency problem of RNNs by implementing a specific memory called "cell state", regulated by structures called gates [10].
- Long Short-Term Memory network with Peepholes (LSTM-P), which is a modification of the LSTM by adding so-called "peephole connections", allowing gate layers to look at the cell state [8].
- Gated Recurrent Units (GRU), which is a noticeable modification of the LSTM, combining the forget and input gates into a single "update gate", resulting in more simpler model [6].

– Simple RNN cell[3] based neural network with no explicit memory implementation, which is known for not learning "long-term dependencies" very well
due to input noise and vanishing gradient problems [4].

Additionally, we use CNN and RNN hybrids, such as CNN-LSTM and CNN-
GRU methods [23]. These hybrid networks benefit from CNN properties to find
patterns in data, prior to feeding the data to RNN cells, as depicted in Fig. 1. We
add one 1D convolutional layer and one max-pooling layer between the embedding layer and the RNN layer. We use a dropout regularization layer[4] before the
last dense layer to prevent overfitting [21].

Additionally, the Naïve-Bayes probabilistic classifier [13] was trained directly
on character encoded strings and used in the ensembles as well.

We use binary cross-entropy loss function, batch size of 200 and dropout rate
of 0.5 for all models in our experiment. Other dissimilar hyper-parameters used
in our models are provided in Table 3.

Table 3. Hyper-parameters of the models.

Method	Hyper-parameters
LSTM	Embedding output dimension: 32; Embedding regularizer: L2 penalty; Output size: 32; Optimizer: Adam (learning rate: 0.01, epsilon: 1e-07); Dropout: 0.5; Penalty: 0.001; Epochs: 40;
LSTM-P	Embedding output dimension: 32; Embedding regularizer: L2 penalty; Output size: 32; Optimizer: Adam (learning rate: 0.01, epsilon: 1e-07); Dropout: 0.5; Penalty: 0.001; Epochs: 64;
GRU	Embedding output dimension: 32; Embedding regularizer: L2 penalty; Output size: 32; Optimizer: Adam (learning rate: 0.01, epsilon: 1e-06); Dropout: 0.5; Penalty: 0.001; Epochs: 40; Loss function: binary cross-entropy;
Simple RNN	Embedding output dimension: 32; Embedding regularizer: L2 penalty; Output size: 32; Optimizer: Adam (learning rate: 0.001, epsilon: 1e-08); Dropout: 0.5; Penalty: 0.001; Epochs: 16;
CNN-LSTM	Embedding output dimension: 64; Embedding regularizer: L2 penalty; Output size: 64; Optimizer: Adam (learning rate: 0.05, epsilon: 1e-06); Dropout: 0.5; GRU layer dropout: 0.35; Penalty: 0.001; Epochs: 40; Kernel size: 3; Pooling size: 4; Convolutional layer activation function: ReLU;
CNN-GRU	Embedding output dimension: 64; Embedding regularizer: L2 penalty; Output size: 64; Optimizer: Adam (learning rate: 0.005, epsilon: 1e-07); Dropout: 0.5; GRU layer dropout: 0.25; Penalty: 0.01; Epochs: 40; Kernel size: 5; Pooling size: 8; Convolutional layer activation function: ReLU;

---

[3] As described in https://www.tensorflow.org/api_docs/python/tf/keras/layers/Simple
RNNCell.

[4] https://www.tensorflow.org/api_docs/python/tf/keras/layers/Dropout.

Prediction is made by the sigmoid function [9] in the last dense layer of the network, giving the real value between 0 and 1, which corresponds to the prediction probability to our classes ('0' for legitimate URL, '1' for phishing URL).

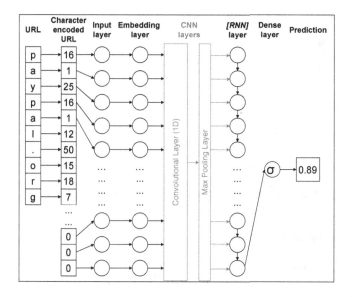

Fig. 1. Configuration of our methods

Stacking Ensemble is used in our experiment to combine predictions of previously trained methods into a unified predictor. As described in the Fig. 2, a new algorithm called "meta classifier" (in our case based on Logistic regression [12]) learns how to combine the predictions from multiple methods and produce a final prediction. The meta-classifier is trained based on predicted probabilities instead of class labels. We used MLxtend 0.17.0 library to build our stacking ensemble methods[5].

3.2   Dataset

In our experiment, we used a dataset from Mendeley Data portal[6], published by Choon Lin Tan (Universiti Malaysia Sarawak) in March 2018. This balanced dataset contains 5,000 phishing and 5,000 legitimate websites URL samples. Additionally, a total of 48 features were extracted from these websites by the authors [5]. We have chosen this dataset for our experiment so that we could compare the performance of the proposed method with the performance of classical classification algorithms from our previous paper [22], where the same dataset was used.

---

[5] http://rasbt.github.io/mlxtend/.
[6] https://data.mendeley.com/datasets/h3cgnj8hft/1.

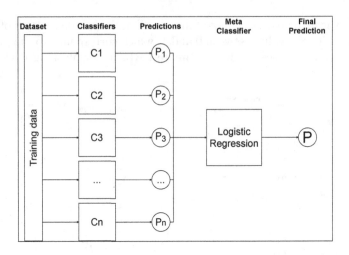

Fig. 2. Configuration of Stacking Ensemble methods

3.3   Measures and Methods

Classification Accuracy in our experiment is the rate of phishing and legitimate websites which are identified correctly with respect to all the websites, defined as follows:

$$ACCURACY = \frac{TP + TN}{TP + FP + TN + FN},\tag{1}$$

where

- TP - number of websites, correctly detected as phishing (True Positive),
- TN - number of websites, correctly detected as benign (True Negative),
- FP - number of legitimate websites, incorrectly detected as phishing (False Positive),
- FN - number of phishing websites, incorrectly detected as legitimate (False Negative).

We chose classification accuracy as our classification quality quantification metric because: (i) most other researchers use classification accuracy to define results of their experiments (see Sect. 2), therefore the comparability of research results is homogeneous throughout our work; (ii) in our experiment, we used a dataset with equal class distributions (there is no disparity between the number of positive and negative labels) therefore we do not have the majority and minority classes; (iii) we used cross-validation function with stratification option, which generates test sets that contain the same distribution of classes, or as close as possible. In these circumstances, classification accuracy is a useful non-bias measure.

Welch's T-Test in our experiment was used to determine whether the means of classification accuracy results produced by any two classifiers have a statistically significant difference. We used *scipy.stats* package for Python to perform a T-test.

Shapiro–Wilk Test was used to check whether samples came from a normally distributed population [20]. We used *scipy.stats* package for Python to perform a Shapiro–Wilk test.

3.4 Experimental Design

In this subsection, we present the experimental design we employed to perform the experiment. The objective is to train all the classifiers from Sect. 3.1 on our chosen dataset from Sect. 3.2 for their best possible classification accuracy described in Sect. 3.3, and to compare classification results. The experiment was divided into two parts: (i) training the classifiers, (ii) comparing the classification results.

We train the classifiers by taking these steps:

1. Configure the classifier in Python's 3.7.5 environment using Tensorflow-GPU 2.0.0 library[7]; we use a computer with Nvidia GeForce RTX 2080 Ti graphical card, Intel Core i7-4770 3.40 GHz processor, and 16 GB of RAM to perform our experiment.
2. Perform the exhaustive grid search to find the best fitting hyper-parameters, using the Scikit Learn 0.22.0 library[8] [17].
3. Train and test the classifier using a cross-validation function with 10 stratified folds from the Scikit Learn 0.22.0 library. Repeat this step 3 times with different seed to get 30 classification accuracy measures.
4. Perform a Wilk-Shapiro test, as described in Sect. 3.3, to check if the accuracy scores are normally distributed. If not, take action to normalize the values (e.g., repeating the training and testing step).
5. Save the results for further actions.

We compare classification results by taking these steps:

1. Using Welch's T-test, described in Sect. 3.3, check every possible pair of classifiers if their mean classification accuracies have statistically significant differences.
2. Arrange all classifiers by their mean classification accuracy in descending order.
3. Evaluate groups of methods that mean classification accuracies have no statistically significant differences.
4. Plot all results in the box plot.
5. Compare the results with our other experiment with classical classification algorithms on the same dataset with manually extracted features [22].

For each algorithm, we perform an experiment with all the steps described above.

---

[7] https://www.tensorflow.org.
[8] https://scikit-learn.org/.

4 Experimental Results

In this section, we present the results of our experiment, conducted following the research design described in Sect. 3.4. We present all RNN-based methods and five best RNN ensemble-based methods of our experiment in the Fig. 3. In this box-plot, the yellow dotted lines group the algorithms which mean accuracy results (assessed with Welch's T-test, as described in Sect. 3.3) have no statistically significant differences with each other.

From this diagram, we can see that:

- the results of ensembles 1, 2, and 3 have no statistically significant difference, but are significantly better than all other models;
- the results of ensembles 4, 5, and CNN-LSTM have no statistically significant difference, but are significantly better than GRU, CNN-GRU, LSTM, LSTM-P, and Simple RNN methods;
- the results of GRU, CNN-GRU, LSTM, and LSTM-P have no statistically significant difference but are significantly better than the Simple RNN method.
- Simple RNN method demonstrated the worst result of RNN-based methods. This result is consistent with the theory, provided in Sect. 3.1, stating that simple RNN with no specifically implemented memory can not learn "long-term dependencies" and is inferior in comparison with LSTM or GRU.

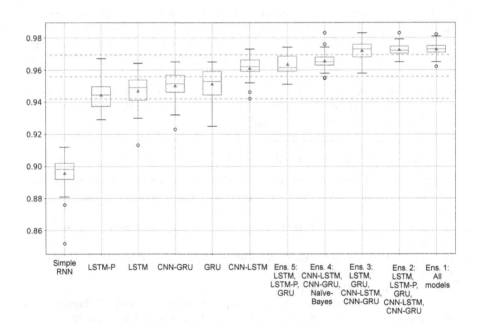

Fig. 3. Classification results

In table 4, we compare the results of this experiment (in the highlighted font) with our previous experiment, were we applied classical classification algorithms on the same dataset with manually extracted features [22].

Table 4. Classification results

Method	Accuracy
Gradient Tree Boosting	0.9742
Ensemble 1 (LSTM, LSTM-P, GRU, CNN-LSTM, CNN-GRU, Naïve-Bayes)	**0.9730**
AdaBoost	0.9728
Ensemble 2 (LSTM, LSTM-P, GRU, CNN-LSTM, CNN-GRU)	**0.9725**
Ensemble 3 (LSTM, GRU, CNN-LSTM, CNN-GRU)	**0.9721**
Random Forest	0.9715
Multilayer Perceptron	0.9671
CNN-LSTM	**0.9612**
Classification and Regression Trees	0.9574
Ensemble 4 (CNN-LSTM, CNN-GRU, Naïve-Bayes)	**0.9657**
Ensemble 5 (LSTM, LSTM-P, GRU)	**0.9634**
Support Vector Machine	0.9549
GRU	**0.9515**
CNN-GRU	**0.9503**
LSTM	**0.9471**
LSTM-P	**0.9443**
Naïve-Bayes	0.9177
SimpleRNN	**0.8958**
Naïve-Bayes (this experiment)	**0.6056**

Welch's T-test has shown that Ensembles 1–3 give the results of the same significance as Gradient Tree Boosting and AdaBoost, applied on the same dataset only with manually selected features. We can see from the results that single RNN methods score 1–2% lower accuracies than the best ensemble-based methods. We also observe that Ensembles 1–3, which scored the best accuracy results, have a higher number of RNN methods, and this confirms theoretical results that the higher number of independent classifiers improve ensemble classification accuracy. We can also see from our results that RNN without memory (SimpleRNN cell) performs worse of all RNNs. The conclusions of our experiment results are provided in Sect. 5.

5   Conclusions

In this paper, we have proposed a new ensemble-based method for phishing websites' URL detection. We have presented the results of our experiment, where we have compared our method with other different types of methods, based on RNNs, CNNs, and different hybrid methods, consisting of these algorithms. From our research, we draw the following conclusions, which are valid on the dataset we have used:

1. Our proposed method, employing RNN-based ensembles, outperform single RNN methods by at least 0.02 difference in classification accuracy, which is statistically significant.
2. Our proposed method performs as well as Gradient Tree Boosting and AdaBoost with human extracted features on the same dataset. The accuracies between our method, Gradient Tree Boosting, and AdaBoost ensembles have no statistically significant difference, according to Welch's T-test.
3. Adding the CNN layer to the method increases classification accuracy by 0.01, and this difference is statistically significant.
4. For phishing websites' URL classification problem, RNNs with explicit memory implementation, like LSTM and GRU, outperform classic RNNs without memory by 0.06 difference in classification accuracy, which is statistically significant.
5. RNNs outperform simple probabilistic classifiers like Naïve-Bayes on URL characters sequence by 0.355 increase of accuracy. Additionally, Naïve-Bayes performs significantly better on manually extracted features rather than string character sequences, with a 0.31 difference of classification accuracy.

References

1. Adebowale, M., Lwin, K., Sánchez, E., Hossain, M.: Intelligent web-phishing detection and protection scheme using integrated features of Images, frames and text. Expert Systems with Applications 115, 300–313 (2019). https://doi.org/10.1016/J.ESWA.2018.07.067, https://www.sciencedirect.com/science/article/pii/S0957417418304925?via%3Dihub
2. Anti-Phishing Working Group, I.: Phishing Activity Trends Reports (2019). https://apwg.org/resources/apwg-reports/
3. Bahnsen, A.C., Bohorquez, E.C., Villegas, S., Vargas, J., Gonzalez, F.A.: Classifying phishing URLs using recurrent neural networks. In: 2017 APWG Symposium on Electronic Crime Research (eCrime), pp. 1–8 (2017). https://doi.org/10.1109/ECRIME.2017.7945048, http://ieeexplore.ieee.org/document/7945048/
4. Bengio, Y., Simard, P., Frasconi, P.: Learning long-term dependencies with gradient descent is difficult. IEEE Trans. Neural Netw. 5(2), 157–166 (1994). https://doi.org/10.1109/72.279181
5. Chiew, K.L., Tan, C.L., Wong, K., Yong, K.S., Tiong, W.K.: A new hybrid ensemble feature selection framework for machine learning-based phishing detection system. Information Sciences 484, 153–166 (2019). https://doi.org/10.1016/j.ins.2019.01.064, https://www.sciencedirect.com/science/article/pii/S0020025519300763?via%3Dihublinkinghub.elsevier.com/retrieve/pii/S0020025519300763
6. Cho, K., et al.: Learning Phrase Representations using RNN Encoder-Decoder for Statistical Machine Translation. arXiv:1406.1078v3 (2014)
7. Cui, B., He, S., Yao, X., Shi, P., Yao, X., He, S., Cui, B.: Malicious URL detection with feature extraction based on machine learning. Int. J. High Performance Comput. Network. 12(2), 166 (2018). https://doi.org/10.1504/ijhpcn.2018.10015545, http://www.inderscience.com/link.php?id=94367

8. Gers, F.A., Urgen Schmidhuber, J.J., Cummins, F.: Learning to forget: continual prediction with LSTM. In: Proceedings ICANN 1999 International Conference on Artificial Neural Network, vol. 2, pp. 850–855. IDSIA (1999). http://www.idsia.ch/www.idsia.ch/

9. Han, J., Moraga, C.: The influence of the sigmoid function parameters on the speed of backpropagation learning. In: Lecture Notes in Computer Science (including subseries Lecture Notes in Artificial Intelligence and Lecture Notes in Bioinformatics), vol. 930, pp. 195–201. Springer, Cham (1995). https://doi.org/10.1007/3-540-59497-3_175

10. Hochreiter, S., Urgen Schmidhuber, J.J.: Long short-term memory. Neural Computation 9(8), 1735–1780 (1997), http://www7.informatik.tu-muenchen.de/~hochreitwww.idsia.ch/~juergen

11. Internet Crime Complaint Center: Internet Crime Report 2019. Tech. rep., Internet Crime Complaint Center at the Federal Bureau of Investigation of United States of America (2020). https://www.ic3.gov/media/annualreport/2019_IC3Report.pdf

12. Kleinbaum, D.G., Klein, M.: Introduction to logistic regression. In: Logistic Regression, pp. 1–39. Springer, New York, NY (2010). https://doi.org/10.1007/978-1-4419-1742-3_1, http://link.springer.com/10.1007/978-1-4419-1742-3_1

13. Lewis, D.D.: Naive (Bayes) at forty: The independence assumption in information retrieval. In: ECML 1998: Machine Learning: ECML-1998, pp. 4–15. Springer, Heidelberg (1998). https://doi.org/10.1007/BFb0026666

14. Lin Tan, C., et al.: PhishWHO: Phishing webpage detection via identity keywords extraction and target domain name finder. Decision Support Systems 88, 18–27 (2016). https://doi.org/10.1016/j.dss.2016.05.005

15. Marchal, S., Armano, G., Grondahl, T., Saari, K., Singh, N., Asokan, N.: Off-the-hook: an efficient and usable client-side phishing prevention application. IEEE Trans. Comput. 66(10), 1717–1733 (2017). https://doi.org/10.1109/TC.2017.2703808

16. Opara, C., Wei, B., Chen, Y.: HTMLPhish: Enabling Accurate Phishing Web Page Detection by Applying Deep Learning Techniques on HTML Analysis. http://arxiv.org/abs/1909.01135arXiv:1909.01135 (2019), http://www.phishtank.com

17. Pedregosa, F., et al.: Scikit-learn: machine learning in Python. J. Mach. Learn. Res. 12, 2825–2830 (2011), http://jmlr.csail.mit.edu/papers/v12/pedregosa11a.html, https://scikit-learn.org/stable/

18. Saxe, J., Berlin, K.: eXpose: A character-level convolutional neural network with embeddings for detecting malicious URLs, file paths and registry keys. arXiv preprint arXiv:1702.08568, February 2017, http://arxiv.org/abs/1702.08568

19. Seifert, C., Welch, I., Komisarczuk, P.: Identification of malicious web pages with static heuristics. In: 2008 Australasian Telecommunication Networks and Applications Conference, pp. 91–96. IEEE, December 2008. https://doi.org/10.1109/ATNAC.2008.4783302, http://ieeexplore.ieee.org/document/4783302/

20. Shapiro, S.S., Wilk, M.B.: An analysis of variance test for normality (complete samples). Biometrika 52(3/4), 591–611 (1965)

21. Srivastava, N., Hinton, G., Krizhevsky, A., Sutskever, I., Salakhutdinov, R.: Dropout: a simple way to prevent neural networks from overfitting. J. Mach. Learn. Res. 15(1), 1929–1958 (2014)

22. Vaitkevicius, P., Marcinkevicius, V.: Comparison of classification algorithms for detection of phishing websites. Informatica 31(1), 143–160 (2020). https://doi.org/10.15388/20-infor404

23. Vazhayil, A., Vinayakumar, R., Soman, K.: Comparative study of the detection of malicious URLs using shallow and deep networks. In: 2018 9th International Conference on Computing, Communication and Networking Technologies (ICC-CNT). pp. 1–6. IEEE, July 2018. https://doi.org/10.1109/ICCCNT.2018.8494159, https://ieeexplore.ieee.org/document/8494159/

24. Verma, R., Das, A.: What's in a URL. In: Proceedings of the 3rd ACM on International Workshop on Security And PrivacyAnalytics - IWSPA 2017, pp. 55–63. ACM Press, New York, New York (2017). https://doi.org/10.1145/3041008.3041016, http://dl.acm.org/citation.cfm?doid=3041008.3041016

25. Wei, B., Hamad, R.A., Yang, L., He, X., Wang, H., Gao, B., Woo, W.L.: A deep-learning-driven light-weight phishing detection sensor. Sensors 19(19), 4258 (2019). https://doi.org/10.3390/s19194258

26. Whittaker, C., Ryner, B., Nazif, M.: Large-scale automatic classification of phishing pages. The 17th Annual Network and Distributed System Security Symposium (NDSS 2010) (2010). https://doi.org/10.1109/TDSC.2013.3, http://www.isoc.org/isoc/conferences/ndss/10/pdf/08.pdf%5Cnresearch.google.com/pubs/pub35580.html

27. Xiang, G., Hong, J., Rose, C.P., Cranor, L.: CANTINA+: A feature-rich machine learning framework for detecting phishing web sites. ACM Trans. Inf. Syst. Secur. 14(2), 1–28 (2011). https://doi.org/10.1145/2019599.2019606, https://www.ml.cmu.edu/research/dap-papers/dap-guang-xiang.pdf

28. Yang, P., Zhao, G., Zeng, P.: Phishing website detection based on multidimensional features driven by deep learning. IEEE Access 7, 15196–15209 (2019). https://doi.org/10.1109/ACCESS.2019.2892066

29. Zhao, J., Wang, N., Ma, Q., Cheng, Z.: Classifying malicious URLs using gated recurrent neural networks. In: International Conference on Innovative Mobile and Internet Services in Ubiquitous Computing, pp. 385–394. Springer, Heidelberg (2019). https://doi.org/10.1007/978-3-319-93554-6_36

30. Zhao, P., Hoi, S.C.: Cost-sensitive online active learning with application to malicious URL detection. In: Proceedings of the 19th ACM SIGKDD International Conference on Knowledge Discovery and Data Mining - KDD 2013, p. 919. ACM Press, New York (2013). https://doi.org/10.1145/2487575.2487647, http://dl.acm.org/citation.cfm?doid=2487575.2487647

Impact of Information Security Training on Recognition of Phishing Attacks: A Case Study of Vilnius Gediminas Technical University

Justinas Rastenis[(✉)], Simona Ramanauskaitė [ORCID], Justinas Janulevičius, and Antanas Čenys

Vilnius Gediminas Technical University, 10223 Vilnius, Lithuania
justinas.rastenis@vgtu.lt

Abstract. Phishing attack is a type of social engineering attack and often used as the initial stage of a larger campaign. It is dangerous as users might inadvertently reveal to the attackers personal data or sensitive corporate information. Therefore, inability to recognize and properly react to phishing attacks must be treated as one of the main security risks in the enterprise. In this paper, we present a methodology for evaluating employees' resistance to phishing attacks. We also analyze the changes to the situation after the employees participated in information security training. Experiments with employees of Vilnius Gediminas Technical University were carried out within a period of one year to gather information on how credulous they are to phishing attacks before and after security training. Results of the experiment reveal the benefit of security training, however there is still room for improvement and need to pay attention in the future.

Keywords: Phishing attack · Credulity · Security · Research · Education

1 Introduction

Phishing is a criminal mechanism employing both social engineering and technical subterfuge to steal consumers' personal identity data and financial account credentials [1]. However real life phishing attacks are aiming to get different type of data – both user personal data as well as enterprise (where the user works or has some connections to it) sensitive data. To deceive the user, attacker sends an e-mail or/and creates a web page to gather users provided information. The information varies from personal data as well as enterprise sensitive data. If the attacker manages to prepare very convincing e-mail in order to get needed data, or if the user is very credulous, no hacking skills are needed to get users or enterprise sensitive data. Therefore phishing attacks are the number one infection vector employed by 71% of organized groups in 2017 according to Internet Security Threat Report [2].

In order to fight against phishing attacks phishing message filtering mechanisms can be very beneficent as they prevent the phishing message to reach the victim. To identify phishing e-mails some solutions exist [3–5]; however, most of them are not able

© Springer Nature Switzerland AG 2020
T. Robal et al. (Eds.): DB&IS 2020, CCIS 1243, pp. 311–324, 2020.
https://doi.org/10.1007/978-3-030-57672-1_23

to identify all possible phishing methods and techniques as variety of possible phishing e-mail vary a lot. Therefore combination of different methods have to be used to fight against phishing attacks. The most effective method to fight against phishing attacks is security training [6]. Well-trained and conscious person can identify the phishing attack with minor efforts. However, not all users have enough knowledge and practice to identify phishing attacks. Therefore it is very important to identify the weak links in the enterprise (or society) and provide needed training on information security and phishing identification.

The aim of this paper is to evaluate how efficient are security training in order to identify phishing attack. We execute the experiment in Vilnius Gediminas Technical University with all the personnel in it. The personnel is composed of different age, different position and education persons, therefore we can identify which groups of the personnel are the most vulnerable to phishing attacks and whom benefits from the security training.

In Sect. 2 we analyze related works in order to get ideas for the design of our experiment. The proposed methodology for user resistance to phishing attacks is provided in Sect. 3, while Sect. 4 presents the results of the experiment and analysis of security training efficiency.

2 Prior and Related Work

2.1 Phishing Attack

Phishing is an alternate of the word "fishing" [7] and it refers to bait used by phishers who are waiting for the victims to be bitten [8]. The beginning of phishing was in 1987 when a detailed description of phishing was introduced while in 1995 started the wider application of phishing attacks in the internet [9]. Phishing is a kind of social engineering attacks, where the attack tries to affect the victim from making rational choices and make the victim to make emotional choices instead [10]. The manipulation of victim's emotions (fear of losing, desire to benefit, etc.) usually is directed to retrieve persons individual, personal data or enterprise sensitive data [11].

However, phishing attack is not a social engineering attack only. There are different media, attack vector and technical approaches used in phishing attacks [12]. Social engineering is adapted to all attack vectors (e-mail, efax, instant messaging, smishing, social network, vishing, website, wifi); however more technical approaches exist for specific attack vectors or/and media. In some cases, hacking skills are needed to get user related data from its computer environment (computer, web browser, etc.). Therefore the information can be gathered not directly from the person (by taking advantage of his or her emotions), but by its environment and interaction with tools, used for the phishing attack.

Some phishing attacks might be specific to target devices. The attack techniques can be divided into initialization, data collection and system penetration [13]. Existence of "ready-to-deploy" packages for creating and configuring phishing content that also provide built-in support for reporting stolen credentials complicated the situation even more [14]. According to the research of Kurt Thomas et al. results [15], the popularity of phishing kits is high and do not decrease.

2.2 Mitigation of Phishing Attacks

Legal [8], technical [18–21], process engineering [16], prevention by detecting malicious or spoofed objects [17] and other methods exist as countermeasure to the phishing attacks. However all authors agree the education is the most important activity at the moment which can outperform any automated solutions in its efficiency.

As the importance of phishing attack and persons credulity to it, some research executed in order to define the properties, influencing a person's credulity to a phishing attack. Daniela Oliveira et al. [23] analyzed the age factor for susceptibility to a phishing attack. The results proved younger adults are more suspicious to phishing attack comparing to older persons. As well multiple studies confirm [24–26] women are more vulnerable to phishing attacks comparing to men. This is related to the fact women are more sensitive to their emotional and social needs and realize the ability of the internet to help fill those needs.

Tzipora Halevi et al. [27] executed research in order to prove some hypotheses, what influences person vulnerability to a phishing attack. The results revealed:

- Conscientious people are hardworking and have high self-control, therefore an appeal to efficiency and order overcome the participant's self-control and raise the likelihood of responding to a spear-phishing attack.
- Women are more likely to respond to the phishing email.
- Users who are more aware of cyber-risks are more resistant to phishing attacks.
- Users are not able to estimate their likelihood of being phished correctly.

Also, the research revealed the internet usage, as well as computer-mediated communication competence, does not correlate with vulnerability to phishing attacks. These findings show the usage and understanding of information technologies are not enough to identify phishing attacks.

Mohamed Alsharnouby et al. [28] confirm users' general technical proficiency does not correlate with improved detection scores. As well they tracked person eye movements in order to define how much attention they spend on factors, identifying the phishing attack. The results were disappointing as people spend very little time looking at security indicators compared to web site content when making assessments whether it is a phishing or not. This fact can serve as a prove phishing related training is needed rather than internet technology understanding.

For solving the problem or phishing-related training different solutions are provided. Even game-based mobile applications is developed [22] in order to educate persons in the phishing identification area. As well as attention training and elaboration system [29] is needed in order to protect against phishing attacks suitably.

2.3 Security and Phishing Attack Awareness Training Solutions

Security awareness training shows positive outcomes in enterprises [30] and different organizations as well as NIST [31] presents programs for security awareness and training. However the results of security awareness training can vary a lot as different methods for training organization, different training format exists [32] as well as different groups of trainees have their own preferences [33]. For example in research with college students' the hypothesis there is no significant relationship between information security awareness training and the students' information security awareness topic were rejected for half of analyzed security topics [34]. Therefore it is important to adjust the security awareness training to a specific audience and topic.

In the field of phishing attack awareness training rule-based training can be applied, when explanation on how to identify phishing attack, how to act in certain cases is provided. Jansen et al. [35] states this kind of training improves organizational defenses against phishing attacks; however, regular repetition of rule-based training may not yield increasing resistance to attacks. Therefore they apply mindfulness theory to develop a novel training approach that can be performed after individuals are familiar with rule-based training. This approach involves analysis of real situations, importance of specific attributes etc.

While mindfulness technique is oriented on more detail explanation, analysis of consequences etc. Dodge et al. [36] recommends practical exercises. Generated fake phishing e-mail can be used to identify key components, directing to not legitimate, phishing attack. However the usage of practical training show persons inability to identify the phishing e-mail by all employees and fully prevent the phishing attack.

One of barriers that bigger enterprises face – inability to provide phishing awareness training to all its users. Therefore embedded, online training can be organized. Caputo et al. [37] analyzed how efficient such a training is. These authors tracked employees' reactions to spear phishing emails and immediate training activities, which were sent just after the clicking on the phishing e-mail link. The embedded awareness training revealed a group of "non-clickers" while the embedded training provided no significant difference for the "clickers" group.

The existing phishing attack awareness training techniques and inability to achieve very significant achievements in resistance to phishing attack presupposes there should be used a combined, multiple methods in order to reach different groups of enterprise users.

3   The Methodology for Testing Employees Resistance to Phishing Attack

In order to test employees' resistance to phishing attack, the best ways is to execute or inspect existing phishing attack and analyze users' reaction to it. However, execution of real phishing attack is not ethical, while inspection of reaction to real phishing attacks from outside is hard to execute, as no user action logging can be executed etc.

The ethics of phishing experiments are summarized by D. B. Resnik and P. R. Finn [38] by stating phishing experiments "… can be conducted ethically if risks are minimized, confidentiality and privacy are protected, potential participants have an opportunity to opt out of the research before it begins, and human subjects are debriefed after their participation ends.". While all requirements are clearly defined and logical, some of them do not align with realistic implementation of phishing attack. For example, the user must be informed about the upcoming attack, meanwhile, results of K. Parsons et al. executed experiments [39] reveal the phishing identification rate is very dependent on whether the user knows he is participating in phishing detecting experiment or no. Therefore, the experiment of phishing attack methodology must be carefully judged and prepared in order to design realistic situation with no ethical issues in the experiment.

We propose a schema of the experiment presented (see Fig. 1) to satisfy all requirements.

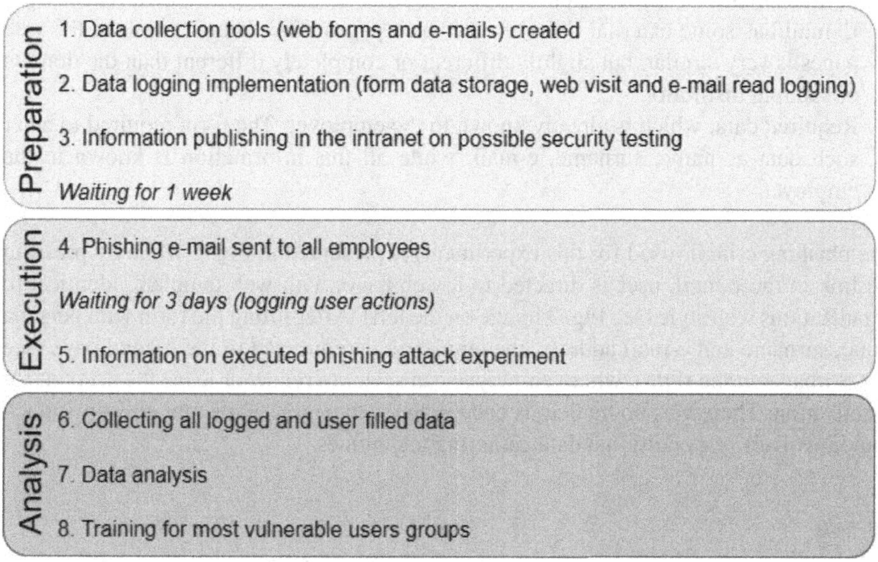

Preparation

1. Data collection tools (web forms and e-mails) created

2. Data logging implementation (form data storage, web visit and e-mail read logging)

3. Information publishing in the intranet on possible security testing

Waiting for 1 week

Execution

4. Phishing e-mail sent to all employees

Waiting for 3 days (logging user actions)

5. Information on executed phishing attack experiment

Analysis

6. Collecting all logged and user filled data

7. Data analysis

8. Training for most vulnerable users groups

Fig. 1. The experiment flow to identify employees ability to recognize the phishing attack

We solve this contradiction between information on executed phishing experiment and a need to imitate realistic situation by informing all employees in the intranet system one week before the experiment. All employees have access to the intranet, where all main news are published. The news flow in the intranet is constant and after couple of days, the news about planned security testing is not in the first page, while period of one week is enough to remember such information. As well employees whom suspect the received e-mail is a part of phishing experiment can view the news archive to find information on it.

It is important to prepare the tools for testing too. We have to be able to collect data on who read the e-mail, who visited the web page and filled required personal or company data.

As well it is important to prepare the content of phishing e-mail. For testing purposes the phishing e-mail should not be too obvious and at the same time should have at least several places, according to what it can be identified as phishing e-mail. We propose to use such elements to identify phishing e-mail:

1. E–mail senders address is very similar to real one but has some minor differences (several letters are different, synonym usage, etc.).

2. The e–mail text has some spelling or style errors. It is usually influences by the fact the text was automatically translated from other language.
3. Sender's institution, affiliation is not mentioned in the e–mail text. There is not enough information to identify the contacts of the sender, his or her institution.
4. Usage of an embedded image. The e-mail included an embedded image which has to be downloaded in order to view it. Usually, images are attached to the e-mail in normal situations while the embedded images allow tracking of e-mail reads.
5. E–mail has some external links to other web pages. The domain name of the web pages is very similar, but slightly different or completely different than the domain of sending institution.
6. Required data, which is already known to the employer. The form required to enter such data as name, surname, e-mail, while all this information is known to the employer.

The phishing e-mail (used for this experiment) is presented in Fig. 2 while by pressing the link in the e-mail, user is directed to a web page, with web template, identical to organizations web style (see Fig. 3 image on the left). After filling the form with persona name, surname and e-mail address, the employee is redirected to the second page (see Fig. 3 image on the right), where employee can select to renew or leave the account for deactivation. There was no malicious code in the web pages, while real phishing attack could involve some additional data gathering techniques.

Fig. 2. E-mail, used for testing of employees resistance to phishing attack

Fig. 3. View of web pages, used in the phishing attack experiment to collect users data (Color figure online)

After the phishing e–mail is sent several days all employees activities, related to the phishing e–mail is logged. The logging should be done in several ways:

1. Logging of e–mail reads. If enterprise is using personalized e–mail viewing system, it can be improved to log when specific users gets the e–mail, what actions he or she takes, does he or she opens it, etc. While its complicated to use in practice, the e–mail embedded image can be used to log e–mail reads – while the user loads the image, server logs the IP address and additional data, if it was attached to the image url address (personalized links, to identify specific user).
2. Logging of web page visits. Visiting the external web page shows, the user is interested and takes some actions. Technically, it is identical as image loading identification.
3. Logging of personal data reveal. In order to identify employees revealed data all entered data must be stored. In some cases employees are testing what the e–mail or web page wants and how it looks. It such cases employees fill fake, incorrect data. Therefore, in data analysis the collected data is compared with employee database data, to identify fake data.
4. Logging of phishing activity reporting. As the experiment is executed on enterprise employees (not individual person) all reports, requests, enquiries to information technology or other departments in the enterprise must be logged to identify users ability to recognize or at least doubt the information, provided in phishing e–mail. In most cases the help desk calls and registered tokens can be used, while personal discussions among several employees are hardly logged.

The possible states of phishing e-mail related actions logging is presented in Fig. 3. The cases in the left of the image (in gray background) are not logged because of employees ignorance to the phishing e mail, used protection mechanisms or because the e mail message was missed, not received. Meanwhile the cases in the right of the image (in green background) are logged as active and conscious phishing attack recognition/suspicious actions. These cases indicate a good understanding of phishing attack importance to the enterprise security and active participation in enterprise security assurance and are welcomed.

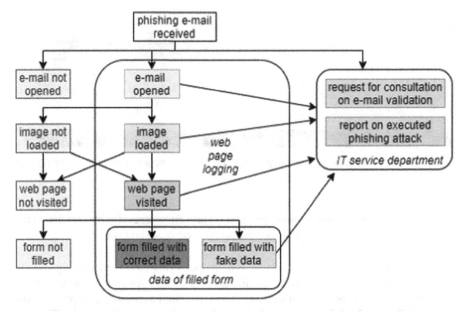

Fig. 4. Experiment execution and data gathering elements (Color figure online)

The most vulnerable to phishing attack employees executed actions presented in the middle of the image (see Fig. 4). The intensity of red background indicated the higher risk to the enterprise and lower phishing recognition skills.

In order to increase the enterprise security level, all employees are notified on executed experiment and its results. As well all employees are invited to take training on enterprise security and its management principles. Meanwhile the persons whom visited the external web page and filled the form with correct personal/enterprise data are contacted personally and involved into individual consultations on phishing attack recognition.

While phishing attack related trainings are very important its influence to the phishing attack recognition is not clear. Therefore, experiments to evaluate the security training efficiency is needed.

4   Security Training Efficiency to Recognize Phishing Attack: Methodology and Results

In order to evaluate how efficient are security training in Vilnius Gediminas Technical University in order to increase phishing attack recognition a combination of repetitive phishing attack experiments, security trainings and employees survey were used.

On 2018 December the first experiment based on proposed methodology for testing employees resistance to phishing attack was executed. During this experiment, a phishing e–mail was sent to request filling personal data into external web page in order to get Christmas present from the employee. After this experiment all employees were invited to participate in security training, held by information technology service department in Vilnius Gediminas technical university.

The information technology service department of Vilnius Gediminas technical university every year organizes multiple trainings for university employees. The trainings are related to information system usage (incident reporting procedures are included in it) as well as security related topics. Phishing attack related training took 1 h and introduces participated employees with 3 topics: phishing attack definition and examples; ways to identify phishing attack; ways how the organizer of phishing attack can gather users data and where it can be used for malicious purposes. The training included theory, rule-based teaching as well as demonstration of different phishing attacks and its identification activities.

After this training, the number of consultations on phishing attack incidents with information technology service department increased. The department gets approximately 74 requests to investigate suspicious e–mail every month, while before the training only 19 request per month were received.

Both increasing number of phishing attacks as well as increasing understanding to report and investigate phishing attacks in the enterprise can explain the increase of phishing attack investigation requests. Therefore additional, second phishing attack experiment was executed in 2019 December. During this phishing attack an e–mail about necessity to confirm accounts non deactivation was sent to all employees. Users were directed to external web page and asked to fill additional form with personal data in order to prevent account deactivation in the future. The second experiment revealed the changes after the first experiment and training.

Additionally with the results of the second experiment an online survey was distributed to all employees to gather their opinion on executed phishing attack experiments and training efficiency.

The summary of both phishing attack experiment results are presented in Table 1. It is nice to see the employees were more active on e–mail reading but the credulity is lower as smaller portion of employees loaded the image, visited the web page and filled data. The number of employees who executed all steps as the attacker expected reduced more than 10 times (from 214 to 21 employees). Meanwhile the reporting of phishing incidents increased drastically too (from 10 to 205 incident reports). These numbers are very presentative, however 1% of fully credulous to attacker employees are too much and needs to be reduced in the future.

The data analysis of fully credulous employees revealed some changes between first and second experiment – management employees were the weakest link in the first experiment, while during the second experiment management personnel were resistant to phishing attack while the teaching staff becomes the most important in order to assure the enterprise security (16 persons from 21 fully credulous persons were from teaching

staff). This change can be explained by analyzing security training attendance data –
about 300 employees participated in the training, while 57% of it was from management,
while teaching staff missed the training, because of their occupation with students.

Table 1. Summary of phishing attack experiment results

Year	2018		2019	
	Count	% from all employees	Count	% from all employees
No of employees/e–mails	1648	100	1618	100
E–mails read	708	43	931	58
Loaded image	405	25	350	22
Visited in the web page	410	25	355	22
Filled personal data	214	13	21	1
Replied to the e-mail	2	1	21	1
Reported as an incident	10	1	205	13

We also divided employees, who filled the web form with personal name, surname
and e-mail address into categories based on the year (younger than 40 years old and
40 or more years old) and gender (female and men). The summary of fully credulous
employees data (numbers) are presented in Table 2.

Table 2. Summary of fully credulous employees data in the second experiment

Classificatory	Numbers	Percentage
Position type in the organization: Teaching staff Management staff	16 5	24% 76%
Gender: Female Male	9 12	43% 57%
Age group: <40 years old >= 40 years old	5 16	76% 24%

Another difference – the second time elder persons more likely were not able to
recognize phishing attacks, while the first time younger persons were more credulous to
phishing attack. This fact can be explained by different type of phishing content of e–mail
– younger persons know the principles of information technology management and do
not trust urgent requests, however are more attracted to getting benefits and presents. As
well, the ability to learn from the first experiments results might be another reason why

younger persons are not so credulous to phishing attack in Vilnius Gediminas technical university too.

After the second phishing attack experiment an e–mail with invitation to participate in a survey about executed phishing attack imitations and security trainings was sent. Only 138 employees responded to it. Some persons just ignored the invitation, while some portion of personnel was suspicious and assumed it is a phishing attack too. The answer distribution to main questions of the survey is provided in Table 3.

Table 3. Answers to survey questions after the second phishing attack experiment.

Question	Answer	Answers
What helped to identify phishing e-mail in the last phishing attack imitation?	Suspicious sender	127
	Improper formatting	86
	Errors in e-mail text	61
	Improper subject of the e-mail	51
	Incorrect data (year)	20
	Other	31
What actions you took after receive of the phishing e-mail in the last phishing attack imitation?	Deleted the e-mail	76
	Informed IT service desk on received improper e-mail	52
	Informed your colleague about improper e-mail	44
	Ignored the e-mail	33
	Other	10
Are imitated phishing attacks needed in the future?	Yes	121
	No	17
Do you feel you have enough IT security knowledge?	Yes	69
	No	69
Did you participated in security training, held in your institution this year?	No	86
	Yes	52

The survey revealed employees notice the senders address and it was the biggest factor to ignore it as a phishing e-mail. As well personnel of Vilnius Gediminas Technical University are suspicious to improper formatting, errors in the e-mail text. Less than half of employees report about the phishing attack, most often, they just delete the e-mail. Vilnius Gediminas technical university has a strategy and policy on managements of information security incidents; however the low number of incident reports show the security incident reporting policy is not strict enough (there are no penalty for not reporting), the policy is not communicated enough among all employees of the organization (not all employees participate in security training or read security related information in the intranet) or personnel just ignore the requirement to report any incident. This situation should be improved and maybe legislative security policy could be applied to increase the number.

The survey results revealed more than 90% of the personnel believe the imitations of phishing attack is necessary in the future. Our institution employees threat it as an education tool, which helps to improve their IT security knowledge as less than half of personnel were able to participate in arranged IT security trainings in the institution.

Both the repetitive phishing experiments with the employees as well survey results show the benefit of security training. In future we plan to repeat the security training as well as experiments in order to trace how effective the security training can be in the long period.

5   Conclusions

Phishing attacks in most cases are directed to all employees of the enterprise and just in some cases, very dedicated personal phishing attacks are executed. The mass phishing e-mail are very effective and just several responses are enough to benefit from it. In Vilnius Gediminas Technical University the efficiency of phishing attack can be efficient as more than 1% of employees are credulous to phishing attack and reveal their personal data. Therefore it is one of top concerns in order to assure enterprise security. In order to eliminate this risk additional security trainings will be executed, all new employees will have to be introduced with enterprise security policy.

In order to reduce the employees' credulity to phishing attack, a series of security related training were executed. The security training resulted up to 10 times better results for employees' ability to identify phishing attacks and response to it. These results are not enough to assure enterprise security as 21 person revealed its personal data (which is up to 1% from all employees). This shows the training is needed to reduce the security risks, however additional countermeasures have to be applied to get zero employees credulity to phishing attacks.

Employees survey on executed security training and phishing attack imitation experiments revealed employees understand the purpose of these actions and are willing to participate in it, however only 50% of the survey respondents were able to participate in the security training. In order to increase the ability to identify phishing attacks and follow the security policy guidelines, the security training could be mandatory for all users, or systemic security related newspapers could be issued to maintain the understanding of security importance for the enterprise.

References

1. Phishing Activity Trends Report—4th Quarter 2018. http://docs.apwg.org/reports/apwg_t rends_report_q4_2018.pdf. Accessed 12 Nov 2019
2. Internet Security Threat Report, vol. 23. https://www.symantec.com/content/dam/symantec/ docs/reports/istr-23-2018-en.pdf. Accessed 12 Nov 2019
3. Chandrasekaran, M., Narayanan, K., Upadhyaya, S.: Phishing email detection based on structural properties. In: NYS Cyber Security Conference, vol. 3 (2006)

4. Gansterer, W.N., Pölz, D.: E-mail classification for phishing defense. In: Boughanem, M., Berrut, C., Mothe, J., Soule-Dupuy, C. (eds.) ECIR 2009. LNCS, vol. 5478, pp. 449–460. Springer, Heidelberg (2009). https://doi.org/10.1007/978-3-642-00958-7_40

5. Mbah, K.F., Lashkari, A.H., Ghorbani, A.A.: A phishing email detection approach using machine learning techniques. Master's Thesis, University of New Brunswick, Fredericton and Saint John, NB, Canada (2017)

6. Stockhardt, S., et al.: Teaching phishing-security: which way is best? In: Hoepman, J., Katzenbeisser, S. (eds.) SEC 2016. IAICT, vol. 471, pp. 135–149. Springer, Cham (2016). https://doi.org/10.1007/978-3-319-33630-5_10

7. Oxford Dictionaries. http://www.oxforddictionaries.com/definition/english/phishing. Accessed14 Nov 2019

8. Mohammad, R.M., Thabtah, F., McCluskey, L.: Tutorial and critical analysis of phishing websites methods. Comput. Sci. Rev. **17**, 1–24 (2015)

9. James, L.: Secure Science Corporation "Phishing Exposed-Uncover secrets from the Dark side". Syngress Publishing (2005)

10. Goel, S., Williams, K., Dincelli, E.: Got phished? Internet security and human vulnerability. J. Assoc. Inf. Syst. **18**(1), 22–44 (2017)

11. Kim, D., Kim, J.H.: Understanding persuasive elements in phishing e-mails: a categorical content and semantic network analysis. Online Inf. Rev. **37**(6), 835–850 (2013)

12. Chiew, K.L., Yong, K.S.C., Tan, C.L.: A survey of phishing attacks: their types vectors and technical approaches. Expert Syst. Appl. **106**, 1–20 (2018)

13. Aleroud, A., Zhou, L.: Phishing environments, techniques, and countermeasures: a survey. Comput. Secur. **68**, 160–196 (2017)

14. Cova, M., Kruegel, C., Vigna, G.: There is no free phish: an analysis of" free" and live phishing kits. Proc. USENIX Workshop Offensive Technol. **8**, 1–8 (2008)

15. Thomas, K., et al.: Data breaches, phishing, or malware? Understanding the risks of stolen credentials. In: Proceedings of the 2017 ACM SIGSAC conference on computer and communications security, pp. 1421–1434 (2017)

16. Chaudhry, J.A., Chaudhry, S.A., Rittenhouse, R.G.: Phishing attacks and defenses. Int. J. Secur. Appl. **10**(1), 247–256 (2016)

17. Gupta, S., Singhal, A., Kapoor, A.: A literature survey on social engineering attacks: phishing attack. In: 2016 International Conference on Computing, Communication and Automation (ICCCA), pp. 537–540. IEEE (2016)

18. Mohammad, R.M., Thabtah, F., McCluskey, L.: Phishing websites features. In: School of Computing and Engineering. University of Huddersfield (2015)

19. Cui, Q., Jourdan, G.V., Bochmann, G.V., Couturier, R., Onut, I.V.: Tracking phishing attacks over time. In: Proceedings of the 26th International Conference on World Wide Web, pp. 667–676 (2017)

20. Aonzo, S., Merlo, A., Tavella, G., Fratantonio, Y.: Phishing attacks on modern android. In: Proceedings of the 2018 ACM SIGSAC Conference on Computer and Communications Security, pp. 1788–1801 (2018)

21. Abdelhamid, N.: Multi-label rules for phishing classification. Appl. Comput. Inform. **11**(1), 29–46 (2015)

22. Arachchilage, N.A.G., Love, S., Beznosov, K.: Phishing threat avoidance behaviour: an empirical investigation. Comput. Hum. Behav. **60**, 185–197 (2016)

23. Oliveira, D., et al.: Dissecting spear phishing emails for older vs young adults: on the interplay of weapons of influence and life domains in predicting susceptibility to phishing. In: Proceedings of the 2017 CHI Conference on Human Factors in Computing Systems, pp. 6412–6424 (2017)

24. Hambyrger, Y.A., Ben-Artzi, E.: Loneliness and internet use. Comput. Hum. Behav. **19**(1), 71–80 (2003)

25. Hamburger, Y.A., Ben-Artzi, E.: The relationship between extraversion and neuroticism and the different uses of the Internet. Comput. Hum. Behav. **16**(4), 441–449 (2000)
26. Sun, J.C.Y., Yu, S.J., Lin, S.S., Tseng, S.S.: The mediating effect of anti-phishing self-efficacy between college students' internet self-efficacy and anti-phishing behavior and gender difference. Comput. Hum. Behav. **59**, 249–257 (2016)
27. Halevi, T., Memon, N., Nov, O.: Spear-phishing in the wild: A real-world study of personality, phishing self-efficacy and vulnerability to spear-phishing attacks. Phishing Self-Efficacy and Vulnerability to Spear-Phishing Attacks (January 2, 2015) (2015)
28. Alsharnouby, M., Alaca, F., Chiasson, S.: Why phishing still works: User strategies for combating phishing attacks. Int. J. Hum Comput Stud. **82**, 69–82 (2015)
29. Harrison, B., Svetieva, E., Vishwanath, A.: Individual processing of phishing emails: how attention and elaboration protect against phishing. Online Inf. Rev. **40**(2), 265–281 (2016)
30. Eminağaoğlu, M., Uçar, E. and Eren, Ş.: The positive outcomes of information security awareness training in companies–a case study. Inf. Secur. Techn. Rep. **14**(4), 223–229 (2009)
31. Wilson, M., Hash, J.: Building an information technology security awareness and training program. NIST Spec. Publ. **800**(50), 1–39 (2003)
32. Shaw, R.S., Chen, C.C., Harris, A.L., Huang, H.J.: The impact of information richness on information security awareness training effectiveness. Comput. Educ. **52**(1), 92–100 (2009)
33. Abawajy, J.: User preference of cyber security awareness delivery methods. Behav. Inf. Technol. **33**(3), 237–248 (2014)
34. Kim, E.B.: Recommendations for information security awareness training for college students. Inf. Manage. Comput. Secur. **22**, 1 (2014)
35. Jensen, M.L., Dinger, M., Wright, R.T., Thatcher, J.B.: Training to mitigate phishing attacks using mindfulness techniques. J. Manage. Inf. Syst. **34**(2), 597–626 (2017)
36. Dodge, R.C., Carver, C., Ferguson, A.J.: Phishing for user security awareness. Comput. Secur. **26**(1), 73–80 (2007)
37. Caputo, D.D., Pfleeger, S.L., Freeman, J.D., Johnson, M.E.: Going spear phishing: exploring embedded training and awareness. IEEE Secur. Priv. **12**(1), 28–38 (2013)
38. Resnik, David B., Finn, Peter R.: Ethics and phishing experiments. Sci. Eng. Ethics **24**(4), 1241–1252 (2017). https://doi.org/10.1007/s11948-017-9952-9
39. Parsons, K., McCormac, A., Pattinson, M., Butavicius, M., Jerram, C.: The design of phishing studies: challenges for researchers. Comput. Secur. **52**, 194–206 (2015)

Managing Security Risks in Post-Trade Matching and Confirmation Using CorDapp

Mubashar Iqbal$^{(\boxtimes)}$ⓘ and Raimundas Matulevičiusⓘ

Institute of Computer Science, University of Tartu, Tartu, Estonia
{mubashar.iqbal,rma}@ut.ee

Abstract. Blockchain technology is ready to revolutionise the financial industry. The financial industry has various security challenges *(e.g., tampering, repudiation, denial of service, etc)*. The Corda platform provides suitable technological infrastructure to build the blockchain-based application (CorDapp) in the financial industry to overcome these challenges. In this paper, we take a case of the capital market post-trade matching and confirmation process to perform security risk management. We compare the countermeasures of centralised application and CorDapp that mitigate the security risks. Furthermore, we explain what security risks appear within the CorDapp.

Keywords: Blockchain · Corda platform · CorDapp · Capital markets · Security risks · Security risk management · FinTech CorDapp.

1 Introduction

The advent of *Blockchain* technology introduces new concepts to revolutionise the financial industry. The European Central Bank (ECB) [12] presents the financial industry interests to use blockchain technology in their infrastructure. The centralised infrastructure that supports the business processes execution is challenged by strict regulations and constant security risks [2,3]. The security risks harm the business processes and valuable assets that could lead to a reputation loss or financial sanctions for the organization. For example, the hackers used SWIFT credentials to stole $81m from the Bangladesh bank [2,25]. Also, the financial industry ranks second in data breaches. Hence, the security risks in capital markets enable manipulative, illegal and abusive trade practices [2].

Blockchain is a distributed ledger technology (DLT) that operates over a peer-to-peer (P2P) network [28]. It eliminates the third-party intermediation and automates the transaction process. Blockchain technology is becoming prominent in the financial industry because of transaction-level integrity. The blockchain-based Corda platform could be an enabler to protect the financial industry from various security risks. The goal of this paper is twofold: firstly, we explain how

© Springer Nature Switzerland AG 2020
T. Robal et al. (Eds.): DB&IS 2020, CCIS 1243, pp. 325–339, 2020.
https://doi.org/10.1007/978-3-030-57672-1_24

Corda-based application (CorDapp) could mitigate the security risks. Secondly, we discuss the security risks that appear within the CorDapp after using the blockchain. Similar to [15,16], we use the security risk management (SRM) domain model [11,19] to identify the assets and their security criteria *(C - Confidentiality, I - Integrity, A - Availability)*. Furthermore, we utilise the STRIDE [27] *(S - Spoofing, T - Tampering, R - Repudiation, Id - Information disclosure, D - Denial of service, E - Elevation of privileges)* threat model that supports a systematic analysis to identify, explain and mitigate the potential security risks. In this paper, we consider the centralised post-trade matching and confirmation case because of the current challenges in the financial industry [2,3].

The rest of the paper is structured as follows: Sect. 2 presents the centralised capital market and post-trade activities. Section 3 introduces the CorDapp as a countermeasure. In Sect. 4, we compare the countermeasures of centralised and blockchain-based applications. Section 5 provides a discussion about security risk management in CorDapp. Section 6 concludes the paper.

2   Centralised Capital Market and Post-Trade

In this section, we present the system context of the centralised capital market and post-trade. Next, we discuss the security risks in centralised post-trade matching and confirmation process and the countermeasures considering both traditional approaches and blockchain-based Corda platform.

2.1   System Context

A capital market is a part of the financial industry and it processes the financial instruments (e.g., securities, futures, options, and other assets). There are a few capital market post-trade activities between the counter-parties [30]. Mainly, the trading system has three modules: front-office, middle-office, and back-office module. The important action in the middle-office is *trade matching and confirmation*. The business process model (Fig. 1) represents the post-trade matching and confirmation process between counter-parties (*e.g., Bank X is a buyer and Bank Y is a seller*) [24]. The trade matching is executed after receiving the trade details from the front-office. The financial organization (*e.g., Bank X*) performs trade matching with *Bank Y*. The confirmation process is run when the trade details are accepted and agreed by each counter-party. In centralised trading system, trade matching is performed manually, so there are high chances of security risks. The third-parties (e.g., regulators and clearinghouses) assure that the trade is valid and all the necessary information is provided [5].

2.2   Security Risks

In this section, we perform a security risks analysis of post-trade matching and confirmation. Firstly, we illustrate the assets and security risks (see Table 1). Secondly, we present what are the security risks vulnerabilities and how a centralised infrastructure mitigates them.

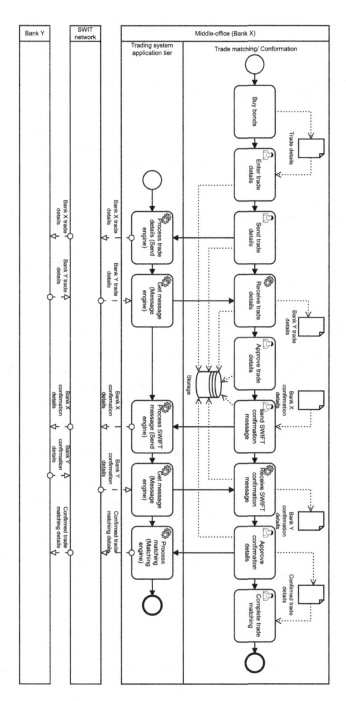

Fig. 1. Post-trade matching and confirmation in centralised infrastructure (adapted from [24])

Table 1. Assets to be secured in post-trade matching and confirmation

Business asset	System asset	Risk
Import message *(I)*	Sender engine, Import message engine	*S*
Trade data *(I)*	Database, Trade matching, Confirmation process	*T, R*
Trade details *(I, A)*	Database, Sender engine, Matching engine	*T, D*
Processed trades *(C, I)*	Trade details, Transactions, Log files	*Id, R*
Trade matching *(I, A)*	Servers, Import message engine, Matching engine	*Id, D*
Confirmation *(A)*	Servers, Trading system, Sender engine	*D*
Trading *(I)*	Access rights, Remote operations, Trade execution	*E*

Security Risks Vulnerabilities: The architecture (Fig. 2) helps to visualise the vulnerable assets in post-trade matching and confirmation [16,24]. The vulnerabilities depict weaknesses of the system assets. The threat agent exploits the vulnerabilities and harms the valuable assets. This way he negates the security criteria. The vulnerabilities are:

V#1: No proper implementation of communication protocols (S) [7,8]
V#2: In-secure transmission of data (S, T) [20,25]
V#3: Inappropriate validation of transmitted data (T) [1,3]
V#4: Poorly implemented access control (S, T, R) [1,20]
V#5: Unprotected logs and ineffective logging controls (R, Id) [1,20]
V#6: No proper mechanism to filter a large number of requests (D) [2,20]
V#7: Weak controls to restrict unauthorised remote operations (E) [1,20]

Security Countermeasures: The architecture (Fig. 3) demonstrates the assets of post-trade matching and confirmation in three different layers. The presentation layer provides the user controlled operations. The application layer includes the post-trade processing and technology details. The data layer consists of database and action logs. The traditional countermeasures (TC) are defined to mitigate the vulnerabilities of centralised post-trade infrastructure:

TC#1: Secure implementation of communication protocols (V#1, V#7)
TC#2: Incorporate the cryptography and digital signatures (V#2, V#3)
TC#3: Authorisation and access control (V#4, V#7)
TC#4: Only authorised administrators could access logs (V#5)
TC#5: The system shall not log sensitive information (V#5)
TC#6: Install a firewall and antivirus software (V#6)

Figure 3 illustrates countermeasures that mitigate the security risks' vulnerabilities. For example, the *V#1* is mitigated by incorporating *TC#1* that relates to a secure implementation of communication protocols [7]. The use of cryptography and digital signatures *(TC#2)* helps to overcome *V#2*. The cryptography schemes (e.g., public-key cryptography) secure the data and communications between intended parties. Similarly, the *V#3* is mitigated by using the *TC#2*.

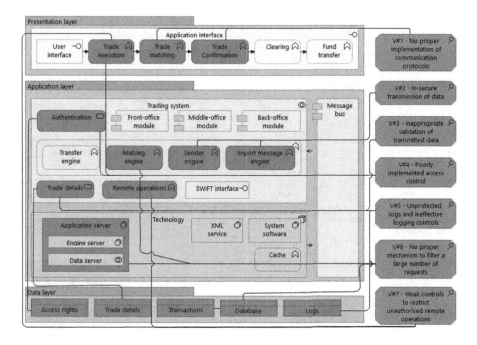

Fig. 2. Security risks vulnerabilities in centralised infrastructure of post-trade

For example, the public-key cryptography-based digital signature RSA validates the authenticity and integrity of the transaction/message [22]. The $V\#4$ is mitigates by authorisation and access control mechanism $(TC\#3)$. The access control mechanism detects and protects against unauthorised access to a system. The logs help in audit and regulatory compliance but unprotected logs $(V\#5)$ could nullify the security of the system. The implementation of $TC\#4$ could protect the logs from unauthorised users. Also, one should also carefully monitor the logs to check if the system is not logging sensitive information $(TC\#5)$. The firewall and antivirus software $(TC\#6)$ help to mitigate the $V\#6$ by monitoring the abnormal traffic requests in the system. The $V\#7$ is attained by $TC\#1$ and $TC\#4$ that restricts the unauthorised remote operations.

3   CorDapp to Mitigate Security Risks

The Corda platform is an example of a permissioned blockchain where only authenticated nodes exchange assets [13]. The Corda platform uses i) validity, and ii) uniqueness [13,17] consensus. The validity consensus ensures the correctness of input & output states and required signatures in a transaction. The uniqueness consensus is performed by notaries. It checks if the transaction is not already consumed (e.g., protection against double-spending [13,17]).

In this section, we present CorDapp as a countermeasure to mitigate vulnerabilities and protect the assets *(see Sect. 2.2 for vulnerabilities and assets).*

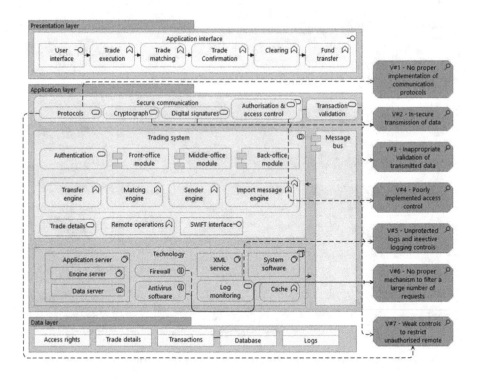

Fig. 3. Security countermeasures in centralised infrastructure of post-trade

The architecture (Fig. 2) is extended to (Fig. 4) by integrating the Corda platform. Similarly, the architecture (Fig. 4) illustrates the assets of post-trade matching and confirmation in three different layers along with the auxiliary components (e.g., client, nodes network, etc). The architecture helps to visualise how the identified vulnerabilities are mitigated and assets are protected by CorDapp. CorDapp leverages the benefits of blockchain and also introduces several other techniques to secure it. We considered those Corda-based countermeasures (CC):

CC#1: Authorised nodes over P2P network (V#1, V#4)
CC#2: Mutually-authenticated TLS connection and PKI (V#1, V#2)
CC#3: A notaries-based consensus model (V#3)
CC#4: Nodes implement an access-control mechanism (V#4, V#7)
CC#5: Actions logs and a traceable immutable distributed ledger (V#5)
CC#6: Deploy a rate-limiting firewall (V#6)
CC#7: Doorman validate and filter malformed requests (V#6)
CC#8: Sandbox to prevent execution of code (V#7)

The countermeasure *(CC#1)* mitigates the vulnerability *(V#1)* related to a lack of proper authentication of the source and destination connection that could trigger the spoofing attack. The *V#2* is mitigated by incorporating the

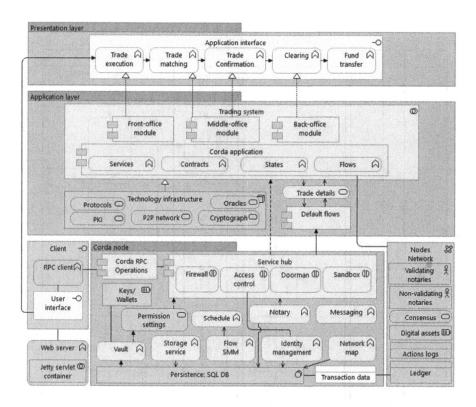

Fig. 4. CorDapp as a countermeasure in post-trade matching and confirmation

mutually-authenticated TLS connection and PKI *(CC#2)*. CorDapp introduces a notaries-based consensus model *(CC#3)* that validates the transmitted data and overcome the *V#3*. The CorDapp provides access control *(CC#4)* by design that helps to mitigate *V#4* and restrict unauthorised access. The *V#5* is overcome by a traceable immutable ledger and keeping the action logs of participant nodes *(CC#5)*. The CorDapp introduce rate limiting firewall *(CC#6)* to protect nodes against the *V#6* by restricting the flooded requests. Also, the CorDapp incorporates the doorman to validate and filter malformed requests *(CC#7)*. The CorDapp brings the concept of the sandbox *(CC#8)* to prevent unauthorised remote operations *(V#7)* and code executions.

The business process model of CorDapp (Fig. 5) enables blockchain-based states, contracts, flows, and vault to interact with counter-parties to perform the assets exchange [24]. The counter-parties *(e.g., Bank X & Y)* perform the operations without relying on the manual operations and trusted third-party intermediation. The Corda platform performs the validation of the transaction by a notaries-based consensus [13]. The counter-parties receive the validated data from the distributed Corda ledger over the P2P network. The involved counter-parties provide necessary details of the transaction by Corda node to CorDapp

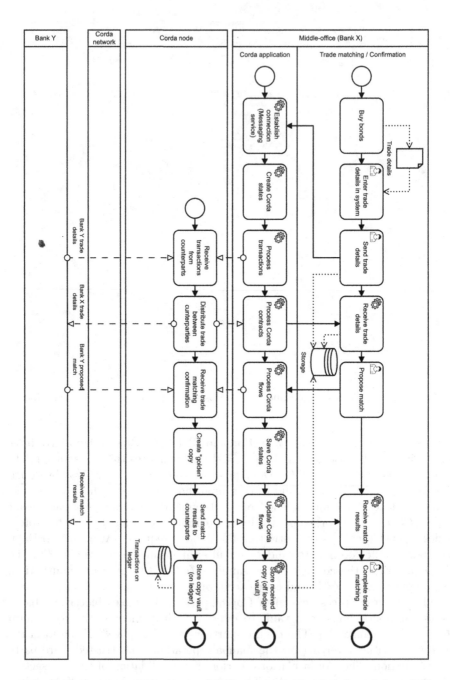

Fig. 5. Post-trade matching and confirmation in CorDapp (adapted from [24])

that validates and completes the post-trade matching and confirmation. The process increases efficiency and reduces the risks of manual operations.

4 Comparison

In this section, we compare the countermeasures with regards to identified vulnerabilities in post-trade matching and confirmation. Table 2 presents the countermeasures of centralised and CorDapp infrastructure.

Table 2. The comparison of countermeasures

	Centralised infrastructure	CorDapp infrastructure
V#1	- Secure communication protocols	- Secure communication protocols - Authorised nodes & P2P network
V#2	- Cryptography & Digital signatures	- Cryptography & P2P network
V#3	- Transaction validation	- Notary-based consensus model
V#4	- Authorisation & Access control	- Authorised nodes & Access control
V#5	- Centralised actions logs - Authorised administrators access	- Decentralised actions logs - Immutable distributed ledger
V#6	- Traffic monitoring - Firewall - Antivirus software	- Rate limiting firewall - Doorman validate requests - Doorman filter malformed requests
V#7	- Secure communication protocols - Authorisation & Access control	- Secure communication protocols - Sandbox to prevent code execution

In order to mitigate $V\#1$, secure communication protocols (e.g., HTTPS/TLS, IPSec, etc.) are applied to ensure the integrity of the secure connection and information exchange between client and server. The communication protocols provide data origin authentication, also encrypting the transmitted data to protect against eavesdropping and tampering. The weak implementation of communication protocols could be broken [7]. In this case, an attacker could intercept the communication and data transmission channel [7]. CorDapp overcomes this by considering only the authorised nodes over a P2P network where nodes behave both as a server and as a client [9]. Also, the CorDapp incorporates mutually authenticated TLS connection [10] as an extra security layer to protect the communication between nodes.

The in-secure transmission of data could lead to spoofing and tampering risks $(V\#2)$ [20,25]. The malicious user may intercept the plain-text data transmission and gain unauthorised access to the system. It would negate the confidentiality and integrity of sensitive data. In order to mitigate $V\#2$, the centralised infrastructure uses cryptography and digital signatures. The CorDapp also incorporates PKI based cryptography schemes. The Corda platform also plans to introduce Intel SGX integration [10] that would bring the CPU P2P encryption and allows one to encrypt the entire ledger [14]. Also, a hardware security module (HSM) could be applied to manage and protect digital keys [10].

To mitigate $V\#3$, the transaction validation mechanism is utilised. The centralised infrastructure introduces the traditional transaction validation process (e.g., RSA signatures, etc.). The Corda platform uses a notaries-based decentralised consensus model to validate a transaction and ensure authenticity and integrity [10,13]. In centralised approach, the attacker can trigger a Man-in-the-Middle (MitM) attack and modify the transaction [18]. Similarly, in CorDapp the attacker can perform MitM to modify the transaction but the notaries-based consensus model protects and guarantee the integrity of transaction [10].

The *vulnerability #4* is mitigated by implementing centralised authorisation and access control mechanisms in traditional infrastructure. It could be error-prone or subject to attacks because of centralisation, password theft or weak implementation of security policies [29]. In contrast, the Corda platform provides a built-in decentralised access-control mechanism to protect against *V#4*. Also, only authorised nodes can join the network that limits this vulnerability.

Multi-user applications are subjects to repudiation because the system allows a user to perform/deny the malformed actions. The system should ensure that the user actions are recorded in order to protect against insider security risks. In order to mitigate *V#5*, centralised post-trade infrastructure implements separate features for keeping and securing the action logs. This protects sensitive data from intentional misuse or harm from the involving parties. The security of logs in the existing infrastructure is weak, vulnerable and subject to attacks [23] because the controls remain to a designated authority and centralised storage. Also, the system logs sensitive information that could leak. In contrast, CorDapp manages the records in a decentralised immutable ledger. It provides tamper-proof transparent traceability and auditing. Also, the CorDapp logs each action of a participant node that replicates over a P2P network with other authorised participant nodes [10].

The *V#6* is mitigated by installing a firewall and antivirus software for traffic monitoring and controlling of abnormal requests. Similarly, the CorDapp introduces requests rate-limiting firewall along with a doorman. The doorman validates and filters malformed requests. In CorDapp the P2P communication is authenticated as a part of the TLS protocol *(CC#1, CC#2)*; it means that the attacker could not join the Corda network to launch a DoS attack [10].

To protect against unauthorised remote operations *(V#7)*, the centralised infrastructure use secure communication protocols *(TC#1)*, authorisation & access control *(TC#3)*. In comparison, the CorDapp also utilise the secure communication protocols *(CC#1)* along with the concept of sandbox [10] to prevent unauthorised remote operations and execution of code.

5   CorDapp Security Risks and Countermeasures

In this section, we perform the security risks analysis to identify what security risks appear within CorDapp. Again we apply the SRM approach to identify the assets, security criteria, associated risks (Table 3), and risks vulnerabilities that are mapped on the architecture (Fig. 6). The architecture helps to visualise which assets are affected by these vulnerabilities. Later, we perform the risk treatment by presenting the security countermeasures (Fig. 7).

5.1   Security Risks and Vulnerabilities

In [15,16], the authors conclude that blockchain technology not only helps to mitigate the security risks but also introduces other security risks. Likewise, the CorDapp mitigates various security risks (see Sect. 3), it also introduces other security risks. For example, the i) endpoint vulnerability (EV) (such as keys lost, weak passwords, physical access to digital wallets and devices), ii) quantum computing threat (QCT), iii) privacy violation (PV), iv) de-anonymization (DA), v) smart contract attack (SCA), vi) denial-of-state attack (DSA).

Table 3. Post-trade CorDapp assets and associated security risks

Business assets	System assets	Risk
CorDapp services *(I, A)*	Wallets, Keys, Computers/devices, User	*EV*
Transactions *(I)*	Trade details, Cryptography	*QCT*
Customer data *(C)*	Trade details, Counter-parties	*PV*
Counter-parties *(C)*	Transaction data, Trade details, Counter-parties	*DA*
Digital assets *(I)*	Smart contracts, Ledger	*SCA*
Transaction valiadtion *(I, C)*	Non-validating notaries, State reference	*DSA*

The vulnerabilities belong to post-trade matching and confirmation in Cor-Dapp, called CorDapp vulnerabilities (CV). These vulnerabilities are:

CV#1: Lack of awareness and knowledge (EV) [31]
CV#2: Not using quantum-resistant cryptography schemes (QCT) [31]
CV#3: Sharing full content of transaction with validating notaries (PV) [17]
CV#4: Possible to link individuals data (DA) [21]
CV#5: Lack of exception handling and error-prone smart contracts (SCA) [26]
CV#6: The malicious actor is able to create a transaction and non-validating notary consumes a state by considering it a valid transaction (DSA) [17]

5.2   Security Countermeasures

We collected various countermeasures to overcome these vulnerabilities. The architecture (Fig. 7) illustrates how the countermeasures for CorDapp vulnerabilities (CCV) are applied to secure the CorDapp.

CCV#1: The knowledge and awareness to educate system users (CV#1) [31]
CCV#2: Hardware security modules to store and protect keys (CV#1) [10,31]
CCV#3: Implement quantum-resistant cryptography schemes (CV#2) [17,32]
CCV#4: Incorporate the concept of transaction tear-off (CV#3, CV#4) [17]
CCV#5: Smart contracts code analyser to detect errors (CV#5) [4]
CCV#6: Trusted execution environment & zero-knowledge proof (CV#6) [17]

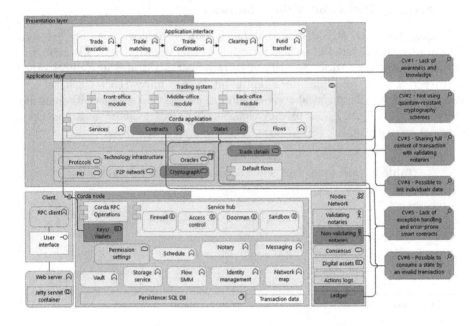

Fig. 6. Security risks that appear within CorDapp

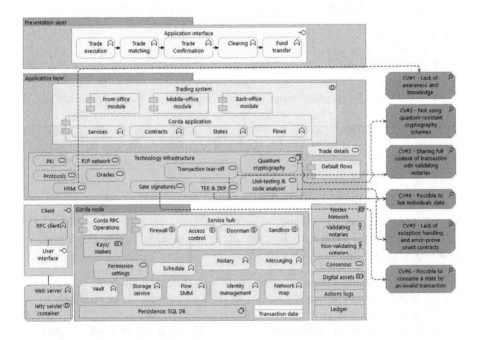

Fig. 7. Security countermeasures to mitigate CorDapp security risks

The lack of knowledge and awareness *(CV#1)* led attackers to steal information [6] by social engineering & phishing [2], or accidentally exposing the secure information [20]. The *CCV#1* is related to educate system users about possible security risks if exposing their protected information. Also, incorporate hardware security modules (HSM) to generate, protect, and store keys *(CCV#2) (Corda will soon support this* [10]). The quantum computing threat [32] is real, however CorDapp does not provide any mechanism *(CV#2)* to tackle this threat in a post-quantum era. The possible way is to implement quantum-resistant cryptography schemes *(CCV#3)*, for example, lattice-based, multivariate, hash-based cryptography and similar in order to secure against quantum computing threats. The author [17] suggested to use transaction tear-off *(CCV#4)* to protect against *CV#3* and *CV#4*. The lack of exception handling and error-prone smart contracts *(CV#5)* could lead to harm valuable assets (e.g., Ethereum smart contract reentrancy attack when an adversary stole $60 million Ethers [4]). The system should include a smart contracts code analyser [4] to detect errors *(CCV#5)*. In *CCV#6*, the author [17] suggested to use trusted execution environments (TEE) and zero-knowledge proof (ZKP) to protect against *CV#6*.

6   Concluding Remark

In this work, we apply the SRM and STRIDE models to explore security risks and their countermeasures associated to the CorDapp. The results illustrate the security risks that are mitigated by the blockchain-based solution – CorDapp, and the security risks that appear in the CorDapp. This work could support the developers' decisions while developing CorDapp applications.

In order to validate the results, the discussions were performed with three experts (manager, software developer & consultant) [24] in the field of post-trade. Overall, the experts endorse using CorDapp to overcome the security risks.

As a part of the future work, we would utilise the findings of this research to build a security risks reference model for blockchain-based applications to evaluate their security. The identified components of CorDapp would be generalised in a way that would not be dependent on the specific blockchain type or platform. This model would explain and help to explore the blockchain-based application assets, security risks, and potential countermeasures.

Acknowledgement. The authors would like to thank Justs Placāns (Riga Technical University) for the constructive comments and significant contribution while preparing this paper.

References

1. AccentureSecurity: Future Cyber Threats: Extreme But Plausible Threat Scenarios In Financial Services (2019)
2. Agarwal, S.: Cybersecurity essentials for capital markets firms in the digital age. http://bit.ly/37rdMTe

3. Al-essa, M.: The Impact of Blockchain Technology on Financial Technology (2019)
4. Atzei, N., Bartoletti, M., Cimoli, T.: A survey of attacks on Ethereum smart contracts (SoK). POST (2017)
5. Baker, R.P.: The Trade Lifecycle: Behind the Scenes of the Trading Process (2015)
6. Bellekens, X., Hamilton, A., Seeam, P., Nieradzinska, K., Franssen, Q., Seeam, A.: Pervasive eHealth services a security and privacy risk awareness survey. CyberSAÍ6 (2016)
7. Brubaker, C., Jana, S., Ray, B., Khurshid, S., Shmatikov, V.: Using frankencerts for automated adversarial testing of certificate validation in SSL/TLS implementations. In: Proceedings - IEEE Symposium on Security and Privacy (2014)
8. CMA: Capital Markets Fraud Investigations Unit. http://bit.ly/2SVxClg
9. Dagan, G.: The Actual Networking behind the Ethereum Network: How It Works (2018). http://bit.ly/2HjtchG
10. Docs, C.: Corda Threat Model. http://bit.ly/39xcuHJ
11. Dubois, É., Heymans, P., Mayer, N., Matulevičius, R.: A Systematic Approach to Define the Domain of Information System Security Risk Management (2010)
12. ECB: Potential Impact of DLTs on Securities Post-Trading Harmonisation and on the Wider EU Financial Market Integration (2017). http://bit.ly/37jMFcG
13. Hearn, M.: Corda: A distributed ledger (Whitepaper) (2016). https://www.corda.net/content/corda-technical-whitepaper.pdf
14. Hearn, M.: The Future of Corda (2018). https://www.r3.com/wp-content/uploads/2018/04/The-Future-of-Corda-ENG.pdf
15. Iqbal, M., Matulevičius, R.: Blockchain-based application security risks: a systematic literature review. In: CAiSE 2019 Workshop (2019)
16. Iqbal, M., Matulevičius, R.: Comparison of blockchain-based solutions to mitigate data tampering security risk. In: Di Ciccio, C., et al. (eds.) BPM 2019. LNBIP, vol. 361, pp. 13–28. Springer, Cham (2019). https://doi.org/10.1007/978-3-030-30429-4_2
17. Koens, T., King, S., Bos, M.V.D., Wijk, C.V., Koren, A.: Solutions for the Corda Security and Privacy Trade-off : Having Your Cake and Eating It (2019)
18. Kubo, R.: Detection and mitigation of false data injection attacks for secure interactive networked control systems. ISR (2018)
19. Matulevicius, R.: Fundamentals of Secure System Modelling. Lecture Notes in Business Information Processing. Springer, Cham (2017). https://doi.org/10.1007/978-3-319-61717-6_12
20. Maurer, T., Levite, A., Perkovich, G.: Toward a global norm against manipulating the integrity of financial data (2017)
21. Moser, J.: The Application and Impact of the European General Data Protection Regulation on Blockchains (2017)
22. Mylrea, M., Gourisetti, S.N.G.: Blockchain for smart grid resilience: Exchanging distributed energy at speed, scale and security. In: RWS (2017)
23. OWASP: A10-Insufficient Logging and Monitoring (2017). http://bit.ly/31P2Du7
24. Placāns, J.: Security risk management in corda-based application for capital markets. Master's thesis, Riga Technical University (2019)
25. Polyviou, A., Velanas, P., Soldatos, J.: Blockchain Technology: Financial Sector Applications Beyond Cryptocurrencies (2019)
26. R3: Corda: Secure Coding Guidelines. http://bit.ly/2TluaiO
27. Ruffy, F., Hommel, W., Eye, F.V.: A STRIDE-based security architecture for software-defined networking. ICN 2016 (c) (2016)
28. Sato, T., Himura, Y.: Smart-contract based system operations for permissioned Blockchain. In: NTMS 2018 (2018)

29. Sweigart, C.: Global Information Assurance Certification Paper (2003)
30. Thulasidas, M.: Principles of Quantitative Development (2010)
31. Velissarios, J., Herzig, J., Didem, U.: Blockchain's potential starts with security. Practice Nurs. **24**(5), 561–568 (2019)
32. Yin, W.E.I., Wen, Q., Li, W., Zhang, H.U.A., Jin, Z.: An Anti-Quantum Transaction Authentication Approach in Blockchain **6** (2018)

Author Index

Printed in the United States
by Baker & Taylor Publisher Services